Peter Hoffmann was educated at]
Oxgangs, Edinburgh and at Boroughmuir Senior Secondary
School. After graduate and post-graduate studies in
Edinburgh he worked for SCVS; the Scottish Episcopal
Church; the private sector and thereafter mainly in local
government as a chief officer in education; culture and sport.
He is the author of *The Stair; A Boroughmuir Schoolboy's
1971 Edinburgh Diary* and other works. In a previous life he
was an Olympic, European and Commonwealth Games
athlete. He is married to Alison and Paw to *Atticus* and
d'Artagnan. In his sixtieth year he represented Scotland at
epee in the Veterans' Home International against England,
Wales and Ireland at Durham. Peter still keeps journals!

For athletics coach, Bill Walker, but for whom there would be no story to tell and to that extraordinary band of volunteers who give up their time to help better young people's lives.

Achilles' Heel

Peter Hoffmann

'When summer's end is nighing'

'When summer's end is nighing
And skies at evening cloud,
I muse on change and fortune
And all the feats I vowed
When I was young and proud…'

A. E. Houseman

'Every past was a present once, and those who lived in past times never
thought of their experiences as bound to become moments in history.'

David Daiches, WAS A Pastime From Time Past

'...*I was much too far out all my life*
And not waving but drowning.'

Stevie Smith

Introduction

Was and If. What was, begs what if? To borrow from David Daiches, this book is about a pastime from time past. *'Sometimes it went so slowly, sometimes it went so fast…His story History. My story Mystery.'*

It's about *Once upon a time*. It's about a search for love. It's about two boys going out to earn their spurs; two errant and flawed young knights in search of the Grail, whatever that might be. It's an Arthurian quest set in more modern days and times. Or more boringly, it's about socialisation. It describes that journey-the ups and the downs; the hopes, the aspirations and the regrets; it's a testament to ambition, resilience and weakness; it's about kindness and support; being young and overwhelmed; a river of chutzpah and a stream of self-doubt, recording it and writing it down in the style of a folded clock, before all the main protagonists are in the earth. As Ben Jones, M.D. says *'The saddest thing about dying is that all the stuff you've learned goes in to the ground with you. Make sure you pass it on before you croak.'*

However, it's like trying to catch the wind, as that younger scribe records fleeting moments about a time and a place and figures in the landscape, perhaps because he doesn't want them to die and become extinct; and whilst it may not be your experience, perhaps at times you may catch a pang of recognition of a broadly felt experience. And yet and staying with Daiches: *'I wasn't always brooding like this you know, mostly I took life as it came, affected by the weather, welcoming Friday, relishing fresh scones and jam, losing myself in books.'*

A Day In A Life In A Year is the final volume of *An Edinburgh Trilogy*, following on from the *The Stair* and *A Boroughmuir Schoolboy's 1971 Diary*.

Whilst it can be read as a sports book, the story is of interest beyond the athletics enthusiast to the more general reader too. Most autobiographical sports memoirs tend to be written by the vainqueurs rather than the vanquished-Olympic and world champions; world record holders; Tour de France and Major winners, whereas I only ever reached the lowly foothills of Olympus, enjoying modest success at international level. However, failure can be as interesting as success, as well as more poignant and the detailed journals which I kept on my athletics journey during the years between 1973 and 1978 give the book a certain uniqueness. And, it could be argued as Stevenson wrote: *'To travel hopefully is a better thing than to arrive.'*

The extracts from the diaries from half a century ago contain details of athletics training and competitions making it of interest to athletes and coaches, but the diaries are about much more than just sport, instead describing a young man's journey from boyhood to becoming a man, set within the culture of 1970s Edinburgh. They capture day to day family, working and student life, making the book a valuable and interesting social document.

Like all good diaries the extracts don't just record events, interesting as they may be, but also the young diarist's observations, thoughts, responses and reactions to the events to which he's party and the individuals with whom he interacts.

Similar to the previous two volumes, the memoir is set mainly within Scotland's capital and is a love letter to Edinburgh as well as to family and friends. My love of the city shines through in the procession of the seasons of the year whether in capturing it at the height of summer or in the depths of winter, as well as describing the surrounding local landscapes of rural Midlothian and the coast and beaches of East Lothian; Broughty Ferry and Dundee feature regularly too.

Sport provided a good vehicle to express myself in writing these journals. Not only did athletics take me outside into the elements, but also on adventurous travels providing the opportunity to meet other people. The 1970s were also a period in history when it was only sportsmen who could travel behind *The Iron Curtain* to the likes of the former East Germany and Czechoslovakia.

Several threads run through the book. One theme is transformation and how the vision of the City Fathers in bringing the 1970 Commonwealth Games to Edinburgh and building Meadowbank Sports Centre, allied to the remarkable contribution of community spirited volunteers help to transform a young man's life for the better and the common good. The story describes the up and down relationship between a coach and a young athlete; and whilst it is a local story, it is also a universal tale too, reflecting the positive impact such individuals can make on others' lives. The book is dedicated to my coach, Bill Walker and to that extraordinary band of volunteers who give up their time to help better young people's lives.

When faced with a significant crossroads in life I take the road less travelled, but rather than the poet, Robert Frost, it instead brings to mind the writer and mythologist, Joseph Campbell, who wrote of following your bliss:

If you do follow your bliss, you put yourself on a kind of track that has been there all the while waiting for you, and the life you ought to be living is the one you are living. When you can see that, you begin to meet people who are in the field of your bliss, and they open the doors to you. I say, follow your bliss and don't be afraid, and doors will open where you didn't know they were going to be. If you follow your bliss, doors will open for you that wouldn't have opened for anyone else.

The crossroads faced is a direct result of an extended period of school truancy, previously described in the two earlier volumes; missing school and the consequences of leaving education with no qualifications had come back to haunt me each day.

In the two years between 1972 and 1974, whilst my peers are enjoying school and university, I go off to work each day in a dead end job as a costing clerk, with its inherent daily grind and toil resulting in an ongoing frustration and soul-destroying *ennui*, colourfully described as my *Dickens blacking factory period*. However, it gave me the time for much self-reflection bringing me to my senses and the realisation that the only way out was to transform my life for the better through the power of education.

The book is also a testament to friendship, in particular between two boys, myself and my good friend, the mercurial Paul Forbes. There's a Tolkien dimension to our story as we set forth in 1971 on a quest from a common and garden existence to one of adventures, tests and magical rewards. It's life-affirming stuff. Because our friendship features so prominently-we often trained, socialised and went off on trips together, an alternative title for the book would have been, *Mainly Peter. And Paul*. Our ongoing friendship (we've been friends now for half a century) is one of the charms of the book. Of course a further alternative title for the book could have been *Wisdom, Madness & Folly* but Laing got there first!

It is also a love story, indeed two love stories, both of which are destined to fail. Because the diary is so transparent and brutally honest, it poetically records a young man's joys and highs when the relationships with *Pixie Mia Farrow lookalike* and *Diana the goddess of love and hunting* are going well, alongside the lows, despair and misery of unrequited love.

Other relationships feature too-the importance of family support from my grandparents and estranged parents; the key role of older role models and mentors, including the well-known Jenkins' brothers David and Roger, as well as sub 4 minute miler Adrian Weatherhead and Norman Gregor, a British international 400 metres hurdler, all of whom have significant walk–on parts.

From a distance of forty years I can now discern patterns and key mistakes made which of course tear at the soul and clutch at the heart. The child is the father of the man. They say *if* is the saddest word in the English language. If I'd played a smarter, less intemperate and more measured hand with the lovely Pixie. If I'd done weights, gym-work and plyometrics one hundred times a year instead of only on a handful of occasions. If I'd raced at 136 rather than 143 pounds. If my diet had been more like Mo Farah's rather than Alf Tupper's! If 1979 had not been such an *annus horribilis*. But back then, knowledge came slowly and athlete support from the authorities, there was none.

Or as rather beautifully expressed by Father Gianni in the recent BBC series set in Tuscanny, *Second Chance Summer*: '*...the problem is you only learn with age and experience, so by the time you realise you have learnt a lot of things unfortunately a lot of time has passed and many chances have been lost.*'

And today, if I had access to a time-machine, what then? Most of all I'd wish to put an arm around my younger self's shoulder and quote Julian of Norwich's words: '*All shall be well, and all shall be well and all manner of things shall be well.*'

And more practically, that with some judicious fine-tuning my athletics career would have been very different, more successful and I might just have gone on to achieve my long term ambition to have raced Coe and Ovett down the home straight in the race of the century at the 1980 Olympic Games 800 metres final in Moscow. Ironically, I ended up watching the drama unfold at Meadowbank Sports Centre in the AV room where a large television had been set up.

However, at what cost would any such sporting success have been? Shades of the film *Sliding Doors* spring to mind. But most likely, life would have been less fulfilling.

But, if I were to be offered some Faustian pact whereby I could travel back in time and change such key staging posts in life, tempting as it might be to accept, I'd probably reject the Devil's offer preferring the way life worked out afterwards and in particular the joy of our two sons, *Atticus* and *d'Artagnan*, the latter of whom we watched win a medal as part of the Scotland Epee Team at the 2014 Commonwealth Championships and t'other a first class honours degree in law.

And yet, and yet, having revisited these journals after four decades and lived with them over the past ten months, as I drift off to sleep of a summer's evening, haunting images of past crossroads in life not taken offer tantalising glimpses of a different life not led with interesting, unexplored avenues, alongside ethereal images of *Pixie* et al occasionally dance across the screen and the night air…

Peter Hoffmann

Jamestown, Strathpeffer, 31st July, 2017

The Journey

One day you finally knew
what you had to do, and began,
though the voices around you
kept shouting
their bad advice --
though the whole house
began to tremble
and you felt the old tug
at your ankles.
"Mend my life!"
each voice cried.
But you didn't stop.
You knew what you had to do,
though the wind pried
with its stiff fingers
at the very foundations,
though their melancholy
was terrible.

*It was already late enough, and a wild
night,
and the road full of fallen
branches and stones.
But little by little,
as you left their voice behind,
the stars began to burn
through the sheets of clouds,
and there was a new voice
which you slowly
recognized as your own,
that kept you company
as you strode deeper and deeper
into the world,
determined to do
the only thing you could do --
determined to save
the only life that you could save.*

Mary Oliver

Preface

As an athlete, internationally, I only ever reached the lowly foothills of Mount Olympus but I was selected for Olympic, European and Commonwealth teams as well as winning a silver medal at the 1975 European Junior Championships. Domestically, in a short career, between 1973 and 1978, I won ten Scottish titles as well as seven AAAs medals at 200, 400 and 800 metres. Looking back, I was perhaps a jack of all trades and master of none; I was able to win national short sprint indoor titles at 50 metres yet also race over 1000 metres too. One of the things which gave me the greatest satisfaction was beating good international athletes over a range of distances including Drew McMaster over 100 metres; being the first Brit to defeat David Jenkins at a national championship over 400 metres; and Paul Forbes and John Robson over a half mile, as well as Steve Ovett on the one occasion I raced against him.

Autumn

Into my heart an air that kills
From yon far country blows:
What are those blue remembered hills,
What spires, what farms are those?
That is the land of lost content,
I see it shining plain,
The happy highways where I went
And cannot come again.

A.E. Houseman, A Shropshire Lad

Michaelmas Day, 29th September, 1974 Today's the day when the harvest and the accounts should be completed and the new farming and athletics cycle begins; the future starts today. I watched Edinburgh Athletic Club (E.A.C.) set a World Best for the 24 hour mile relay and later I helped tidy up afterwards. Coach Bill Walker gave me a lift home.

<u>Morning:</u> **600/500/400/300/200/100 metres; walk a lap recovery; Nigel Seymour joined me**

<u>Afternoon:</u> **8x150s (2minutes recovery); on my own**

<u>Evening:</u> **Stewart Togher gym circuit**

30th September, 1974 A frosty morn, but lovely out running early and easily around Portobello Park 'n Golf Course. What could be better in the life of a young man? A morning massage at the physio and then I got myself organised for the long haul ahead, putting the first building blocks in place-library work; academic supplies and bus pass bought in. It's an exciting time in the cycle of the year when I begin to think ahead to what may be possible. I've left work now and started academia and after some serious training this past year I've improved hand over fist. Come the evening, a nice session.

Morning: 19 minutes run

Evening: Gym exercises warm-up followed by 10 x 400 metres (90 seconds recovery) average 66 seconds-last run, 61 secs

Before Bed: Arm-action; leg-work; sit-ups

1975 I thought *Pixie Mia Farrow lookalike* would be down at the track this evening, but she wasn't. I was disappointed. I jogged around Arthurs Seat on my own, feeling rather lonely.

1st October, 1977 Yesterday a nice letter arrived in the post from Roger Jenkins-some extracts herewith:

'Have you decided to run 800m next year? Oh yeah Coe was supreme wasn't he?-incredibly tough guy but with a lot of hard work-early a.m. runs and lots of short recovery and fast 600/700/800/1000's you're as good. Whatever you decide don't get caught as you did last year-early Nov/Dec/Jan you were going to run 800s then as the indoor programme looked good-back to the security of 400-but you'd lost valuable speed-to run 400-you've gotta do speed all year-decide then and stay by your decision as the work involved in 800's is very different from 400-unless you're V.O.5 (Juantorena)! I'm off to Marseille very soon...got some pretty good work set by Nallet etc....regards to 'Diana'. and to Paul.'

Coach Walker drove his squad hopefuls, Norman Gregor; Peter Little; Paul Forbes and me out to Army H.Q. at South Queensferry for the Scotland Commonwealth Games weekend. Having made the decision to move up to the half mile I joined the distance guys including the marathon runners! In the evening, *Diana, the goddess of love and*

hunting made my dinner before I collapsed into bed-
EXHAUSTED!

Morning: **9 miles run around Corstorphine Hill**

Evening: **4 miles easy**

2nd October, 1976 I'm in pretty poor shape, which is probably how it should be at the start of winter training.

On a wet, windy and cold day I got beaten up on the track by sub-4 minute miler, Adrian Weatherhead; but later, an enjoyable steady run with him afterwards on Craigentinny Golf Course which was quiet. We discussed approaches to training and generally sorted the world out. I admire Adrian's discipline, which, given I'm still young-he's 12 years older, I've emulated, but also his resilience, which I can't replicate-that hardiness-that inner steel, is something inner-born; it's either there or not. What I can do to alleviate it is to be disciplined; I would never drop out of a session and I'm motivated. Also, because I'm more talented than him, with the blessing of speed, means that I can do very well.

Resilience is an interesting aspect. I often speak to Coach Walker about it expressing my view that because I'm a bit of a wimp, relatively speaking, compared to Adrian, but not others, that I'm not pushing myself hard enough and just cruising on talent. Although it sounds immodest, but because I seem to have an unusual ability to train with sprinters like Drew McMaster or Gus McKenzie; quarter milers such as Roger and David Jenkins; half-milers like Paul; as well as milers like Dave Moorcroft and Adrian, gives me an insight into their strengths and their weaknesses. None of the sprinters would have made it if they were destined to run middle distance, but if Adrian had been born with fast twitch fibres he would very much have made it either way. He's a strong influence on me and one of the key mentors who have helped me to partly overcome my frailties and the lack of such influential figures around when I was younger.

In the evening *Diana the goddess of love and hunting* and I went to see Halpern the Hypnotist. He was absolutely brilliant. I was pissing myself laughing, rolling about the aisles. It was as well Paul wasn't along as we'd have set each other off and probably been carried out on a stretcher! But what a laugh-stooges eating onions; driving racing cars; acting as policemen-you name it. I must get Paul along to see him.

Morning: **600 metres (85 seconds); 500 metres (72 secs-died); 400 metres (60 secs-died); 300 metres (41 secs) with 4 minutes recovery**

Afternoon: **5 miles steady run around Craigentinny Golf Course with Adrian and Ross Nicol**

Before Bed: **Press-ups; sit-ups; squats**

3rd October, 1972 After six months of going down to Meadowbank to the training I've had a surprisingly good first season at the athletics including two seconds in the Scottish Boys Clubs Championship 100 metres and 200 metres even though it's kind of second division stuff. But now that I've turned sixteen and had a wee taste of what it's all about with Coach Walker's squad, I've decided to start training regularly. However, I fancy moving from sprinting up to the half mile where I want to make an impact; good as they are, I think I could make an impression against the likes of Paul, John Scott et al. It's a big leap up. But I've run the occasional 400 metres for the club in relays and run not badly, including getting my first medal at the Scottish Eastern District Championships in the Youth 400/200/200/400 Relay.

Evening: Winter training with Mr Walker's squad

4ᵗʰ October, 1973 I got in at a reasonable hour from my work as a junior cost clerk at Thomas Graham & Sons, Builders & Plumbers Merchants after the usual long dizzy trek across town from Balcarres Street, Morningside to Portobello. The journey sees me running up through the Morningside Graveyard to the 41 bus stop at the foot of Morningside Drive to catch the bus to just past Blackford Pond from where I alight and run like the deer over a mile to the Kings Buildings to jump on a number 42 bus back home to Duddingston. If the driver doesn't let me on the bus at the traffic lights at Mayfield I think *Fuck him!* and run down to Cameron Toll where to his chagrin he has to let me on; all followed by a swift jog up Durham Road so that I can get my dinner before going training at Meadowbank Sports Centre. It's almost a session in itself. But I'm highly motivated to do something with my life that I don't really think about it. Winning this summer's Scottish Youth 400 metres title has given me the taste and is just the start; although I won it in 52.0 seconds, I only did enough to win; in a time trial last month I ran 50.8 seconds against Keith Ridley who beat me and got the final spot on the EAC British Cup Final relay team. By next summer I am sure that I'll become an automatic choice for the club; already in training I'm starting to become increasingly confident against athletes like Keith and ready to leave them behind.

Meanwhile at work I've got a lot of time to reflect on my foolishness at skiving school and leaving with only two O Levels. Like Charles Dickens at the blacking factory I feel ready to transform my life for the better and become a serious student. I often sit idly in the office dreaming of how nice it would be to be a student and to train on a Wednesday afternoon with Roger et al. I need to come up with a strategy to make it happen. After Sunday's E.A.C. annual sponsored walk, followed by three hard track sessions in a row this week, my blisters were hurting a bit in training tonight. But it didn't stop me running a hard session.

Evening: 10 x 400 metres (45 seconds recovery) average 68 seconds

Before Bed: Arm-action; leg-work; press-ups; sit-ups

5th October, 1974 After a Saturday breakfast I lay down listening to *Junior Choice* with Ed *'Stewpot'* Stewart on BBC Radio 1. Brian Gordon wasn't down from Aberdeen, but Norman and I ran a solid session together. I spent the early afternoon at Coach Walker's and then we went out to watch Derek Innes win the schools cross-country race. Paul and I really enjoyed our evening out at *The Corries*. Songs such as *Bonnie Dundee* don't half make the hairs on the backs of your neck stand up, as did listening to Ronnie Browne's sweet tenor voice on *Dumbarton's Drums* and *Mothers, Daughters, Wives*; pure class. Once again it was the usual wonderful evening with a rich mix of music, fun, romance, history touching all the emotions creating a sense of Scottish identity and community; they're quite inspirational. Ronnie's wife, Pat, had sent me complimentary tickets and invited us to the after show party too. As ever Ronnie was interested and supportive of our athletics saying how well we're both doing and to keep it up, as well as teasing Paul about filching beer when we left the New Year Eve Party two years ago!

Morning: 4 x 500 metres (6 minutes recovery) 70.0; 68.4; 68.3; 71.6 seconds; I was absolutely shattered

1975 *Pixie Mia Farrow lookalike* ran fantastically well at Balloch finishing 6th! However, she had her purse stolen; back in Edinburgh we drove her back out to Dunf with pots of home-made jam etc.

6th October, 1975 A large group of us set off for a run around Arthurs Seat. It turned in to a bit of a burn up over the last mile with only Mark Wilson; Paul and me there at the death; as the only sprinter there, I'll take that!

Evening: **Gym circuit followed by 4 miles run around Arthurs Seat**

7th October, 1973 Whilst I was in working at Thomas Graham & Sons yesterday Paul phoned to say he'd won the cross-country race-brilliant stuff! I was pleased for him. He phoned me again later in the evening suggesting that we should move to Australia. Of course now that he's got a Scottish Schools title and me a Scottish Youth Championship I'm sure Australia would welcome us with open arms; as if! We're still searching for a way forward in our lives; so if it's not the likes of Australia, then we're in and out of the Army, Navy and Air-Force revolving doors. But, are the forces ready for us? Could they cope? Do you still need a criminal record to get in to Oz? What's the meaning of the universe? Let's see what next week brings. Meanwhile I ran a cross-country today. Dougie McLean drove a group of us through to Balloch in the west of Scotland in his wee Austin 1100. As usual it wasn't very good and once again I didn't win a prize. There were a lot of spectators out on the course. A few of them cheered me on, probably recognising my forlorn hopes towards the back of the field; still, it's good discipline mentally and toughens me up a wee bit and brings me back down to reality keeping my feet on the ground and tempering my highfalutin aspirations. I sometimes have this mad-cap idea of taking off at the start of a cross-country race running flat out for the first half mile and opening up a 100 metres gap and seeing what happens next; aye and then I wake up!

Afternoon: 3,500 metres Cross Country, Balloch (44th)

The Road Not Taken

'I shall be telling this with a sigh
Somewhere ages and ages hence:
Two roads diverged in a wood, and I-
I took the one less travelled by,
And that has made all the difference...'

Robert Frost

8th October, 1976 Well, I started at Loughborough
University on Wednesday and packed it in today, only two
days later. It's a key day in my life. Out with committing to
athletics and leaving work two years ago, it's the biggest
decision I've ever made. Everything I've worked for and
achieved these past two years by going out and getting five
good Highers and going from being a good junior athlete to
making the Olympic team put me in a position where
universities were making me offers, accompanied by four
page missives from the likes of C.K. Lipton and others.
Anyway, it was George Gandy who tempted me to come
down and join the star-studded Loughborough line up. He
said he was looking forward to me training with some of the
other new students there including Sebastian Coe. The
course appealed to me too as it was a triple whammy-a
degree in Sports Science, Physical Education and English
and the prospect of teaching English really appealed to me.
The course would see me continuing to devour books;
deconstruction and the writing of critical essays. However, in
the two days I've been down here I've been stuck away from
everyone in the East Tower and basically haven't seen hide
nor hair of any bugger until I went along to my first class
today; ironically, I enjoyed the swimming. Removed from my
Edinburgh friends and family and *Diana the goddess of love and
hunting* I've felt somewhat overwhelmed lacking that sense of
love and belonging. I've been increasingly lonely and
insecure. I've longed for home and for Edinburgh which I

love. I received a couple of lovely letters from Grandma Jo which perhaps hindered rather than helped me and influenced my decision. The notes painted charming wee cameos of ordinary day to day life back home at Portobello- my brother Iain helping grandfather out with the car; the terrible wet and windy autumn weather; and the dog and cat asleep in front of the fire. And, if I'm being absolutely truthful, most of all, I've been missing *Diana* who I only met in August, but who has bewitched me. Long distance relationships don't work and I feel this romance is special and I want to give it my best shot and to have no regrets. That said I haven't been overly-impressed with the athletics set up here and they've still to build the tartan track. I may come to regret not training with Coe et al, but I've reasoned I'm very happy with life in Edinburgh; the set-up there has enabled me to make the Olympic team this year; I've got a great international training group with athletes such as Forbes; Weatherhead; Gregor; and the two Jenkins' to train with and a great coach too. Meadowbank Sports Centre is on my doorstep, only two miles away; I've friends and family; and my new girlfriend. To quote Lord Melbourne *Why not leave it alone?* There's also the additional pressure of my Scottish Education Department grant, which I've not touched so far. As soon as I made the decision at lunchtime I felt better for it because it lifted a great weight from my shoulders; and so, *Let the dice fly high!* Travelling back on the night train I thought of a Norman Macaig poem:

Crossing the Border

'I sit with my back to the engine, watching the landscape pouring away out of my eyes. I think I know where I'm going and have some choice in the matter...'

Norman Macaig

And then later as we crossed in to Scotland:

The Lay Of The Last Minstrel

'Breathes there the man, with soul so dead,
Who never to himself hath said,
This is my own, my native land!'

Sir Walter Scott

9th October, 1973 It was a rotten, cold morning. I made my way along Balcarres Street; allied to it being a wind-tunnel, it's surely the most miserable street in Morningside. I've been at Thomas Graham & Sons for a year now, so I've had plenty of time to reflect on my massive mistake of leaving school with no qualifications having spent the previous two years skiving off school, playing hooky. Of course it's now come back to haunt me. The combination of reflecting on that youthful misjudgement; working in a dead-end job in a windowless and airless 'office' in a warehouse straight out of Dickens, which is roasting in the summer months and freezing in winter, whilst sitting amongst a line of cost clerks all seated in a row, working at a worktop surface, where we price interminable invoices is a daily reminder and a slap in the face.

The clerks range in age from seventeen years old (me), to sixty five year old, Tommy Drummond, with all ages in between. As in John Buchan's *The Gap in the Curtain* where the future is revealed, so it is to me each day-the working equivalent of the cradle to the grave; unless of course I take some decisive steps to change the way the earth is spinning. Thus, the first thing I did this morning was to write off for the job which I saw advertised in yesterday's Scotsman newspaper. The post is with Grahams' big rival, S.C.K. However, I had to change the envelope as my boss Roy Wallace stuck a Grahams' stamp on the envelope! He's a funny guy and likes me, but he can be a bit of a bastard too. That said, it was quite amusing; he must think I'm as thick as shite if he thought I was going to post it with the company's logo on it! I feel good that I've done something practical and positive; it's a start.

Evening: 800 metres; 600 metres; 500 metres; 400 metres with jog lap recovery; Coach Walker was away to a meeting, so we did the session by ourselves

Before Bed: Arm-work; press-ups; sit-ups

1975 *Pixie Mia Farrow lookalike* and I enjoyed The Corries concert; later we sat in the car park at Cramond talking for hours.

10th October, 1976 I went up to Meadowbank late morning; David and Roger Jenkins were there so I was speaking to them. Despite feeling very tired before starting the session I still managed to put in a good shift. Now that I've packed up Loughborough I'll have to map a new way forward. *Diana, the goddess of love and hunting* and I went for a stroll around the Princes Street shops; later on we enjoyed tea at Meadowbank and then watched the karate championships.

Lunchtime: 600 metres (90 seconds); 500 metres (71 secs); 400 metres (53 secs); 300 metres (37 secs) with a 4 minutes recovery; on my own

11th October, 1974 It's all change. Labour has won the General Election-well, when I say *all change* they've just scraped a majority of three after it being a hung parliament back in February. Crikey, just imagine two elections in less than a year-that can't happen very often. I played table tennis with Anders at college, but I need to ensure I'm not led astray from my studies now that I've quit work at Thomas Graham & Sons; like my athletics, I need to focus on getting a handful of good Highers. I've been speaking to Coach

Walker about future goals. Although I just scraped the fourth spot this past summer on the British Junior 4 x 400 metres relay team (Roger Jenkins is the U.K.'s number one)- anyway, I put in such an excellent workout this evening, that I've decided that if I can keep up this work-rate and focus, then I'd like to try to win next year's European Junior Championships 400 metres title! Now that's ambitious! I'll mention it to Paul next time I see him, just to give him a wee chortle!

Evening: **Gym circuit; some half squats and mobility**

Before Bed: **Arm-action; leg-work; press-ups**

Height: **1.78** **Weight:** **145 lbs**

12th October, 1974 I enjoyed a long lie in bed before travelling down with the club to the Scottish East District Cross Country League at Hawick, made all the more fun for winning 80p at cards. We're well in to the autumn, so as ever I'm doing a few cross country races. I'm the only sprinter out on the ploughed fields. I finished 74th out of 109 runners; just a little bit different from running in Madrid back in August for the British Junior Team against Portugal and Spain. My legs are very stiff now, especially my hamstrings and quadriceps. Aye, we're wimps compared to the iron men of the iron ground. In the evening I went out to our *local*, the Waverley Bar, St Mary's Street, with Paul and a dozen others. Thereafter we went dancing at the Watsonians Rugby Club followed by a long walk home to Portobello in the early hours of the morning. Unsurprisingly, it didn't exactly ease my legs off.

Afternoon: **4 miles cross country**

13th October, 1975 The Monday after a good weekend. On Saturday I ran in the Scottish East District League Cross

Country race down at Galashiels in the Scottish Borders on the most hellish course. We were trudging through, rather than over, wet, muddy, ploughed fields. It was bloody miserable. As usual I finished way back-21st counter for the club. Although it was a real plod over the fields I actually ran well along the road toward the end of the race and much to the amusement of the spectators out-kicked Jim Dingwall. I don't think Jim enjoyed the course much either. Galashiels in the cool autumn is just a slight change from being second in Europe in sunny Athens just six weeks ago. Later in the evening I caught the amusing Billy Connolly on Parkinson. Yesterday we were training at Arthurs Seat and this evening we re-commenced winter training on the track. I worked very hard and was suitably *rewarded* as I felt as sick as a dog.

Evening: Gym session warm-up followed by: 2 x 800 metres (2 minutes 6 seconds and 2 minutes 11 seconds); 2 x 400 metres (61 and 57 seconds) and 2 x 200 metres (slow) 5 minutes recovery between runs

14th October, 1975 A sweet and sour day. On a beautiful crisp golden autumn morning I ran up to Meadowbank. In the afternoon Uncle Andy Ross drove us out to Cramond to collect grandfather's car; it had broken down when I was visiting *Pixie Mia Farrow lookalike* at Dunfermline College of P.E last night. Andy's a gem-a one in a million bloke who over the years has regularly come to the rescue of Gaga and his temperamental second-hand cars. When we got back home to Portobello, over tea and scones, Grandma Jo tried to give him some monies for his help. Andy said *Listen, if I were to take anything for it, it would take away all the fun I've had; I've had a braw afternoon with Willie and Peter!* I think it's a way for him to do something for Nana and Gaga for the kindnesses which they did for him and Aunt Margaret when they were young and first married. I guess, it's an example of

Gaga's homespun wisdom: *What's round, goes around!* Later on, a miserable, drunken evening at a 21st birthday party; the ongoing highs and lows of my relationship with the temperamental *Pixie* and my ongoing search for love and belonging. But amongst it all, there's training. Always.

Morning: 4 miles steady run

Evening: 8 x 120 metres with a walk back recovery

15th October, 1973 As autumn progresses the Edinburgh weather is getting colder and colder each morning. The journey to work at Thomas Graham & Sons along Balcarres Street is no fun and the miserable wind tunnel only exaggerates it. As I stride along to work, the westerly wind cuts straight through me like a knife.

A Northern Morning

'…Head down in my new coat
I dodge to the High Street conscious of my fellows
Damp and sad in their vegetable fibres.'

Alastair Elliot

I've been offered the job at S.C.K. at seventeen pounds a week, plus their offices are at Meadowbank, so it should be a no-brainer. It's almost double what I'm getting here at Graham's, but I want to speak to Mr Rogan the manager to see if I can use it as a bargaining tool. He was away all day, so I've kept the opposition on hold. Being offered the post has increased my confidence and sense of self-worth. Also, it's made me more hopeful, optimistic and positive about the future. It's another wee step on the ladder to getting on in life and starting to overcome my unfortunate start to post-school life. A year on from leaving Boroughmuir School I've got a Scottish title to my name and the prospect of a reasonable wage. It's a start.

Evening: **20 x 200 metres slow-fasts all in 30 seconds (90 secs jog 200m recovery); my blisters were killing me!**

16th October, 1976 I travelled down from Silverknowes by the sea and *Diana the goddess of love and hunting* to Meadowbank and ran a very poor session. I just couldn't handle Adrian Weatherhead or Paul Forbes come the last run of the session. I was pretty knackered. I just blew-up! The last run was a bit of a struggle, but there was no way I wasn't going to complete the session. But the lactic acid made for a painful last 300 metres. I've still got this hankering to continue half-mile training, but I know if I don't give it 100% there's a danger of getting caught between two events, the quarter mile and the half mile. Still, at this time of the year it's all good background work and more money in the bank. And although I lost contact on the last run, Adrian and Paul are quality international middle-distance athletes, so I'm not completely disheartened. In the evening I went to the ABC Cinema Lothian Road with *Diana* to watch a couple of Clint Eastwood movies.

Morning: **4 x 600 metres (4 minutes recovery) 91; 91; 91; 104! seconds; very windy**

Afternoon: **6 miles run with Adrian around Craigentinny Golf Course**

Before Bed: **Leg-work; sit-ups**

17th October, 1976 It was a fresh, crisp, autumn morning. Before going up to join Adrian and Paul for round two I *enjoyed* a cold bath. This time I was able to run with the boys all the way, which was quite encouraging and has raised my expectations; perhaps I really can crack this middle distance thing. In the afternoon I enjoyed an easy steady run round Arthurs Seat with Ann Clarkson. I had an enjoyable blether with her, followed by a relaxed afternoon of reading-the life of the athlete-scholar.

Morning: **600 metres (84 seconds); 500 metres (70 secs); 400 metres (56 secs); 300 metres (39 secs) with a 4 minutes recovery**

Afternoon: 4 miles steady run

Before Bed: Arm Action; leg-work; press-ups; sit-ups

18th October, 1975 I picked up an excellent Diana Ross L.P. After last night's hill session with Roger at Arthur's Seat my calves were still pretty sore this morning. Alongside Paul, the three of us ran a solid, workmanlike session. It's really the start of the journey for Roger and me as we aim for a place on next year's G.B. Olympic 4 x 400 metres relay team for Montreal next year. Roger's one of the firm favourites after running 46.49 seconds this season winning a silver medal at the World Student Games. Meanwhile, I'm slower on paper with my 47.27 silver medal at the European Junior Championships, but I'm stronger than him in training, although he's still basically quicker than me. However, I'm not intimidated and I feel I've a lot more to come next year; but then he does too. It's a good pairing in training, particularly when Dave Jenkins joins us at weekends, plus Norman; Adrian; and Paul make up what is the best training squad in Britain. We're competitive, but supportive and not silly. The other thing which gives me a quiet confidence is thinking *Crikey, I'm almost on a par with the Jenkins', I'm younger* *and it's not (really) my main event as at some time I'm going to give the half mile a serious go.* Happy days. After the session Roger gave me a lift home. I enjoyed a relaxing evening aiding the recovery progress. I lounged back in the big armchair enjoying the interesting Bette Davis and Ron Moody on Parkinson.

<u>Morning:</u> Good gym warm-up before 6 x 500 metres with 5 minutes recovery in 75; 75; 77; 75; 72; 71 seconds

<u>Afternoon:</u> Gym circuit

19th October, 1974 Brian Gordon is down from Aberdeen for the weekend so we maximised the opportunity. He's a very good athlete. He's about eight years older than me and quite a serious bloke. He finished ahead of me when I ran the Scottish Senior Championships 400 metres for the first time taking the bronze to Brian's silver and Roger's gold. However, he's focusing on the half mile and ran 1 minute 50.4 seconds this past summer. We ran in each other's shadow, but I sense I'm getting better and would get very close to matching him in a race. I dropped him slightly on the last repetition whilst running within myself, cruising an effortless 24.7 seconds last 200 metres after fifteen previous repetitions. Knowing I still have another gear is an exhilarating feeling and makes me wonder what I might run for a half mile. Brian's aiming for a sub 1.49 half mile next year. I feel I might just hold on to his coat-tails. It makes me think whether I could just as easily aim for the half mile at next year's European Junior Championships rather than the quarter? That sounds a bit daft given my best is only 1 minute 57.4 seconds set six weeks ago at the Northern Trophy, but I was only half a second behind Paul and based on this morning's session, anything seems possible. Happy and exciting times!

<u>Morning:</u> 2 sets 8 x 200 metres (90 seconds recovery)

(Set 1) 27; 27; 27; 26.7; 27; 25.9; 26.7; 26.1 seconds (13 minutes recovery between the sets)
(Set 2) 28.3; 25.9; 25.9; 25.9; 27.2; 26.4; 28; 24.7 seconds

20th October, 1974 After a solid morning's track session at Meadowbank come the afternoon I put in a fantastic session up on Arthurs Seat. Alongside some good discussions with Coach Walker, overall, it's been a satisfying weekend of training.

<u>Morning:</u> 4 x 500 metres (4 minutes recovery) 73; 73; 72; 70 seconds

<u>Afternoon:</u> Arthurs Seat circuit; one single hard effort: (Gordon 1 min 34 secs; Hoffmann 1.43; the rest further back); hopping; 2 x 6 x 20 secs hill runs with jog down recovery: set 1 (Gordon 5 mins 40 secs; Hoffmann 5.41) set 2 (Hoffmann 5.20-a course record!; Gordon 5.36)

<u>Before Bed:</u> Arm-action; press-ups; sit-ups

1975 I think my relationship with *Pixie Mia Farrow lookalike* is doomed.

21st October, 1975 I met *Pixie Mia Farrow lookalike* this evening; she's still as gorgeous as ever.

1977 A perfect autumn day. Early morn I studied hard and also in the early afternoon too, interspersed with an exhilarating morning run through an aromatic Hermitage along the riverside.

To Autumn

'Season of mists and mellow fruitfulness!
Close bosom-friend of the maturing sun…'

John Keats

The path was covered by a blanket of leaves. Thereafter I climbed high up and ran over the Braid Hills Golf Course. I was just floating along effortlessly over the bouncy, parkland turf. Towards dusk I went up to a quiet Meadowbank at 4.00 p.m. to do some gym work, arriving there earlier than usual whilst others were at work. If I train there in the evening I can't always get on to a machine which can be frustrating as I like to keep the programme and recoveries disciplined. It's great being able to train when it best suits. This lifestyle is the outcome of the decision I made to quit work at Thomas Graham & Sons three years ago. I'm now benefiting from the realisation of these little perks; it's all in direct contrast to when I sat for two long miserable years at my office work-bench dreaming of how life might be: *Alea iacta est!*

My *raison d'etre* has changed dramatically giving me motivation, focus and a disciplined approach which was lacking when I had no goals and was skiving off Boroughmuir School only a couple of years back. Life was floundering and spiralling out of control with no real hope for the future other than an ordinary working life. Life now has a purpose. The combination of having an objective; motivation; habit and a little bit of talent is a powerful combination and a heady mix. I love the life of the scholar-athlete. My old school-teachers would be shocked at the transformation. Meeting Coach Walker and others was the catalyst-serendipity or destiny?

Morning: Burpees; press-ups; sit-ups followed by a 7 miles run through the Hermitage Park and over the Braid Hills

Afternoon: Gym circuit followed by 6 x 100 metres strides

22nd October, 1973 Before training started at Meadowbank we played football and cards. I was running well. Coach Walker gave me a lift to the bus stop. I was staying at Oxgangs tonight. We chatted in the car for quite a while- mainly about how I need to lift my horizons and move up several notches next year onto the senior international stage. Crikey all I've won so far is a Scottish Youth title in 52.0 seconds; but he's got faith in me and it's exciting and encouraging to hear someone saying such nice things compared to when I was at school.

Evening: 10 x 300 metres (walk 100 recovery) averaging 45-46 seconds

23rd October, 1974 Paul and I had lunch at Porty and then went up to Meadowbank to train. The 1980 Olympic Games are being held in Moscow, but after speaking to Grandpa Willie this evening I've decided to aim for Montreal in 1976! The conversation went like this:

I told Gaga I was aiming for Moscow.

He said: *That's no use!*

I asked: *Why?*

He replied: *Because I won't be around then!*

I love my grandfather. I'm determined to become as good as I can be for him and to try to make the team, very long shot that it is, given I'm only ranked in the top six of the British Junior rankings, never mind the senior rankings. And it's less than two years away. I better not mention this one to Paul as his eyes will birl around so much they might just fa' oot! He's always bemused at my latest proposals for our future. I did a lot of exercises before bed. I'm feeling very loose.

Afternoon: **12 x 150 yards (90 seconds recovery) 19; 18; 17; 17; 17; 17; 17; 17; 18; 16.5; 16.5; 17 seconds**

Evening: **Gym circuit**

Before Bed: **Mobility and hundreds of arm-action; leg-work; press-ups; sit-ups**

1975 *Pixie Mia Farrow lookalike* annoyed me like never before; she phoned later to say she was sorry; I rang her later; she said she was glad I did…

24th October, 1975 I spent the morning at college. In the afternoon I did a session at Meadowbank with *Pixie Mia Farrow lookalike*. She was up to her nonsense and annoying me. Afterwards I met Roger to run another of our hard hill sessions at Arthurs Seat. We finished just as dusk was falling. I love these Friday afternoon sessions. We work well together and are pretty much level as we push each other hard on each hill run to exhaustion. Afterwards, I enjoy the sense of camaraderie, friendship and shared intimacy as we engage in friendly conversation and laughter, as we slowly jog-walk back, tired, but content, to Meadowbank, for a long hot shower.

Happiness

'So early it's still almost dark out.
I'm near the window with coffee,
and the usual early morning stuff
that passes for thought.

When I see the boy and his friend
walking up the road
to deliver the newspaper.

They wear caps and sweaters,
and one boy has a bag over his shoulder.
They are so happy
they aren't saying anything, these boys.
I think if they could, they would take
each other's arm.
It's early in the morning,
and they are doing this thing together.

They come on, slowly.
The sky is taking on light,
though the moon still hangs pale over the water.

Such beauty that for a minute
death and ambition, even love,
doesn't enter into this.

Happiness. It comes on
unexpectedly. And goes beyond, really,
any early morning talk about it.'

Raymond Carver

Enveloped in the cool air with the temperature dropping like
a stone, there's the most tremendous blissful feeling of
satisfaction; a warm after-glow, both physical and mental,

which emanates from knowing we've hammered ourselves. It's partly the endorphins kicking in, but it's also a joyful serenity that comes from realising and appreciating that our lives have a real purpose. There's something pure about undertaking a shared venture with someone who I like and admire and for which there is no guaranteed outcome. The rest of the city of Edinburgh carry on with their day-to-day lives oblivious to the extreme and unusual adventure we're on. We're two young men pursuing a dream of Olympia 1976 next summer; a dream across the water; across the Atlantic Ocean; I feel I'm on an Arthurian quest. Meanwhile, the drivers make their way home, snakelike, through Arthurs Seat at the end of the working week. Their car headlamps light our path back to Meadowbank Stadium. Somehow, being a Friday, enhances it all and the way I feel. As they drive past us they are of course quite unaware to what we're doing and of my feelings. And all our fellow athletes throughout the world too, many of whom, as **Longfellow** wrote: *'The heights by great men reached and kept were not attained by sudden flight, but they, while their companions slept, were toiling upward in the night.'*

Early afternoon: 6 x 120 metres relaxed

Later: 6 x 40 seconds hill runs at Arthurs Seat at the *Holyrood Bowl*

25th October, 1973 I've been on holiday this past week which has allowed me to join some of my old Oxgangs pals, Gilbert; Les; my brother Iain who are all enjoying the tattie-holidays. We chummed Iain into Princes Street to buy a pair of Levis.
I bought a pair of *Adidas Tokyo* spikes at Lilywhites. I got six pounds knocked off them which is pretty considerable. I've also ordered a pair of *Adidas Weltrekord* which are a pretty

cool and unusual pair of spikes. I've not seen anyone else wearing them at Meadowbank. I like to be that wee bit different so I'm looking forward to wearing them. Now that I've been working for a year, the only positive thing is my wage of eight pounds and forty nine pence after tax. I'm putting it to good use. It's also showing that I'm committed to the athletics project in hand.

In the afternoon Paul came round. We all had a hell of a laugh hitting poor Les with comics! Paul wasn't training in the evening but I put in a workmanlike session with the middle distance runners. After training Coach Walker gave me a lift into town. Once again we sat talking in his car until 11.30 p.m. It was mainly about athletics, but also about my keenness to improve my future prospects through education-to get a better job and to make a good future for myself. He was saying that I've come on well and am starting to mature in my approach to training and that not many sprinters would have hung in with the middle distance runners the way I did tonight. Once again he encouraged me to think about my athletics in the longer term too; and although I'm only a first year junior athlete next year he thinks I have to look beyond Scotland and instead try to make the British Junior Team-a G.B. vest-God, that sounds FANTASTIC! At last someone is mentoring me compared to the absence of such pastoral care at home from my father or some of my teachers at school who all thought I was pretty useless; but whilst it brings a mixture of excitement there's a fear of failure too; I don't want to let anyone down; but I guess you can't have it both ways. I got the 12.45 a.m. late night bus back to Oxgangs, where I've been staying all week.

Evening: 1000 metres; 800m ; 600m ; 500m (80 seconds); 400m (59 secs); 3 x 150m (16-17 secs) with a jog lap

recovery; I seemed to get stronger as the session progressed and left others trailing on the 150s

26ᵗʰ October, 1976 I'm enjoying reading David Hemery's autobiography *Another Hurdle*. I suspect that today's sessions are closer to his type of training at this time of the year when he was based at Boston University than to many other one lappers out there. His book adds a third volume to the two other athletics books which have had the greatest influence on me: Peter Snell's *No Bugles, No Drums* and Cordner Nelson's *The Jim Ryun Story*. They're the three athletes who I most aspire to be like. Hemery's book confirms everything I've felt about him. I first became aware of athletics in 1968. I was twelve years old. It was the Olympic Games in Mexico City. Hemery's victory in the 400 metres hurdles where he destroyed the field was stirring stuff. It resonated all the more for David Coleman's great commentary. And today, whenever I'm struggling through a tough training session and wanting to give up; and come these last few repetitions I *hear* Coleman's voice in my mind's-eye *'...and it's Hemery (Hoffmann) gambling on everything...he's really flying down the back straight...Hemery (Hoffmann) leads...it's Hemery (Hoffmann) Great Britain...it's Hemery (Hoffmann) Great Britain...and Hemery (Hoffmann) takes the gold...he killed the rest...he paralysed them...Hemery (Hoffmann) won that from start to finish...'*

And before I know it, the session's over. And I've run as best as I can and got through another tough session. I guess it's called motivation-self-motivation; although a Canadian professor at Dunfermline College of P.E. might call it a phenomenological approach. Whatever it is, it's important and helps to push and propel me forward. If that inner fire ever stops burning and dies then that's the time and the day to retire and stop training purposefully. On the day after the Mexico final I arranged oil drums (which belonged to an

Irish navvie gang of road-menders based in Oxgangs for a month) at strategic points around the circular path of the four blocks of flats (Numbers 2, 4, 6 and 8 Oxgangs Avenue). I thereafter arranged *400 metres hurdles races* for my pals. Hemery is a hero without feet of clay and an absolute inspiration. He's modest and unassuming. He's someone who strives to continually achieve, but also contribute too. He was a fierce competitor, but as straight as a post. And he showed how you can reach the heights with a modicum of talent combined with focus, discipline, good planning, hard work and resilience.

Morning: 5 miles run

Evening: 10 x 400 metres (1 minute recovery) 63; 63; 61; 64; 64; 63; 64; 63; 63; 62 seconds

Before Bed: Press-ups; sit-ups; squats

27th October, 1975 It's amazing how much the world has moved on in only a year. Last year I was in love or was it just like with the *Mary Rand lookalike from the south-west*. I could have continued with that long-distance, but steady relationship, but instead moved on to the roller-coaster ride with the enchanting and bewitching *Pixie Mia Farrow lookalike* with whom I'm head over heels in love. She can be madly annoying, irritating and inconsistent, but she's great fun, personable and highly intelligent-I adore her.

Code Poem For The French Revolution

'The life that I have is all that I have,
And the life that I have is yours.
The love that I have of the life that I have
Is yours and yours and yours…'

Leo Marks

I'm no longer working and I'm into a second year of college to help enable me to apply go to university. On the athletics front, at the start of last year my official best for a quarter was only 52 seconds; but I've now run 47 seconds. On the debit side of the ledger I've had to make do with very little money, but thanks to Mum buying me a bus pass each month; Dad sending me 25 pounds each month from abroad; receiving my Edinburgh Corporation scholarship card giving me free access to Meadowbank; and Coach Walker giving up his time and expertise to us all for free, have enabled me to transform my life. I won't forget the kindnesses shown to me.

Although I'm still classified as a junior athlete I picked up my first British senior vest against Sweden last month at Meadowbank. David Jenkins did me a big favour. I was only selected as the reserve for the 4 x 400 metres relay team for the match at Meadowbank; however, when I was warming up with the squad, David told me to make sure I was fully ready to race as he felt a small pull coming on! He duly pulled-out allowing me to get my first senior G.B. vest. It was really great of him and another kindness which I'll not forget; when I thanked him afterwards he said *You deserve it Peter*. I guess it's a reward for training with him and helping out over the past 18 months to where he is today, the best quarter miler on the planet. I think he thought I deserved it after getting a silver medal at the European Junior

Championships; but also because he thought I'd run well and wouldn't let the team down. And further, he was confident that his brother Roger would win for G.B. on the last leg which he duly did in an exciting finale for the home crowd. I was happy with my run, sitting in on the Swede and handing the baton over just a stride behind, which was perfect. I've made big strides forward including matching David in many of the training sessions. It's not often in life you get to team up with a boyhood hero.

This evening I trained straight from college with Norrie. Because he's always trying to improve his time-management we did our session much earlier on and before the others came down; it allowed me to get home much earlier than the normal 9.30 p.m.

Evening: 4 x 300 metres with a two stride run-in (10 minutes recovery) 39.5; 36.5; 36.1; 35.3 seconds. It was very cold and windy; a smooth controlled session. I could probably have run quicker as indicated by the progressive nature of the times, but it's satisfactory given it's late October

28th October, 1973 Last night we put up the Perth athletics statistician Bryan Webster and this morning we took him up to Meadowbank to watch Coach Walker's Sunday session. In the afternoon Coach had a group get-together to discuss our future plans and to watch an athletics film. I trained with the middle-distance guys again. It was the first occasion I've bested them in a purely middle distance session and it included Stewart Walters; John Scott; and Paul who are all solid performers, so I was quietly pleased. But I'm still learning my trade. However, I think one of the keys when training with these guys is to adopt the right mental attitude; if you're a reflective practitioner and wanting to improve you need to think about these things. I've noticed that some people are naturally harder than others-more resilient if you like and all these guys are naturally tougher than me. I guess some things are inherent within you, but other things can be developed-training the mind as well as the body. And today I was focused and found the best way to handle the session was to just take one run at a time and not think about how tired I was feeling at the end of each repetition and instead only consider how I was feeling shortly before the next run started i.e. towards the end of the two minutes active rest. I think that's a mistake some athletes make, particularly sprinters, where they end up dropping out of a session. It's almost as if they've thrown in the towel too early, when they're feeling immediately buggered and at their worst. You *always* feel better after a couple of minutes rest and recovery and therefore you should never make an impetuous decision, particularly when it's hurting most. And whilst I'm aware that I'm soft as shite, I feel I can overcome some of my general wimpiness by adopting various intelligent and disciplined coping stratagems. It's all interesting stuff and I'm learning my trade and reflecting all the time. Beforehand I was speaking briefly to the great Dave Jenkins so perhaps I was hoping to impress him too and that helped to motivate me. He said *Well done on winning the Scottish Youth title in 52 seconds but you should be breaking 50 seconds with your ability!* What a lift that gave me!

Morning: 6 x 600 metres (walk back 2 minutes recovery) 103; 104; 103; 102; 100; 95 seconds followed by 6 x 4 back to back 75 metres (1; 2; 3; 2; 1 minutes rest between sets); a very solid session

1975 *Pixie Mia Farrow lookalike* asked me if I would take her to see *The Way We Were* tomorrow...

29th October, 1975 We've got a big race coming up on Saturday at Parkhead, Glasgow. It's being held at half-time during the Celtic v Rangers match so there will be a capacity crowd to cheer us on. It's being billed as an attack on the world 500 metres best, but given it's on a cinder surface on the outside of the Parkhead football pitch, I'll be very surprised. Given the world's number one ranked quarter miler, David Jenkins, is running I suppose they're justified and at liberty to publicise it in that way. It also features Alan Pascoe the European and Commonwealth 400 metres hurdles champion and Bill Hartley the 400 metres hurdler and European Gold Medallist in the 4 x 400 metres. The distance should suit both of them as they're very strong; plus there's Roger and Norman so it's a great field. I'm the youngest in the race and nobody would put their money on me, but 500 metres is an interesting distance and I've matched David in training. I'm really looking forward to it and am quietly confident of running well. Because the race is at such an unusual time of the year it's meant we've tweaked our training slightly.

Pixie, Mia Farrow lookalike asked me to take her out to see *The Way We Were* tonight so I trained earlier in the afternoon with the university guys; it meant missing college, but it's just a one off. We saw the film at the Cameo Cinema, Tollcross. It was incredibly popular, with a long queue tailing around the corner. We just managed to squeeze in getting the last two seats; fortunately a very thoughtful person kindly moved their seat to allow us to sit together. The film was quite beautiful and we spent the most wonderful evening together.

Sonnet XLIII: 'How Do I Love Thee?'

'How do I love thee? Let me count the ways.
I love thee to the depth and breadth and height
My soul can reach, when feeling out of sight....'

Elizabeth Barrett Browning

It's on such evenings we seem destined to be together. We get on so well and then for no apparent reason the relationship becomes fragile and teeters on the brink. But tonight was quite unforgettable; I'll remember it always.

<u>Afternoon:</u> 3 sets 4 x 120 metres (jog 80 metres 30 seconds recovery); all between 14 and 16 seconds shouting out time; for me nearer the former

30th October, 1977 Two years ago I did an indoors session in the Meadowbank weights room and then went back home to watch Ali sensationally defeat George Foreman. Today, now that I've decided to move up to the half mile I was outside plodding a very miserable five miles struggling to get going in the wind and the rain of an autumn day. Arthurs Seat was unnaturally quiet with most people staying indoors. From high up on the hill looking eastward, the sea was raging and wild.

Lines Composd In A Wood On A Windy Day

'...For, above, and around me, the wild wind is roaring
Arousing to rapture the earth and the seas.
...I wish I could see how the ocean is lashing
The foam of its billows to whirlwinds of spray,
I wish I could see how its proud waves are dashing
And hear the wild roar of their thunder today!'

Anne Bronte

I struggled back home. I felt exhausted, mentally and physically, but felt much better after a massage. I was glad to have trained and disciplined myself to get out early to get it over and done with-more money in the bank. *Diana the goddess of hunting and love* and I spent much of the time working on our essays interspersed with a short family visit to Oxgangs. This evening the wind is howling and the rain is lashing down. Meanwhile we're snug and warm in with only the light of two candles. Mid-evening I saw *Diana* on to her bus home; on the way back I noticed Wattie (the lovely guy who looks after the equipment at Meadowbank) awaiting his bus, so I picked him up and gave him a lift home.

<u>Morning</u>: 5 miles run Arthurs Seat including 6 hill runs

31st October, 1976 After a month of winter training, I'm gradually getting a wee bit fitter, however there's still a very long way to go. Yesterday I blew up on the last repetition of 4 x 600 metres with a 4 minutes recovery, after running 88 seconds for the first few runs. I was well and truly dropped by Adrian and Paul. It stung mentally as well as the physical effects of the lactic acid, however I saw it through and struggled through a last painful 300 metres. Today I felt a little more in control and a bit more like myself, although the session was nothing to shout home about-workmanlike is perhaps the most apt description.

Morning: **600 metres (88 seconds); 500 metres (72 secs); 400 metres (52 secs); 300 metres (38 secs) with a 4 minutes recovery**

1st November, 1975 The day of the big race. Because Dave Jenkins is giving a lecture at Frank Dick's annual International Coaching Convention, Paul Forbes got a late call up to replace him to make up the field of six internationals. Roger; Norman; Paul and I travelled through to Glasgow together to Parkhead Stadium; meanwhile Alan Pascoe and Bill Hartley flew into Glasgow from Nice, France. Because of the religious divide, the only instruction we were given by the organisers was to not wear either blue or green in case it antagonised any Celtic or Rangers fans who might throw missiles at us! We shared the same dressing room as the Celtic players. I was quite bemused at how the *professionals* prepare for a game with not much of a warm up at all and a few of them were enjoying the odd cigarette! We watched a little bit of the game, but being *amateurs* we needed to use the first half to get properly warmed up. It was quite a challenge as there was a very limited fenced in area out the back of the stadium; there was only about 80 metres to do some jogging, stretching and strides-not the usual large 400 metres arena, but it made for an interesting challenge. It was surprisingly quiet out there and we were shielded from the noise and then of a sudden a loud roar would arise. Being quite an enclosed area we were all close together. There was some talking, but I'd adopted my usual approach of becoming slightly withdrawn and focusing on what I had to do.

With David Jenkins not running I quite fancied my chances, European and Commonwealth gold medallists or not. Before the race Pascoe gathered us all together suggesting that because of the tight bends and being a cinders surface that we should forget any world record attempt; instead we should all run together for the first 300 metres to give the fans value for money and then it would be every-man for themselves. It didn't affect me one way or t'other; fast or slow I intended to sit in on the group and kick the last 100 metres, turning on the turbo-jets! Half time arrived and we emerged through the tunnel in front of 55,000 fans. What an atmosphere! It was an all-ticket sell-out. Both sets of fans were in a happy frame of mind as the score remained at 0-0 at half-time. We were introduced to the crowd and a massive cheer went up. I don't think I'd really considered just how close the crowd would be to us-within touching distance. I was feeling good-reasonably well warmed up and the adrenaline was flowing. The gun fired and Pascoe took the race out; meanwhile I settled in at the back of the group. Although we were running at around 53 seconds pace I was just cruising along, concentrating on running the shortest distance. I wore an outfit which I would never normally wear-a t-bar brown vest, white G.B. shorts and my long white socks and headband.

Sitting in Wottle-style, the biggest challenge was to be patient. Half way through Roger Jenkins took the race by the scruff of the neck with a strong burst, but eventually faded to fifth. Coming out of the final bend, everyone spread out to launch a long drive for home. According to the press I was at least ten metres down on the leader, with Paul running well and now holding the front alongside Gregor with Pascoe and Hartley a stride behind. 80 metres from the tape I put the foot down. I could hardly believe it. Inside 15 metres I easily accelerated past everyone; it was like a knife going through butter and I was still running away from the field at the finish. Once through the finish line I continued to stride around the bend to acknowledge the crowd. Paul ran well to take second place and Norrie Gregor was third-a victory for Coach Walker's squad and our preparation. Hartley was fourth and Pascoe brought up the rear. Scottish Television (STV) were filming the football match and the race too; Alex Cameron interviewed me track-side. I was still bubbling away with excitement and said *I could easily have kept that pace going for at least another 100 metres if necessary*. I guess that will be tomorrow's headline! He asked me if I thought I could make next year's Olympic team and with youthful candour and excitement and a lack of circumspection, I said *Yes!* Whilst it puts some pressure on me, why not, as half the field, Jenkins, Hartley and Pascoe are all likely to be in the mix for the Great Britain 4 x 400 metres relay team next year. I'm looking forward to watching a re-run of the race on *Scotsport* on the television tomorrow afternoon. For winning the race I received an alarm clock and twenty five pounds for travel expenses. Meanwhile Pascoe received five hundred pounds-Ce la vie...one day!

Because we left during the second half we were able to get a very smooth run out of a quiet Glasgow and back down the M8 to the King James Hotel in Edinburgh to catch Jenkins' lecture and interview which I really enjoyed. He's an intelligent, reflective individual blessed with enormous talent. Indeed, he's the greatest natural talent I've come across and an inspiration to me in many ways. He was genuinely pleased to hear of my win and said he was unsurprised-good to have his confidence. A rather wonderful day was soured slightly later on. In the evening I went out with *Pixie Mia Farrow lookalike* who was in a bloody awful mood going off in the huff about her spots. After I'd dropped her later in the evening, the *Ford Cortina* courtesy car which I'd had the loan of as one of the convention's chauffeurs for the international guests ran out of petrol; given I'd run into the back of Coach Walker's Cortina the night before when he'd braked suddenly, all made for an interesting weekend. I guess you can't have everything in life; although it doesn't remove my youthful optimism. A full on day.

International 500 metres Parkhead, Glasgow

1. P. Hoffmann (EAC) 67.4 seconds

Postscript: I'm writing this on the day after (Sunday afternoon); this morning Roger and David Jenkins and I followed up yesterday with: **2 x 3 x 500 metres with a 5 minutes recovery and 10 minutes between sets all between 70 and 73 seconds**

And *Pixie* was in a great mood too. I can keep up with *Jenks*, but not her!

2nd November, 1973 Last evening I was running very well and I'm starting to slowly improve. I ran:

1200 metres (3 minutes 48 seconds-a personal best, although it's probably the first one I've ever run); 800 metres (2 mins 19 secs); 400 metres (58 secs) all with a walk a lap recovery; then 2 x 300 metres (42.0; 42.5 secs) with a walk 100 metres recovery; a 5 minutes rest then 4 x 200 metres (20 secs recovery) 27; 29; 30; 28 seconds

I was very tired at work today which given last night's session is hardly surprising. Combined with having to get up at half past six each morning to go out to work early isn't the best thing for my athletics, but for the time being I have to thole it. However, Nana's great- preparing my breakfast of porridge and bacon as well as making up my snacks and lunch each day; she's incredibly supportive. I got my pay-rise through so I'm no longer on nine pounds a week, however there was no rise for poor Scott Wallace. Scott's like me-he's the same age, he's not stupid and he also didn't really work hard at school either. I like Scott and having him in the office makes life more bearable. As he lives at Rankin Drive, Blackford, we often journey part of the way home together.

My boss, Roy Wallace, told me that I can have the 7th December off to allow me to travel down to Cosford to take part in indoor athletics for the first time. I'm fair looking forward to it. I met Coach Walker at Meadowbank. Being a Friday it was very quiet so he spent a lot of time with me; he's given me my first weights type session to do. It will be interesting to see if it helps me to improve. My sister, Anne, is down staying with us again this evening. I went to bed after watching David Dimbleby's *Talk-In*. I'm looking forward to David Hemery's talk at the International Coaching Convention tomorrow.

Evening: Weights session

3rd November, 1973 A day immersed in athletics. This time last year Coach Walker arranged a wee job for Paul and me. It was with a company undertaking a survey of Meadowbank Sports Centre users. We spent the weekend recording and gathering hundreds of statistics by clicking little metal counters as each person passed by. We had a bit of a laugh sitting at opposite doorways chatting to hundreds of people, particularly the girls. We must be some of the best kent faces at Meadowbank-often for the wrong reasons! A year on, Coach Walker held a session for us at noon. Before we started, he introduced me to David Hemery the former Olympic champion. Today's session was a hard middle distance one which takes a lot of concentration-something which sprinters are not that good at and therefore have to learn. It's an area I need to continue developing further. It's not just training the body, but the mind too, as well as generally toughening up. I felt I was running quite well, but I'm still somewhat apprehensive and should have been a little more aggressive at the start and run the earlier repetitions more quickly. However, to be fair it was kind of unknown territory. Afterwards Paul and I joined Coach Walker and Mr Dalgleish to go out to watch the cross country before coming back to hear David Hemery give a great talk at the International Coaching Convention. What an inspiration he is. In the evening Paul and I went to the ABC Cinema. I ended up staying at his home out at Broomhouse.

Lunchtime: 8 x 600 metres (4 minutes recovery) 109; 112; 103; 100; 97; 97; 97; 99 seconds

4th November, 1977 A perfect day. Life has changed and been transformed for the better these past four years. Because of my upbringing and traumatised relationship with my father I'm aware there's a basic fragility in my make-up, but by dint of luck, application and desire I've made life so much better. Being thrown out of the family home and moving to stay with my grandparents five years ago was the catalyst for change. Living there meets all my basic needs in terms of a secure, steady home environment where there are lovely meals on the table produced as if by magic all based around my training routines. Grandma Jo hand-washes my clothes and training kit; she has an old, cranky and temperamental washing machine, but only uses it occasionally. Both Grandma Jo and Grandpa Willie take an interest and pride in my athletics achievement, but it's only ever a measured interest; non-judgemental and supportive. Willie often loans me his car to go up to Meadowbank.

Overall, there's a good sense of security, love and belonging. Athletics and Meadowbank have given me what Boroughmuir School never could-a sense of acceptance and friendship within the larger Meadowbank community as well as within smaller groups and with individuals such as Paul; Norman; Roger et al. I've also been fortunate to find good role models too such as Adrian who were missing from my life. Becoming friends with people who I admire such as Roger who are pursuing academia in tandem with athletics has lit a fire within me. It's given me the confidence to follow a similar pathway in life too. But the greatest search over the past five years has been for love and intimacy. *Pixie Mia Farrow lookalike* was the love of my life but that relationship was a doomed roller-coaster ride with great highs and bigger lows depending on her mood and how she chose to relate to me on any given day. Today I've been going out with *Diana the goddess of love and hunting* for fifteen months now and it's provided me with the security, love and fun I've been seeking.

When I started out on this odyssey the reservations were whether I had the physical ability to go all the way; now it's whether I have the mental toughness and resilience to push myself and the self-discipline to stay the course. Anyway, that's a long prelude to where I began this entry-that it was close to being a perfect day-the life of the scholar/athlete/lover. I was up before dawn and studied for several hours getting stuck into the early chapters of McCormick (Economics). I then ran up to and around Duddingston Golf Course. And for November it was a remarkably fine, but cool morning; it was really very lovely to be out running on the grass parklands and through the carpets of leaves strewn across the path the dying embers of summer which had fallen down from the increasingly barer tree branches up above.

What could be better than to be young, fit and healthy with a purpose in life? It's only a few years ago that I was stuck in Grahams' office and unable to do this, enduring the *ennui* of my miserable Dickens blacking factory period. Thereafter, home for lunch and more studying whilst Josephine and Willie took a wee tootle out to the watchmaker at the country village of Pathhead. When they returned home I went up to Meadowbank and did a wee blend of circuit work and a light track session. Tomorrow, I'm running at the Scottish East District Cross-Country Relays, but I'm really just treating it as another session so I didn't bother resting and easing down for it today or indeed this week. Afterwards I drove from Meadowbank up to Polwarth to see Denis Davidson (the physio) for a rub. On the journey a maniac went flying past and just about killed a cyclist. Come the evening I smartened up and had a lovely outing with *Diana*-a baked potato at the Meadows followed by a delightful Woody Allen movie, *Annie Hall*, which was funny and romantic, not to mention all the charming neuroses too. Talking of neuroses the only sour note was the way *Diana* was scolded by her mother when I dropped her off later. She got an absolute roasting. Ouch!

Morning: 5 miles run Duddingston Golf Course

Afternoon: Gym circuit followed by 5 x 200 metres (2 minutes recovery) all in 24-25 seconds

5th November, 1975 *Pixie Mia Farrow lookalike* and I went to see *Love Story*…we had a good time…then a hellish time…then a fabulous time…

1977 I managed to put in an hour's studying before leaving for the Scottish East District Relay Championships. It was a miserable wet day and pouring with rain when the club bus left Meadowbank at noon. *Diana* had decided to come along as she wanted to spend the whole day with me. With the inclement weather the course was very slippy and quite marshy in parts, which hardly played to any strengths that I may have. There were 36 teams running and I handed over in the middle of the pack in eighteenth place; considering it was over two and a half miles, it was a satisfactory outcome. After the first leg Andy McKean came over to speak to me- he's a lovely guy.

Diana and I enjoyed an intimate evening in and watched *The Howard Hughes Story*-what a fascinating character, but highly unusual guy. It was so late and miserable outwith, Grandma Jo suggested *Diana* should just stay over, but her mother was very nippit on the phone, so she decided to travel the long way back home to the other side of the city to Silverknowes by the sea. I'm reading Joe Haines' *The Politics of Power;* it's excellent.

Afternoon: Scottish East District Relay Championships 2.5 miles (14 mins 2 secs) (McKean 12.04; Paul 13.01)

6th November, 1977 I've enjoyed some good sleeps over the weekend which is great. Rest and recovery are as important as pushing myself in training. It was only the lovely sound of the peal of church bells ringing out over Portobello that awoke me. Today was a big day in the calendar as it was the first group track session of the winter. This past month Coach Walker has just left me to get on with some background work-essentially steady running and some circuit work on my own. So, it was with a keen sense of anticipation and a little trepidation that I ventured up to the Meadowbank track for the first session of the winter with Adrian and Paul. I was intrigued to see how I might get on. Running the half mile next year involves considerable risk with it being both a Commonwealth Games and European Championships year. But it's now or never, especially given my long term goal is to make the Moscow 1980 Olympics 800 metres final. My best 800 metres was as a first year junior when 1 ran 1 minute 53 seconds indoors on the tight 150 metres Perth track three years ago. So I'm a very long way off making Scottish never mind British teams. However, that run was a single outing. I just sat in behind Brian Gordon and followed him all the way round and finished 0.1 of a second behind. Ironically, I ended up ranked in the top five in the U.K. Junior Rankings with that time; mind you if I were to use that as a guide, I ran my first and only 400 metres hurdles that year too and was ranked second in the UK so it may not be that useful a guiding light.

Whilst the odds are against me and I have severe doubts, on the other hand in the previous two years I've done middle-distance training in the early winter months with a view to stepping up to the half before chickening out and deciding to stick with the quarter mile. So, there is more background there than everyone realises. Another positive is that even as a youngster I've often hung out with the tougher middle distance guys. It's an informed decision and there's some basis to it; and I've always been the strongest quarter miler in training sessions. But I'm aware too there have been a lot of failed attempts to move up a distance. In conversation with Steve Ovett he joked to me how the quarter milers just don't have what it takes. However, I believe if I can make the transition then I can make very quick and significant leaps forward rather than the traditional slow progress of most athletes. When I told Paul I was aiming to run one minute 46 seconds he and Davie Reid had a good laugh about it! I don't blame Paul at all. Ovett's best is only 1:45.4, so I would only be half a second slower than him; and Paul is coming at it from an informed position having run 1:48.8 back in

1976. However, I've often been a catalyst for Paul's improvement to think big and to think out of the box. I've raised the bar each year with new goals on my annual horizons and he's followed suit. Although he's not quite achieved what I've done so far it's led to him getting into G.B. teams and winning an AAA Championships which he wouldn't have initially contemplated. Anyway, interesting days; interesting times; and an interesting future-*Let the dice fly high!*

Today's session went well. It was as good a start as I've made. The key thing I was looking for was to see how well I recovered throughout the session against Adrian. Speed is never going to be a problem for me, but Adrian, being a 3 minutes 57 seconds miler has a superb recovery. I thought it would be interesting to see if the recent steady running has had any kind of a positive effect. All I can say is I ran with him for the whole session. It's a positive start. After lunch, on a soft autumn afternoon *Diana the goddess of love and hunting* and I went for a lovely outing. Whilst she walked our Smooth Fox Terrier through the Hermitage Park, I ran five miles over the Braid Hills; being a Sunday there were no golfers out so I could run where and how I pleased.

Leisure

'What is this life, if full of care,
We have no time to stand and stare...'

W.H. Davies

On such a day it's a wonderful privilege to be out there with the panoramic views across the city of Edinburgh and down the coast of East Lothian. What more could I want in life-to be young, in love and out running freely. After a late afternoon tea and with dusk falling earlier and earlier as the calendar disappears into the last two months of 1977, I read some economics. The only shadow in life is Grandpa Willie no longer has his wee part-time butchering job. I worry at what the future holds for him. He's 72 years old now and in increasingly poor health. He's finding it very difficult to breathe with severe bronchitis and emphysema. He never complains. When I see him bent over coughing it breaks my heart. He's been such a kind, loving presence in my life and supportive of me since I was born. From the health and rest perspective it's good that he isn't going out to his part-time job anymore. Yet having that day to day pattern has been good for him giving him a purpose and structure. It kept him active physically. He also needs the money to keep his wee car going. I sometimes have idle day-dreams that I'm out working and earning good monies and that I'm able to help him out for all the endless kindnesses he's done for all of us over the past twenty years. Yet because of my delayed education I know that's a long way off and that I have to be patient. He knows that too and the balm is that my small successes at athletics has given him a lot of pleasure. In his wallet he carries an article that a journalist wrote about me a few years back. *Diana* and I watched the second part of the *Howard Hughes Story* before I gave her a lift up to Easter Road to get the number 1 bus home to Silverknowes.

Morning: 8 x 300 metres (75 seconds recovery) average 43.7 seconds

Afternoon: 5 miles run over the Braid Hills Golf Course

7th November, 1973 Another freezing morning as I walked along Balcarres Street to work at Thomas Grahams & Sons with yet another cold wind cutting me to the quick. As usual the lines took up the morning; the work hardly taxes or stretches my intellect allowing me to switch off and dream of how life might be. I'm gradually beginning to formulate plans as to how I might turn my future around; the launch pad is to go out and get myself 5 good Highers. At lunchtime I borrowed a quid off Joan Campbell to go across to the Heating Department to play stud poker, coming back later to our Plumbing Department, 11p to the good. As I was travelling straight down to Meadowbank tonight, mid-afternoon I enjoyed the soup which Grandma Jo had made up for me. I ran an average session and I'm back home now; I've had my tea and I'm off to bed early.

Evening: 2 sets 10 x 150 yards (1 minute jog back recovery) all in 20 seconds; walk a lap recovery between sets, followed by a gym circuit

8th November, 1977 One of the things about keeping journals is being able to see the subtle changing patterns of the years. Five years ago in 1972 after only a few months in post I still had the tiniest vestige of enthusiasm for work, however it was ebbing away. Getting in to the life-changing habit of training at Meadowbank was the main catalyst for change. Four years ago in 1973 I was enthusiastically on board the athletics train and completely fed up with the *ennui* of work and desperately planning the great escape. Come this November Friday back in 1974 I was still trying to get the overall balance in life right. I'd left work and begun studying. On this day I called in to Drew McMaster's shop at St James Centre to buy a pair of shorts; visited Grandma Hoffmann at Dean Park Street, Stockbridge before meeting up with Paul to go and see *Butch Cassidy and the Sundance Kid*. Two years ago I was running a hard quality session of repetition 500 metres and recovering with an aerotone bath at Portobello Baths, followed by a quiet evening in, enjoying a visitation from Aunt Margaret and Andy Ross. Today was no different in the general busyness of life. At our student digs in Broughty Ferry, Dundee, Tom Morgan, Derek Anderson and I enjoyed a full breakfast from our land-lady of porridge, bacon and eggs and toast before the academic day began. During Economics I decided to make my way back to Edinburgh at lunchtime instead of at tea-time and I therefore gave my Accounts tutorial a miss. You might say old habits die hard, but the difference today is I'm ahead of schedule in terms of reading and course-work. I studied on the train for most of the journey back home to the capital. When travelling, I try to study assiduously, apart from the odd bit of contemplation as I gaze out the window or occasionally nod off because of riding the twin-train of academia and athletics. From the comfort of the train I enjoyed looking out on to the late autumn season glancing out the window as the train wound its way through the farmlands of the Fife countryside. Although it was very cold out the sun shone strongly and then weakly, before it began to slowly and then quickly sink in to the west, a giant yellow, then orange-red ball, which became a half circle, before disappearing altogether from the horizon.

Encounter

'We were riding through frozen fields in a wagon at dawn.
A red wing rose in the darkness.

And suddenly a hare ran across the road.
One of us pointed to it with his hand.

That was long ago. Today neither of them is alive,
Not the hare, nor the man who made the gesture.

Oh my love, where are they, where are they going
The flash of a hand, streak of movement, rustle of pebbles.
I ask not out of sorrow, but in wonder.'

Czeslaw Milosz

At Meadowbank, Adrian and I ran a session of 200 metres. Normally it's a strong suit for me, but this tea-time, 27 seconds for each run seemed unusually quick. In the evening I picked up *Diana the goddess of love and hunting* at the west end and we went to see The Corries folk group who were, as usual, excellent. During the interval I met my former Boroughmuir P.E. teacher, the great T.A.S. Taylor. He was saying he's been going along to watch them perform for years. Of course Ronnie Browne will be an ex-pupil of his too. It's changed days since T.A.S. had a quiet, stern word with me in 1971 about the need to *Pull your socks up!* After the interval I got a mention in one of their jokes; I wonder what T.A.S. thought; changed days indeed. After the show we went backstage for ten minutes before I drove *Diana* back home to Silverknowes by the sea. It's been a packed and full-on day, but enjoyable too. I'll have to pay for my sins, getting up at 5.40 a.m. tomorrow to catch the early morning train at Waverley Station back to Dundee to get in on time for my Economic Development lecture and then to run seven miles in the afternoon. I see heavy rain is predicted.

Evening: 10 x 200 metres (90 seconds recovery) all in 27 seconds; with Adrian

9th November, 1975 A lovely frosty morning out. Before and after breakfast I studied until the church bells could be heard ringing out. Grandpa Willie gave me a loan of his little white Ford Escort, with the go faster Mexico thin red stripes so I was able to take some of Coach Walker's squad down the East Lothian coast to Gullane to train on the sands. Big Norrie sat in the front so we were able to enjoy some good craic; whilst Ann Sowersby; Linda Waite; and *Pixie Mia Farrow lookalike* were able to blether away in the back. The weather was glorious. It was crisp and cool, but the sun shone all day. As ever it was great fun and a fantastic workout. Coach Walker led us on the usual fast jog warm-up run before we did a variety of stretching; sprints; bounding and then an Indian relay along the shore to finish the session as usual with an intensive and competitive relay race on the Big Dipper dune. For most of us we reach that point where your legs just give way and you collapse on to the sand. The terrain is a great leveller and athletes who I might normally out-run quite easily on the track can be surprisingly close to you on the beach sands. That natural spring which gives you an advantage is taken away and instead it becomes solely a matter of raw strength. A few of the athletes were sick. I tend to feel sick, dizzy and with the usual feeling of a burning lactic sensation. However, I don't feel the same intensity and nauseousness which you get from a longer flat out effort on the athletics track. Coach Walker is smart in getting everyone working hard through a subtle peer pressure by organising us into team relays; the athletes end up going the extra mile and pushing themselves harder than they might otherwise do so. And it's all within a fun environment with your team-mates cheering you on and of course it's all taking place within the glorious setting of golden sands, clear blue sky and sea. At the end of the two hour session I ran into the cold winter sea for a quick splash and cold dip. I was just showing off; as usual. Thereafter, we trudged back up to the car park and headed back home to the capital, via Musselburgh and Lucas ice cream shop, the finest in Scotland, where we all stopped off for a slider or a tub of Italy's finest export. After dropping off the others I gave *Pixie* a lift out to Cramond to Dunfermline College of P.E. On this Sunday afternoon we're gloriously in love and sat in the car for a couple of hours enjoying magical moments together.

When You Are Old

'When you are old and grey and full of sleep,
And nodding by the fire, take down this book,
And slowly read, and dream of the soft look
Your eyes had once, and of their shadows deep;'

W.B. Yeats

A lovely and memorable day; one not to be forgotten.

<u>Afternoon:</u> 2 hours session on Gullane Sands; the usual leg-sapping, mind-numbing session to exhaustion!

10th November, 1977 Next year I have to *really start delivering* and reaping the rewards of the commitment revealed in these earlier entries. It's commensurate with looking over a bank-book and the monies deposited over the years and the interest and capital accumulated, from which I hope to draw upon in 1978. The journals proper began in 1971; the training diaries were first written up toward the end of December, 1972. They're like yokes in harness. A matching, but different pair, which when harnessed together provide a rounded picture-*The Top Secret Diary of Retep Nnnamffoh*.

Although I was only sixteen when I started the athletics journal, looking back, it may have been an unconscious statement of intent or purpose and one of the first intimacies of a growing maturity. It marked a moment in time. It was a statement, that after dabbling with the sport, that YES, I'm serious about this athletics venture.

On this day four years ago in 1973 I was down at Musselburgh Racecourse taking part in a team cross-country relay. The race wasn't much fun, but I enjoyed the afternoon out having spent all morning working within the confines of Dickensian Thomas Graham & Sons. I ran **6 minutes 24 seconds.** I was a second quicker than Paul, which must have been a first. And last! However, we were both ten seconds slower than John who was the *Star in the East* at the time and also Stewart Walters. 1974 was a breakthrough year. I spent the morning cruising: **2 sets of 5 x 200 metres (2 mins recovery) in 24 or 25 seconds followed by mobility, hurdling and hill repetitions** In the afternoon it was tea at Coach Walker's home, courtesy of his wife, Kay, followed by us sitting down together for three and a half hours to agree my targets for 1975.

On this day in 1976; '…I sat and watched the American tennis player, Jimmy Connors play tennis at Meadowbank for half an hour…he's an impressive athlete...' Today, I'm riding the twin horses of academia and international athletics. It's hard work. I slept in this morning, not arising until 7.25 a.m. When the alarm proper went off at 7.15 a.m. I thought *What's an alarm going off at five o'clock for!*

Psychology was fun. We conducted food taste and colour experiments on the good citizens of Dundee before I travelled back home to the capital on the train, but studying all the way. At Waverley Station I bumped into our elderly bachelor neighbour, Howard Anderson. He's a real character. I'm very fond of him. He's been working as a chiropodist at *Binns' Department Store* for almost half a century now. On the bus home he told me that he's only just started getting every second Saturday off. He deserves it! As on several previous tenths of November the weather was foul, wet and windy. I struggled through an evening run down to Eastfield and then ran along the Joppa and Portobello promenade and sea-front; the sea was raging and the wind howling against me until I turned into the relatively sheltered cobbled streets of Brighton Crescent and jogged back to the sanctuary of home. But there, it's done. And I feel all the better for it.

<u>Evening:</u> 4 miles run

11th November, 1975 A difficult day. After college Gaga gave me the loan of his car and I went up to Meadowbank to train. I wasn't running well. Coach Walker and I had a major fall-out. As you might expect I was told in no uncertain terms that I needed to pull the finger out and if not perhaps I should consider looking for another coach. So I'm feeling pretty fragile at the moment on that front, not to mention the roller-coaster ride with *Pixie Mia Farrow lookalike*. There's a basic fragility and insecurity at the heart of me. Whilst I may come across as someone who is confident and out-going with a lot going for me, perhaps even a little bit cocky, I don't think I'm brash in say the Drew McMaster class as I'm sensitive to others' moods and needs. And whilst I've been described as cocky in newspaper articles, it's really just a *joie de vivre* at winning races. Afterwards I drove out to Cramond and Dunfermline College of P.E. after giving Ann Sowersby a lift en-route. *Pixie* and I sat for several hours having a lovely conversation. God, she's so beautiful; I love her.

Sonnet 18: Shall I compare thee to a summer's day?

'Shall I compare thee to a summer's day?
Thou art more lovely and more temperate:
Rough winds do shake the darling buds of May,
And summer's lease hath all too short a date;
Sometime too hot the eye of heavan shines,
And often is his gold complexion dimm'd;
And every fair from fair sometime declines,
By chance or nature's changing course untrimm'd;
But thy eternal summer shall not fade,
Nor lose possession of that fair thou ow'st;
Nor shall death brag thou wander'st in his shade,
When in eternal lines to time thou grow'st;
So long as men can breathe or eyes can see,
So long lives this, and this gives life to thee.'

William Shakespeare

Evening: 4 x 200 metres (2 minutes recovery) all in 26 seconds; (8 minutes rest) 3 x 200 metres 24; 29; 29 seconds (2 minutes recovery)

Afterthought: From a distance, given the poor quality of the session and me supposedly aiming for the Olympics next year, Coach Walker has a point. It's a bit of a wakeup call.

12th November, 1973 *Aaarrrgh!*-Mondays! It was very windy this morning. I walked along Balcarres Street to Thomas Graham & Sons. When I arrived there I was surprised to see all the ware-housemen outside the premises on strike! Well, that was a slightly different start to the week. It meant that none of the plumbing and heating businesses in the city could buy their wares. I assume that Davie Rogan the Manager must have gone outside to negotiate with them; it certainly wouldn't have been wee Mills the Director. He would have been too feart and then too combustible! Man, he just blows-a *Mr Krook'* (*Bleak House*) waiting to happen! He sits in his room all morning reading *The Scotsman* newspaper; nice work if you can get it. He would have called Mr Rogan through and begun in his languorous home-spun way, infused with his Glaswegian accent, *'Eh.......Davie!'* Anyway, the guys were back inside by 11.00 am. I'd bought a wee cassette recorder off Marion's catalogue and she brought it in today; it's alright. It's nice and compact for my wee bedroom at Nana's. Need I say it, but work was once again very boring, allowing me to go off on flights of fancy as to how life might and WILL be! Come the end of a slow day I was quite lucky as Scott Wallace's old boy gave us both a lift, so I was back home to 45 Durham Road by 5.30 p.m.-a luxury for me! Because of the inclement weather-not only was it windy, but it poured with rain all evening too, Coach Walker had us train indoors; afterwards I didn't hang around with the crew so I was back home by 9.00 p.m.

Evening: Weights/Gym Session followed by 4 x 6 x back to back 60 metres-all competitive with several of us vying for the front; I wanted to win every one!

1975 I telephoned *Pixie Mia Farrow lookalike*...we had a really good chat...

13th November, 1977 At 8.30 a.m. our Fox-Terrier, Jill, was at my bedroom door excitedly saying *Get up*! I let her in and sleepily drew back the curtains and opened the window for her to sniff the late autumn morning air. It's a Sunday, so a nice moment. I jumped up, pulled on a pair of jeans and rubbers and took the car up Durham Road to collect the milk and papers and then took the dog to Portobello Park and Golf Course for a walk. It was very quiet out. I could see only one old man and his dog in the far distance. It was surprisingly bright, but crisp and cold and promised to be a lovely day given the time of the year. It was timeous as Adrian; Paul; John and I were running a middle distance session; perfect conditions and it turned into a fair old session too.

Diana, the goddess of love and hunting came down and joined me for lunch. We picked up some ice cream at *Arcari's*; she went through to the back shop to adore the kittens. It was such a lovely afternoon we went for a stroll with the dog through the Figgate Park. We were reminiscing on our primary schooldays. For once she was dominating the conversation, which was lovely. On our travels we met the physiotherapist and masseur, Davie Campbell. It was great to see him; he wants me to have a chat with him next Sunday. We fell out and it would be good to patch things up as we always got on well and he was another part of the jigsaw that helped my small successes, as well as being supportive on the *Pixie Mia Farrow lookalike* roller-coaster ride. In the evening *Diana* copied out my study notes. She's such a beautiful, neat, stylist. Afterwards I dropped her off at Easter Road to get her bus home; fortunately there was no hanging around this time as the wind was biting. Thereafter, dressed up in mittens, trackie bottoms and a white jumper I went out for a miserable steady run,

Morning: 8 x 300 metres (2 minutes recovery) all between 40 and 42 seconds

Evening: 4 miles steady run

14th November, 1975 *Pixie Mia Farrow lookalike* and I had the most wonderful evening listening to records with her ending up naked as the day she was born...

How my true love and I lay without touching

How my true love and I lay without touching
How my hand journeyed to the drumlin of his hip
My pelvis aching
Just like two saints or priests or nuns
my true love and I lay without touching.
How I would long for the brush of a kiss
to travel my cheek or the cheek of my groin
my heart aching
But like two saints or priests or nuns
my true love and I lay without touching.

...and I aching
in our cold single beds with many seas dividing
as we think of the years that we spent without touching.

Leland Bardwell

1977 Hell on earth as the Monday morning alarm rang out telling me to get up from my cosy warm Edinburgh bed to travel up to Dundee; however, Grandma Jo's bowl of porridge, brown sugar and cream puts a smile on my face. Once again, it was very cold out. I set off from Portobello for Waverley Station to catch the early morning train. Grandpa Willie is so very good getting up to give me a lift, especially as he no longer has to go out to work anymore.

Those Winter Sundays

Sundays too my father got up early
and put his clothes on in the blueblack cold,
then with cracked hands that ached
from labour in the weekday weather made
banked fires blaze. No one thanked him.

I'd wake and hear the cold splintering, breaking.
When the rooms were warm, he'd call,
and slowly I would rise and dress,
fearing the chronic angers of that house,

Speaking indifferently to him
who had driven out the cold
and polished my good shoes as well.
What did I know, what did I know
Of love's austere and lonely offices?

Robert Hayden

It's a greater struggle for him nowadays, but I know how much he still likes to help me out in whatever small way he can. However, once he's up and heading back home to Portobello he collects his *Scottish Daily Express* newspaper and it sets him up for the rest of the day. I studied for most of the train journey and fortunately the train was on time. Lectures were pretty good today. I found Mike Swanson's Psychology tutorial on the impact of birth order and personality illuminating. As only three of us turned up it was good to be able to participate more too. Before dinner I ran four miles. We've got a new student bringing the quota at our student digs back up to four once again. He's a cheerful lad called Jimi from Malaysia. After dinner the four of us wandered down to the local Broughty Ferry Cinema to watch *Everything You Ever Wanted to Know about Sex but Were Afraid to Ask*! It was absolutely disgusting-actually we had a good laugh! On the way back to our digs I bumped into Barbara Lyall. She's absolutely lovely and told me to look in for coffee. Coach Walker used to coach her back in the 1960s when she made two Scotland Commonwealth Games teams. She was interested to hear I've decided to move up to the half mile next year; she says she's going to follow my progress.

Evening: 4 miles steady run

15th November, 1977 Like a river the years flow by with various twists and turns, but I'm in a good place. Three years ago I went down to visit Nana Hoffmann at 14 Dean Park Street, Stockbridge, but she wasn't in and I'd wondered whether something was up. Today, she's no longer with us. Two years ago I'd had a temporary fall out with Coach Walker and looked round to see the national coach, Frank Dick for some advice and recorded *He was really good*. This evening I'm sitting in my room in dark Broughty Ferry. I was out early this morning at 6.40 a.m. for a run along the flat coastal plain and quiet coastal roads of the Ferry. A man alone. There was no other soul out. I ran along the dark sea-front, past the harbour. Looking out to sea it was bitterly cold. I can't say I'm looking forward to Thursday morning's run. Meanwhile, Accounts was fine this morning; it's Conventional Accounting, so, intellectually, it was pretty straightforward. At lunchtime I ate in the refectory for the first time. It was a wee change as I'm getting fed up with ham salads. The chap Sharpe sat at the next table to me. He's a quiet sort of a lad. I suspect there's a lot to him. In the afternoon I did another steady run. It's fucking great discipline. In the evening I went out for a meal and a couple of drinks with my room-mate, Derek Anderson. He's a lovely lad and you can't but like him. He was talking about pensioners not getting enough money to live on, making some astute points. Bed by 10.00 p.m. I'm very sleepy, which isn't surprising.

Morning: 4 miles steady run

Afternoon: 6 miles steady run

16th November, 1976 *Pixie Mia Farrow lookalike* and I travelled down to Hawick together…we didn't get on too well…something is spoiling things and it's definitely emanating from her-I'd like things to work…

1977 At this time of the year I often used to venture down to Hawick for the cross country league races. On one occasion Paul and I went off for a three course meal at a local café; I assume that was after the race! And on another day wrote …*Pixie Mia Farrow lookalike was her usual enigmatic self.* Anyway, it's a Wednesday and today I'm at our Broughty Ferry digs at the end of a full day. I've enjoyed our land-lady's breakfast these past few winter mornings; the porridge is a good start, but it's the well-cooked bacon 'n eggs which are the stars. It was quite nippy out and the heating was full on making student life challenging and boring. Our Economic Development lecturer, Mr Ingram, seems to read out sentences in no apparent logical order. And there was a lot of information to take in on binomial theory. Later on as I headed down to the university facilities for my first workout of the winter on the cinder track I felt somewhat lethargic but ran a 600 metres session, all in the aimed for times. Towards dusk I walked back to the changing rooms. Looking out over an overcast River Tay I reflected on how running alone on such a miserable wet, cold November afternoon is in many ways a masochistic existence. But I guess it will be worth it all come the heat of Edmonton, Canada next summer. Back at our digs we were served up a fish and potato meal with a white sauce; our land-lady, Mrs Neve, takes her role seriously. She's a no-nonsense, tall, strong woman who is very much the matriarch of the family; whereas her husband is a pleasant, down to earth, straightforward guy. They're a good family doing the best that they can; and although when she sallies back and forth from the dining room and I make the other lads roar with laughter about my flights of fancy about their 16 year old daughter and *the horn!*, I actually have a tremendous respect for their family unit and their wee boy, Glen, is a super wee lad. He's very fond of me and I make a bit of a fuss of him. Afterwards I lay and soaked in the bath for a while reading *Punch*. My calfs are tight which is unsurprising as I'm unused to running on my toes, not to mention the gym-work too. Before lights out I managed to read a sizeable amount of Psychology. I'm in bed now listening to the England v Italy World Cup qualifier on the radio; so far 1-0 to the Englanders with Italy playing a very physical game and breaking the rules; what do you expect-is the Pope Catholic!

Afternoon (1.00 p.m.): Gym circuit

Afternoon (2.00 p.m.): 6 x 600 metres (3 minutes recovery walk a lap of the 200 metres cinder track) all between 97 and 103 seconds

17th November, 1974 Last year I ran one of my better cross country races down at Hawick and finished sixteenth. I got a couple of shouts from the lovely Jan McCall which put a spring in my step. I won 50p at cards on the bus, so it was a bright day. Yesterday I went down to the border-lands, but this time just to watch Paul and the rest of the club's athletes. Last night, on a beezer of an evening, Gaga dropped Paul and me off at a dance at Watsonians Rugby Club, but it was a pretty disappointing affair. Afterwards I ended up staying the night at Mother's. It was like old times. First thing this morning I walked up to Ewarts Newsagents at Oxgangs Broadway to buy in some Sunday rolls. It was lovely having breakfast and a blether with Mother and the family indoors on such a frosty morn. But, before I knew it the St John's Church bell was ringing out calling me to *worship* at Meadowbank. I wandered across to the bus stop and took the number 4 bus across the city to Meadowbank to join Roger Jenkins for a workmanlike session. Coach Walker's session was much more suited to me and I ended up running Rodge into the ground. We had to sweep him off the track afterwards, but fair play to him, he completed the session. After a wee snack in the Meadowbank café, a blether and some recovery, we did a circuit in the gym. Come the evening I didn't feel too well so I only did a few sit-ups and went to bed early.

Morning: **2 x 4 x 150s (jog back recovery) in our tracksuits, but the runs felt quite fast (walk/jog 2 laps rest); 4 differential 400 metres (walk a lap recovery) (1) 52 seconds (28/24 secs); (2) 53 secs (28/25 secs); (3) 57 secs (34/23 secs); (4) 58 secs (31/27 secs)**

Afternoon: **Gym circuit**

Before Bed: **Sit-ups**

1975 I went to Paul's party…*Pixie Mia Farrow lookalike* was in a foul mood…

18ᵗʰ November, 1977 1973 becomes 1974 and then '75 becomes '76; and now here we are in 1977. I'm never quite sure why I keep these journals and for what purpose. It's not as if they'll ever see the light of day. Some people say it's a way of putting the world in order or at least a way of ordering it in one's mind and thus making sense of it-recording events and one's reactions to them. When I flick through the pages I stray across long forgotten posts from the mists of time e.g. four years ago I joined a scratch 4 x 100 metres relay team who ran against the Scotland team that will be travelling across the globe to New Zealand for the Commonwealth Games in early 1974. On a tragic and heart-breaking note, in 1974, Trevor Cole's brother, Chris, died in his sleep-devastating for the family; I felt so sorry for them. Two years ago I was on another roller-coaster with *Pixie Mia Farrow lookalike*. I became so exasperated with her mood swings and attitude toward me that I suggested a break, which I accurately predicted would become permanent and over which I'm still heartbroken. By this time last year Nana Hoffmann had died. Dad posted out the wee Stockbridge Trustee Savings Bank, bank-books in which she'd placed forty pounds for each of the three of us (Anne; Iain; and me) many years before, when she must have come into a little money. What a wonderful thing. It wasn't the money that really counted; and instead it was the gesture, the forethought and the kindness. It's one of these little things in life which others do for you that you don't forget. I was thinking there's a danger of me becoming too focused, too isolated and too serious. Grandma Jo and Grandpa Willie had dropped me off at a wet and windy Meadowbank on their way to *Safeways*. I ran a miserable session. Once back home I enjoyed a lovely steak dinner and then made some inroads on my Economic Development reading, before going back up to Meadowbank in the late afternoon to do a circuit. Paul; John; and Fritz were all there and tried to persuade me to go out drinking with them, but I said no, that I was too busy and didn't really have the time-FFS, it's a Friday night! I looked into Denis's for a rub. He was saying he'd received a postcard from Roger Jenkins who's settled down well at the Sporting Club de Paris with their excellent training facilities. I miss our sessions together, but I guess the world has moved on. On the way home to Portobello I grabbed a small 12p ice cream from *Demarco's* at Tollcross-it's still as flavoursome. In the evening I sat in with Willie watching *Superstars*. I suppose a small positive from not going out is that it gives my grandfather some company and I treasure these wee moments together. I sat up late into the night and completed the research needed for my Economic Development essay.

Morning (10.00 a.m.): **15 x 200 metres slow/fasts all in 28-30 seconds (90 seconds jog 200 metres recovery)**

Afternoon (4.00 p.m.): **Gym circuit**

19th November, 1977 Although it falls tomorrow we celebrated Paul Forbes' 21st birthday today. Directly after breakfast I ran five miles; well that was a big mistake as half way round I felt very dizzy. Once back home to 45 Durham Road we discovered Grandpa Willie's car had two flat tyres. I pumped them up for him and we went off to the local *Kwikfit* to get them repaired. The lad said someone had thrown a couple of darts at them and repaired the tyres for free. It was very decent of him and was especially helpful given Will is not well off. Willie thereafter dropped me off in town and I bought some shoes, a couple of shirts and ties. The weather was an atypically wet and windy November day-very blustery. Whilst doing my afternoon session towards dusk out the back of Meadowbank (Meadowbank Thistle FC were playing under the floodlights in the stadium) it reminded me of running there in the G.B v USSR match, which was a similarly miserable evening too. Afterwards I looked into the weights room and found Paul was already there-he was down early. I belted up town and bought him an Oxford Dictionary for his 21st; I hope he likes it. *Diana the goddess of love and hunting* wrote out the inscription from us in her inimitable, beautiful hand. Paul; Lorraine; Mark; Davie; John; Lorna; Earl; Fritz; *Diana*; and I travelled down to Tranent to George McNeil's restaurant. We had a great time-loads o' laughs and far tae much to drink! Later on we went back to Elsie's (Elsie Morris-Lorraine's mum) at Mountcastle for food. She'd put on a great spread. She's such a lovely woman. Suddenly it hit me; I felt absolutely terrible. I'm clearly just an amateur on the drinking front. *Diana* and I walked the mile home; the cold fresh air helped me, but not poor *Diana!*

Morning (10.00 a.m.): **5 miles run**

Afternoon (3.00 p.m.): **4 x 6 back to back 60 metres sprints with a 10 seconds recovery and 2 minutes between sets; followed by a small gym circuit**

20th November, 1977 The morning after the night before. *Diana the goddess of love and hunting* and I were somewhat fragile from Paul's 21st birthday celebrations the night before. I was a little light-headed, but poor *Diana* felt terrible. Meanwhile, Nana and Aunt Heather were away for the day, hunting agates in the ploughed fields of Fife. Between 10.00 a.m. and 5.00 p.m. there was a mix of light and heavy snowfalls. I chose the early afternoon as the best time to go out and train. There were no other athletes out. Meadowbank was cold and miserable; it snowed for much of the session, but I struggled through it, mainly going through the motions; still it was better than doing nothing at all. On the way home and as requested last Sunday, I called into see the physio, Davie Campbell. He said no more appointments until I pay him 20 quid! *How much! Aye, that'll be right.* I looked into Lorraine's to collect my cap; they were all a little fragile, but looked fine. Once back home *Diana* made my meal and we all had some Arcari's ice cream; she'd looked after Willie all day, hand and foot! *Diana* wasn't looking forward to going home; it's no wonder as her father had smashed her head through a window pane. I'm in bed now; outside it's cold and a light snow is falling; it's beautiful to look out at; parts of the neighbourhood have a distinctly Edwardian feel to them.

Afternoon: 5 x 500 metres (3 minutes recovery) 75 seconds; cold, snowing and windy

21st November, 1976 The usual *Pleasant Valley Sunday* with breakfast, newspapers and up to Meadowbank. Because my left Achilles tendon is giving me gyp I decided not to train. Instead I took *Diana the goddess of love and hunting* out to the quiet country lanes of Carrington, Midlothian to give her a wee driving lesson in Willie's *Ford Escort*. Although it's late autumn, the countryside is still gorgeous, clothed in a range of browns; the hedgerows remain full; and the ancient trees that line the country roads testament to the legacy of the farmers who planted them centuries previously. *Diana* enjoyed herself and did very well for her first drive-especially being a woman! On the way back we stopped off for Lucas (Craigmillar) ice cream and then parked the car at Arthurs Seat before I ran her home to Silverknowes.

Having abandoned Loughborough University I've picked up a one year contract at the Scottish Council Social Service at Claremont Crescent to produce a handbook of voluntary services in Scotland. It will give me the opportunity to decide whether I want to go to St Andrews University to study next year; Frank Dick has kindly spoken with the Director, Archie Strachan. In the evening I watched John Osborne's *Look*

Back in Anger. Parts of the main protagonist's character reminded me of myself-disaffected, educated, working class...etc. No training to report today, but two years ago a good session on my own, as detailed below; and I note Kim Roberts' perceptive comment *You fancy Pixie Mia Farrow lookalike!*

Evening: 2 sets 3 x 300 metres (4 minutes recovery) (1) 38 seconds (wearing tracksuit and wetsuit!); (2) 37 secs; (3) 37 secs; (12 minutes rest between sets) (1) 36.5 secs; (2) 37 secs; (3) 36.9 secs; the weather, cold, wet and windy, thus I ran two bends

Before Bed: Arm-action; leg-work; press-ups; sit-ups

22nd November, 1975 This morning, despite completely blowing up on the last run I ran an excellent training session. I'm taking it as a positive, showing I've pushed myself pretty hard. I felt particularity good early on floating through the first half of the session. In the afternoon I warmed down with a saunter up to the Scottish Cross Country Relays to watch the iron hard men of the iron hard ground. I spent the evening reading, resisting the temptation to phone *Pixie Mia Farrow lookalike.*

Morning: 6 x 500 metres (5 minutes recovery) 71; 69; 69; 73; 72.7; 97 seconds-OUCH!!!

Before Bed: Mobility

23rd November, 1975 Coach Walker and I haven't patched things up since we fell out, so I'm mostly training on my own. It's not ideal, particularly if I'm aiming for Montreal. It's certainly a wakeup call and causing me to reflect on things. First thing I wandered up to the karate session at George Kerr's Edinburgh Club at Hillside Crescent; well that was an interesting session! Immediately afterwards I went straight down to Meadowbank and ran a solitary session-not much to write home about. However, on a very lovely late autumn day, an upbeat afternoon as *Pixie Mia Farrow lookalike* and I walked the dog for a few hours up on Arthurs Seat. After collecting Nana and Aunt Heather from Waverley Station I enjoyed *A Streetcar Named Desire;* my cultural education continues apace.

Morning (9.30 a.m.): One hour of karate including a lot of mobility followed by 1000 metres (2 minutes 50 seconds); 600m (84 secs); 300m (39 secs) (10 minutes recovery)

Afternoon: Arthurs Seat hill runs 2 sets 6 x 20 second repetitions with jog recovery (10 mins between sets) (6.03; 5.34) followed by gym-work

24th November, 1977 Yesterday I awoke with a raw, sore throat. Because it's such a big year ahead and I want to be as professional as possible I immediately began a course of antibiotics and took a rest from training. In the past I would have done the opposite! It was a very cold and nippy morning out, however the world of academia was fine and at lunchtime I had lunch with Anne McCartney. She's a nice person and a good mixer. She wants to do Personnel. She's well suited to it and will thrive in her future career. I worked all afternoon on Computing, eventually getting the hang of it, but I'm still not entirely *au fait* with Programming. I took the 5.22 p.m. train home to Edinburgh and sat and read the newspapers. It was a scruffy wee train, getting into the capital at seven o'clock. Emerging from Waverley Station I clocked the 44 bus and had to make an awkward dash along Princes Street lugging my bag and briefcase. Will gave me the loan of the car. I looked into Meadowbank for a chat with

Coach Walker. He's advised me to register a fast 800 metres time very early in the season to help ensure I get selected ahead of the established middle distance runners for Scotland's match in Greece. It seems a long way off; as Hemery's coach said *It's hard to get enthusiastic about the summer in the winter.* In the evening I went along to the Old Augustians Rugby Club with Paul; Davie; and John and had a half pint of beer and a game of darts; back home there's a poetry film on about running which should appeal to me. No training to report, but on this day in 1974:

Morning: 500 metres 66.2 seconds (12 minutes recovery); 4 x 150 yards (4 mins rec) 15.8; 15.6; 15.5; 15.9 secs

Afternoon: 2 x 6 hill runs on Arthurs Seat followed by a gym circuit

Before Bed: Arm-action; press-ups; sit-ups and mobility stretching

25th November, 1977 Because of my sore throat I went out to Oxgangs to visit the doctor and also called in to see Mother; she was in a cheerful mood. A lovely surprise-*Diana the goddess of love and hunting* turned up. As usual Dr Motley was in an excellent mood-what a cheerful persona; we were both laughing and chuckling away. He's such a character and a tonic. If you could only bottle his positive attitude to life and prescribe it to everyone, then all would be well with the world. Driving through the Queen's Park *Diana* and I were staggered at the beauty of the morning. On a fresh cold morning the scenery was stunning; the sun shone on Arthurs Seat bathing the hill in a warm and soft yellow winter glow; Duddingston Loch was as still as a millpond. Holyrood Park hasn't really changed much since Robert Louis Stevenson used to visit the park a century ago. *Diana* and I visited John Macpherson. He's an old bachelor and a former maths teacher at Boroughmuir. Last summer, he contacted me out of the blue and kindly offered me his golf clubs; because of old age he can no longer play at Prestonfield. He showed us an old photograph album from the 1920s with a lot of pictures of him hiking; there were also a few photographs of Dad, who looked remarkably like me. We stayed there until four o'clock when *Diana* had to go off to work at Safeways. I dropped in to Denis's for a rub; he'd received a letter from Roger in Paris; he's doing fine and aiming for the indoors. Homeward bound for a wee bit telly and some studying. No training to report again, but detailed below from a younger me back in 1973 complaining *'I wasn't running too well.'*

Morning: **300 meters (39.0 seconds); 200 metres (25.0 secs); 10 x 60 metres fast**

Evening: **Gym circuit**

26ᵗʰ November, 1973 I went back to work today. As Gaga is on holiday from his wee part time job at James Waugh & Son Butchers, Morningside I had to get the number 5 bus across town. I hadn't been looking forward to work, but it wasn't too bad. Having been off on Friday I got my pay-packet-a nice wee start to the day; I also received my contract too. The overtime, or should I say, stock-taking started today, so I worked on until 5.45 p.m. Stepping out into the night air from the relative warmth of Thomas Graham & Sons showroom on to Balcarres Street, I was hit by the cold. It quite took my breath away; it was FREEZING! In the evening a group track session at Meadowbank, but no weights tonight. Afterwards, Tom Drever gave me a lift part of the way home to Duddingston Crossroads from whence I walked the remaining half mile back to Durham Road. It was a still, dark evening with a clear dark sky and the stars glittered in the heavens. The temperature is well below freezing. It was good to get home to the welcoming warmth of the coal fire and bosom of the house and a little supper.

Evening: 6 x 300 metres (4 minutes recovery) 41; 43; 40; 40; 43; 45 seconds; it was FREEZING!

November Night, Edinburgh

The night tinkles like ice in glasses.
Leaves are glued to the pavements with frost.
The brown air fumes at the shop windows,
Tries the door, and sidles past.

I gulp down winter raw.
The heady Darkness swirls with tenements.
In a brown fuzz of cotton wool
Lamps fade up crags, die into pits.

Frost in my lungs is harsh as leaves
Scraped up on paths. — I look up, there,
A high roof sails, at the mast-head
Fluttering a grey and ragged star.

The world's a bear shrugged in his den.
It's snug and close in the snoring night.
And outside like Chrysanthemums
The fog unfolds its bitter scent.

Norman Macaig

27th November, 1977 With two variables there are always four potential outcomes. So taking antibiotics at the start of my sore throat may have resulted in me picking up remarkably quickly within a few days and I was able to join Adrian and Paul for training today. I awoke at half past eight.

It was a glorious Sunday morning out-really wonderful.
There wasn't a breath of wind, not even a zephyr, which is
most unusual for Edinburgh. The ground was hard as iron
with a heavy white hoar frost covering the landscape. The
pond I'd created for Grandma Jo over the warm summer
months was frozen over for the first time. I collected the
Sunday newspapers and took our Fox-Terrier to Portobello
Park. The temperature was minus three yet it didn't feel that
cold so long as you kept on the move. The dog and I had
fun trying to catch leaves as they fluttered downwards from
the tree branches high up above. All things considered I ran
a fair session at lunchtime, but I blew up on the last run.
Because of the freezing temperature we decided to half the
length of the recoveries so that we didn't get too cold
hanging around in between repetitions. Afterwards the three
of us ran a steady six miles around Craigintinny Golf Course
which was closed to the golfers. It's always a great way to
finish off a Sunday. I'm enjoying some aspects of half mile
training and because Adrian ensures we only do a recovery
run at an easy pace there's some great craic between us. We
discuss ideas about training and racing, but also talk about
politics-the whole gamut and in between some good laughs
too. It was one of my most enjoyable runs ever, all enhanced
with it being a cold, still and crisp afternoon with a beautiful
orange globe sun sinking into the west. I've come to the
conclusion that you need to learn to enjoy steady running-
perhaps Psychology is going to be useful after all. Back home
at Durham Road we had a late Sunday lunch. It was good of
the household to delay the meal until I got home from
training. Afterwards, *Diana the goddess of love and hunting* wrote
out my Economic Development essay in her perfect
penmanship; it took two hours to dictate and it gave the
poor girl a headache. I would like to reward her with an
Alpha mark. We had bought *Mull of Kintyre* earlier-at least the
record! and later on sat listening to it in the darkness of the

front room with the lights off and the electric fire aglow-a lovely moment. However, before we knew it I had to see *Diana* on to the bus back home to Silverknowes; come a Sunday evening she's always so sad and usually a bit fed up. The temperature has dropped to minus four degrees below. I'm away out to put the old coat on the car engine so that the car will start tomorrow morning to take me up to Waverley Station at 6.00 a.m.

Lunchtime: 4 x 600 metres (2 minutes rec) 91; 93; 93; 100 seconds!

Afternoon (2.00 p.m.): 6 miles steady run with Adrian and Paul, Craigintinny Golf Course

28th November, 1977 On this day, 1974, I'd escaped over the walls of Thomas Graham & Sons. And, I'd even managed to get 88% for my APH exam too, so things were definitely looking up. My teachers at Boroughmuir School would have been astounded at the class dunce's progress. Similarly, in training I'd also run a personal best **300 metres in 34.5 seconds**-pretty wild for a late November evening, followed by **2 x 200 metres in 22.8 secs and 22.9 secs and then 6 x 60 metres**

Given that two years prior I was only breaking 60 seconds for 400 metres for the first time, I don't think I'd quite appreciated the literal and metaphorical strides I'd made. Why should that be? Perhaps it's emblematic of the culture and sensibility which Coach Walker has engendered. Within the squad there's an expectation, but not an arrogance, that if you set challenging, but realistic goals and apply yourself in the right way then success will follow as surely as day follows night. Part of that ethos stems from Coach Walker's close relationship with John Anderson from earlier years. It meant we were able to associate and occasionally train with John's squad of older international athletes. That good fortune rubbed off on us and is definitely a strong influence on me. They say imitation is the greatest form of flattery e.g. Coach Walker had been working with me on my technique; sometime later I heard a comment second-hand on my running style-great positive reinforcement, because I'd been modelling myself on aspects of David Jenkins. I recall watching some of John's athletes quite closely-how they prepared themselves for training-the way they warmed up-the way they carried themselves-the way they applied themselves to their training sessions and the attitude which they brought to the table. And I was already beginning to discriminate, in that most were very positive, but others slightly less so and one or two could even be a bit whiny. I began to copy some of the positive things which I liked and thought were valuable. At the start of the process I often *smiled to myself* thinking, *What are you doing Peter!* However, by sticking at it, day in day out, it really does start to become the new you. A professor told me later that there were aspects there of what's termed a phenomenological approach. However, there's a fine balance in adopting the right sensibility. I recall Paul, a few others and me being bemused by Drew McMaster and his great conceit of himself; at his cockiness and confidence; his grand predictions; his over-the-top behaviour, behaving like a mini-man, but in the body of a youth. And yet, whilst we naturally laughed, I sensed that beneath his flamboyant bravado and silly crude persona, there was something important and valuable there too that was worth exploring, harnessing and adopting, but in a more sensible and sensitive way and with a more modest demeanour. But, what was important-what was vital-was that you needed to believe in yourself.

Anyway, from the philosophical to the practical. This morning it was minus six at 6.00 a.m. Outside there was a very heavy frost. I went out and broke the ice on the garden pond; it must have been at least a quarter of an inch thick. I'm never quite sure whether it's the right thing to do by the goldfish. Meanwhile the dog follows me around and is always quite fascinated at what I'm up to. Will ran me up to Waverley Station to get the early morning train to Dundee. I bought him a *Scottish Daily Express*. On the train I envisaged him back home at Durham Road sitting reading it by the coal fire, whilst outside the bare winter garden was enveloped in a deep white frost. It gave me a warm glow to picture the scene-Willie sitting there with the dog by his side, whilst I ventured out to make my way in the world; two worlds and no doubt at times he'll think of me with a warm glow too, both of us enriching each other's lives. I hadn't slept well overnight, with a few nightmares about sleeping in, so I had to discipline myself to study and not fall asleep like several of my fellow passengers. I think part of the reason is a fear of sleeping through the alarm and missing the train; certainly that featured in a variety of formats. Another regular dream is waking up with a start as I jump from a great height. I wonder if there's a deep set fear there of breaking my legs-who knows! The world of academia was fine; our wee group won the Sociology/Psychology prize-a large tube of *Jellytots*-competitive-who, moi! I dashed down to the railway station and just managed to catch the 3.33 p.m. train out to Broughty Ferry. I may be an athlete, but it's no easy task when carrying bags as well as groceries! Once back to my room I did some stretching and then ran a pretty quick four miles-probably a personal best. Catching the early train enabled me to run on a very still late afternoon just as the light was beginning to fade. It was cold out and the thermometer was dropping like a stone. For me it's a great time of the day to run and probably when I feel at my very best. At this time of the season I was aware of that as a kid when I used to run down from home at 6/2 Oxgangs Avenue to the shops at Colinton Mains I always felt as if I were just floating across the ground. I trust the Olympic final is around this time of the day! Bath, dinner and then I studied until eight. I felt very sorry for Derek tonight; he heard his grandfather had died. It came as a bit of a shock and I tried to offer him what comfort I could. Since we began sharing digs a few months ago I've grown very fond of him and we're pretty close pals now. I guess this is where those with a religious disposition find comfort and solace; their deep faith keeps them strong. Derek was on the phone for hours so Tom and I had a pint at the local

<u>Afternoon (4.00 p.m.):</u> 4 miles run; pretty quick, followed by arm; leg; and core exercises

29th November, 1977 In 1973, Coach Walker told us to go for a steady run around the Meadowbank area. Paul had set off a bit earlier and a few minutes ahead of me; anyway, towards Jock's Lodge I noticed he'd been grabbed by a group of youths about our age. Without thinking I ran straight at the guy who had a hold of Paul and hit him so hard I broke his tooth. They all got such a shock at this *madman* they all scattered. Afterwards I was saying to Paul how bad I felt about it; however, he made me laugh saying *Fuck him, what aboot me!* Two years later, Paul crops up again and I write that I wasn't looking forward to the session at all, but managed to run with him all the way:

6 x 500 metres with a 5 minutes recovery in 73.7; 74.2; 72.4; 71.9; 72; 71.8 seconds; it was a very wet, cold, windy and an icy track; we jogged non-stop in between each run

Today we had an amusing start to the morning. The four of us all trooped down to Broughty Ferry Railway Station to take the train into Dundee; however Derek had forgotten his books-daft bugger-and had to belt back to our digs. I probably should have volunteered as I would have been quicker; anyway, he just made it careering along the platform with Jimi; Tom and me cheering him on! Later, we all met up for lunch. Naturally, Derek is still down about the death of his grandfather. It will take a wee while for him to get over it. The Accounts tutorial-Conventional Accounting, was fine, with one amusing moment. We thought the tutorial had finished, then the lecturer said *Now Mr Mackenzie...* and asked a rather challenging question which the normally laid back and cool Derek Mackenzie floundered over. Late afternoon I took the train back to Broughty Ferry in the company of Fonzie who's a very likeable, amusing and well balanced sort of a character. He's originally from Glasgow, but now lives in Castle Douglas. He's staying with his auntie out at Carnoustie. Later, a wee steak pie for dinner after my run. I'd telephoned *Diana the goddess of love and hunting* but she was out. I'm waiting for her to ring back, but suspect she won't before I go to bed.

Evening: 4 miles run in my tracksuit; it was raw and very cold out

Before Bed: Arm and leg-work

30th November, 1977 The bedrooms in our digs are so cold that I slept in a tracksuit all night. I'm still taking cold baths first thing in the morning and I keep thinking I'm about to have a heart attack. I took the train in for Economic Development; as usual, it was very boring. I was glad to escape for the afternoon to do a gym session followed by a track session on the 200 metres cinder track at Riverside

Park. Out with it was a lovely afternoon with the ground still hard frozen over and covered in a white frost; once again I had the place to myself. And although it was cold, the sun was out and there was no wind. These sessions really just keep me ticking over until I'm back in the capital at weekends, but perhaps it's a better balance than hammering myself night after night? And afterwards, it was nice to be able to walk back contemplatively to have a long hot shower at the changing rooms. I took the train back to Broughty Ferry and managed to put in a good shift of Economics; later I telephoned *Diana the goddess of love and hunting* and then nipped out for a quick pint with Tom. It was a raw, damp, frosty night; still I'm back to Edinburgh tomorrow. It's an unusual habit for me, but I'm re-reading my favourite book, *The Ginger Man,* by J.P. Donleavy. Mother introduced Donleavy to Paul and me when we were only sixteen.

<u>Afternoon (1.30 p.m.):</u> Gym circuit

<u>Afternoon (2.15 p.m.):</u> 600 metres (89.9 seconds) 10 minutes rest followed by 8 x 200 metres with a short walk recovery

1st December, 1974 makes me think of *Sweet Baby James*; the last line in the first verse seems appropriate:

Sweet Baby James

'…With ten miles behind me and ten thousand more to go…'

James Taylor

Last year on this day Paul and I had a bit of a laugh. We commandeered a taxi out to a cross country race at Esk Valley where *I ran rubbishly over hill 'n dale.* I'd been working at

Thomas Graham & Sons until 11.00 a.m. helping out with their stocktaking, before nipping into town with the overtime monies to buy my first wet-suit

It's quite poignant to look back on this day because Paul and I went to see a film with Chris Cole, who died only a couple of weeks ago. It was an enjoyable evening; we watched *Shaft in Africa*; but today it's a sobering thought and certainly puts things into perspective. Talking of sobering, last night was Bob Sinclair's birthday party which I greatly enjoyed. *The Mary Rand lookalike from the south-west* had too much to drink and was sick. I ended up chatting with a lovely girl called Aileen Gordon, before giving Ann Clarkson a hand to wash up the dishes in the early hours.

I put in a good double session. In the morning Coach Walker asked me to help out a guy who was undertaking a coaching exam. I think he was required to work with someone who is an international athlete; he didn't bat an eye at the session, assuming it was standard fayre. I thought it was pretty solid myself; I couldn't see many teenagers doing it, but there you go-nonchalant!

In the afternoon Coach took the group across to Arthurs Seat where we ran a very hard hill session on the usual '20 seconds' hill' just beyond St Anthony's Chapel. In the evening I sat in playing some music and thinking about last evening's conversation with Aileen.

<u>Morning:</u> 6 x 200 metres (3 minutes 30 seconds recovery) 24.5; 24.2; 24.5; 24.7; 24.6; 24.5 secs

<u>Afternoon:</u> Arthurs Seat 6 hill runs (jog recovery) 5 minutes 42 seconds-my legs were killing me!

Before Bed: **Arm action; press-ups; sit-ups and mobility stretching**

2nd December, 1977 Although back then I didn't keep any training diaries in my 1972 diary Paul and I went out to the Esk Valley Cross Country five years ago today and recorded he was 4th and I was 20th; never mind the former, 20th wasn't too shabby! In 1973 I wrote 'Thank goodness Bill isn't throwing me out!' so I must have been up to no-good and he gave me the dubious pleasure of running:

6 x 200 metres in 25-27 seconds with a 2 minutes recovery

In 1975 we'd still fallen out at this stage of the year and not resolved our differences-the ups and downs and ebb 'n flow of life. Anyway, nothing to report on the training front today as it was a rest day, but much more interesting on the non-athletics front. I kicked off the day with an hour of Economics reading when Mother phoned-*Would I come out to Oxgangs to have a wee chat with Iain?* He's wanting to return home, perhaps hardly surprising given how young he was in getting married. At lunchtime I went out to Oxgangs. Anne was there-she'd had her Physics prelim in the morning. Along with Mum the three of us had a fun afternoon. At four o'clock I popped down to Denis Davidson's for a rub and then came back to Oxgangs for my tea. Iain and I then went down to Morningside for a pint or three! We met our old neighbour from 6/6 Oxgangs Avenue, Gail Blades, and her pal and we all went back to her flat at Balcarres Street and met up with Fiona Blades. I haven't seen her for years since we used to do morning papers together at Bairds Newsagents five years before and that last summer of my boyhood when we'd camped at Stobo, Peebleshire, along with Paul, Iain and Ali Blades. Around 10 p.m. I took the number 5 bus home to Portobello. I thought how thin Fiona looked and unhappy at the way life was panning out; she was such a bright girl. Our paths have taken such diverse routes. I always liked Fifi and we got on pretty well. It was strange to see her again and to reflect on the twists and turns of life's path. If you think about it too much it's disconcerting. It's a bitterly cold evening and a tough session awaits me tomorrow at Meadowbank with Adrian and Paul.

Rest Day

3rd December, 1977 I managed an hour of Economics before going up to Meadowbank to run a good session. On a cold winter's Saturday morning as we ran a session of 500s it felt like old times. We had a good group out-Paul; Adrian; Norrie Gregor; and John Scott. I was running quite well and only got dropped on the last repetition. Afterwards I had a good chat with Coach Walker before doing a gym circuit. I got back to Portobello around three in the afternoon, but only Will was in; he rattled up my lunch, a plate of fish and potatoes. He was telling me that Jimmy Sneddon reckons his car is knackered; poor Will; if anyone deserves a wee car it's him. I lay on Jo's bed in the front room and read some Economics, mainly the theory of pricing, although I ended up nodding off for half an hour-hardly surprising given being out in the fresh air and having exercised hard.

Diana the goddess of love and hunting arrived around five o'clock, just before Josephine and Aunt Heather came home. She was in a poor mood early on-it takes two of us to make things right. Will crushed the two of us at our wee game of dominoes before the *Two Ronnies*. I counted 45 laughs for Corbett on his one man spot! *Diana* was staying the night; she didn't want to leave the warmth of the bed!

Lunchtime (12.00 p.m.): 6 x 500 metres (3 minutes recovery) 76; 75; 75; 75; 75; 80 seconds; the track was icy with a a very cold wind; I ran with Paul and Adrian until the last repetition-not unhappy with that

Afternoon (1.30 p.m.): Gym circuit

4th December, 1977 In 1973 after our session I wrote *...as usual Norrie Gregor was praising me yet he's miles better than me, but I'm trying to keep up with him in training.* Come 1975 Ann Sowersby told me I've *'...to finish with Pixie Mia Farrow lookalike on Saturday as I'm too much for her. I don't know what I'll do.'* And then, rather ironically *'...I was just settling back with a book when Pixie phoned me.'* Huh-women! And on now to '76. Iain's motorbike had broken down at Meggetland, so we towed it back over the ice-what a laugh that was! This morning *Diana the goddess of love and hunting* and I cleaned out the garden pond. Only one of my fish is dead-result! I ran a fair session of 300s with Paul and Adrian, however I should have gone for a jog yesterday afternoon. When I got up this morning my legs were very stiff from yesterday's session; my pins felt as if they still had some lactic acid in them. It was cold, wet and rather miserable. *Diana* came up to watch the session. In the afternoon we went for a six miles run around Craigintinny Golf Course whilst she went down to Arcari's to get some ice cream. I really enjoyed the run; a nice steady recovery run and good company. When I got home I felt pretty knackered. I had some dinner, packed my stuff and *Diana* chummed me up to Waverley Station. I met Tom Morgan and we had a quick beer before getting the mobbed London-Aberdeen train, alighting at Dundee. I managed to gather in six of the *Sundays* so lots of reading. Fortunately we got a bus out to Broughty Ferry right away. A cup of tea, a cracker 'n cheese, then bed. A new week awaits.

Afternoon (1.00 p.m.): 8 x 300 metres (90 seconds recovery) 42-43 seconds; last two nearer 44; with Adrian all the way

Afternoon (2.30 p.m.): 6 miles steady run Craigintinny Golf Course with Adrian and Paul

5th December, 1977 In 1973 I was becoming pretty keen. My boss at work, Roy Wallace, told me to stay on at Thomas Graham & Sons late in to the evening to work overtime, but I couldn't as training was starting at 6.00 p.m. I'd gone off to train instead hoping I wouldn't get in to trouble.

4 x 60s; 4 x 100s; 4 x 60s all fast with good technique followed by 4 x 50s back to back then a gym circuit.

In 1974 there were some interesting people in town. I'd bumped into Steve Green, the top English sprinter; Mike Farrell the English athletics official who'll be an important guy if I make next year's Great Britain Junior team; whilst Sandy Sutherland the journalist treated me to an orange juice and gave me a lift home. In 1975 Laurie Gray was advising me to *Say nothing to Pixie Mia Farrow lookalike and that if she wanted to end it all then it was up to her.* And Puma were taking an interest in me as a pair of *Puma Jumbo* and also *Puma Munchen '72* had arrived in the post from the great Derek Ibbotson.

Last year, 1976, Roger and I hammered ourselves on Arthurs Seat doing a hill session, but complained about how poor the session had been as we were both feeling buggered. Meanwhile in the here and now, 1977, Tom and I took the train to Dundee together this morning. An old boy went charging past us on the platform to catch the train-it was rather amusing to watch as he bustled and bundled fellow passengers oot the way!

Our Economics lecturer, McGillivray, was off today so another chap took us for the theory of indifference. Intellectually, McGillivray is a class apart, so I missed him. When Derek and I went for our messages we pulled the old trick. We pointed to the plums and asked for a pound of tomatoes. *'But Sir, these are plums!'* *'Aye we ken that, but we want a poond o' tomatoes!'* Aye, pathetic, easily amused students. Still we all had a good laugh. Derek and I went to the Golden Fry for some lunch of fish 'n chips. He's now getting over the funeral; it's well behind him and he's coping fine. The family are all off to Bermuda for ten days at New Year-can't be bad. I managed a little studying before bed. I'm back home to Edinburgh on Wednesday-bravo! Before bed I rang Aunt Heather and *Diana the goddess of love and hunting.* A rest day today so from 1974 toward the end of being a first year junior athlete, Coach Walker put me through the mill:

Evening: 2 sets 4 x 200 metres (2 minutes recovery) (10 mins between sets) Set 1: 22.9; 23.8; 24.8; 25.2 seconds: Set 2: 24.1; 24.8; 24.9; 25.3 secs; the weather was cold with the wind against for the first 60 metres; I was shattered at the end feeling it simulated the way I feel at the end of a 400 metres race

Before Bed: Arm-action; leg jump-squats; press-ups; sit-ups

6th December, 1975 I was up relatively early today because we needed to start the session at Meadowbank at 9.45 a.m. On arrival both Coach Walker and Roger Jenkins immediately put my back up annoying me. At lunchtime I met *Pixie Mia Farrow lookalike* and we went to Murrayfield to watch Scotland beat Australia 10-3. Taking Laurie's advice I decided not to say anything to her, but she brought the subject up briefly. In the evening, Davie Reid came down for a game of chess, a bite to eat and a blether, before we went up to Meg Ritchie's party. I didn't feel like staying long, so came back home early and went to bed with Agatha Christie's *Dead Man's Folly*.

Morning (9.45 a.m.): 6 x 500 metres (5 minutes recovery) 73; 70; 70; 75; 70; 75 seconds I didn't feel very good, but the slower repetitions were mainly the ones that Roger Jenkins led out

7th December, 1974 Today's training session really highlights the difference a year can make. Last year, 1973, my best official 400 metres was 52 seconds, whereas this morning I was probably running through the quarter in that time en-route to a 500 metres. And to really put it in context, the year before in 1972, Coach Walker had us running 4 x 2 x 400 metres and I noted down that I'd run one of them in 63 seconds! Another difference is the change in the weather. Last year I wrote: 'Gaga had the car back which was good. However, at 1.30 p.m. the flamin' snow came tumbling down and stayed on for the rest of the day. There was about four inches in total, carpeting Edinburgh; even the Corporation busses had stopped running. I've decided to give Marion two weeks catalogue money plus Grandma Jo two weeks digs money so that I can get my shoes next week. On the way back home from Morningside to Portobello travelling through the Queen's Park Gaga drove very slowly. I didn't bother going up to Meadowbank this evening.'

Looking back it was quite Dickensian, but with a 1972 twist. Because Friday was the one day Gaga worked all day I would meet him at Nile Grove where he always parked the car across from James Waugh & Son, Butchers. He wandered across to the car watching how he went in the snow, wrapped snuggly under a cap and in his tweed jacket. His watch-words on foot, when driving the car and in life was *Gang-ginger!* Fridays alongside Wednesdays are the two evenings Coach Walker's squad take off and I do a gym circuit on my own; I suspect Meadowbank would have closed that evening. Anyway, today the weather was somewhat fairer, but quite windy; and because Brian Gordon was down from Aberdeen we did a double session going up to Arthurs Seat in the afternoon.

Morning: **500 metres: Brian Gordon 65.7 seconds; Hoffmann 65.8 secs; Paul Forbes 66.8 secs (15 minutes recovery); 2 x 3 x 200 metres (2 mins rec) 23.6; 24; 24 (15 mins between sets) 24; 23.5; 22.8 secs; come the last run a good feeling, cruising, in control, with another gear there if necessary!**

Afternoon: **Arthurs Seat 5 fast repetitions on the usual 120 metres hill including a 20.6 seconds effort**

Before Bed: **Press-ups; sit-ups and mobility stretching**

8ᵗʰ December, 1977 Yesterday when I got back from Dundee, Grandpa Willie wasn't feeling too well and had a pain in his chest. I accompanied him to the Deaconess Hospital where they will keep him in for a few days, but are hopeful of patching him up. I hope so as his health is so poor; he deserves some care and attention. Despite worrying about him I managed to put in a good shift today. In the morning I read some Sociology-not my favourite subject. Come lunchtime I did a hill session on my own up on Arthurs Seat. I was running reasonably well. It was damp and cold. A couple of swans flew overhead-necks craned out, beating their wings noisily, the sound akin to *The Flying Machine* in *Noggin of the Nogs*. Afterwards I took some money out and had lunch at Meadowbank, before Grandma Jo and I went to the hospital to visit Will. He was looking so much better, had a bit of colour to him and was very cheerful-all very good news. Jo and I walked down the High Street to take a bus home to Portobello. In the evening I ran a relaxed session at Meadowbank, managing to fit it in just before the rain started to come down-always a small victory. A relaxed evening home in front of the box; *Diana the goddess of love and hunting* telephoned.

Lunch: **4 miles run to Arthurs Seat and back including 8 x 20 seconds hill runs**

Evening: **6 x 150s fast (90 seconds-2 min 30 secs recovery); an easy session**

9th December, 1975 Ouch! An early 7.15 a.m. rise on a December morning. Another wee surprise with the post this morning with yet another parcel from Puma-I'm being bombarded! It included an interesting variation of previous pairs of spikes sent to me-this time Puma Munchen top, but Puma Jumbo sole. Interesting! Different! There was also another small Puma top which I'll give to *Pixie Mia Farrow lookalike* for her Christmas. Presciently, two years ago in 1973 I wrote in my diary *I wonder if Pixie fancies me at all.*

I spoke briefly with Iain this morning, but spent much of the day reading Arthur Ashe's *Portrait in Motion*, but I also managed to read a chapter of Biology. I've set myself a couple of goals over the festive season: (i) get lots of studying done to kick start the process of getting some good Highers next May; and (ii) reduce my weight-crikey, I'm 10 stone 10 lbs!

Rest Day

10th December, 1977 Just a wee difference to training three years ago. I'd been up at Bill's all afternoon, but when I went to the stadium, the track was frozen over; I ran: **2 x 4 x 50**

metres in between 5.8 and 5.9 seconds indoors on the concrete floor of the Meadowbank Concourse in my training shoes. Today was rather harder. I eased into the morning with a stroll with the dog around Portobello Park. I was going to take either the 5 or 44 bus up to Meadowbank, but perchance tried starting Will's car and lo and behold, the engine turned over. I put a pound's worth of petrol in the tank and took it up to Meadowbank. Before the session even started my thighs felt weak and tired, but I ended up running a good session; come the end of the last run the lactic acid in my legs was incredible! After lunch I took Willie's car up to the Wisp Garage and walked back with the dog. I enjoyed the couple of miles walk, reflecting on all the new square boxes appearing as the developers eat up the countryside. Back home I sat and read Accounts with the International Cross Country on the television in the background. *Diana the goddess of love and hunting* arrived at five and thereafter Josephine and Heather direct from the hospital. They said Will was comfortable. I went in yesterday and I thought he looked well; he was cheerful to see me. *Diana* and I had a fun *Eros* evening; television and a Chinese carry out. Mid-evening Susan Rettie phoned to say she was leaving for Canada. Josephine gave me a lovely silver pendant which she had made to give to Susan; it had an agate insert. I nipped down to Brighton Crescent and handed it in to her brother; an atypically generous gesture from Jo.

Lunchtime (1.00 p.m.): 4 x 600 metres (4 minutes recovery) 88; 88; 88; 93 seconds

Afternoon: Two miles walk

11th December, 1977 Three years ago Dougie McLean gave Keith Ridley and me a lift home; I shouted out the car window at (Petrina) Cox and (Fiona) McCaulay who are perhaps the female equivalent of Forbes 'n Hoffmann-anyway it gave them a bit of a laugh! Last year I began working in the one year post at the Scottish Council for Social Service and made up my mind to buy a wee *Triumph Spitfire* sportscar. Come the evening Iain and I went to our cousin David Ross's 21st birthday party.

It was wet, damp and dreich this morning. *Diana the goddess of love and hunting* stayed overnight. After breakfast she went for the Sunday newspapers whilst I glanced over some Economics as I've an exam tomorrow. We took an SMT bus to Meadowbank. My legs were still feeling heavy after yesterday's 600s session so I ran an easy session today. Adrian dropped me slightly on the last run. Afterwards Norrie Gregor gave us a lift home. Grandma Jo was just leaving for the hospital so whilst I got my bags packed *Diana* cooked my lunch. I couldn't take the risk of travelling up for an exam tomorrow. I caught the 4.50 p.m. train at Waverley; it was a bit grim. I was very sleepy on the train and nodded off for a little while. On arrival in Dundee it was raining heavily and the Sunday church bells were ringing out, calling people to worship. At our digs our landlady Mrs Neve cooked me some meat, potatoes and tomato. She also served up some tea and cake. Sitting there reading the *Sunday Times*, eating sponge cake whilst daintily pouring out tea from the rose petal teapot made me feel like a throwback to 1950s Oxbridge. I studied hard until ten o'clock when Tom's cheery face appeared. Unlike me, he usually always arrives on a Sunday, but late on.

Morning: 8 x 300 metres (75 seconds recovery) 42-43 seconds; I lost Adrian slightly on the last run

12th December, 1973 The ongoing atypically windy weather continues with Edinburgh residents having to batten doon the hatches. The day's dull grimness and *ennui* of work at Grahams was temporarily set aside at lunchtime when I played Willie Fernie at chess. Willie's a late middle aged man with a wife and a child who came along to bless them late in life. He assists Jim Hughes in the design and drawing of kitchens. He's a wee gem of a bloke and has the lovely knack of getting on well with everyone with whom he interfaces. At one level I really admire that quality. But at another level I don't want to be like Willie in that he seems to be too ready to go along with others' views; on some issues he fundamentally disagrees, but will keep that to himself. I get on fine with everyone but I tend to be a little more challenging. Willie's got a fine mind and is much smarter than everyone realises. Others pigeonhole him because of his lowly role in the company and therefore lowly status at Graham's especially given he's in his early 50s; but I respect him and like him a lot. He's much more mature and sensible than me and is aware of his family responsibilities so he doesn't want to rock the boat. He's not well paid and my heart goes out to him. Like my grandfather, he's subject to the way the winds blow and has to adjust the sails accordingly. We regularly enjoy a game or two of chess at lunchtime. We trade wins; today I beat him twice, so I must be improving.

Later I phoned Mother at the Civil Service at St Andrews House to say I would look round to Oxgangs tomorrow after work for my tea. I had an age to wait at Morningside Station for the number 15 bus to take me across town to Meadowbank; not only did it not arrive until 5.25 p.m. but it broke down twice en-route. Paul; David and Alistair Scott were the only ones down this evening so we just trained indoors in the concourse. Paul and I were in fits of laughter as we went off on surreal wild flights of fancy and innuendo entertaining the Edinburgh Southern girls, Cox 'n McCaulay et al with our white pudding stories! Absolutely brilliant fun. Back home I watched the great Jackie Stewart win the BBC Sports Personality of the Year.

Evening: **Gym circuit followed by 2 x 4 x 80 metres technique, but fast; 4 x 80 metres flat out!**

13ᵗʰ December, 1977 Four years ago there was the most odd thing. I received a call at Thomas Graham & Sons to be told that I should visit the doctor. It was a locum who shortly thereafter took off for New Zealand because of his incompetence. When I called round he told me that I had a diseased liver and that I wasn't fit for hard training! I of course was pretty worried about this and Coach Walker said he'd accompany me to the doctor the following week. Later on, Mother and I surmised perhaps the doctor had got my notes mixed up with Father who is an alcoholic. Two years ago I wasn't feeling well either, but for different reasons writing that even at midnight I had not recovered properly from the morning's session when I felt terrible for 15 minutes afterwards-dizzy, sick and tired. On a cold and breezy day we had run: **5 x 500 metres (5 minutes recovery) in 71; 71; 72; 73; 72 seconds**

Today's Accounts exam went really well and there's no chance I've failed it. At lunchtime, Derek, Tom and I went to *Menzies* where we bought wee Glen our land-lady's son a magic set for his Christmas. We enjoyed lunch at The Golden Fry. I left to come back to our digs early on, but no one was in so I took a wee tootle up to Broughty Ferry and looked around the shops. Later I ran five miles. My Achilles tendon is a little tender which is worrying-perhaps it's due to interchanging training shoes? In the evening we were served up a three course meal including a mince dish with a mashed potatoes and a cheese topping. I studied for an hour and a half for tomorrow's Economic Development exam. I had the radio on; there was an excellent programme on called *All*

Things Considered. One of my heroes was on, Jimmy Reid, who was brilliant; Chris Bonnington was fair; Bob Langley was poor; and a minister, James McKay was good. Late on I had a pint on my own. Tom and I had a long chat and a good laugh on the stairwell with Laura, the land-lady's 16 year old-going on 24 year old daughter!

<u>Afternoon:</u> 5 miles run followed by leg-work; press-ups; sit-ups

14th December, 1977 Two years ago I was thinking about an upcoming 600 metres race at Cosford in January. I didn't enjoy the session; it was too open-ended for my liking. I much prefer a set distance where I can more accurately distribute my effort. In each of the runs I felt I could still have kept running on at a similar pace; also I had to run the whole session from the front too, which again is not my forte. The weather was cold, wet and windy which makes it look even better from afar. Looking back it was pretty good running and hopefully indicative of what I might be able to run next season when I move up to the 800 metres. The session comprised of: **90 seconds run (I covered 670 metres); 50 seconds (413 metres); 40 seconds (325 metres); and 24 seconds (215 metres) with a 12 minutes recovery**

Pixie Mia Farrow lookalike had given me the brush-off on the phone so it was a sweet and sour day.

Remember

'…Remember me when no more day by day
You tell me of our future that you planned:
Only remember me; you understand
It will be late to counsel then or pray.
Yet if you should forget me for a while
And afterwards remember do not grieve:
For if the darkness and corruption leave
A vestige of the thoughts that once I had,
Better by far you should forget and smile
Than you should remember and be sad.'

Christina Rossetti

In the evening Davie Reid came down to visit me. We watched an athletics programme about the Kenyans. I was surprised to see myself appear on the screen. They showed a race clip of the 400 metres at the AAA v Borough Road College invitation meeting at Crystal Palace back in June where I finished second to Kenya's Stephen Chepkwony; after that race I knew I could run well at the European Junior Championships in August.

I wasn't looking forward to my Economic Development exam, but it went really well. I thought I wrote two solid essays. History was my best subject at school and the quality of my essay writing has come on hand over fist; mind you, I put that down to *The Secret Journals of Retep Nnamffoh* as much as to 'attending' school!

Mathematics was cancelled so I was able to get my Statistics exam written out and handed in. I was supposed to see my personal tutor, Tina, but missed her so I just left her a wee note. And now, that's me free for the holidays-YES!

Tom and I went out to Broughty Ferry to collect all our gear. Our land-lady, Mrs Neve, gave each of us a card and a 1978 diary. Tom and I got the 2.06 p.m. train back to the capital. Back home to Portobello I heated up my lunch and saw Jo before I left later on for Meadowbank. The chap from the Wisp Garage brought Willie's car back; he's a really nice guy. The car is running okay so I took it up to Meadowbank and ran a fair session with Norman Gregor; he was delighted to hear my exams had gone okay-he said I had to do well as I'm representing the athletics fraternity! *Diana the goddess of love and hunting* and I had a super evening out in a bar uptown-lots of laughs followed by a small meal of chicken chow mein and sweet 'n sour at the *Ping On* restaurant in Stockbridge before I ran her home to Silverknowes.

Evening: 8 x 200 metres (2 minutes recovery) all in 25 seconds

15th December, 1977 Life's internal journey oft taken in the gaps between life itself. Three years ago in 1974 I wrote in my training journal: **'START OF BUILD-UP TOWARDS COSFORD'** and kicked off with a personal best; given it was the start of winter that wasn't too shabby! The session was part of a training course the SAAA's had put on.

Morning: 6 x 60 metres; I led Drew McMaster and Bryan Dickson on each run

Afternoon (1.30 p.m.): 300 metres time trial (1) Hoffmann 34.2 seconds (p.b.) (2) B Dickson 35.7 (3) Albert Ree 36.0

Afternoon (2.30 p.m.): Arthurs Seat 2 x 6 Hill Session; 5.37 and 5.39; good going against a strong wind

Before Bed: Arm-action; press-ups; sit-ups

Looking back I essentially did three separate sessions in the one day; training with the 100 metres guys in the morning; the quarter milers in the afternoon; and then the middle distance guys late afternoon and each a very solid session in its own right, not to mention something before bed. The following year, 1975, was slightly different; I'd taken severe cramp in my right calf overnight and ended up going along to see Mr C. the physio. He'd also offered me some fatherly advice not to phone *Pixie Mia Farrow lookalike*. Ironically, that evening, whilst resisting the temptation to phone her, I watched a Dustin Hoffman-Mia Farrow film called *John and Mary* and couldn't get over how much the actress looked like *Pixie*; with the added irony of a mix of our heroes' names-Farrow and Hoffman! Anyway, back to today. After taking the dog to Portobello Park, I took a bus uptown to get Will's road tax. It turned out I did not have some of the required documents so took a wee tootle along Princes Street where I had a *Eureka!* moment. Looking in a shop window it dawned on me what I would most like to give *Diana the goddess of love and hunting* for her Christmas-a beautiful nurse's fob-watch. It's gold plated. It costs forty pounds. The only small problem is I'm penniless. Skint! God, walking doesn't have take it out of you; crazy as it sounds, I find it quite wearing! At lunchtime in just a pair of shorts and a rugby jersey I ran the few miles from the house to Holyrood Palace. It was a glorious and really lovely bright sunny day out. I met Norrie; it was difficult to see him at first especially as I was looking in to the sun-he was like a Red Indian hiding up in the hills, but he whistled down to attract my attention. He was his usual exuberant self and is in a very happy place just now which is lovely to see. I can empathise as I'm in a pretty happy place myself too. We ran a very solid hill session, pretty much eaksy-peaksy exchanging blows the way Roger and I did when we ran together on previous winter afternoons.

Now that I'm off I'm really looking forward to enjoying the seasonal break. Later, I returned back to town to collect Will's road tax and also looked into Drew McMaster's where I was able to swap a pair of spikes from the shop's stock. It was good of him to do that for me. Now that the car is officially back on the road I took the dog with me and we collected Will from the hospital; I'd taken Jill thinking it would give him a wee fillip. I thought he didn't look too bad; fingers crossed. In the evening I ran an easy track session on my own. *Diana* just called to say she has a Safeways shopping voucher for Josephine-that's great! A relaxed evening in; Jo and I watched *Meet Me In St Louis*. 35 years on it remains a delightful wee film structured around seasonal vignettes-a year in the life; meanwhile Aunt Heather is out at a Civil Service office party; Grandma Jo will have the breathalyser on her when she gets in; either that or she'll have to be road-tested to confirm she can walk in a straight line.

Afternoon (1.00 p.m.): 6 miles run, including 8 hill runs at Arthurs Seat with Norrie Gregor

Evening: 1200 metres (3 minutes 28 seconds); 800m (2:03); 600m (89 secs); 400m (54 secs)

16th December, 1977 The 16th December-yet another of those sweet and sour days. Come the end of 1973 the athletics was progressing nicely. My personal best 400 metres of 52 seconds set earlier in the summer equated to an even paced 39 seconds 300 metres. Yet six months later I was able to run at that pace in a session on a mid-winter's evening. How the world moves on:

Mobility work; 2 x 4 x 60 metres flat out; 5 x 300 metres (5 minutes recovery) 40; 40; 39; 40; 39 seconds

Two years later and two years ago I wasn't exactly chirpy. *Pixie Mia Farrow lookalike* had essentially given me the heave-ho. We were out together that Tuesday; when I suggested we might meet up come the weekend or the following Wednesday she said she was *Too busy*, so I guess I got the message. As she got out the car I said: *Where did I go wrong?* She said *Peter...nothing...you did everything right.* I was pretty upset driving back, but in the evening I managed to run a reasonable session at Meadowbank. It's been a roller coaster ride over the previous couple of years with the most delicious and delightful highs as well as some lows thrown in there too. She's not someone I'll forget-from our first kiss at the Carnethy Hill Race disco whilst dancing to *The Hollies'*, *The Air That I Breath*; my first, my true love.

Twelve Songs

'...The stars are not wanted now: put out every one;
Pack up the moon and dismantle the sun:
Pour away the ocean and sweep up the wood.
For nothing now can ever come to any good.'

W.H. Auden

There was one small consolation. Coach Walker's got me an invite to the 600 metres invitation race at Cosford next month. I'm looking to win it and I want the world's best time! I better not tell Paul that one as he'll go in to paroxysmal hysterics! However, the reality is that whilst the world best is 77.8 seconds, back on 1 February of this year at Cosford in the AAA Junior Medley Championships I took almost twenty yards off Gary Cook; it went almost un-noticed but my official split was 78.5 seconds for my 600 metres leg against Gary's 81.0. So although I'll be regarded as an outsider to G.B. internationals Ainsley Bennett; Jim Aukett; with David Jenkins the heavy favourite, I know I can run the time. Plus I'm surely a better runner now, as I'm a year older. Come last year I was in a much happier place.

Pixie had drifted out of my life, if not my thoughts; she seemed to have quit the athletics scene to concentrate on her Dunf. studies. A lovely period of seeing her at training had come to an end. As Jackson Browne wrote in the elegiac:

For A Dancer

'..I don't remember losing track of you. You were always dancing in and out of view I must've always thought you'd be around...'

Jackson Browne

My most treasured possession is the card and lovely message *Pixie* sent me last year when she heard of my selection for Montreal. Rather ironically when I came back across the Atlantic she was keen to meet up; on a late summer evening in Edinburgh we had a lovely night out together. By then I had been going out with several girls at once; interspersed within the nine months from when we separated, for the first and last time in my life, most unusually there was a plethora of girls vying for my attention, including a six months period with the *Simone de Beauvoir Philosopher Queen* in the first half of the year.

Juxtaposing women for men:

Bloody Men

Bloody men are like bloody buses -
You wait for about a year
And as soon as one approaches your stop
Two or three others appear.

You look at them flashing their indicators,
Offering you a ride.
You're trying to read the destination,
You haven't much time to decide.

If you make a mistake, there is no turning back.
Jump off, and you'll stand there and gaze
While the cars and the taxis and lorries go by
And the minutes, the hours, the days.

Wendy Cope

Anyway, when *Pixie* and I departed late on to go our separate
ways she was quite emotional and tearful...ce la vie...I guess
she knew more than me that a line had been drawn in the
sand and we were both going off to lead separate lives and
follow separate paths in life, perhaps never to meet up
again...or perhaps, one day, years hence...who knows; there is
a light there that will not be extinguished. And by September
I'd been seeing *Diana the goddess of love and hunting.* However, if
I were ever to be offered a Faustian pact, what then…or
to perhaps reach a deal whereby the reward for an Olympic
medal might be a sex-filled London weekend with
Pixie...she's such a free spirit I suspect that kind of offer
might meet with her approval! Last year on this day I used
my wee one year job to buy a Triumph Spitfire car which
was great fun for the short period of time I had it. Anyway,
back to the here and now, 1977. In the lead up to Christmas,

Jo and I got in the messages from Safeways. I took Will's car. For once it's going well; I'd adjusted the idling speed and the volume of petrol mix going in to the engine, so it was ticking over nicely. I couldn't get over the cost of the messages-sixteen pounds! *Diana's* voucher was a God-send.

Since it's the student holidays I've signed on the dole. I played an hour of squash with Coach Walker and then after a shower looked in to see Will at the hospital. I brought him in some ginger beer. He seems to be doing fine, well at least all things considered. He was glad to see me; he means everything to me. Afterwards I looked round to see the physio, Denis Davidson. He was steamboats as was his wife, Sarah, who promptly sold me a Charlie Chaplin figure-well I felt obliged and what could I say! They had an old lawyer friend there too and he was in a similar state; aye you can take the Christmas spirit tae far! After a fry-up tea at Oxgangs, I drove my sister, Anne, down to Henderson Row to Andy and Maggie Ross' where Anne was staying overnight; we went via Demarco's Cafe at Tollcross where we stopped off for a wee ice cream. Andy had just sat his finals today, so fingers crossed. He's a remarkable bloke doing an Open University degree at his age whilst simultaneously running J & R Glen Highland Bagpipe Makers in the High Street. It would be great to see him pass; I'm so proud of him. I had a half pint at Deacon Brodie's Tavern before going round the corner to collect Jo; Aunt Heather; and Frances from the lapidary club to give them a lift home to Porty. I'd missed Dad; he'd phoned earlier from abroad. He's back home in a week's time, but I managed to speak to his wife on the phone. Over a *7-up* and cracker and cheese I sat and watched a Columbo movie-not like me at all. A very different sort of day and somewhat happier than that somewhat haunted day with *Pixie* two years previously. And tomorrow? Well, more standard fayre awaits me with Adrian on the Meadowbank track; I'm already steeling myself mentally!

Afternoon: One hour game of squash

17th December, 1977 A very long and boring day at work at Grahams. The Prime Minister, Edward Heath, announced the Three Day Week Order to help conserve stocks of coal. It comes into being on Hogmanay. Meanwhile we've been told we will have to continue working, cold or not, or we'll only be paid for three days. On a happier note Josephine had phoned Angus who passed on the message to me that Gaga is working this afternoon so I was able to get a lift back home to Portobello and be in for dinner at a luxurious 5.30 p.m. Just before I was leaving for Meadowbank Mum telephoned to say that I've got to go to the hospital tomorrow about this so called liver condition. I've arranged with Coach Walker to come along with me.

Evening: Gym circuit followed by 8 x 200 metres (2 minutes recovery) all in 26-27 seconds

18th December, 1973 I must have picked up a bug as I was up twice during the night with diarrhoea, not to mention five times this morning! Nana phoned Graham's to say I wouldn't manage in to work. Fortunately, by lunch time I felt better and Gaga ran me out to Colinton to meet up with Coach Walker. We went to see the doctor together. The news was really good and I can restart training immediately. What a fiasco it's been. At night I celebrated by buying a new Meadowbank Sports Centre membership. After the training session I had a good chat with Coach Walker before coming home. Earlier Paul and I had a bit of a laugh with me ending up bursting his balloon! I also gave Dougie McLean the dance tickets money. I'm really looking forward to the Edinburgh Athletic Club Christmas Eve Dance; it should be one of the highlights of the year.

Evening: Gym circuit followed by 2 x 6 x 40 metres

concentrating on technique; then 6 x 60 back to back sprints

19th December, 1977 Three years ago I started my student holiday job working for the Royal Mail on the Christmas post. Well that was a big mistake. In the week afterwards I ended up spending much of my pay at the physio getting my shoulder massaged and sorted out. Wimp. Gaga had driven me out to the end of London Road very early in the morning. In the bowels of the building I sorted out the mail amongst the regular posties (many of whom are great characters and enjoy taking the piss out of the students) before venturing out for hours with a heavy bag, traipsing up and down the various stairs in the locale. Mother said she had a similar job twenty years before when she was at Edinburgh University. I finished at two o'clock and slept all afternoon. In the evening I went up to Meadowbank, but complained of feeling '...shattered before I even started'. However, I managed to run a good session.

Evening: 300 metres 34.6 seconds (12 minutes recovery) 2 x 200 metres (bend to bend) in 22.9 secs (4 mins rec) but with my tracksuit on; followed by 4 x 100 metres very fast

Before Bed: Arm-action; press-ups; sit-ups

Today was just a little bit different; definitely no holiday jobs with the Royal Mail and Willie is still in hospital. I drove Josephine up to the dentist for 9.00 a.m. We took the dog along with us. On the way back home we stopped off at the Deaconess Hospital and I dropped off a bottle of Coke for Will. At lunchtime I ran the two miles up to Meadowbank and did a gym circuit before going across to Arthurs Seat to do the usual hill session, but this time with a major difference; I ran the session with a 20lbs weights jacket.

What a REVELATION! I'm convinced this type of work is going to make me world class! When I ran a single rep at the end without the jacket on I felt like I was flying! I ran home for lunch before Jo and I went back up to the hospital. Could you believe it-we weren't allowed in as it wasn't a set visiting hour and they are very strict on adhering to the rules. In the evening I did a run round Arthurs Seat. It was quite enjoyable although my quadriceps were a bit sore on the big climb, resulting from the lunchtime session. I was back home by 7.30 p.m. to watch a wee bit television; there was nothing on so I read the second volume of David Niven's *Bring On The Empty Horses*. It's not as amusing and funny as *The Moon's A Balloon*. *Diana the goddess of love and hunting* telephoned halfway through my fish supper.

Lunchtime: **Ran 2 miles to Meadowbank; gym circuit followed by 6 x 20 seconds Arthurs Seat hill runs; 2 miles run home**

Evening: **4 miles around Arthurs Seat**

20th December, 1977 Four years ago in 1973 I was unhappy at work at Thomas Graham & Sons. I wrote: 'It was a hellish day at work. Roy was really picking on me and very annoying. He has put me on the lines permanently-the worse job in the section. On a whim he moved me to the far side of the room; I've been banished! Normally he likes me sitting next to him, because I'm probably his favourite amongst all the cost clerks. However, I've become aware over the past year that he can change like the wind-on a whim, so I don't really anticipate being on the lines permanently. He is the perfect encapsulation of a *mercurial character*-quick, lively, amusing and often very funny; but in tandem there is a nasty side to him too, which sometimes bubbles to the surface. At heart he's actually a nice guy, but a trace of *Schadenfreude* sometimes comes through. Anyway, bugger him, I'm working on the great escape. Come next summer, I'm going to put in my notice and go off to college to get 5 Highers.

A year later, my wee world had been transformed. I'd picked up my *Athletics Weekly* magazine and got a wee boost. There was a long interview with Bill Hartley and he said: '...*Last week I won a 600 at Wolverhampton in 79.6 and that was pleasing as it proves my over-distance conditioning is coming along okay. I needed that confidence booster because at the end of October Alan (Pascoe) and I came back from a week in Nice and ran a lousy 500m race in Glasgow during a Celtic-Rangers football match. We got screwed by these two good Scottish youngsters, Forbes and Hoffmann, but as we'd gone straight up from France without a break it wasn't really surprising...*'

Perhaps that gave me some motivation because I sat down and wrote out my objectives for the 1975 season and then sealed the note in an envelope which said 'Not to be opened until end of September, 1975'. The single page stated the following: (I've added what actually happened:

Aims for Indoor and Outdoor Track Season 1975

Indoor Objectives

Cosford
60 metres: 7.0 seconds
400 metres: 48.0 secs. British Junior Record
600 metres: 80.0 secs.　　　　"
800 metres: 1min. 51 secs.　　"
AAA British Junior 400 metres title

Perth
50 metres: 6.2 Scottish Junior Record
300 metres: 35.0 secs. Scottish Senior Record
Scottish Junior Indoor 50 and 600 metres titles

Actual Indoor Results

Cosford
600 metres British Junior Record 80.6 secs.
600 metres leg AAA Medley Relay 78.5 secs official split
800 metres 1 min: 53 secs Scottish Junior Record
AAA Junior 400 metres gold and AAA Junior 200 metres silver (Disappointed to draw the tight inside lane in 200 final otherwise I would have won the double, but with 6 races inside 24 hours, I was relatively happy.)

Perth
Scottish Junior 50 metres gold 6.2 secs and 300 metres gold 35.2 secs

Outdoor Objectives

100 metres 10.8 secs.
200 metres: 21.3 secs.
400 metres 46.8 secs.
800 metres 1 min 50 secs.
1500 metres sub 4 minutes
East District Junior 200 metres title

Scottish and British Junior 400 metres titles
Scottish Junior 800 metres title
European Junior 400 metres final
Scotland v Switzerland

Actual Outdoor Results

100 metres 10.8
200 metres 21.8
400 metres 47.2
800 metres 1 min 53 secs (indoors)
400 metres hurdles 54.2 (Ranked number 2 in UK Junior
Rankings off debut run!)
No East District Champs as it clashed with me winning
British Games, London on same day
No Scottish Junior Champs as representing UK v GDR
in Dresden
AAA Junior 200 metres bronze and 400 metres silver
(Unwell-sick, temperature and severe migraine
headache)
European Junior Silver Medal 400 metres
UK v Sweden Senior International

Anyway, back to today, 1977. Jo and I picked up Will from
the hospital. I used the stairs to come down; however they
ended up getting stuck in the lift for 10 minutes-just as well
it wasn't an emergency! I find that at this time of the year,
11.00 a.m. in the morning is the best part of a winter's day.
The sun always seems to catch Arthurs Seat and it was
bathed in a lovely soft warm glow. I played squash for an
hour with Coach Walker; it was too long and I lost a bit
interest as it wasn't very competitive. *Diana the goddess of love
and hunting* came down mid-afternoon. We sat in the front
room by the light of the Christmas tree playing bagatelle-
always good fun. The tree is lovely and Aunt Heather bought
replacement bulbs. In the evening I ran a good session with
John Scott-he was running well. Along with Paul the three of

us are running the half mile at the AAA Indoor Championships next month at Cosford-my first serious attempt at the distance.

A mist descended so quickly and was so thick that we couldn't see parts of the track which made it interesting for running in-a real peasouper; I wouldn't have been surprised to see Sherlock Holmes emerge from the gloom. I hate to imagine how Arthurs Seat looked; you would have been stumbling around in the dark. I gave *Diana* a lift home to Silverknowes before driving carefully back to Portobello. I'm now lying in bed with the Christmas version of the *Radio Times*. To borrow from John Masefield's *The Box of Delights* and more appropriately on this foggy evening-*When The Wolves Were Running*...

Lunchtime: 1 hour squash

Evening: 3 x 4 x 200 metres (20 seconds recovery) 27-28 seconds (8 and 10 minutes between sets); the weather was cold frosty with a heavy mist

Winter is coming...

Journey of the Magi

'A cold coming we had of it,
Just the worst time of the year
For a journey, and such a long journey:
The ways deep and the weather sharp,
The very dead of winter.'

T.S. Elliot

Winter

21st December, 1976 Given it's the winter solstice and as
we move towards the mid-winter festivals and the end of the
year, a wet, but relatively mild day for this time of the season.
On the way back from work at the Scottish Council of Social
Service, Claremont Crescent the Triumph Spitfire was giving
me a little bit bother and I ended up putting the battery on a
charge overnight. Three years ago, Roy Wallace, my former
boss at Thomas Graham & Sons was implementing a new
regime; I wrote 'Oh well, back to the hole today. It was really
bad having to do the lines all day. Roy was taking the crap
out of me for much of the day-an abuse of power, still I just
had to thole it until I escape over the wall. However, the
afternoon was leavened and improved for the better; at
lunchtime I popped along to *McGillivrays* at Morningside for
a hamburger supper before Willie (Fernie) and I went out in
his wee *Hillman Imp* to the cash 'n carry where I bought three
boxes of chocolate liqueurs as Christmas presents.' Being a
Friday I was able to get a lift home from Nile Grove to Porty
as it's Gaga's full working day at the butcher's shop; wee
Anne (sister) joined us. I telephoned Coach Walker to check
if I could join Stewart McCallum after my gym circuit.

**Evening: Gym Circuit followed by 10 x 100 metres fast
with a walk back recovery with Stewart McCallum**

On that 1973 Friday evening, I was clearly keen to keep my
nose clean; you can get punished by Coach Walker just as
easily for being keen and enthusiastic as you can for being
apathetic!

**1976 Evening: 6 x 300 metres (2 minutes recovery) 39;
40; 39; 41; 41; 42 seconds; a solid session**

22nd December, 1973 Dougie McLean gave me a lift out to Fernieside for the Edinburgh Southern Harriers Road Relays. Given my dismal distance running ability I'm not sure why, but I was given a spot on the Edinburgh Athletic Club Youth B team; I ran okay. We almost pulled off a shock result only losing to the more fancied A team by one second. It may not have made much of a difference, but I would have quite fancied running that last leg. Coach Walker gave me a lift back home; I phoned Paul, but he had already gone out.

Afternoon: ESH Road Relays 2.5 miles 14 minutes 13 seconds

23rd December, 1975 Today was a very lazy sort of a morning; still I am on holiday. Davie Reid phoned me and I went up to Meadowbank. We sat around for an hour listening to the 'Pros' and the bookies arguing about the professional athletics and the New Year Sprint. They were all pretty animated; it was fun and interesting being a fly on the wall. I thereafter did an average sort of a session. I'm feeling a bit of a cold coming on which is a bugger given I've got this big race at Cosford. In the evening I relaxed at home enjoying watching the enigmatic *Lawrence of Arabia*; what a man; what a life; what a film. Magnificent stuff. He's Grandma Jo's hero; she's suggested I read *The Seven Pillars of Wisdom* from her library

Lunchtime: 6 x 200 metres (3 minutes easy jog recovery) all in 24 seconds

Christmas Eve

Birth: the coming into existence of something

1973 The Dickensian world of Thomas Graham & Sons was in full swing and alive and well. I wrote 'It didn't seem to be so bad a Monday morning at work as it was Christmas Eve.

And because it was the office Christmas lunch (which I couldn't afford to attend), because of the two hour break, I managed to travel home with Willie from Waugh & Son, Butchers at Morningside to Portobello for our lunch together.' Then later, Bob Cratchitt was alive and well because in true Ebenezer Scrooge fashion, 'They let us away early at four o'clock.' In the evening I'd missed everyone at Meadowbank, but Stuart Gillies and his wife gave Paul and me a lift to the dance. Mark (Wilson), Paul and I got stoned. I got off with Petrina Cox. I also necked Fiona Macaulay. Dougie gave me a lift home from Mountcastle.

1974 <u>Afternoon</u>: 500 metres 64.6 seconds a personal best, 51.8 at 400 metres (15 minutes recovery); 300m 35.6 secs; the weather was wet, cold and windy

I Started Early-Took My Dog

I started Early-Took my Dog-
And visited the Sea-
The Mermaids in the Basement
Came out to look at me-

And Frigates-in the Upper Floor
Extended Hempen Hands-
Presuming Me to be a Mouse-
Aground-upon the Sands

Emily Dickinson

1976 A Christmas Eve to remember. The weather was remarkably fine, bright and mild. I drove the Triumph Spitfire down the East Lothian coastline to Gullane. I ran a good session on the sands with the dog skipping along beside me. It felt magical to be by the sea once again on Christmas Eve. It felt good to be alive and healthy and outside in the fresh air and to be out running on such a special day. I wanted to affix the moment in my mind's-eye. After the session it was with a dreamy sense of an inner glow and satisfaction that I walked back along the sands to the car parked high on the cliff. On the way I glimpsed a couple of boats gliding along the Forth upon a calm sea; and although the weather was far finer and kinder I thought of Stevenson's poem, *Christmas at Sea:*

Christmas at Sea

'...The bells upon the church were rung with a mighty jovial cheer;
For it's just that I should tell you how (of all the days in the year)
This day of our adversity was blessed Christmas morn, And the
house above the coastguard's was the house where I was born...'

Robert Louis Stevenson

Later on *Diana the goddess of love and hunting* and I visited old John Macpherson before going to a Watchnight service at Davidsons Mains.

<u>Morning:</u> 3 miles run on Gullane Sands followed by 4 x 2 x sand dune runs (3-4 minutes recovery)

1977 On a less happy note I awoke with a ghastly sore throat and a burning session in my chest. It's a bugger with the AAA Indoor Championships next month and my debut over 800 metres. I seem to collect so many colds and viruses but more worrying still is my inability to throw them off. It's my biggest flaw and my greatest weakness. The doctor was closed for the holiday but I managed to get some Ampicillin from Dr Hislop. I took it very easy just sitting in reading David Niven. *Diana* arrived around five o'clock. After tea we played bagatelle before taking Christmas cards and some Harvey's Bristol Cream to the Rosses at 6 Henderson Row and then the same to the Walker family at 54 Claremont Crescent. Coach Walker's wife Kay served up some red wine and mincemeat pies; we sat around chatting with the kids until eleven o'clock before we left to go to the midnight service at Davidsons Mains; once again it was packed out and was so busy we had to sit opposite each other on aisle pews. I didn't get home until one o'clock in the morning. A Happy Christmas to one and all!

Christmas Day, 1973 My second Christmas Day away from Oxgangs and on which I reflected upon later. After we exchanged presents Nana; Gaga; Aunt Heather and I travelled the seven miles along the quiet country back-roads from Portobello to Dalkeith Cemetery. Josephine laid a beautiful home-made winter wreath on Pumpa and Wee Nana's graves. From Dalkeith, once more on to quiet back-roads, but this time traversing Midlothian to Oxgangs arriving just after mid-day. Mother gave me a Christmas stocking containing lots of thoughtful presents. For the second year we had our Christmas dinner at the Harp Hotel at Corstorphine; it was fine, but it's not the same as the usual family Christmas Day at Porty. To save on a taxi Gaga made two separate trips back to Oxgangs. I was thinking how much I miss being with Anne and Iain at home, but I guess the world has moved on and the clock can't be turned back.

Boxing Day, 1972 I was back to work at Dickensian Thomas Graham & Sons; no such thing as a Boxing Day holiday. Having started my first training journal two days before I wrote that I was out in the evening putting in an indoor session with Robin Morris on the concrete floor of the indoor concourse at Meadowbank running:

Evening: 3 x 6 x 100 metres at three-quarters speed

27th December, 1975 Having taken three days off to recover from the cold and with the prospect of the Phillips' Invitational Indoor 600 metres approaching I lay in bed until about ten thinking about this 600 metres time trial. I wandered up to Meadowbank. I ran well, sitting on Norman Gregor and kicking past him on the final bend. It was a good time given the poor conditions; it was very windy and cold, but at least it was dry.

Morning: 600 metres 78.8 seconds (personal best) 10-15 minutes recovery; 4 x 150m (jog 250m recovery) all in 15 seconds; a good day's running

28th December, 1976 I ran with Adrian all the way. In the afternoon I picked up *Diana the goddess of love and hunting* and we went out to Carrington where she did some driving practice. Is a sports car really the best vehicle for this! However, whatever the weather, it's always lovely to be out in the deep Midlothian countryside; mid-winter is as lovely as any other season; the beech hedges are still dressed in their clothes of leaves and many of the fields are now under the plough. Late afternoon, just before dusk began to fall we travelled out to Silverknowes to enjoy afternoon tea. And then home. Under a sparkly sky.

Lunchtime: 8 x 200 metres (70 seconds jog recovery) 26-27 secs; I ran with Adrian all the way

1977 My first day back training after being side-lined with the cold for several days. At ten o'clock Jo and I went up to the Lilywhites, Princes Street sale-grandmother and grandson battling it out. I bought her a pair of trousers as a Christmas present and I picked up a T-shirt; thereafter next door to Murray Bros. where we both got a jumper each. With it being my first day back I took it pretty easy and ran a 150s session with Olympian Dave Wilson and Kevin McGuire. Dave's back home for his annual Festive holiday to visit his parents in Edinburgh. Because my cold is still there, I ran very much within myself, whereas poor Dave was out the box at the end, feeling sick and dizzy. It shows the difference between our different metabolisms, but also the progress

I've made since I first came along as a wee boy five years ago, admiring Dave and his best friend, David Jenkins.

Dave was amusing us all with his tales of a three weeks trip to Venezuela back in October and his adventures in the prostitute belt and on how to avoid and keep away from them! I was also speaking to Bob Sinclair who is working on a 25,000 words dissertation on local county councils. In the afternoon I skimmed several chapters of Charles Lipsey's Economics textbook. *Diana* phoned me in the evening. I thought she might have been down today. In the evening I enjoyed the first part of a superior programme called *Washington Behind Closed Doors*. I am fascinated by American politics. Thereafter I sat on the big old squishy armchair enjoying Grandma Jo's delicious home-made (cake-like) Christmas shortbread and continued to read Mr David Niven, interspersed with pauses for laughter as I chuckled away.

Afternoon: 2 x 5 x 150s ((90 seconds recovery)

29th December, 1977 Today was a rest day, but some interesting developments on the home front. *Diana the goddess of love and hunting* and I drove up to the West End and went shopping. Princes Street was bustling with the crowds. I picked up some clothes; books and the *Business Game* whereas poor *Diana* didn't get any clothes. We played *Monopoly* all afternoon. Her father phoned, raging away, telling her *To get home right away!* Well that did it! The balloon went up! It's not something I'd witnessed before, but Grandma Jo got on the phone to him and left him without a name! She thereafter did the same to *Diana's* mother too! She told them straight that until they agreed to treat her decently then she wouldn't be coming home! Well, it seemed to have quite an effect because they relented, calmed down and said she would be treated well. I gave her a lift home to Silverknowes. From there I went for a pint with Alistair

Hutton who's travelling out to Spain tomorrow along with Chris Black, Meg Ritchie and Stewart Togher. Whilst out Roger Jenkins had phoned from London so I unfortunately missed him; *Washington Behind Closed Doors* was excellent once ·again.

30ᵗʰ December, 1972 Having committed to training regularly I ran dismally in the Queen's Drive Races finishing toward the back of the field.

Afternoon: Queen's Drive Race 3.25 miles followed by some weights

Evening: One hour indoor football plus exercises before bed

1974 I bought some science magazines in the morning, for no other reason than to extend my knowledge beyond the arts. Gaga gave me a lift up to Meadowbank at lunchtime. I played some table tennis with Paul and then ran a fantastic 300 metres. Given it's the middle of winter, Bill was *really pleased*. I don't often write that! I hung around until 9.30 p.m. when Bob Sinclair gave me a lift home.

Evening: 300 metres with a short 5 metres rolling start: 33.2 seconds! I was timed through 200 metres in 21.3 secs; 2 x 100m (7 minutes recovery) 10.8; 11.0 (rest); 2 x 60m

Before Bed: Arm-action; press-ups; sit-ups; mobility

1976 *Diana the goddess of love and hunting,* her mother and I went to see *The Nutcracker* ballet; it was exquisite and Tchaikovsky's score was rather wonderful.

Hogmanay, 1972 We went to the Ross' Hogmanay Party; both Paul and Iain (brother) were stoned! It was less memorable for Mother's embarrassment; as Paul was waving a cheery goodbye to our hosts on their doorstep, four stolen cans of beer gradually slid down his jacket sleeve dropping out falling downwards one by one on to the stony floor in stony silence; it was as if time had stood still-a moment frozen in time with the clock-hands still. I laughed out loud which broke the silence; as they say, you have tae laugh, which we boys did on the bus back home to Oxgangs. The following day, Mother said she had never been so black-affronted!

Morning: 8 x 300 metres (2 minutes recovery) 44; 48; 49; 49; 44; 45; 49; 44 seconds

1973 The start of a trend of going to Coach Walker's annual Hogmanay parties at East Claremont Street; as the years have gone by they have become as legendary as Mr Fezziwig's annual party in Dickens' *A Christmas Carol.*

Twenty of us took a pub crawl up the Royal Mile; mostly the usual suspects who meet up at the Waverley Bar at weekends. Just after the pubs closed at ten o'clock we split up into small groups to go for a bite to eat. I was with Dougie McLean; Alistair Grant and his girlfriend Elspeth; we managed to find a table and got some Chinese food. We all managed to reconvene later and met up again at the Tron Church to hear the bells and welcome in New Year, 1974. Pat and Mary were enthusiastically kissing me. Thereafter, we all headed down to Coach Walker's house until 2.00 a.m. Paul and I had to sprint for the number 2 night bus which took us all the way out to Oxgangs. We bumped into Les Ramage and Steve Westbrook, before going to our beds at 3.30 a.m.

1976 I was keen to repeat previous Christmas Eves and went down to Gullane Sands in the Spitfire on this the last day of the year. In the evening Iain; *Diana the goddess of love and* *hunting* and I went for some drinks to The Steading Inn at Hillend; then The Buckstone; and on to the Hunters Tryst before going down to the Walkers' Hogmanay party. We got home at 2.00 a.m. We had a wonderful time. The years seem to be getting better and better; happy days!

Sea Fever

I must go down to the seas again, to the lonely sea and the sky,
And all I ask is a tall ship and a star to steer her by;
And the wheel's kick and the wind's song and the white sail's shaking,
And a grey mist on the sea's face, and a grey dawn breaking.

I must go down to the seas again, for the call of the running tide
Is a wild call and a clear call that may not be denied;
And all I ask is a windy day with the white clouds flying,
And the flung spray and the blown spume, and the sea-gulls crying.

I must go down to the seas again, to the vagrant gypsy life,
To the gull's way and the whale's way where the wind's like a whetted knife;
And all I ask is a merry yarn from a laughing fellow-rover,
And quiet sleep and a sweet dream when the log trick's over.

John Masefield

Morning: **Gullane Sands 2.5 miles run; bounding; set of 4; 3; 2; 1 sand-dune hill runs; worked very hard till I felt sick**

Lunchtime: **Gym circuit**

1977 Late morning there was a surprisingly large group of us out for our 300 metres session-Norrie; John Scott; Paul; Adrian and me. However, with the after-effects of the cold I had to drop out after only six runs; possibly the first time I've dropped out of a session; it doesn't augur well given I'll be racing both Paul and John over a half mile at the AAA's Championships in January.

I dropped Paul off up at the Bridges and drove home through a quiet Arthurs Seat reflecting on the year gone by and the year ahead, with the uncertain promise of the 1978 Commonwealth Games in Edmonton and the European Championships behind the Iron Curtain in Prague. Given Steve Ovett has a personal best of 1 minute 45.4 seconds and Sebastian Coe is the current number one Brit, am I getting just a little ahead of myself, given my best is a pedestrian 1 minute 53 seconds from an indoors Perth run three years ago? I'm crossing the Rubicon, so, *Let the dice fly high!*

Having driven back in a reflective *dwam* (to paraphrase Robert Louie from *Catriona*) I arrived back home to find that *Diana* was already down at Porty enjoying a sherry. We sat and played Monopoly and then had a lot of fun making up an imaginary guest list for our wedding-who's in and who's out! I phoned Dad and in between Paul phoned several times; later we collected Paul and Lorraine and went to the local Three Inns; as I was driving I only had one small drink, but we had a lot of fun and laughter at The Great Wall Restaurant in Portobello. The waitresses didn't quite know what to make of Paul who was gently outrageous! Very late on *Diana* and I went to a party at Dad's.

<u>Lunchtime:</u> 6 x 300 metres (90 seconds recovery) 42; 42; 42; 42; 44; 46 seconds: I had to drop out after 6 of a planned 8 runs; my worst session for years; a little dispiriting, but I suspect it's mainly to do with not properly shaking off this ongoing cold-a bit of a bugger and an unfortunate way to complete a mixed year on the athletics front where I got into *No-Man's Land* as astutely identified by Roger in his letter to me at the end of September.

New Year's Day, 1978 After a lovely buffet at Mum's we drove back in the dark and cold to Portobello; however disaster struck. Just as we were approaching the traffic lights at the start of Peffermill Road, Gaga's car had a puncture-the rear inside wheel. The tyre deflated and didn't respond to any attempts at resuscitation. The icy wind cut straight through me further hampering any efforts on my part. Meanwhile it made sense for Jo, Aunt Heather and the dog to leap on to a passing number 42 bus much to the dog's relief! We weren't able to retrieve the situation so Will, *Diana the goddess of love and hunting* and I managed to thereafter commandeer a passing taxi and travelled home in style, but not before poor *Diana* almost went her length on the ice, with me ungentlemanly laughing at the scenario. We were going to go to Mark Wilson's party, but I was too tired. *Diana* was in tears as she walked up Durham Road to head for home; she wasn't looking forward to seeing her folks...

2ⁿᵈ January, 1973 As I was staying over at Oxgangs, Iain; Les; Keith and I were up at 6.00 a.m. to do the milk run. There were no busses running until 7.00 a.m. so we had to walk down to Morningside. What a fucking laugh we had! Les and Keith were throwing pints of milk at each other; they were dripping with the white stuff; later on Les and I were dropping half pint three-sided tetra-packs from the top landings of the Morningside flats; if you got them to land just right on their corner there was the most almighty bang with milk splashing everywhere. We had to race downstairs, tumbling and laughing as we went and out into Morningside Road before the tenants opened their front doors to find out what the fuck was going on. It was absolute carnage. A great start to the year with loads of belly laughs. I trust the boys won't get the sack from Berry's Dairy!

Toward lunchtime Paul and I met up with Coach Walker and some of his athletes at Paties Road Sports Centre from whence we went for a nine miles run through Colinton Dell and over the Pentland Hills. Although it was wet and windy it was lovely being high up on the hills looking down and out over the city below. I found the run really hard going, however Eric Fisher was very supportive and nursed me along, staying alongside encouraging me right to the finish, whilst the likes of Paul quite rightly waltzed off into the distance. Eric's a lovely guy.

Lunchtime: 9 miles run through Colinton Dell and over the Pentland Hills

1978 The phone rang at 9.30 a.m. Guess who? Wrong! It was Andy Ross about Gaga's abandoned car at Peffermill Road. Andy arrived at the house at 10.00 a.m. and we went out to mend the puncture. Andy was underneath the car lying on the cold, wet road, putting the jack underneath and holding it in place, whilst I loosened the wheel. I don't know how he managed it as it was bitterly cold; I couldn't feel my hands. However, we got the job done fairly quickly, but not without a fair share of tension that the jack would remain in place and hold the car upright! Thereafter Andy came back to Durham Road for some coffee and shortie and was full of his usual good cheer making us all laugh and delighting the household.

Meanwhile *Diana the goddess of love and hunting* had telephoned whilst I was out; her father would not run her down to the New Year Sprint so I went out and picked her up. We met the gang there including Coach Walker; Paul; Lorraine; Davie etc. It was an enjoyable day and I thought the winner, Roy Heron, was very impressive-10.79 seconds for the 110 metres, off 8.5 metres.

After giving Paul and Lorraine a lift home I went out and ran five miles as I start to try to regain full fitness after this debilitating cold. It was good to be out and running over the wintry Duddingston Golf Course; there were only one or two golfers out so I essentially had the parkland to myself. After being in company for much of the day I enjoyed the solitariness and contemplation. As I ran through the Figgate Park, on the way back I bumped into *Diana*-she was out walking the dog. I felt pretty knackered, but I had at least run at a pretty steady pace throughout. Thereafter back home for a bath; a bowl of soup; and then I gave *Diana* a lift home to Silverknowes before travelling back to enjoy another instalment of *Washington Behind Closed Doors*. A life in a day.

Afternoon: 5 miles run Duddingston Golf Course

3rd January, 1974 We're off for an adventure to Cosford. The bus left Meadowbank at 8.45 a.m. My first impression was that it looked like an old ice cream van! However, it was a pretty good trip down and the morning passed very quickly. When we arrived in Wolverhampton the first thing Paul and I did was to go off to buy a bottle of cough mixture and then joined everyone for a meal; the waitress was gorgeous!

Meeting in a Lift

We stepped into the lift. The two of us, alone
We looked at each other and that was all.
Two lives, a moment, fullness, bliss.
At the fifth floor she got out and I went on up
knowing I would never see her again,
that it was a meeting once and for all,
that if I followed her I would be like a dead man in her tracks
and that if she came back to me
it would only be from the other world.

Vladimir Holan

When we got out to Cosford, after looking at the programme, Kim Roberts and Brian Gordon were terrified of their opposition! My heat went well and I handled Cecil Moven easily, but I took an unusually long time to recover. The semi-final was loaded, but that was no excuse-I just ran badly; with only a 20 metres or so home straight to the finish I just couldn't get past either Mike Delaney who's a very shrewd indoor tactician and Glen Cohen. Afterwards we went for a Chinese meal and I then sat up playing poker with Keith Ridley and Drew Hislop until 3.00 a.m. in the morning.

Evening: Cosford Phillips Games

400 metres Heat (7.40 pm) 1. Hoffmann 50.8 seconds; I felt a bit hot and tired;

400 metres Semi-final (9.20 pm) 1. Glen Cohen 49.3; 2. Mike Delaney 49.38; 3. Hoffmann 49.6 (p.b.)

1976 After a long lie in bed I went up to Meadowbank and ran a scorcher of a race-oops, not a race, but a session-I'm getting a touch excited! Come the afternoon I worked out in the gym. At night I didn't feel too well as I had trained so hard, so I sat in front of the telly all evening.

Morning: 600 metres: 78.6 seconds (pb); 500m 63.6 secs; 400m 49.8 secs (12 minutes recovery); it was cold and windy with a very icy bend

Afternoon: Gym Session

1978 Around 10.00 a.m. I drove up to Meadowbank early doors. I warmed up and ran a better session than a few days back; this time I ran with Norman; Paul and Adrian all the way-a good workmanlike session so I'm on the road to recovery. Towards the end of our session a lot of people were arriving to watch the second day of the *Powderhall* New Year Meeting. I grabbed a quick shower then joined the others in the stand to enjoy the athletics. Bill took us into the VIP lounge for a nice salad lunch before we went back out to watch Roy Herron win a very exciting sprint race for Wilson Young's school. After the meeting I joined Duncan McKechnie and we went along to see what Tom McNab had to say about the new professional set up in Dubai. In two words-not much! I came home for a meal before settling down to study all evening.

Morning (11.00 a.m.): 10 x 200 metres (1 minute 45 seconds recovery) all in 26 seconds

4th January, 1975 After breakfast I got a call from Bob Sinclair to say Colin O'Neil is injured and may not run in the Phillips Cosford Games 400 metres final and as the fastest loser I may get a call up. However, he recovered sufficiently to run; meanwhile I was invited to run in the 600 metres which was televised; it was my first appearance on the box much to the delight of my grandfather who I phoned later from a transport cafe. David Coleman gave me a good crit, saying how promising he thought I was! Because I was an extra I had to start behind the top American, Mark Winzenreid and in the same lane; despite being bundled off the track after 400 metres I came through well to run a U.K Junior Record. Coach Walker was really pleased-in fact everyone was genuinely pleased for me. I received a nice wee dish as a prize. We arrived home in Edinburgh at 1.00 a.m. in the morning.

Invitation 600 metres

(3rd) Hoffmann 80.6 seconds (UK Junior Record), 51.3 at 400 metres; got knocked off the track

1976 I had another long lie in bed this morn; I felt exhausted from yesterday's effort, but still ran a superb session.

<u>Morning:</u> **4 x 300 metres (15 minutes recovery) 33.9; 33.9; 34.2; 34.8 seconds; the track was wet, but no wind today**

1977 I watched our own Robert Louis Stevenson's *Weir of Hermiston* on the box-excellent. Overnight the temperature had been well below zero. During the morning I broke the ice on the pond; one fish had died, so we're down to only eight now. As the hose was frozen too I was back and forward re-filling the pond with buckets of water. Come two o'clock in the afternoon I ran the 2 miles to Meadowbank and did a gym circuit, before venturing across to Arthurs Seat with the weights jacket to run a good hill session. It was lovely up there. Dusk was fast approaching and the landscape glistened with a white frost that had not lifted all day. At such moments I feel at one with the world, although it was a solitary and lonely feeling too; I felt like the last man alive as there was no one else to be seen in a quiet Queen's Park.

Stopping by Woods on a Snowy Evening

'…The woods are lovely, dark and deep,
But I have promises to keep,
And miles to go before I sleep,
And miles to go before I sleep.'

Robert Frost

Afterwards, I ran home, studied and saw the doctor about why I was picking up so many colds. I was impressed with him; he wonders whether it may be to do with my dry skin- an interesting theory.

Afternoon (2.00 p.m.): 2 miles warm up; Gym circuit; 8 x 20 seconds hill runs (with weights jacket); 2 miles warm down

5th January, 1975 The day after the night before's UK Junior Record over 600 metres. Despite having raced the past two days and travelling up to Edinburgh in the early morning from Wolverhampton I was keen to go training at Meadowbank. I was running really well over very short distances; afterwards Paul and I took on John Kerr and Davie at table tennis and then in the afternoon I ran a fantastic 60 metres time-trial; come the evening Aileen didn't seem keen to go out, which suited me...Ce la vie!

Morning: 6 x 30 metres all in 4.0 seconds; equates to 10.8 100 metres or quicker

Afternoon: 3 x 150m in 15.5 seconds; 60 metres time-trial race 6.7 seconds!

6th January, 1975 After all the excitement and good running of the past few days Coach Walker brought me back down to earth today with a bang as we ran a tough speed endurance session; I felt terrible at the end, feeling dizzy with a sore head.

Morning (10.30 a.m.): Clock 2 x 160 metres; 2 x 180m; 2 x 200m; 2 x 210m; 1 x 200m; 1 x 180m; 1 x 160m with a walk/jog back recovery

7th January, 1974 It was a horrible day at work-wet 'n windy. It was also the start of the Three day working week. We had Calor gas lamps on all day which gave me a headache; hardly surprising given it's an internal office with no windows or fresh air. It was a boring day, making me reflect on how I'm wasting my youth here; I need to break the cycle. We were allowed away early at 4.30 p.m. so I was home for dinner by 5.15 p.m.

Evening: 6 x 200 metres (2 minutes recovery) 27; 26; 26; 26; 25; 25 seconds all in my tracksuit because of the cold; followed by gym circuit.

1975 I passed my driving test today; it was a great feeling. I phoned Kay Walker-she was delighted for me.

1978 Sitting in the car in Portobello with the rain tumbling down made me think of such Saturdays as a boy, either working on my bicycle in the back shed or lying in front of the coal fire watching Grandstand whilst munching on Golden Wonder crisps and drinking Globe Sun Kool Kola. I ran a fair, but very hard session at Meadowbank; after lunch, around three in the afternoon, Aunt Heather; Grandma Jo and I took a wee tootle out to Carrington, Midlothian. Whilst I ran 4 miles along the quiet country lanes they went for a walk with the dog. It was just starting to get dark as we headed for home; in the evening a nice meal with *Diana the goddess of love and hunting* before we drove out to see Dad.

Afternoon (1.00 p.m.): 4 x 600 metres (4 minutes recovery) 91; 91; 92; 96 seconds. It was windy; there was a high lactic acid build-up on the last run; I'm not used to running 600m at a fair pace; I need regular sessions of 500/600/700 metres repetitions and some fartlek work

Afternoon: 4 miles fartlek

8th **January, 1978** *Diana the goddess of love and hunting* was sleepwalking in the night and what noisy floorboards! I ran a very hard session which stretched me mentally as well as physically. Dad drove me to Dundee for the start of the academic term; his wife and young Roddy were there as was *Diana*. On a lovely winter afternoon it was an enjoyable drive through the Fife countryside and newly ploughed fields. It was good of him to drive me; I think he's wanting to try to do the best by me now as a father as we start to repair the despair of all the previous damaged and lost years. After dropping all my gear off at my land-lady's he took us all out for a meal to the Hong Kong Restaurant. After everyone left to head back to Edinburgh the feeling of loneliness suddenly hit me. I settled down and studied for a few hours; outwith it was very cold when I ventured out later on to the phone box to check that *Diana* had got back safely. Thank goodness she had; I don't know what I'd ever do without her; she's irreplaceable; she feels very flat too. I lay in bed listening to Radio Forth and reading the Sunday Times.

<u>Morning:</u> 8 x 300 metres (90 seconds recovery) all in 42 secs; it was cold and windy; I just managed to run with Adrian all the way, but I was whacked at the end

9th January, 1973 I was pretty tired when I got up this morning; half the crew were absent from work. It was a long day, especially as I was there until 5.50 p.m. although Roy marked my card as finishing at 6.30 p.m. as I had nipped out to get him an Edinburgh Evening News. On the bus I saw an old school-friend Graham McKiernan; he used to be part of our annual winning relay team at Hunters Tryst Primary School; he's a bright lad and unlike me he's buckled down at school and is doing well. Paul, John Kerr and I had a bit of a laugh at Meadowbank; dinner inside me I'm now tucked up in bed with Radio Luxembourg on. A day in the life of a 16 year old working loon, trying to find his way in life.

<u>Evening:</u> 12 x 200 metres (2 minutes recovery) all between 29 and 32 seconds; there was a damp mist hovering which made it difficult to breathe

10ᵗʰ January, 1976, Athletics Weekly Report Phillips Cosford Games:

'The men's 600 proved to be a slowish race, although rather more competitive than anticipated. David Jenkins had hoped to run the first 200 in about 24.5, the second in 25.5 (50 at 400) and the last in 27-odd. The final lap was covered in 27.2 as it turned out but the initial pace was far off what was required. Jenkins and Ainsley Bennett were abreast at 200 in 25.6 ('that shows a diabolical lack of speed' mutterred Jenkins) while at 400, reached in 52.5, Jenkins was a stride ahead of Bennett, with Peter Hoffmann a similar margin behind Bennett. The young Scot overtook Bennett halfway round the last lap and started closing on Jenkins but the final result was never in doubt. Hoffmann, the European Junior silver medallist, ran splendidly even if he was disappointed with his time. Having run the distance outdoors at Meadowbank in very cold weather recently in 78sec he had hoped to duplicate that time in the warmth of Cosford. His target for 1976 is to lower his best 400 mark (47.27) to around 46.5, as well as running a few more 800's.'

Invitation 600 metres

1, D. Jenkins (Gates) 79.7 seconds; 2, P. Hoffmann (EAC) 79.9 secs; 3, A. Bennett (Bir) 81.7 secs; 4, J. Aukett (W&B) 83.1 secs

1978 We had to run to catch the train from Broughty Ferry in to Dundee; it arrives two minutes earlier now. Although I passed my Accounts exam I was very disappointed with the mark-more facts and less eloquence! To take my mind off the result I went out to Riverside to train. As I made my way there, a blizzard of snow came tumbling down. The cinder 200 metres track surface was covered in white. There was no other person to be seen out, but I managed to run a good session, which I enjoyed. Afterwards it was a strange feeling taking refuge in the empty Riverside changing room to remove my spikes. As Captain Scott said *Snow's a strange thing*.

Stopping by Woods on a Snowy Evening

'...The only other sound's the sweep
Of easy wind and downy flake.'

Robert Frost

I jogged back for a shower and thereafter caught the 5.10 p.m. train back to Broughty Ferry. I felt a bit low. *Diana the goddess of love and hunting* telephoned me from outside Meadowbank on her way to training. Tom, Derek and I enjoyed an animated and lively discussion tonight.

Afternoon: 10 x 160 metres (jog back recovery) on a snow covered Riverside track

11th January 1978 Well, I managed to get out early this morn, but not without a few miss-starts. The alarm clock is still dodgy and I had to awaken myself. First of all I awoke at 5.00 a.m. and then several more times.

Things

'...It is 5 a.m. All the worse things come stalking in
and stand icily about the bed looking worse and worse and worse.'

Fleur Adcock

It was cold out; everything was covered in a hoar frost with a light dusting of snow. I ran along the beach road out beyond Broughty Ferry harbour. I ran around 4 miles at a good pace. I kept my red tracksuit and blue hooded top on to keep the cold at bay. Afterwards, a cold bath and then some yoga and all before breakfast.

I noticed in the year register that I came third top of the year in Economic Development; I also got a good mark for Economics too. In Maths we've moved on to quadratic equations. In the afternoon I did a circuit in the university gym and showed Albert Ree the Riverside track. However, there was no chance of running any 600s as there was a blanket of snow covering it and there was no chance of the snow storm abating; it won't be like this in California. Late afternoon I studied hard. In the evening after Mrs Neve served up all our dinners we had good fun playing with her young son, Glen, showing him how to do hand-stands. When we looked out afterwards the streets were covered in a blanket of snow-gosh, that was quick!

Snow

'The room was suddenly rich and the great bay-window was
Spawning snow and pink roses against it
Soundlessly collateral and incompatible:
World is suddener than we fancy it.

...There is more than glass between the snow and the huge roses.'

Louis MacNeice

Diana the goddess of love and hunting telephoned me from a Davidsons Mains phone box, spending 50 pence.

Morning (7.00 a.m.): 4 miles-good pace

Lunchtime (1.30 p.m.): Gym circuit

12th January, 1976 I was running superbly well this evening; later I went out to Oxgangs to give Mother the Philips stereo I received for finishing second to Jenkins at the weekend.

Evening: 2 x 4 x 200 metres: (1) 21.5 seconds; 21.5 secs;

22 secs; 22 secs; (2) 21.5 secs; 21.5 secs; 22 secs; 24 secs
with a couple of yards rolling start, crown to crown, as it
was very windy

1977 I trained with Roger at lunchtime. I finished the final
Hercule Poirot book, *Last Case, Curtain.* After reading half a
dozen of them in the flat library in Montreal I've now read
them all-Christie back to her best. It was poignant to see him
die-he's become a friend.

<u>Lunchtime:</u> **4 x 800 metres, striding the straights,
jogging the bends**

1978 At 7.00 a.m. I stepped out into the Broughty Ferry
snow in just my red tracksuit to run four miles. It wasn't
quite as cold as I'd anticipated and there was little wind. I
had been thinking of scaring the sleepy milk-boy, but
decided not to. The only other people out were a couple of
paper-girls. In the afternoon I endured the most boring
experiment in Psychology, before disappearing to catch the
late afternoon Edinburgh train; it was packed full of posh
school kids. The train was an old grunter-cold and bumpy
making it impossible to study on. Edinburgh was raw-
absolutely freezing; I arrived back at Porty just as Will was
about to run Jo up to her painting class.

<u>Morning (7.00 a.m.):</u> **4 miles**

13th January, 1974 Scrubs and I were singing coming home
on the bus. I think I've managed to get back in with Coach
Walker again-let's make it permanent this time.

<u>Morning:</u> **4 x 200 metres (4 minutes recovery) 23.8; 24;
23; 23 seconds; (12 mins rest) 2 x 200m 23; 23 secs**

<u>Afternoon:</u> **Gym circuit**

1978 I ran a solid session of 600s; after losing a bit of fitness and confidence with my cold two weeks ago, I'm picking up; my debut at the AAAs Indoors may not be so forlorn after all; thereafter I got a rub at Denis's. Iain has started working at the meat market; he gave me three sirloin steaks and is keen to help me each week. We had a pint at The Merlin where we bumped into Les and his girlfriend. I dropped him off at Kim's; on leaving I felt a twinge of sadness for days gone by. I'd like to be in a position one day to help him out.

Afternoon: 5 x 600 metres (8 mins recovery) all between 90-92 seconds

14th January, 1978 I slept soundly straight through until 9.00 a.m. I went up Durham Road first thing before breakfast to collect my *Athletics Weekly*. I spent much of the morning gathering facts for my Business Studies essay before dropping Heather and Josephine off at the Royal Mile and then drove down to Meadowbank. It was a cold, wet and windy day. We ran a tough breakdown session; Paul was dominating the group; he's looking an increasingly good bet for the AAAs indoor championships. I wasn't unhappy with my session and feel I can only get better and better with this type of work. Also, because I was running in the pack there was a cold spray on my legs which didn't help any. I always find it difficult to run well when I'm feeling that cold. I also feel I'm lacking a wee bit on the speed side too.

After enjoying Iain's sirloin steak for lunch Josephine and I went out to Carrington. Whilst she sat and sketched I ran four miles on the country roads and lanes. On a wet and overcast winter's afternoon the countryside is stark and bare; yet with several of the fields already under the plough, there is the hope and anticipation of spring. Athletics and the farming cycle of the year share much in common-athletes and farmers hope to reap what they sow come the late summer-early autumn:

Ode to the West Wind

'...Oh Wind,
If Winter comes, can Spring be far behind?'

Percy Shelley

I felt a bit tired over the last mile of the run, especially in my front thighs; I need to fine tune and temper this so that I become much more efficient. *Diana the godess of love and hunting* was down at the house when we arrived home; a lovely passionate evening in together; later laughing out aloud and later still, me dictating an essay, whilst she wrote it out beautifully; a pretty zany scene as I paced up and down, intermittently lying down and thereafter getting back up again, all the while, she with a cider and *Babycham* in her hand and me with a lemonade and ginger beer and a handful of hazelnuts; you have to laugh! When Willie; Josephine and Heather came back we all enjoyed some St Andrews fish 'n chips; we completed the essay and I drove *Diana* home to Silverknowes before watching Parkinson on the box. Happy days.

Lunchtime (12.00 p.m.): 700 metres (98 secs); (12 minute recovery) 600m (83 secs); (10 mins rec); 500m (69 secs); it was cold, wet and windy; a lot of splashback

Afternoon (3.00 p.m.): 4 miles run at Carrington

15th January, 1978 Josephine awoke me at 8.30 a.m. I was sound asleep and otherwise would have slept on until 10.00 a.m. After breakfast I collected the papers, rolls and milk and took the dog for a run in Portobello Park. It was a cold, wet, windy and nasty January morning. There was a very strange red light around creating an unusual shadow across the winter landscape. I managed a little studying before going up to Meadowbank and all things considered ran a pretty good

session, including running a 1200 metres, a distance which I've never run before. Norman brought down a couple of books on Accounts which was very good of him.
Diana the goddess of love and hunting and I picked up some Arcaris ice cream and then had Sunday lunch.
Thereafter I packed my bags for another week in Dundee. Will ran us up to Waverley Station. I was going to get the 4.50 p.m. train, but I sensed *Diana* was a little down so asked her if she wanted me to stay on a little later. We went out to Morningside for a small meal at the Mei Kwei-she loves the Morningside area, particularly at this time of the year. We took a 23 bus to the bottom of the Mound and then strolled hand in hand along Princes Street. I bumped into Tom at the station; we had a half pint and then boarded the 8.30 p.m. London-Aberdeen train. We got to our digs at 11.00 p.m. So went the day.

Lunchtime: 1200 metres 3 mins 10 secs (20 minutes recovery); 4 x 300m (5 mins rec) all in 38.0 secs; the weather was wet and windy

Up in the Morning Early

'Up in the morning's no for me,
Up in the morning early;
When a' the hills are cover'd in snaw,
I'm sure it's winter fairly...'

Robert Burns

16th January, 1973 Once again, it was a real struggle to get up early in the middle of winter. As I had my Adidas training bag, Gaga was very good giving me a lift all the way along Balcarres Street and dropping me off at Thomas Graham & Sons. Being dropped off around 7.30 a.m. and working through until 6.30 p.m. made for a long day, however it wasn't too bad and passed reasonably quickly. By the same token I don't want to be wishing my life away. What also helped was that we had another game of *Scrabble* at lunchtime; this time I managed to win. Jim; Roy; and Rhona gave me a lift to the Bridges. I was running quite well tonight.

Evening: 2 x 6 x 200 metres (90 secs-2 minutes recovery); all in between 28 and 30 seconds

17th January, 1975 There was a lovely wee note in the post this morning from the charming C. K. Lipton (Borough Road College):

'...If there is any hold-up or delay or difficulty, do not hesitate to let me know. I shall endeavour to be entirely impartial and advise as an educationist and not as someone who seeks to press-gang a fine athlete. Don't forget: it is your interest alone that you should be serving. Decisions are rarely irrevocable early on in life, but it is preferable to make the right one. Keep on working hard at school...'

I feel fortunate to be able to have met such wonderful people as him-and all because of athletics.

18th January, 1976 Whilst getting a Pink News last night I bumped into Mr C. and he told me to come around for a rub before today's big session. David Jenkins was up, but unfortunately the wind was howling and it bucketed rain.

Morning: With Dave Jenkins; Norrie; Paul; John; very cold; wet; and windy: 5 x 500 metres (10 minutes recovery) (1) 65.0 seconds-I led it out; (2) 68.6 secs-Dave led it out; (3) 65.0 secs-Norrie led it out. I ran across the line level with Dave on each run-a good session

1977 Hellish news; Dougal Haston was killed in an avalanche. He's been one of my heroes for years; often I sat up into the night in bed reading of his exploits. When the going got rough it was usually Haston who they passed the baton on to, to see it through.

19ᵗʰ January, 1973 I'm already starting to get nervous about tomorrow's cross-country race!

1975 It was very frosty this morning. Heather and Nana are away on a 'stone trip' to the ploughed fields of Fife. After getting in some groceries I phoned Coach Walker and picked him up; I also gave him a lift home. In training I ran a good 300 metres. We were looking at the programme for the Scottish Indoor Championships next Saturday; it should be a cakewalk. Later I gave the lovely *Pixie Mia Farrow lookalike* a lift home to the Braid Hills.

Toilet

'I wonder will I speak to the girl
sitting opposite me on this train.
I wonder will my mouth open and say,
'Are you going all the way
to Newcastle? or 'Can I get you a coffee?
Or will it simply go 'aaaaah'
as if it had a mind of its own?

...A tunnel finds us looking out the window
into one another's eyes. She leaves her seat,
but I know that she likes me...'

Hugo Williams

I have a sore throat so I went to bed early.

Morning: 300 metres with a short rolling start: 34.1 seconds; 2 x 150m: 15.5/15.8 secs and 4 x 100m all with a walk back recovery

1978 This morning I ran three miles along the Broughty Ferry coast. It wasn't cold out; but it was windy with lots of snow in the sky. After breakfast Tom and I went in for only Integrated Studies and then headed back to Edinburgh together. It was a great feeling to be back in the capital. After a light lunch I drove up to Meadowbank; Coach Walker and Davie Reid were there. I did a weights jacket circuit on my own and thereafter went across to Arthurs Seat to do some hill runs. Thursdays have been following this pattern and I feel my quads are very strong. Holyrood Park was at its majestic wintry best. It was a pity that I didn't have a camera with me. The ice on the frozen Dunsapie Loch was thick enough for me to walk on. At the far end there was an old man with what looked like his grandchildren. As I made my way to the usual hill beyond St Anthony's Chapel, dusk was beginning to fall. On the slope parallel to where I was running, two ladies were out with three young children. They were sliding on the light snow and laughing happily together; it was rather charming to watch, partly taking my mind off the hard work. I came home for tea and then studied all evening. Meanwhile Jo and Heather are away up to Cannonball House on the Royal Mile at the Edinburgh Sketching Club. I phoned *Diana goddess of love and hunting...*

Morning: 3 miles run

Afternoon (3.30 p.m.): Gym circuit with 20 lbs weights jacket; followed by 8 x 80 metres Arthurs Seat hill runs with weights jacket

20ᵗʰ January, 1973 I ran in the Scottish East Districts Youth Cross Country Championships. I didn't get a medal, but I ran okay. I was 19th. I now realise I was kidding myself about getting a medal, but I can't fault the ambition! Afterwards I stayed the night at Paul's home at Broomhouse. We enjoyed ourselves.

Afternoon: Scottish East District Youth
Championships 4 miles (19th) 22 minutes 39 seconds

1975 I'm in bed with a very heavy cold; my throat is
particularly sore; it's a bugger with the Scottish Indoor
Championships only five days away.

1976 I was sprinting really well this evening. I was
entertaining Ann Sowersby and Jackie Grounwater reading
out extracts from J.P Donleavy's *The Ginger Man*. I'm away to
phone Roger.

Evening: 10 x 40 metres sprint starts; I was cooking!

1978 *Diana the goddess of love and hunting* and I went to
Demarco's for a coke float and rolls then for a drive in the
wintry countryside; later we went for a walk along the
Cramond coast. Despite the sea-air, everywhere was covered
under a blanket of snow.

ANNABEL LEE

'It was many and many a year ago,
In a kingdom by the sea,
That a maiden there lived whom you may know
By the name of ANNABEL LEE:
And this maiden she lived with no other thought
Than to love and be loved by me.'

Edgar Allan Poe

21ˢᵗ January, 1975 I lay abed for hours with this hellish cold,
temperature and sore throat. It's unlikely I'll be fit for
Saturday's Scottish Championships. I gave Paul a ring at
Thomas Graham & Sons; what a bloody laugh. I
impersonated Tam Paton, the Bay City Rollers manager:

'*Afternoon-whit's yir name young man?*'

'*Eh, Paul.*'

'*Right Paul-Tam Paton here, manager o' the Bay City Rollers.*'

'*Oh, right Mr Paton. Hello Mr Paton, sir.*'

'*Just call me Tam. Now Paul, two things; first of a' how's ma rubber shite pan coming oan?*'

'*Just a minute Mr Paton, a' mean Tam.*'

Pause.

I hear Paul turning around to his boss Ian Slater*:*

'*Ian, that's Mr Paton on the phone-he's wondering how his rubber shite pan is coming on?*'

'*His WHAT?-Fuck off Paul!*''

'*Hello Mr Paton, sorry I mean Tam; eh, my boss doesn't know.*'

'*Okay, nae worries Paul; mair important, how are the boys' tartan bathroom suites coming on?*'

'*Just a minute Tam.*'

Pause.

'*Ian, Tam's wondering how the boys' tartan bathroom suites are coming on?*'

'*WHAT...are you taking the fuckin' piss Paul?*'

What a laugh.

I was lying on my back howling with laughter...*'You fuckin' bastard Peter!'*

22nd January, 1974 Oh how my heart soared. After work, I walked up to the foot of Morningside Drive to get the 41 bus. *Pixie Mia Farrow lookalike* was on her way home from Mary Erskine's School. She saw me and came across the road to talk to me. She's such a nice girl. I would love to go about with her. For once the bus came too soon. I thought about her for much of the journey home, but forlornly; *Pixie* in her public school uniform, bubbling and sparkling with intelligence and prospects, while little old me is working as a lowly cost clerk at Tommy Graham's. I can but dream; as Yeats says:

He Wishes For The Clothes Of Heaven

'...But I, being poor, have only my dreams:
I have spread my dreams under your feet;
Tread softly because you tread on my dreams.'

W.B. Yeats

<u>Evening</u>: Weights session; followed by 30 x 200 metres slow-fasts! All between 31 and 35 seconds

1976 I managed to buy the complete set of J.P. Donleavy books today, costing the grand total of three quid. Roger arrived late, around 7.00 p.m. to give me a lift to the Lorimer's Breweries Scottish Sportsman of the Year Dinner. It was quite good. We had a heck of a lot of fun on the way back, laughing all the way home.

1978 I wandered through in my dressing gown to awaken *Diana*; she always looks so beautiful when she's asleep. Before breakfast I walked up to Swann's to collect the Sunday newspapers. I managed a little studying before Gaga ran us up to Meadowbank. Coach Walker was giving us a lift through to Grangemouth for an Open Graded Meeting-a useful blow-out and test before next weekend's AAA Indoor Championships.

Blimey! *Diana* and I had to share a front seat, whilst Peter Little; Ann Sowersby; Florence; and Owen Quinn were all in the back! It was very cold, wet and windy. I was fairly happy with my runs although I felt a bit woozy after the 300 metres. Barry Craighead gave *Diana* and me a lift back to Edinburgh. He was telling us that he is changing jobs to begin working as a site agent. Afterwards *Diana* said she thinks he is a very nice man. He is a nice man.

After a large steak dinner, *Diana* and I took the dog to Portobello Park. Whilst there we watched the moon rising in the sky. I managed a little Economics then come 7.00 p.m. Will ran me up to Waverley Station; on the way up he explained to *Diana* de meanin of jammin! The London-Aberdeen train was on time, so there was no Tom. There was a fascinating man on the train; he was from Australia. I bet he had an interesting tale to tell; if I'd been a news reporter I'd have asked him.

<u>Afternoon:</u> Grangemouth Open Graded Meeting (1.30 p.m.) 300 metres 1st 37.0 seconds; (2.25 p.m.) 600 metres 1st 83.0 secs; very cold; wet; windy

23rd January, 1973 George Foreman beat Joe Frasier in round 2. What a sensation. He had him down six times.

<u>Evening:</u> 2 x 6 x 150 yards; the early runs were relaxed with the later ones flat out; 20 seconds reducing to 17 secs

1975 I was feeling even better today. Nana was feeding everything into me in an effort to make the Championships on Saturday.

1976 Coach Walker picked up Paul and me and then Graham Malcolm and Norrie and we set off for Cosford. On the motorway one of the tyres blew at 80mph; I thought the end had come. We were heading straight for a metal pole in the central reservation, which I thought would slice the car in two; as it was fast approaching I thought, well it's not going to slice me as I'm not in the middle! Somehow Coach Walker wrestled the car's steering wheel and we eventually ground to a halt. Thereafter we managed to change the wheel thanks to a lorry driver who stopped to give us a hand. We just got to Cosford on time after further miscalculations. I ran miserably and just scraped into the final. Meanwhile Paul and Norrie got knocked out in their semi-finals. Everyone's nerves were frayed, so perhaps no wonder. I met up with Helen Barnett from London and we were talking for a while after my race; she's an engaging, bubbly, highly intelligent girl.

Evening: 1976 AAA Indoor Championships Cosford

(7.30 p.m.) Heat 1st 50.2 seconds Semi-final (9.10 p.m.) 2nd 49.3 secs (winner Steve Scutt 49.3 secs)

24ᵗʰ January, 1975 I felt very much better after being floored by this heavy cold all week. I think I'll be okay to run on Saturday.

1976 We sat about the hotel all morning playing cards. I finished about a pound up. Outside, everything was covered in snow-a rather lovely English winter scene as we travelled out to Cosford for the men's 400 metres final. I ran abysmally, finishing last. God Almighty! As the *Athletics Weekly* said: *'...as Peter Hoffmann faded to last after blazing the first*

200 in 22.5...' If I'd run the 200 metres instead, with that first lap, I would have won the bronze medal; I suspect I would actually have come close to winning it! Afterwards I walked around for half an hour with Helen Barnet, before we left for Edinburgh at tea-time. I'm not using it as an excuse as I know this is a race I should have won, but I'm going to take most of next week off to try to shake off this cold. My Achilles Heel? Certainly the propensity to not only keep picking up colds and infections, but it's my inability to throw them off too; it's certainly up there as a weakness in my arsenal.

We had a hell of a laugh on the way back home as we took one another to task over the miserableness of the performances. I was the only one of the four of us who made a final. Did the tyre blow out affect the others? Paul and I are a deadly combination when we get together and poor Norman in particular was toast. He may be the intellectual academic along with Graham Malcolm, but when they come under the combined working-class Oxgangs street wit and humour of the two of us, they just melt-they cannae keep up-putty in our hands! Still it cheered everyone up and my sides were sore with laughing. Even Coach Walker was laughing! We got back to Edinburgh at 11.30 p.m. which wasn't bad going. When I got home, sitting amongst the post was a fantastic offer from Loughborough University; I'm 95% certain of accepting it.

AAA Indoor 400 metres

(4th) 50.9 secs (22.5 first 200 metres!)

25th January, 1975 Well, staying in bed all week seemed to do the trick. I travelled up to Perth for the Scottish Indoor Championships. I sat beside Robert Sinclair. Outside the rain was teeming down. I managed to pick up a couple of titles, but afterwards I felt terrible. Back home at Portobello I was feeling so bad that Grandma Jo gave me a small glass of brandy; so it looks like more time off to recover, but I would have hated to sit the championships out.

1975 Scottish Junior Indoor Championships

300 metres heat 36.4 seconds (1st); 50 metres heat 6.3 secs (1st); 50m semi-final 6.3 secs (1st); 50m final 6.2 secs (1st); 300m final 35.2 secs (1st)

26ᵗʰ January, 1973 I was very tired this morning. Will and I had to go to work via Oxgangs to let Anne know the Mineral Club is cancelled-aye we could do with telephones. It was a rotten day at the Dickens blacking factory.

We gotta get out of this place

'...We gotta get out of this place
If it's the last thing we ever do
We gotta get out of this place
'cause girl, there's a better life for me and you...'

Barry Mann/Cynthia Weil

Scott and I went along to the Jester Restaurant for lunch. I paid so he's going to treat me next week.

1977 *Diana the goddess of love and hunting* and I had a few drinks too many, but much fun too. Earlier in the day she tried to hunt down a copy of *Evita* for me. I'd caught Julie Covington singing on the radio a quite stunning and beautiful version of *Don't Cry For Me Argentina*. Diana bought me this new journal-she's just great!

Don't Cry For Me Argentina

'...I love you and hope you love me...
...Have I said too much?
There's nothing more I can think of to say to you.
But all you have to do is look at me to know
That every word is true.'

Lloyd-Webber/Rice

<u>Evening:</u> 6 x 150 metres; first 40 metres building up, last 110 metres flat out

1978 Jo gave me my breakfast at 8.30 a.m. Together we cleared out the pond-another fish has died-is it the cold? I took the dog to Portobello Park and then met up with Coach Walker. He was saying if this new Edinburgh indoor arena comes off that he would most likely manage it and that there might be a chance of me becoming the assistant manager one day; that would be fabulous! I set off for Cosford and the AAA Indoor Championships. Will drove me up to Waverley Station to get the train. The very fact I'm travelling down on my own the day before shows I'm treating my first proper race over the half mile seriously. Based on training, Paul must be a big favourite. John Scott's also travelling down tomorrow and he's running well too. I managed to do a couple of hours of Accounts reading. Meanwhile out with there was a lot of snow particularly as the train passed through the Borders. Being so well versed in Agatha Christie, I felt I was on the Orient Express and wouldn't have been surprised to see Hercule Poirot (Albert Finney) and Colonel Arbuthnot (Sean Connery) come wandering through the carriage! I arrived at Wolverhampton at 5.30 p.m. and booked into the Old Vic Hotel. After dinner I lay on my bed reading and watched a bit of television. At 9.00 p.m. I telephoned *Diana*. I dialled the wrong number-what am I like! Believe it or not, but I had to call Directory of Enquiries to get her number! Clearly I'm focusing on this race. I know it's very important if I want to make an initial impression if I'm serious about making the Commonwealth and European Championships at the half mile and to challenge Coe and Ovett.

27th January, 1974 Whee! P*ixie Mia Farrow lookalike* was squeezing up to me at Meadowbank. I spend idle hours thinking of her. Will I ever take her out? I don't agree with Barrie! Hmmm, perhaps I do.

The Little Minister

"Let no one who loves be called altogether unhappy. Even love un-returned has its rainbow."

James Barrie

Morning: 6 x 150 metres flat out; walk round the track recovery; a very hard session

1975 The rain was teeming down. Our new kitten, Tiki, looks as if she's heading for the happy hunting ground. I was given a good headline in *The Herald* for Saturday's double win at Perth. Mid-morning I went along to the physio; Paul arrived halfway through and we went up town together. For *artistic reasons* we went to see *Emmanuele* to see what all the fuss was about! Back home I listened to Bryan Ferry's *Those Foolish Things* album; the title track makes me think of *Pixie*. I lay back idly day-dreaming of being her boyfriend and spending fun outings and lovely days out with her:

Those Foolish Things

'...The beauty that is Spring
These foolish things remind me of you
How strange how sweet to find you still
These things are dear me
They seem to bring you near to me...'

Eric Maschwitz

In the evening I trained at Meadowbank. I was high as a kite; of course I blame the presence of the fabulous *Pixie*. Unfortunately she was there with her boyfriend.

Evening: 300 metres (36.2 seconds); 200m (24 secs); 2 x 150m (17 secs); the track was covered in ice

1977 At 10.00 a.m. I met Paul at Waverley Station. The journey down was fine and quite relaxing. We had a bite to eat; I read and we also played the *Mastermind* code-breaking game. Adrian Weatherhead arrived at 6.00 p.m. and we had an excellent meal. We walked out in the rain to a local cinema; we watched one and a half pornographic movies; they were indescribably awful. Of course I blame Paul-Grandma Jo always said he was a bad influence-only joking! I tried to telephone *Diana the goddess of love and hunting* but her line was engaged. I lay down and read a Hercule Poirot-*Death on the Nile*.

1978 I went for breakfast a little after 9.00 a.m., but not before I wandered down and picked up *The Times*. I took a wee tootle to the shops and picked up a running magazine and two bottles of Dynamo-a glucose drink. I lay on my bed for the rest of the morning. There's always that fine balance about worrying and preparing for the evening's race ahead, but not exhausting yourself either. If I'm getting nervous I must believe that I have a chance. At lunchtime I was turfed out by the cleaner, so went down to the bar for an orange and lemonade. *Diana the goddess of love and hunting's* train was late so I had some lunch, then lay back for half an hour listening to Neil Diamond's Rainbow album which is packed full of wonderful material from some great song-writers-Joni Mitchell; Leonard Cohen; Fred Neil; Buffy St. Marie; Tom Paxton; Rod McKuen et al. I went down to the railway station to meet *Diana*, but was told the train was delayed by 90 minutes. I was going back and forth like a yo-yo. I met her at 3.00 p.m. but she had been there for 20 minutes. Perhaps it was a mistake to take such a vamp back to the hotel room. I put it out of my mind-it was just so lovely to see her; she's so supportive. She was starving and had some hamburger and chips whilst I made do with a small slice of toasted cheese. By accident we ended up getting the 4.41 p.m. train out to Cosford. I lay on the bleacher seating at Cosford for half an hour blocking everything out to focus on the race. I drank a little Dynamo and began my warm-up.

Paul ran beautifully to win Heat 1 in 1:52:7 easily holding off Colin Szwed; John Scott ran well-1:54.4 but was knocked out by Julian Spooner. Meanwhile I drew Heat 3; with no 800 metres pedigree I wasn't seeded and only finished third to John Goodacre and Pete Browne. However, it was a blanket finish in 1:53.4 with us all given the same time. My inexperience and slight lack of confidence probably cost me, however the good news is that I qualified in the single fastest loser spot. I also felt surprisingly easy so haven't ruled anything out for tomorrow's final. Afterwards I felt quite high about the whole experience. My heart-rate was up all night. We collected our suitcases from the Old Vic Hotel and Coach Walker drove us in the minibus out to the County Hotel. A group of us went out for an Indian curry-it wasn't up to much. After a quick game of cards we all hit the sack, only to be seduced by a siren in the night.

1978 AAA Indoor Championships

800 metres Heat 3 1, J. Goodacre (Notts) 1.53.4; 2, P Browne (TVH) 1.53.4; 3, P. Hoffmann (EAC) 1.53.4

28th January, 1975 Travelling home on the bus from college it was still light-always an uplifting moment in the calendar year-if this be winter and all that. I had a really good time at Meadowbank this evening, getting on well with everyone and I was running well too. I reckon I could take *Pixie Mia Farrow lookalike* out. I'm buying her some earrings. I fell asleep listening to Bryan Ferry, *Those stumbling words that told you what my heart meant...*

Evening: 2 x 4 x 150 yards-all in 16 seconds; it was so cold I ran with two tracksuits on

1978 Because of the constant flow of water outside I didn't sleep well; also I was still on a high after last night's race. Racing so close to 10.00 p.m. with all the adrenalin etc. means there's little likelihood of sleeping properly; still, it won't matter too much; it's what I've been doing over the previous weeks that counts. After a shower I phoned Denis to bring him up to speed on last night's results; he said he would look out for me on the television this afternoon. I put a good breakfast inside me-some scrambled eggs and sausage and then *Diana the goddess of love and hunting* and I wandered down to buy a newspaper. We arrived at Cosford at mid-day. I sat and watched the proceedings; had a snack; spoke to one or two people and then lay back and began to focus on the final. As I went out for the race start there was the most almighty hassle. An official said I couldn't run in my Puma Sprint spikes because of the cleats. Yet I'd worn them in the heats last night. God I could have hit him! There was a short delay; the other finalists were already stripped, so some of us ended up putting tracksuits back on, whilst a group of helpers desperately dashed about trying to avail themselves of a pair of spikes for me that I could borrow for the race. But no luck. The clock was ticking down in all senses of the word, particularly as the race was going out live on BBC. It looked as if I would have to pull out. Just as I was walking away from the start, of a sudden Coach Walker ran over with a pair of spikes. The starter delayed the race again. I tried on the spikes, but they were too big. Well that did it! I was so fucking annoyed that I decided I would just run in my bare feet at the back of the field to keep out of trouble. Running around the first lap was so dispiriting because not only was the surface burning my feet, but it just felt so alien, awkward and uncoordinated running in bare feet on the boards. It was very frustrating when I'm someone who normally just flows along. In disgust I felt like pulling out at the end of lap one, but decided to thole it. I continued for another two laps in a similar frustrated vein but was buoyed by shouts of encouragement from Coach Walker; John Anderson and many others. As the race unfolded I thought let's just hang in here; and there's less and less to go. Come the start of the fourth and last lap, despite the discomfort in my feet I felt okay out with that and began to move past several of the faltering finalists. I cut through much of the field down the back straight, including passing Paul who surprisingly was starting to go backwards. Going into the last bend I moved into third place and felt if I could just get on to the two leaders' shoulders at the start of the home straight that I could edge past them.

I won!

I could hardly believe it at the finish. Quite incredible-British 800 metres champion! I was so bloody happy and it seemed like the whole of the Cosford arena felt that way too having witnessed all the toing and froing at the start. *Diana* couldn't believe it. John Anderson was delighted-over the moon as the footballers say.

Afterwards, rather than travelling back to Edinburgh by train *Diana* and I decided to travel home in the team bus with everyone. I wanted to be in everyone's company to celebrate and enjoy the moment. I telephoned Dad and Grandma Jo from a service station outside Preston; they were delighted too and had watched the drama unfold on BBC Grandstand. We had to drive through a blizzard at the Borders, but I was oblivious to it all. We didn't arrive back home to Edinburgh until past midnight where we had some lemon chicken. A very happy and an unforgettable day.

1978 AAA Indoor Championships

800 metres: 1, P. Hoffmann 1.51.4; 2, J. Goodacre 1.51.8; 3, P Browne 1.51.9; 4, M. Francis 1.52.4; 5, C. Szwed 1.52.5; 6, J. Spooner 1.55.9; 7, P. Forbes 1.56.3.

Athletics Weekly: 'Peter Hoffmann, who only made the final as fastest loser and seemed right out of it after the first lap, produced a storming finish (he can claim 10.7 100m speed) to win his first championship at this distance-and he was running barefoot after the referee had failed to approve his spikes. His time of 1.51.4 was a personal best. Colin Szwed set a 53.5/81.8 pace before fading.'

29th January, 1978 I was up at 9.00 a.m. The whole household was delighted with yesterday's win and had enjoyed watching the drama unfold on BBC. I picked up a few newspapers at Swann's. Coach Walker arranged for a doctor to treat my blisters as my feet are wrecked; they're so badly blistered that I can't even walk properly never mind run. I saw Mum before heading up to Waverley Station to travel back to Dundee. It's never much fun on a Sunday evening. Broughty Ferry was freezing; my land-lady, Mrs Neve, was delighted with Saturday's run, so much so she gave me some tea and gingerbread cake-at no extra charge! I managed to study some Accounts.

30ᵗʰ January, 1973 Considering my feet were hurting so much I was running okay this evening. I really need to buy a new pair of spikes. I think I will go for Adidas Tokyo. At first I didn't like the look of them, but after seeing Gus McKenzies's I think they look good.

Evening: 12 x 180 metres (90 seconds recovery) 25-26 secs; I was running well, but my feet were hurting me

1976 After college Laurence Gray dropped me off at Meadowbank. I met Roger Jenkins and Graham Malcolm. It was cold and very still, but pleasant out. The three of us went across to Arthurs Seat and ran a good hill session together. It's a very strong wee group. We all may be rivals on the track over 200 metres, but it's great that we're able to set that aside and train together. Although it's a mature and logical approach, that culture doesn't exist elsewhere in Scotland; too often there's a silo mentality with people training only with their own coach and squad.
Afterwards I took the 44 bus home and walked down Durham Road with old Howard Anderson the Binns' chiropodist; a light snow was just beginning to fall.

Afternoon: 2 x 4 x 120 metres hill runs at Arthurs Seat followed by a gym circuit

1977 I'm feeling terrible with a bad cold; no training.

1978 My feet are still very badly blistered. I bathed them first thing and then hobbled down to Broughty Ferry Station. En-route I picked up some newspapers. My bare-foot exploits have garnered considerable publicity and the papers made it prominent news including a big headline in The Scotsman. That will have pleased Dad and Josephine. The world of academia was fine-at least you don't have much time to think on Mondays. As I'm unable to train I used the time to my advantage by studying hard in the library. At tea-time I took the 4.50 p.m. train back to Broughty Ferry. I bought an *Edinburgh Evening News* at the railway station and noticed I've been selected to run for Britain against West Germany in the 800 metres and have also been selected for the 4 x 400 metres relay too. In the evening I studied hard and bathed my feet further; it was quite funny with Derek down on his hunkers applying a spray on to my blisters. An early bed at 9.30 p.m.

31st January 1976 An easy morning preparing for today's session. Dave Jenkins was up; we ran a good session. It was cold, but quite pleasant. I read all afternoon and for part of the evening too.

4 x 500 metres (10 minutes recovery) 69; 68; 68; 68 seconds; it was cold with a slight breeze

1978 It began to snow this morning-it had to come. My feet are still very sore. I took the train into Dundee and spent most of the day studying in the library other than an Accounts tutorial. I felt a bit low after it. I took the 4.25 p.m. train back to Broughty. After carefully padding up my blisters I ventured out for a wee run. There was snow everywhere including a good four inches in the park. However I ran at a good pace and it was just great to be back out running again. Coming back I passed Derek and Tom-*Keep it up Mr!* I studied for much of the evening before we went out for a ginger beer and lime. Oh, I've been selected for the international against East Germany in Senftenberg-whoo-hoo!

Evening: 4 miles run

1st February, 1975 We went down to the shops before coming back for a bite to eat at the Old Vic Hotel and then travelled out to Cosford for the AAA Junior Medley Relay Championships final. On the opening leg Paul ran a great leg against the UK's top junior half miler, Malcolm Edwards and passed me the baton just over a yard down against Garry Cook. With the baton in my hand I just flew around the 3 laps and destroyed Cook handing over a 20 yards lead to John Scott on the 400 metres leg. My split was 78.5 seconds which was less than a second outside the world best of 77.7 seconds! I ran fairly even splits and felt very strong not really tiring at the end at all.

I don't think I've ever run as well as that; not only was I just flowing along, but I really felt within myself too; perhaps my aim to win the European Junior Championships isn't such a wild dream after all. Unfortunately John lost the 20 yards and we ended up finishing second to a brilliant Wolverhampton & Bilston team. If we'd had the top EAC team out including Drew McMaster on the 200 metres leg I think we could beat them. Anyway our time in second place was faster by over six seconds than any of the previous winners going back to the 1960s, so it was no disgrace, but slightly disappointing.

1975 AAA Junior Medley Relay (2000 metres)

1. Wolverhampton & Bilston 4.26.0; 2. EAC 4.27.4; 3. Epsom & E 4.37.9 (On the 800 metres leg: Malcolm Edwards 1.53.8; Paul Forbes 1.54.0; 600 metres leg: Garry Cook 81.0; Peter Hoffmann 78.5 seconds)

2nd February, 1974 I've just heard that Filbert Bayi has broken the world record.

1975 Although I raced at Cosford the past two days with two quarters on the Friday night and yesterday's 600 metres relay leg and then not getting home until the early hours of this morning, I decided to go up to Perth to race a third day. Robert Sinclair drove Stewart Walters; Davie Reid and me up in his mum's large Fort Cortina estate; it doesn't half fly and was the usual three figure five white knuckle ride!

It's the Scottish Universities Championships. Roger had a good double in the 300 meters and 600 metres. If we'd raced against each other it would have been interesting over the shorter distance; he ran 35.5 seconds and then 80.9. I ran in two of the invitation races over wildly different distances. I dead-heated with AAA Junior 200 metres champion, Drew Harley, over 50 metres. We were given the same time, but he was given the nod. I was quite happy with the performance as I slipped at the start. Running on what's essentially a concrete gym floor in flats isn't really ideal, but it's good fun. I then ran a big personal best over the half mile. I just sat on Brian Gordon the whole way round; on the tight 150 metres boards and with the short straight I couldn't really move past him but I was quite happy with the run. It makes me think what I might run for the distance. I think I could win the AAA Junior Championships 800 metres, but I'm equally confident that I can win the 200 metres and 400 metres so will go for that as a double. I'm actually running so well just now over 60 metres that I feel if I were to just focus on pure speed-work then I could win that too!

Scottish Universities Invitation

**50 metres 1, A. Harley 6.2 seconds; 2. P. Hoffmann 6.2
800 metres 1. B. Gordon 1.52.9; 2, P. Hoffmann 1.53.0**

**Before Bed: Arm action; press-ups; sit-ups; mobility
stretching**

1978 I was out early for my regular three miles run. I'm glad it's Thursday. Tom and I took the 12.20 p.m. train back to Edinburgh. I met Dad at Waverley Station. He was having to collect a visa from the Australian Office. We sat and had a coffee and a good blether before I saw him on to his train. Whilst he's away I've been given the loan of his wee Opel Kadett Coupe which should help my passage in several senses. I spoke to Coach Walker for an hour at Meadowbank before going across to Arthurs Seat with the weights jacket to run a hill session. Considering it was 4.45 p.m. it was still reasonably light which is encouraging. It also means that very shortly I will be able to run this session with Norman Gregor. Afterwards I did a gym circuit, gave Florence and another girl a lift to Princes Street and then I looked out to see *Diana the goddess of love and hunting*. She was in bed having come home from her wee Safeways job feeling unwell. I sat with her for an hour before driving home picking up a Chinese carry out en-route.

Morning (7.00 a.m.): 3 miles steady run

Afternoon (4.30 p.m.): 8 x 100 metres hill runs with weights jacket followed by gym circuit

3rd February, 1975 I gave *Pixie Mia Farrow lookalike* a pair of earrings; she gave me a choker in return.

Evening: 10 x 100 metres (walk back recovery) all between 11.8 and 12.5 seconds

Before Bed: Arm-action; press-ups; sit-ups

1978 I visited the doctor and he gave me a nasal spray for my cold. With me having Dad's car Josephine and I took a wee tootle down to Stow. It was a very pleasant drive down through the snow covered Borders landscape. I suspect the Lauder road may have been blocked as there was some thick ice; in the afternoon I ran a session with Roger Cauldwell at Meadowbank-the first since I blistered my feet at the weekend. I felt pretty flat. Afterwards I had a chat with Coach Walker. Anne has passed her orange belt at karate. Les Ramage and I went to see *One Flew Over The Cuckoo's Nest*.

Afternoon (1.00 p.m.): 3 x 600 metres (10 minutes recovery) 84.7; 85.3; 87.1 seconds; I felt flat; sore legs; afterwards a few weights

4th February, 1974 Mr Kerr went off his nut at me-he's a cranky old bugger.

Evening: **Weights followed by 6 x 200 metres (5 minutes recovery) 26; 25; 26; 24; 24; 24 seconds. I was feeling slightly tired tonight; possibly the effects of yesterday's invitation indoor races at Perth; Paul ran a big personal best of 1.54.8 for the half! After the final of the 50 metres I ran the 800 metres for fun finishing second in a p.b. of 1.58.0**

5th February, 1975 With Valentine's Day on the horizon I sketched out a poem for *Pixie Mia Farrow lookalike.*

Evening: **Gym session; fartlek; my body is looking in great condition**

Before Bed: **Arm-action; press-ups; sit-ups; stretching/mobility**

6th February, 1976 There was quite a good photo of David Jenkins and me in the Athletics Weekly. I ran an excellent hill session with Norrie.

Afternoon: **30 minutes mobility; 5 x 20 seconds Arthurs Seat hill runs-bouncy and fast (2 minutes 30 seconds recovery); weight session**

Before Bed: **Arm-action; press-ups; sit-ups**

7th February, 1973 I met Scott at the National Gallery and we went to the Carron Company do; there was lots of drink and most of the Grahams' staff were pretty tipsy; afterwards

Scott and I went to The White Cockade in the Grassmarket. Aged 16 years I ordered my first drink-a vodka and bitter lemon; afterwards we got jumped by some guys and Scott lost his ring.

1976 I ran a very good 500 session and then worked hard in the gym...

Morning: **3 x 500 metres (12 minutes recovery) 66.6; 65.4; 66.6 seconds; the track was wet, but it was mild with little wind**

Afternoon: **Gym session**

8th February, 1973 Well that will teach me to drink; I felt absolutely terrible this morning; I tried to make myself sick, but couldn't bring anything up. Gaga gave me a lift out to work. Scott told me that after I left him last night he got jumped again. I felt very delicate all day, but worked through until 6.00 p.m. We trained indoors this evening. In the Meadowbank cafe four thugs said they were going to knife me and were making cutting signs across their throats; anyway Coach Walker must have noticed them and soon sorted it out. They followed me out to the bus stop. Coach Walker was leaving Meadowbank when he saw what was happening; well it was like something out of the movies-tyres screeching, he turned the car around on London Road and mounted the pavement; he ran straight at the biggest guy and grabbed a hold of him-well the guy just panicked and squealed out that it was his mate! Anyway they all ran off as fast as they could, clearly wondering who the fuck this guy was! You have to laugh, but God what's Edinburgh like; here's me minding my own business, but getting jumped twice inside 24 hours.

Evening: **6 x 60 metres fast (10 minutes recovery) 2 x 6 x 60m back to back**

1975 I did a really hard session this morning. I had a chat with Coach Walker in the afternoon-he's only going to coach for a short time into the future.

Afternoon (12.00 p.m.): **6 x 500 metres relaxed first 300 metres in 46 seconds followed by a fast 200 metres in 24 seconds (6 minutes recovery); with Brian Gordon; a good session**

1976 I ran a reasonably good session with Roger. I got in a bit of a mix-up with one of the Heriots boys; they're a bit up their own arses, but I shouldn't have got involved and should have just ignored them; it was a bit upsetting...

Morning: **2 x 200 metres (30 seconds recovery) 24.2/25.0 seconds; followed by jog 100m/sprint 100m/jog 100m/sprint 100m (10 mins rec); 300m 34.9 secs, jog 100m/sprint 100m (10 mins rec); 200m 23.1 secs, jog 200m/sprint 100m /jog 50m/sprint 150m; an interestingly different sort of a session**

1978 I felt a bit sleepy this morning. I more or less don't seem to need the alarm. I awoke at 4.30 a.m. and then 6.00 a.m. bursting for a pee! Whilst out running this morn I thought *Is this run too short?* However, I need to remember that I'm still building up and easing into half miling. Perhaps I might extend the distance once I get these indoor internationals out of the way. But I must make the Commonwealth Games team so any strategy needs to be determined by that primary objective. I did a light session at Riverside with the Edinburgh Southern Harriers sprinter, John Wilson. Afterwards he gave me a lift in his Mini to the railway station. In the evening I went into Broughty Ferry and spent a fortune on sweets and some chocolates for Josephine and *Diana the goddess of love and hunting*. There's no Tom tonight; after he'd hobbled along to the hospital with his sore foot this morning caused by last evening's run, he just headed back in the snow to Edinburgh. Dad phoned. I'm to collect his car tomorrow as he's leaving to fly out to Australia. I'm sorry to see him go. The last few months have been great and we've got a much better relationship. I really hope both our fortunes keep going well; to bed at 9.30 p.m.

Morning (7.00 a.m.): 3 miles steady run

Afternoon (4.30 p.m.): Light gym circuit followed by 8 x 100 metres strides with John Wilson

9th February, 1978 I ran a slightly different route this morning; a full circle around Broughty Ferry. I think I'll incorporate it into my future runs. I was really looking forward to going back to Edinburgh and collecting Dad's car. I'm a bit worried about Computing Studies; I'm supposed to be handing in some classwork and I really haven't got a clue how to do it; Tom's probably in a similar position. I managed to catch the London train, which was surprising given I'd stopped off for a fish supper. Will collected me at Waverley Station; he brought the dog along. I always look forward to seeing him and enjoy when he collects me. Out with it was a lovely sunny afternoon; the snow is still lying on the Edinburgh streets.

As I've got this international on Saturday I went down to Portobello Baths for an aerotone bath. Before I went in I stood outside the glass doors for a while watching a smashing swimming teacher; she was about 50 years old and was such a good teacher she was just a joy to watch. I ended up talking to an elderly lady who turned out to be an ex-teacher. I had a nice chat with her; in fact it was so interesting I was reluctant to drag myself away. I looked into Meadowbank for quarter of an hour for a chat with Coach Walker, before Will and I travelled out to Livingstone to collect the *Opel Kadett*. The snow was much deeper out there. It was all go and I gave Bett a hand to move the remaining items out to the new house; meanwhile young Roddy belted Willie across the shins with a broom; he wasn't amused. I tailed Will back to Edinburgh just to make sure he got back okay and then branched off to collect *Diana the goddess of love and hunting*. We went to Morningside to the Mei Kwei for a meal. I hit the sack at midnight.

Morning: 3 miles steady run

10ᵗʰ February, 1974 From now on I'm going to try to do mobility stretching every evening to see if it will help prevent me getting any more injuries. Also, if I'm wanting to do well this season I better get the finger out and start to train really hard. I mean the last few weeks I've been slacking. So from now on I am going to work hard. Coach Walker gave Sandy Sutherland and me a lift home; later on I drove Will's car out to Oxgangs. I saw *Pixie Mia Farrow lookalike* on the way-how my heart soared or is that sored! (sic)

Morning: 5 x 150 yards (8 minutes recovery) 16.3; 16.5; 17.0; 16.0; 17.0 seconds; I couldn't run very fast as my left hamstring was really niggling; however on a positive note I've got my starting blocks position and numbers off to a T

Before Bed: Mobility stretching

1978 Josephine was unhappy that *Diana the goddess of love and hunting* stayed overnight. I was out at Dr Motley's. Mum seemed to be a bit down so I took her out for the day. We drove down to Peebles and then over to Stobo. It was a beautiful day. There was a glorious warm sun out and we went for a stroll; I showed her where Alison and Fiona Blades; Paul; Iain; and I had camped for the week six years previously in 1972. Afterwards we drove back through Peebles to Eddleston and the Horseshoe Inn for a nice lunch; on a winter's day the creamy soup was excellent. If it's

good enough for Princess Margaret it's good enough for me!
We got back to Portobello at 2.00 p.m. It began to snow. At
4.00 p.m. Will and Josephine drove me out toward
Edinburgh Airport for my flight to Birmingham, but at 5.00
p.m. I was sitting in Davidsons Mains Village! Disaster! The
accelerator cable in Will's car snapped and the car broke
down at Parkgrove Terrace. There was now a formidable
snowstorm-the snow was just tumbling down reducing
visibility to a few feet and Edinburgh was encased in a
blanket of white. We managed to hail a taxi on Barnton
Road to Waverley Station. The Birmingham train was about
to depart so I didn't have the time to buy a ticket. We
somehow managed to talk my way on to the train. It was
Grandma Jo who did the trick saying to the ticket collector
that I was running for Britain and that it was imperative that
I get on board!

Anyway, all's well that ends well. The journey was rather
enjoyable and passed quickly. I had a meal in the dining car-
most civilised. I no longer felt like a poor student and instead
felt part of an Agatha Christie novel. I dined with a very
interesting chap who worked for the Gas Board. Later I met
Netta Sinclair and Betty Steedman on board; they're both
officiating tomorrow. We took a taxi together to the hotel. I
was in bed by 11.00 a.m. I'm sharing with Keith Connor and
Frank Attoh. Quite a day.

11th February, 1973 Paul and I headed up to Perth for the
Scottish Universities Indoor Championships. We helped
John Anderson out all day. He was brilliant as the M.C.
When we were lining up to take part in the invitation races
he gave me a great build up even though I've never won
anything; yet he was saying what a great prospect I was; it
made me feel a million dollars! I ran really well in the 300
and 800 metres.

Afternoon: 300 metres 38.3 seconds (p.b.); 800 metres 2 minutes 5.9 secs (p.b.)

1978 I felt fairly good this morning; not a bad sleep after yesterday's adventures. I went down to breakfast with Peter Little and Karen Williams. Peter and I then strolled down to some shops to buy some newspapers; surprisingly I was the main athletics headline in several of the nationals-*Hot Foot Hoffmann* said the *The Guardian*; *Peter plans to beat these blisters* from the Daily Express!

It was the most beautiful morning; crisp, fresh, cold and sunny. The Mount Hotel is located in the stockbroker belt. We joined the team meeting. The team manager, Jim Biddle, read out one of the headlines which gave us all a laugh. I'm feeling pretty good. I lay down for half an hour and then had an omelette for lunch. I took the early team bus down to Cosford. I lay around for a while before beginning my warm up. I ran poorly. I got away a bit quicker this time although I was still at the back of the field. I felt tired after 400 metres. On the third lap I should have taken one of the Germans cleanly, but dithered about and got a bit of a bashing. Come the last lap I managed to kick a little at the end, but I was just too tired. After the race I had one hell of a sore throat. I felt a bit down after the race. I spoke to John Anderson who was there. Coach Walker said nothing, but nothing can often say a lot! On the train journey back to Edinburgh Jimmy Bryce and Coach Walker went into a 10 minutes rage and gave me an absolute lambasting over my tactics and told me that if I continued to run like that I'd be better searching for a new coach. I couldn't get over the amount of snow in Edinburgh. It was completely encased in the white stuff. Emerging onto an ethereal Princes Street was like walking into a fairy tale setting-a winter wonderland with the capital's majestic, otherworldly and mysterious dark silhouettes all a twinkle under the street lights and the stars; it could just as easily be a 1948 film set than 1978. And now I'm back at

Porty and to the bosom of home; Grandma Jo prepared my supper and of course was nothing but supportive and non-judgemental. I guess you need both in life-someone offering you unconditional love and support, but also someone there to kick your arse.

U.K. v Germany (Cosford)

800 metres: 1, D. Rebe 1:51.1; 2, John Goodacre 1.51:3; 3, Peter Hoffmann 1:51.4; R. Aechtle 1:52.0

London Snow

*'When men were all asleep the snow came flying,
In large white flakes falling on the city brown,
Stealthily and perpetually settling and loosely lying,
Hushing the latest traffic of the drowsy town…'*

Robert Bridges

12th February, 1978 I got up to find just how much snow there was! It was quite incredible, perhaps the worse Edinburgh's seen for many decades. Aunt Heather was out first thing clearing the paths, whilst I knocked the snow off the rhones. Josephine was concerned that with the added weight they might come down. I was about to set off for Meadowbank when *Diana the goddess of love and hunting* surprised us. Meanwhile Mr Paul from across the road gave me a hand to get the car out the driveway. I had to come out Steve McQueen style! Actually I don't mind skidding about in the snow. I ran a session on the two cleared inside lanes at Meadowbank; the staff had made a fantastic job of it-full credit to them. In the afternoon I played squash with Paul and Davie, eventually grinding them down, although I probably played for too long. I went home and had a chat with Jo about *Diana* and then we enjoyed afternoon tea.

Whilst *Diana* copied out my essay I went up to Meadowbank for a shower. As I was going in Coach Walker; R.R. and Paul were emerging-in for the old hypnosis, no less! They're trying to get to grips with Paul's erratic performances. The last theory didn't work. They'd notice just before he was about to drop back in a race he would start to look down at his feet; so the stratagem was that when he looked at his feet he would get an energy boost. I joked with Paul that when I saw him glance down I pissed past him! Afterwards I went up to Denis's for a rub; it was really very good of him to take me on a Sunday evening. I picked up *Diana* and we enjoyed a lovely meal at the Ping On Restaurant in Stockbridge, spending the evening gazing into each other's eyes.

Afternoon (12.00 p.m.): 8 x 200 metres (2 minutes recovery) all in 25 seconds

13th February, 1973 I went up to Pentland Community Centre to find out about Sunday's Edinburgh Boys Clubs' Cross Country Championships. Although I'm 16 it turns out I've to run in the under 19 age group. Paul's 16 too, but scrapes into the under 16 age group. I went training at Meadowbank; it was quite good, but we could only train on the grass as the snow was falling heavily and the track was too slippy. It's really cold out tonight.

Evening: 6 x 100 metres sprints; 12 short and long sprints; non-stop relay

1975 Coach Walker gave the group a long talk; he's decided to keep coaching.

1976 Roger dropped me slightly on the hill session at Arthurs Seat.

Afternoon: 2 x 4 Arthurs Seat hill runs; average session

1978 Because of the adverse weather I'm not going back to Dundee this week; at least that's my excuse. I sat and studied for an hour and then ran four miles. I was very stiff, particularly around the backside. I studied until mid-afternoon before going up to Meadowbank where I ran a speed endurance clock. I found it tough going. Afterwards I enjoyed a wee discussion on training theory with Wilson Young and Stuart Togher-two interesting individuals and strong characters, both of whom I like. Back home for dinner and some Mathematics coursework, before going up to the west end to meet *Diana the goddess of love and hunting*. We went to the Three Inns for a drink-me on the ginger beer and lime as usual. We shared a bag of L'Albo D'oro chips at Henderson Row, before I dropped her off at Silverknowes. En-route home I stopped off at Portobello and picked up a delicious baked potato-the girl kept asking *Is it only one potato?* Perhaps she thought I needed feeding up!

Morning (10.30 a.m.): 4 miles run

Afternoon (4.30 p.m.): 150; 160; 170; 180; 190; 200; 190; 180; 170; 160; 150 metres (2 minutes recovery)

14th February, 1974 Although I sent a Valentine card to *Pixie Mia Farrow lookalike* I didn't receive one in return. After training Paul and I went with Dougie McLean and Scott Brodie to the Waverley Bar and then on to the St Valentine's dance; it was really good. If I'd wanted I could have got off with three girls. It finished at 2.30 a.m. and I didn't get to bed until 3.30 a.m. I'll pay for it!

Evening: 2 x 8 x 70 metres technique at 80% effort (walk back recovery; 10 minutes between sets)

1975 I received a large Valentine card this morning which I think came from *Pixie* although that may be wishful thinking on my part. I had posted off a couple of cards. I managed to beat the good Swedish table tennis player, Anders, at college today; I now think I'm better than him.

1976 Everything was crisp and white covered in a heavy Jack Frost. We ran 500s at nine o'clock in the morning! I ran averagely. In the afternoon I went down to Portobello Baths for an aerotone bath; as well as helping me recover from the aches and pains from training I enjoy sauntering down there on a Saturday afternoon. I'm on my own and it gives me time to think and reflect on things; old habits die hard; a legacy from early Edinburgh schoolboy days and times spent as the peripatetic philosopher.

<u>Morning (9.20 a.m.):</u> 3 x 500 metres (10 minutes recovery) 69; 68; 66 seconds; cold, no wind, very frosty with the odd touch of ice on the track

15th February, 1975 I received another Valentine card this morning-this one **is** from *Pixie Mia Farrow lookalike* so yesterday's one was from X. The giveaway was the humour, the wit, the intelligence and the charm:

An Ode

To the most fertile athlete on the track,
The one who's got the running ~~act~~ knack,
Lives on vitamins C and E,
Cool and classy-unlike me.
Runs 200's in sub-fifty
For his bulk, that's quite nifty.
As he hits the final bend
The crowds all roar 'There's the trend'
Thousands gather round the telly.
Hoping to see his big pot belly.
With sweatband, beads and Kung-Fu pyjamas
He's the cause of all girls' traumas.
Please your body's so divine
Won't you be my Valentine?

from A. HARDWORKING GIRL,
17a DANUBE STREET,
EDINBURGH 7
Tel. 031-229-6315 (anytime after 7 o'clock)

I felt very sick after this morning's training session. Once I started to recover I was chatting to Helen Golden; Ann Clarkson; and Bob Sinclair. Paul phoned at night but I decided not to bother going out.

Morning: 500 metres 69.1 seconds (8 minutes recovery); 350m 42.9 secs (7 mins rec); 300m 37.9 secs (10 mins rec); 200m 24.6 secs; I was really shattered, sore head and dizziness

1977 I looked in to see Frank Dick at lunchtime. In the evening I joined the middle-distance boys and ran a good session; I felt I was concentrating well.

Evening: **8 x 400 metres (1 minute recovery) all in 62 seconds; really tough mentally on the last two runs but I concentrated really well; pleased with the session. This last week and a half is really bringing me on!**

1978 It was a lovely sunny morning; the cat and the dog were out in the back garden playing in the snow. I did some Computer Studies in the afternoon before looking in to Frank Dick's office at Frederick Street to enquire about the cost of a trip to Estepona in the spring, but no one was there. Later I went out for a four miles run with Dave Curry and Paul but they soon dropped me; after seeing *Diana the goddess of love and hunting* I went home and packed my bags for East Germany-we're off behind the Iron-Curtain.

Morning (11.00 a.m.): **4 miles steady run**

Evening (7.00 p.m.): **4 miles steady run**

16th February, 1978, Dresden, East Germany Jo awoke me at 7.00 a.m. After a good breakfast I got an SMT bus up to Edinburgh. The airport bus left at 8.25 a.m. I met Peter Little on board the London flight. It was a very bumpy landing with the pilot bringing us down with a real belt before we skidded along the runway. I was waiting on my backside catching fire. Peter and I joined Karen Williams for a snack and I sat and read for a while as we awaited Marea Hartman the team manager to arrive at 2.00 p.m. She was actually very good and told us to go off and have a meal. I had a delicious prawn cocktail in the most exquisite sauce, but it wasn't worth 96p, especially given how small it was. Clearly I'm living up to my Scottish stereotype.

The chartered flight to Dresden left at 4.00 p.m. Dave Wilson, Cherry Hanson and I had a great laugh on the flight over. Sitting at 26,000 feet eating an English afternoon tea of scones, Devon cream and raspberry jam with a pot of tea felt so civilised and unreal. Outside the window there were glorious clear blue skies and the sun, a red orange ball, was sinking in the west; just a slight difference to normal student life; but more than that it occurred to me no medieval king ever experienced anything like this. We touched down in Dresden which is one hour ahead of the United Kingdom. Being central Europe, there was some snow, but really only a light dusting. From Dresden it was a long bus journey-over an hour to Senftenberg. We were allocated our rooms. I'm sharing with Peter-room 209 and with the added bonus of a lovely set of towels to steal; trust it doesn't cause a diplomatic incident. I guess it's the novelty of getting something labelled from behind the Iron Curtain. We had to go to dinner immediately. It was awful. A terrible tasting soup with hair at the bottom of the bowl, followed by chips; eggs; meat; and pickled veg-clearly we're being sabotaged! I got to bed at 11.30 p.m. and read some more of Lord Home's autobiography.

17th February, 1973 I bought a new pair of Adidas Titan spikes-fucking hell, what a price-£9.40; that's more than I get each week for my wages from Thomas Graham & Sons; later on I went through to Coatbridge for the Scottish Cross Country Championships; I didn't run because of my infected leg; meanwhile Paul was 69th. I stayed at Paul's overnight.

1976 Having had *Pixie Mia Farrow lookalike* break my heart back in December I thought I should take some positive steps forward rather than pining away. I was chatting up the *Simone de Beauvoir Philosopher Queen* this evening and gave her a lift home after training. She's one of the Edinburgh Southern Harriers stars. We've known each other since I started going along to Meadowbank 5 years ago. Along with Petrina Cox they're the nearest to a Peter 'n Paul double-act. From one angle she's part of the standard fayre of girls there, but she's also very different too-bright as a button. She's got an excellent and highly elevated sense of humour and is going off to study philosophy at our finest yooni. I would imagine she's probably been bemused by me and our behaviour over the years. Although we've had a few laughs with her, she's probably only been doing a little slumming when she's engaged with us. Anyway, she was happy to take a lift and we seemed to get on quite well together. She perhaps thinks I'm now sufficiently house-trained and reached the first stage of maturity. I don't think she would have countenanced a lift in the past, but perhaps what's helped is that with a little application, I've slowly become a better athlete, and am now matching her achievements and even going past her. So, the peripatetic philosopher (3rd class) meets the philosopher queen. Watch this space!

<u>Evening:</u> **2 x 4 x 300 metres (2 minutes' walk/jog 100 recovery; 10 mins between sets) Set 1: 39; 40; 41; 40 seconds Set 2: 39; 42; 42; 38.5 secs**

1978, Senftenberg, East Germany After a good breakfast I wandered along to the team meeting. Lynn Davies gave an excellent team talk. Afterwards, late morning, Dave Wilson; Ian Radcliffe; Peter Little and I walked down to a large department store for twenty minutes. It was cold out, but I was quite taken with Senftenberg. Being part of East Germany and behind the Iron Curtain it's a time warp. Seeing the old trams rattling along against the background of the snow covered streets and houses was rather beautiful. It's as if time has stood still since the Second World War-oops, don't mention the war Retep! Peter and I picked up some small pieces to take home to Edinburgh as presents. I had lunch with Mike Farrell and a good wee blether; he was interested to see how quickly I'd got into the British team after moving up to the half mile, but very supportive.

The team bus left the hotel at 2.00 p.m. We were packed in like sardines. Keith Stock, the pole-vaulter, was telling me he runs a car business in London-he's quite the entrepreneur.

The indoor track was a revelation. The whole of the arena floor is covered with a tartan track and the oval track itself is 250 metres long. It's an athlete's winter dream rather than a wet dream! I'm sure I could come on a bomb if I could train in such a venue, rather than dependent on clearing snow off a Meadowbank track. I was too nervous before the race and ran too conservatively and negatively. Basically I got stuck behind John Goodacre all the way round. I came wide off the final turn and it was another blanket finish. I equalled my personal best-outdoors and indoors-another 1:51.4. I've not shone since winning the AAAs title other than stabilising that performance time-wise. But neither have I disgraced myself either; despite poor running tactics I've been there or there about at the finish against established half-milers. And if I continue I suspect I can leave some of these guys behind when we move outdoors and I get more middle-distance work in the bank and improve my self-confidence for the event. After the race I gave two young girls a couple of good quality Puma and Adidas T shirts each. They were absolutely delighted; and of course I was equally delighted to see their joy. It won't exactly bring down the Iron Curtain, but who knows-one day when they grow up political life may be different and it's something which might remain with them. It was a long journey back to Cottbus with some terrifying fog; at moments the bus driver literally could not see a thing! The evening buffet was fine. Dave Wilson and I were at the heart of a group, with each of us trying to out-do each other telling jokes and aiming for the biggest laugh. I had very little to drink and was disciplined enough to pack my bags just after midnight.

East Germany v United Kingdom Indoor International 800 metres 3rd Hoffmann 1:51.4

18th February, 1973 We went to the Edinburgh Boys Clubs' Cross Country Championships which were being held up on the Braid Hills. Paul won the Under 16 race quite easily.

Meanwhile I picked up only my second ever medal after getting one in last summer's Scottish East Districts Youth medley relay. There were only two medals going. The guy who won it was too far ahead, but somehow I managed to keep in contact with Edinburgh Southern Harriers' Alec Robertson and with half a mile to go he was still in sight. I didn't think I could do it, but I was so determined to get that medal I gradually narrowed the gap over the last half mile. I drew level with Alec with about 80 metres to go and somehow managed to sprint past. The psychology of racing is amazing, because with the effort of making up a hundred metres or so had really buggered me, but I think Alec just assumed I would out-sprint him as I'm essentially a 100/200 metres runner. If he had really challenged me he might well have beaten me. He was really sporting afterwards and genuinely pleased to see my delight at getting a treasured wee medal; it's already in Grandma Jo's cabinet!

Edinburgh Boys Clubs Cross Country Championships, Braid Hills 4 miles 2nd P. Hoffmann; 3rd A. Robertson

1975: There was a letter in the post from *Pixie Mia Farrow lookalike*:

Dear Peter,

I had to write you a note to thank you for the flowers-they were absolutely super. I wasn't at home when they arrived but my Mum phoned me and I went up on Sunday night to collect them. Not only did the flowers make my day but they made my Mum's as well-she was over the moon!

I must apologise for not sending you a card, at least, but I have no excuse really except that due to my financial situation I decided not to bother sending any at all. I hope you don't think it's because I've forgotten you because I haven't.

I hope you are still training well and I am keeping my fingers crossed that I will see you at Montreal.

I watched your run at Cosford and although you're no doubt disappointed I hope you're not unduly so as perhaps it's best to have your only defeat now and use it to push you harder. For God sake don't allow it to upset your training etc. although I'm sure you wouldn't with a split time of 22.3 seconds and despite this, not feeling tired at the end- it cannot have been a bad defeat.

I hope your family-including the cat and dog-are all well, and I'll perhaps see you if you go to the E.A.C. disco. However, until then

Yours faithfully

Pixie x

p.s. I'll give Lorna 'The Moon's a Balloon' for you. Sorry it's been so long.

During the session I felt shattered, but it's a good start to me working very hard in every session. My new philosophy is to attack every session right from the gun. I'm feeling a bit low this evening. There was another letter and card in the post from Oslo from Bjorg Larsen; she included a nice photograph.

Evening: 4 x 200 metres (2-2.30 minutes' walk 200m recovery) 22.5; 22.8; 23.2; 25 seconds; I was shattered; 30 minutes *recovery* 4 x 150m relaxed

Before Bed: Arm-action; press-ups; sit-ups

1978, Senftenberg, East Germany Oh! a 6.30 a.m. rise this morning. I glanced at Peter Little's watch and realised it was still set at British time, so at least I had another hour in bed. With my bags, bottles etc I staggered onto the bus at

7.30 a.m. It was a long drive to the airport-over an hour; I slept for some of the way, but enjoyed looking out at the East German countryside with bare trees set against a background of snowy white. There were few cars on the road and those that we saw were all going off skiing. Once again passport control was very rigid, but this time I got to the front of the queue. They had a good look at mine; with my Germanic last name and full-strength Hoffmann they were clearly wondering whether this was a double bluff-was I trying to defect to the West!

The flight back was fine and I sat with Dave Wilson and Cherry Hanson, both of whom have a bit of life to them. We were served up a lovely meal, half of which I managed to knock over. The cabin crew gave me half a dozen little miniatures of perfume which will make nice presents for the ladies. Karen, Peter and I arrived back in Edinburgh where it was colder than East Germany; according to the *Edinburgh Evening News* the temperature in the capital last night was minus 18 degrees! I took the airport bus to Waverley Station then a taxi back down to Durham Road. It's always nice coming home; Jo prepared a meal whilst I drove up to Swann's Newsagents to collect my Athletics Weekly. In the evening I pottered around watching television etc I retired to bed at 10.30 p.m. I feel a bit tired. I'm training with Adrian and Paul tomorrow; no rest for the wicked!

19th February, 1978 I was up at 7.30 a.m.-early to bed early to rise. I walked up with the dog to Swann's to collect the Sunday papers returning home via Portobello Park. It was very cold out and the ground was covered with a hard packed snow. At 11.00 am. I drove up to Meadowbank in Dad's new *Opel Kadett*. The car was running along so sweetly. I felt like a rich playboy-or at least akin to Bob Sinclair and Roger Jenkins who are the only two peers who run around in cars. I ran a fairly good session with Adrian and Paul.

Great news! I got my USA Olympic vest back, after over a year of it being lost. I was shocked to see George McNeil wearing it. He gave it back to me immediately saying that someone had given it to him. In the afternoon I ran five miles with Adrian and Paul. I felt knackered and come the last mile and a half from Mountcastle I had to hold on for dear life! On the way home I gave an Edinburgh Southern Harriers coach a lift; she was saying she was travelling down to High Wycombe next weekend.

I had a large Sunday roast pork lunch courtesy of Iain. *Diana* phoned and met me at Waverley Station. She was a bit down. It's no wonder, we've hardly seen each other. She was really looking forward to seeing me and vice-versa. Still, we've got next weekend to look forward to. I managed 90 minutes of Sociology on the train before arriving in Dundee. It turned out that Tom had been on board, but on a different part of the train. I was surprised to hear he hadn't been in Dundee last week either. These are busy days. As John Lennon said 'Life is what happens when you're making other plans.'

Afternoon (12.00 p.m.): 8 x 200 metres (2 minutes recovery) 25 seconds

Afternoon (2.00 p.m.): 5 miles run with Adrian and Paul

20th February, 1974 On the way from work to Meadowbank I was speaking to the Boroughmuir Rugby Club president, Ronnie Tait. I've always liked him and found him to be interesting since Dad used to take us along in the 1960s during the summer months to watch and help out with the scoring at the cricket at Meggetland. I had to nip out to Coach Walker's car to collect my bag. I've got the most brilliant library book on the go which Petrina Cox loaned me. It's called *No Bugles, No Drums* by Peter Snell; I'm happy as Larry sitting up in bed devouring it; it's definitely the half mile for me one day.

Evening: 8 x 120 metres (walk back recovery) all in 14-15 seconds

1975 What a bloody laugh we all had. Paul pinched Jackie Groundwater's knickers and was careering around waving them in the air with Jackie in hot pursuit. Crikey I've never seen her move so fast-she must have recorded a p.b.!

Evening: 8 x 150 yards (walk 250 recovery) all in 16 seconds

1976 After we picked Netta Sinclair up Coach Walker drove me down to Largs. I'm sharing with three other guys. Dave Gormal's a nice lad, however I won't show him any mercy on the track.

1978 I'm back in Broughty Ferry again after a week's break and was out running at 6.45 a.m. When I first set out this morning there was the merest hint of light and by the time I got back to my digs dawn had broken; whew, I was glad to hear that most of the lectures and tutorials were cancelled last week so I haven't missed too much; both Economics and Psychology were cancelled today because of the lack of heating, so I spent a lot of time in the library; mid-afternoon Tom and I ventured down to Boots to see Diana Dors signing her book-the crowds were so large we couldn't really see her-not even her bosom! It may have been partly due to the schoolkids being off today. Tom joined me for a run in the afternoon. I was surprised at how fit he is although we just ran at a steady pace...after a full-on three course meal from Mrs Neve we went down to the Regal to watch the James Bond film, *The Spy Who Loved Me*-very entertaining. On the way down to the cinema I phoned *Diana* to save her going out into the cold to phone me and finding I wasn't in.

Morning (6.45 a.m.): 4 miles run

Afternoon: 4 miles steady run

21st February, 1973 Gaga is putting my cross country medal in for engraving tomorrow. It costs 2p a word so it will come to 62p. I went training and was running quite well. We did a queer sort of a session, but age 16 what do I know. After my shower I was speaking to Mr Kerr on how he became a football scout for East Fife. If you catch him in the right mood his bark is worse than his bite and he can be quite entertaining. He's often pretty gruff with me and very straight talking. He's often bemused-*Walker straightened you all out!*, etc., but my instinct tells me that at heart he's quite fond of me; well, perhaps.

Evening: 2 x 200 metres (90 seconds recovery) 27 and 29 secs; 2 x 300m (2 minutes rec) 44 and 45 secs; 2 x 400m (3 mins rec) 62 and 60 secs; 3 x 4 x 60m back to back

22nd February, 1978 I was very stiff this morning so just decided to run a steady 3 miles. Once I got back to the digs I had a bit of fun throwing snowballs at Tom and Derek's bedroom windows; each of them sleepily pulling back the curtains to find out what the fuck was going on. In Maths we were doing calculus. Riverside is unusable and because of feeling so stiff it suited me not to do anything. I spent a while in the bookshop and bought *Diana the goddess of love and hunting* a rather charming autobiography by a nurse. Whilst back in the library Tom came up to ask if I fancied going along to watch the Scotland v Bulgaria match at Hampden. As Derek said he'd go I said yes and phoned Mrs Neve to give her our plans; she was great and rattled up a super early meal before we left Broughty Ferry at 4.30 p.m. We were picked up by a friend of Tom's who'd travelled down from Aberdeen. The thaw had started and it rained all the way. Christ! the boy's driving was a bit wild, however we arrived there in good time. Derek and I joined the snobs in the stand whilst Tom and his pal went to the ground. I enjoyed the game and my pie and coke; Scotland emerged victorious with a 2-1 win. We finally got back to Broughty Ferry at 1.30 a.m. no thanks to the driver. I slept for part of the way, whilst poor Tom sat rigidly awake in the front passenger seat awaiting imminent death!

Morning (7.00 a.m.): 3 miles run

Jenny kiss'd me

Jenny kiss'd me when we met,
Jumping from the chair she sat in;
Time, you thief, who love to get
Sweets into your list, put that in!
Say I'm weary, say I'm sad,
Say that health and wealth have miss'd me,
Say I'm growing old, but add,
Jenny kiss'd me.

Leigh Hunt

23rd February, 1974 Although it was a Saturday I went to work at Graham's all morning. Mark Wilson and Paul arrived outside the showroom at 11.45 a.m., but we didn't manage to get a Penicuik bus until 12.40 p.m. I ran really well in the Carnethy Hill Race cross country getting the bronze medal with Paul winning it. The three of us had tea at Mr Scott's. When I heard that *Pixie Mia Farrow lookalike* was going to the disco, God! I could hardly disguise my excitement! Well, after all those years of holding a candle for her the night went fabulously well and I got off with *Pixie*. Even though the disco wasn't that good I just loved spending the whole evening in her company and most delicious of all we had a long kiss whilst we danced in each other's arms to The Hollies' *The Air That I Breathe*. The evening was just fabulous and went like a dream; I didn't want it to end. I walked her down the road to where her Dad was collecting her. I've never felt so happy in all my life! However, that wasn't the end of the evening as several of us got jumped by a large gang of local youths and I ended up getting my head kicked in. The police picked up two of the guys. Paul and I went round to Mr McCauley's house where we stayed the night. My head is really sore, but I'm not really bothered as I'm sitting well above Cloud 9, I'm just so pleased to be off with the girl of my dreams! We stayed up until 1.45 a.m. before retiring to our beds. Quite a day. I don't think I'll ever forget it!

Carnethy Hill Race 4 miles

1st. P. Forbes; 3rd P. Hoffmann; I ran really well beating many of the more fancied distance guys and won a medal!

1978 Well, despite Tom and Derek's doubts after getting back so late from the Scotland v Bulgaria match I was still out running early doors; mind you it was only for 3 miles. Tom and I took the 12.20 p.m. train back to Edinburgh. Tom slept for much of the way; I read some Marx, but also fell asleep for a bit too. Will greeted me at Waverley Station and ran me home. After lunch I met Norman at Meadowbank and we ran another good hill session at Arthurs Seat. There was a nice surprise awaiting me in Coach Walker's office-£180 worth of Puma gear and that's me who intends to race in Adistar spikes this season! Anyway it included two leisure suits, one of which I'll give to Grandma Jo; it will be a nice surprise for her. With a little needlework it will fit her fine. It's the least I can do for her with all the hard, selfless work she does for me to ease my passage. In the evening I ran Jo to the Edinburgh Sketching Club and then looked out to Oxgangs to see if my sister, Anne, wanted to see the Bruce Lee movie, however her hair was plastered with henna-she's going for a Star Wars look and creation. I watched the film on my own, then picked up Janice and *Diana the goddess of love and hunting*. We had a drink and then *Diana* and I drove out to Carrington. She was dancing about on the country lanes in just her knickers-she's MAD! We had a meal at the Ping On in Stockbride. Bon soir!

Morning (7.00 a.m.): 3 miles run

Afternoon (4.10 p.m.): 8 x 20 seconds Arthurs Seat hill runs with weights jacket; ran with Norman Gregor

24th February, 1974 The day after the night before when I got off with *Pixie Mia Farrow lookalike*. After such an ethereal dream-like evening I could only come back down to planet Earth with a bang; it felt a funny sort of a day. Paul and I breakfasted with the McCauley family then phoned Mr Scott at 9.30 a.m. to get a lift in from Penicuik to Meadowbank. I wasn't talking with *Pixie* for all that long; it was slightly awkward being back in the group situation and I didn't like to spend more time with her than anyone else, however we've arranged to go out together on Friday evening. I think the best way to stay off with her is to just sort of play it cool and not to try to monopolise her or anything like that.

Morning: 5 x 500 metres (6 minutes recovery) 79; 82; 81; 80; 79 seconds

Afternoon: 8 x 200 metres (2 mins rec) 27 secs; I was feeling very tired and just sort of plodded along although the times weren't too bad

1975 I wonder if I need to reduce the amount of carbohydrates I eat each day as my weight is 146 lbs.

Evening: **4 x 300 metres (6 mins rec) 39; 38; 38; 37 secs tracksuit on for the first run; a very misty evening**

1978 I went up to Meadowbank and had a long chat for an hour and a half with Coach Walker; it's the first time we've really spoken since the lambasting I recieved after my 800 metres international debut against West Germany. We'll see how things go, but I think it's to my advantage to stay with him in Commonwealth Games year. Afterwards I did some weights and then some 40 metres sprints indoors. *Diana* and I met up at Waverley Station; I've been invited down to join the Great Britain 400 metres squad training weekend. The train was busy but we managed to get a double seat together; after Carstairs we enjoyed a meal together. *Diana* said a man spent the whole journey staring at her. For the remainder of the journey I studied Accounts whilst *Diana* read. We arrived at Wolverhampton at 9.45 p.m. and took our bags to the Old Vic Hotel. We had a drink together in the bar. *Diana* finally getting a cider 'n Babycham; we then hit the sack.

25th February, 1976 I ran a good session with Jenks (Roger). It was a pity to see Vernon Sollas knocked out; also to see Bayi beaten. On the box there was a very good play about the discovery of insulin.

Afternoon: **2 x 4 x 200 metres (2 minutes recovery) (15 mins between sets) 23.9; 23.4; 23.0; 23.2; 23.2; 23.0; 23.4; 23.2 seconds; the same session as yesterday, but with Roger Jenkins; interestingly, an inferior session to running on my own, but still a pretty good session**

1978, Wolverhampton Before breakfast *Diana the goddess of love and hunting* and I had a lot of fun. We were mucking about, wrestling and play-fighting; what a laugh! After breakfast, hand in hand we wandered around Wolverhampton looking at different shops-furniture; jewellers etc. We bumped into the national coach, Bill

Marlowe, in the Mander Centre; he was sauntering around, pipe in mouth, without an apparent care in the world. Charles Taylor picked us up outside the hotel at mid-day; Steve Wymark was already waiting.

At Aldersley, *Diana* and I had a game of pool before settling down for lunch; Dave Jenkins; Donna Murray etc. were all there. I ran a fair session of 200s with Glen Cohen; Ainsley Bennett etc. Although I ran okay and with the pack I was slightly disappointed with the session. I felt it was the kind of session which I really should have destroyed everyone on, especialy once we moved beyond half-way. A definite lack of speed and speed endurance there; perhaps it's unsurprising in that I'm the only one in the squad who's out doing steady running; still a wee bit of a wakeup call. Two years ago I would have averaged 23 seconds for this session and run the quarter milers into the ground. We got a lift back to room 56 at the County Hotel and enjoyed a long hot bath-*gentleman (athletes) before ladies for pampering!* before the two of us went out for a walk. It's great to see the light starting to stretch out; as dusk began to fall it was lovely looking into the shops' lit windows at this time of the week and the season of the year; we were quite taken with some furniture in a little antique shop. When we stepped outside we were lucky to have brought an umbrella with us-that's the royal we. We laughed and cuddled up underneath the brolly and strolled back to the hotel for the evening meal. Beforehand, there was a nice wee surprise; some kit which I'd lost a while back had been returned, including the Polish vest I'd exchanged with Henryk Galant when we'd finished first and second at the Europeans three years ago. *Diana* and I enjoyed a lovely meal including a bottle of Mateus Rose; we were pretty light-headed. We retired to bed to watch Mike Yarwood etc. etc....

Afternoon: 400 meters national squad, Aldersley 8 x 200 metres (3 minutes recovery) all in 24.5 seconds apart from the last two in 26 secs; okay, but disappointed; I

should be able to run an average of 23-24 secs with only a 2 minutes recovery

26th February, 1974 I was talking with *Pixie Mia Farrow lookalike* in the Meadowbank café; we've arranged to meet on Friday at 6.30 p.m.-our first official date!

<u>Evening:</u> **8 x 300 metres (45 seconds recovery) average 47 seconds**

<u>Before Bed:</u> **Arm-action; press-ups; sit-ups; mobility**

1977 I ran with the middle distance guys today. I felt it was the best I've run with them; in the afternoon I took the dog down to Gullane and did a lot of running; an Eros evening with *Diana the goddess of love and hunting.*

<u>Afternoon (12.00 pm.):</u> **4 x 600 metres (5 minutes recovery) 87; 89; 89; 90 seconds; the first real sign the hard work is paying off**

<u>Afternoon (3.00 p.m.):</u> **Gullane Sands 5 miles run; 2 x 4 x hill dune runs**

1978 I ran another session at Aldersley with Dave Jenkins and Steve Scutt; nothing spectacular. *Diana* and I sat for a while in the waiting room at Crewe where she wrote out five letters for me. We arrived back in Edinburgh at nine o'clock and went for a meal to the Ping On in Stockbridge.

<u>Morning:</u> **3 x 600 metres (10 minutes recovery) 87-89 seconds**

27th February, 1973 I phoned up Edinburgh Boys Clubs to say I would run for them in the SABC cross country championships on Sunday. I changed my mind and did not go training and worked late at Thomas Graham & Sons. I discovered how much Andrew Curran the manager of the kitchen department got for his wages this month-£150.23. After tea I watched *The Likely Lads*-pretty good and gently amusing. I then pottered away with my running spikes.

1975 In the Anatomy, Physiology and Health class they did an oxygen uptake test on me-it was very high. In the evening I ran a fair sort of session.

Evening: 6 x 200 metres (walk 200 metres recovery approx 2.30 mins) 24-25 seconds

1976 A rest day; a pity as it was a cracker of a day; lunch with Dad. Paul and I went to see the film Roger had been raving about-*Rollerball*-interesting, entertaining and fast moving concept of a dystopian future. I studied all evening.

1977 An excellent Meadowbank session followed by an Arthurs Seat hill session. After a Chinese meal, in the confines of the car *Diana the goddess of love and hunting* and I gave a contortionist performance Harry Houdini would have been proud of.

Afternoon (12.00 p.m.): 600 metres 86 seconds (10 minutes recovery); 500m 66 secs (8 mins rec); 400m 52 secs (8 mins rec); 300m 36.5 secs

Afternoon (1.30 p.m.): 6 x 20 seconds Arthurs Seat hill runs (walk/jog rec)

28th February, 1974 With thinking about taking *Pixie Mia Farrow lookalike* out to the pictures tomorrow the day at Thomas Graham & Sons passed really quickly. Because of the General Election there is no training this evening so as I was in no rush to get home I just took the number 5 bus from Morningside Station to the top of Durham Road.

1976 Perhaps my best 500 metres session; in this Olympic year, I feel I'm starting to get my act together.

Morning: 3 x 500 metres (12 minutes recovery) 64.8; 64.5; 64.5 seconds; pretty good!

1977 I found it hard to get motivated this evening.

Evening: 16 x 200 metres (2 minutes recovery) average 26 seconds

1978 I only ran two and a half miles around Broughty Ferry this morning, partly because I was plodding and also because I'm still considering going down to Cosford to run in tomorrow evening's Phillips' Spectacular Meeting. I rang Coach Walker and thereafter sped back to Edinburgh; mid-evening I made the decision to race tomorrow; it may be a mistake; my legs are tired and my calves are tight; to help I did a few strides, went for an aerotone bath at Portobello Baths, then Denis Davidson gave me a very good massage.

Morning (7.00 a.m.): 3 miles

Evening: Strides

1st March, 1974 Great stuff, I'll soon be going out with *Pixie Mia Farrow lookalike*. At lunchtime there was an amazing snow blizzard outside Graham's on Balcarres Street with the largest snow-flakes I've ever seen. I met *Pixie* outside the pictures at half past six; by dint of nerves or just that I'm so thick I bought the wrong tickets and discovered as we were going in that the tickets were for *Enter the Dragon*; well that was embarrassing. I had to go back to change the tickets for *Paper Moon*. The film wasn't very good, but we ended up having a smashing time. I took *Pixie* home on the bus and walked her up the hill to Buckstone. On the way she said she can't go out very often as she has to study hard for her exams. What could I say to that-an unarguable position? A disappointing journey back home from the Braid Hills to Oxgangs where I was staying overnight; especially after all the keen anticipation and promise of the day.

2nd March, 1975 Stuart Hogg says the reason for my sore legs is because I'm still growing.

<u>Morning:</u> **5 x 200 metres (5 minutes recovery) 23; 23.8; 23.5; 23.2; 23.1 seconds**

<u>Afternoon:</u> **3 x 300 metres (no warm up; 8 mins rec) 37.0; 36.0; 36.2 secs**

<u>Before Bed:</u> **Arm-action; press-ups; sit-ups**

1976 I completed *Watership Down*; an interesting concept and a surprisingly good read.

<u>Evening:</u> **3 x 2 x 300 metres (walk/jog 100m recovery) (1) 39/39 seconds; (2) 38/40 secs; (3) 39/40 secs**

1978 Jeez, when the alarm went off at 5.00 a.m. I could hardly keep my eyes open. Nigel picked Karen and me up and drove us out to Birmingham Airport. He's quite amazing the way he drives the car with only one arm. There's a weighted devise attached to the steering wheel which seems to propel it back into position. I would guess that means the wheels are going into a straight linear direction; fascinating as it was, I was slightly apprehensive and glad it was early in the morning and the roads were quiet. The aeroplane was an old Viscount; I slept all the way and it was a great landing back in Edinburgh from whence I drove home. It's uncanny to think I was sitting eating my breakfast in Portobello before the mantelpiece clock chimed out 8.30 a.m. I studied all morning and then did a further hour in the afternoon out in the greenhouse. Come three o'clock I went up to Meadowbank to do a gym circuit before going across to Arthurs Seat to run a hill session. I was very flat-a bit tired.

Afternoon (3.30 p.m.): Gym circuit; followed by 8 x 20 seconds Arthurs Seat 70 metres hill runs with a 20 lbs weight jacket, before finishing off with a 200 metres hill run which killed me

3rd March, 1973 We travelled up to Perth. I ran well, especially in my 300 metres; Paul ran not badly; whilst John Scott ran great. My name was in this week's Athletics Weekly-fame at last. I stayed at Paul's house.

Perth Indoors Meeting: 50 metres (2nd) 6.6 seconds; 300 metres (1st) 38.4 secs; 600 metres (3rd) 88.8 secs (personal best)

1974 I wandered up to Meadowbank and ran a surprisingly good session. I felt a bit down about not being able to go about with *Pixie Mia Farrow lookalike* but I guess I'll just have to move on. I can tell that both Ann Sowersby and Petrina Cox both want off with me; Petrina gave me a loan of her Jim Ryun book.

Morning: 300 metres 35.9 seconds; 200m 23.6 secs; 150m 16.8 secs; 100m 11.4 secs; 6 x 6 x 60 metres back to back (20 secs rec)

Afternoon: Weights session

Before Bed: Arm-action; leg-work; press-ups; sit-ups

1975 I'd forgotten my headband, but Gaga and Nana dropped it off en-route to the Edinburgh Mineral Club.

Evening: 2 x 150 metres (4 minutes recovery) 16.0; 16.1 seconds (6 mins rec) 3 x 120 m (6 mins rec) 13.0; 13.0; 13.2 secs (6 mins rec) 3 x 100m (4 mins rec) 10.9; 10.5 (one step roll-in); 11.0 secs (6 mins rec) 4 x 60m (walk back rec) 7.2; 7.2; 7.2; 7.1 secs

Before Bed: Arm-action; press-ups; sit-ups; mobility stretching

1976 A bad day at black rock. I had to drop out of this evening's session halfway through with a bad right Achilles tendon; later I went along to the Edinburgh Athletic Club St Valentine's Dance. *Pixie* was there; it's the first time I've seen her since last year; whilst the dance was fine I went home on a bit of a low.

Let me not to the marriage of true minds

Let me not to the marriage of true minds
Admit impediments: Love is not love
Which alters when it alteration finds;
Or bends with the remover to remove.
O no! it is an ever-fixed mark
That looks on tempest and is never shaken;
It is the star to every wand'ring bark,
Whose worth's unknown, although his weight be taken,
Love's not Time's fool, though rosy lips and cheeks
Within his bending sickle's compass come;
Love alters not with his brief hours and weeks,
But bears it out even to the edge of doom.
If this be error and upon me prov'd.
I never writ, nor no man ever lov'd.

William Shakespeare

Evening: 4 x 200 metres 24 seconds; dropped out after first run of second set; my right Achilles is bad

1978 When Josephine awoke me this morning I was still very tired. There was a letter from Dr Motley. I went out to see him; he'd received some further correspondence from J. D. Martin at Oklahoma University, but there's still nothing concrete. In the afternoon Josephine and I went for a wee tootle down to Gullane; while she went for a walk looking out for agates or shells I ran five miles with the dog, getting back to the car just as the rain was starting; once back home to Portobello I slept all afternoon; I was pretty knackered.

Afternoon: 5 miles run Gullane Beach

4th March, 1974 In the evening I ran quite a good session. I decided to run the whole way in lane 3 with the group inside me to make me work harder. I felt quite tired after it, but pleased. I'm going to do at least a mile warm down every evening. I'm feeling in pretty good shape and I'm looking forward to competing in the British Junior Indoor Championships for the first time later this month as a first year athlete. I smiled at and spoke once with *Pixie Mia Farrow lookalike*. I think that I'm already beginning to forget her.

I Do Not Love Thee

'...I know I do not love thee! yet, alas!
Others will scarcely trust my candid heart:
And oft I catch them smiling as they pass,
Because they see me gazing where though art.'

Lady Caroline Norton

Evening: 6 x 150 metres 16; 16; 16; 16; 17; 17 seconds

Before Bed: Circuit

1978 A lovely March morning so much so I was up studying at 7.00 a.m. including an hour in the greenhouse taking notes with Radio Forth on in the background. I'm conscious of savouring these moments with Josephine and Heather pottering away in the background enjoying coffee and a blether before heading up town for their regular Saturday jaunt to Edinburgh's antique shops, Laigh Bakehouse, fish shop etc.; meanwhile Grandpa Willie is settled back on the big armchair reading his Daily Express, hot drink and the dog by his side. And I've the Scotsman literary section to look forward to. In a way you think such regular Saturday mornings will last for ever, but without warning, one day they will just disappear for good. Is that one of the reasons I keep these journals? I really don't know. To be honest I never really reflect on why I write them; there's an odd conundrum there, but then again I enjoy paradoxes.

Come 11.00 a.m. I left for Meadowbank to run a hard session with Paul and Norrie. I'm lacking a bit on speed endurance, but I'm sure it will come, especially as I adapt to a new phase of training. Afterwards and with it being such a grand day Paul and I played a set of tennis out the back-great fun! In the afternoon I studied intermittently; watched the Scotland v England rugby match and washed the car too. Come teatime a most enjoyable five miles run with the dog around Portobello Park and Golf Course. I was just flowing along. When it happens you just enjoy the moment. What enhanced it was the early smell of summer with the grass responding to having had the sun on its face all day long. A bath and an evening devoted to working on an Economics essay.

Afternoon (12.00 p.m.): 3 x 3 x 300 metres (1 minute recovery; 7 and 11 mins between sets) all between 41 and 44 seconds. Whacked! A lack of speed endurance. It'll come around nicely though

Evening (5.30 p.m.): 5 miles run; flowing along

5th March, 1977 Coach Walker and I conducted a 400 metres discussion with some athletes. Afterwards I ran a fair session. After lunch I took the dog with me and we went down to Gullane Beach to do a first class session on the sands-the dog loved it too; driving homewards to Portobello was pure tranquillity-a mix of tiredness and content-the endorphins kicking in; being in the happy company of the dog; feeling I'm doing something positive with my life etc. etc. and the prospect of picking up *Diana the goddess of love and hunting*. Later, we collected a bottle of wine and went round to Bob Sinclair's for a meal; a nice evening and a really super day.

Afternoon (12.00 p.m.): 8 x 200 metres (2 minutes recovery) all in 24 seconds

Afternoon (3.00 p.m.): Gullane Beach 6 miles running including 16 x 40 yards sand dunes session to exhaustion-a great session!

6th March, 1975 Half way through this evening's session there was a cloudburst and it poured with rain.

Evening: 5 x 150 yards (5-12 minutes recovery) 15.0; 15.1; 15.2; 15.0; 14.8 seconds

Before Bed: Arm-action; press-ups; sit-ups

1976 After several days off and visits to the physio my Achilles tendons were slightly better, but still niggly. It was cold and windy. I was ahead of Roger Jenkins on each run. I'm very strong down the home straight.

Morning: 500 metres 65.0 seconds (53 secs through 400m before moving up a gear effortlessly kicking down the home straight); 400m 48.1 secs (24.5/23.6 secs!);

300m 34.5 secs; 200m 22.1 secs all with standing starts; a pretty good session

1977 Although I'm not planning to run the half mile I think if I did I could go out right now and run 1 minute 49 seconds. After lunch *Diana the goddess of love and hunting* and I went to see *Emmanuele 2*-a lot of hokum; still it must have had something going for it as I drove *Diana* home via Silverknowes by the sea!

Afternoon (12.00 p.m.): 600 metres 81 seconds (10 minutes recovery); 500m 68 secs (8 mins rec); 400m 51 secs (6 mins rec); 300m 37 secs

1978 Josephine got me up at 6.45 a.m. and after breakfast I left for Dundee; it's light out so it's a bit easier; from the breakfast table I looked out at Rusty the cat sauntering around his estate in the back garden-he's got a fine life. I arrived in Dundee city centre by 8.30 a.m. and straight away began working in the library on my Sociology seminar. It's looking like a bit of a struggle. I met up with Derek and a couple of others and we had lunch at Andrew Kidd's and then picked up some messages. Come the afternoon I got my sleeves rolled up and by the end of the day had really got to grip with the Sociology topic and cracked it. I decided not to train in the evening-the weather; the time; the sore legs etc. *Diana the goddess of love and hunting* telephoned after dinner. I'd also received the letter she sent last week. I enjoy reading her letters. They brighten up my day with the added bonus of having something which you can re-read and go back to. I studied until 9.30 p.m. before Tom, Derek and I hit Jolly's! Tom was drunk and Derek was on the way; I was somewhere in between. We had a brilliant evening with lots of laughs. We dashed across to the Chinese restaurant for a bite; it's pretty mediocre. On the way back to our digs we made a bit of a racket in Broughty Ferry High Street. The odd curtain was pulled back and an old chap in an

Ebeneezer Scrooge white cap glanced down. The town clock rang out and chimed the midnight hour. The scenario reminded me of something out of the film *Hobson's Choice* especially as we climbed up the stairs to our digs; guess who was waiting with folded arms and a dirty scowl? Wrong! No, not Mrs Neve, but her sixteen year old daughter, Laura, who was standing there with arms folded across her enchanting chest and a disapproving, withering look. She gave us a bit of a nagging. I shuddered at the thought of being married to her. I wondered what Paul would have said to her!

7th March, 1978 Well, I showed the boys, the morning after the night before. I was up at 6.30 a.m. to do a circuit and then ran four miles around Broughty Ferry and sweated the alcohol out. Derek couldn't face his breakfast so I ate his eggs 'n bacon-plenty protein. Academia was fine and I got a lot of studying done and also wrote and posted a letter off to *Diana*. In the afternoon I did a gym circuit and then went down to Riverside and ran a good session, especially given it was on my own. I drove back to Broughty Ferry. There was a large envelope there from *Diana* containing a super drawing; my essay copied out and a letter-happy days! Out with a wet 'n windy evening. Derek and I put some petrol in the car then I did two and a half hours of Maths whilst Tom and Derek went off to Jolly's; they brought me back a chocolate Topic bar.

Morning (6.30 a.m.): Arm-action; press-ups; sit-ups; squats and squat-jumps; 4 miles run

Afternoon (4.00 p.m.): Gym circuit; 90; 140; 180; 240; 280; 240; 180; 140; 90 metres (3 minutes recovery)

8th March 1973 I've been relegated to tying up the lines (invoices) worst luck. And until the end of the month, such are the vagaries of life at Thomas Graham & Sons. I'm having to bend with the way the winds blow at any one moment. Meanwhile Scott got his pay rise and is now getting £10.50 basic a week. I was running averagely this evening. Paul and I might be going to Cosford for the British Youth and Junior Championships, but only as spectators. We're not regarded as being good enough to compete.

Evening: 1000 metres 3 minutes 3 seconds (8 mins recovery); 600m 94 secs (10 mins rec); 500m 76 secs (7 mins rec); 400m 58 secs

Before Bed: Press-ups and sit-ups

1974 Whilst at work I telephoned the Midland Counties AAAs at lunchtime; thank goodness I'm entered for my first British Junior Indoor Championships. Last night I dreamt of *Pixie Mia Farrow lookalike*. I thought I'd got her out of my mind, but no. I think it was probably all the references to Mary Rand's daughter, Alison, in her book that triggered it. All today at work I've been thinking about her; in the evening I went up to Meadowbank to do my weights session; usually I'm the only athlete there on a Friday evening, so I got a pleasant surprise to see that *Pixie* was there doing a session with her coach Stuart Gillies. I only managed to speak to her very briefly adding to the general miserableness and dissonance; once back home I felt rather lonely.

Evening: Gym/weights session

9th March, 1978 I went out for a bit of a burn-up around Broughty Ferry on the morning run, but ended up being disappointed with the overall time. As people begin to think ahead to exams, the world of academia is starting to wind down After Psychology I drove back to Edinburgh. I took it easy wending my way through the Fife countryside on a wet 'n windy afternoon. At Davidson's Mains I stopped off briefly at Safeway to see *Diana the goddess of love and hunting*. I thought how lovely she looked.

The Avenue

Who has not seen their lover
Walking at ease,
Walking like any other
A pavement under trees,
Not singular, apart,
But footed, featured, dressed,
Approaching like the rest
In the same dapple of the summer caught;
Who has not suddenly thought
With swift surprise:
There walks in cool disguise,
There comes, my heart

Frances Cornford

In the evening I ran a very good session with Paul which has improved my confidence no end. Afterwards I gave Florence a lift up to Princes Street; she was telling me all about this girl who always thinks of me in glowing terms. I picked up Jo and Heather from the Edinburgh Sketching Club. Later, I watched a debate on immigration on BBC 2 chaired by Robin Day. There are two million immigrants and the debate was on future policy and whether the numbers should be cut. I was disappointed with the quality of the discussion.

Morning (6.30 a.m.): 4 miles run

Evening (7.30 p.m.): 10 x 300 metres (1 minute recovery) 43 seconds; pleasing

10th March, 1973 I did some overtime at Thomas Graham & Sons until 11.30 a.m. and then looked out Oxgangs for lunch. On the way back down to Portobello I stopped off at Meadowbank. Dave Bedford was there and I was speaking to him. Parkinson was fantastic this evening with Jimmy

Reid delivering a knockout blow in a debate with Kenneth Williams; I love the pair of them, but for different reasons.

1974 I was talking with *Pixie Mia Farrow lookalike* for a bit. I wish I could forget about her, especially as there are others who stand a better chance of getting off with her...Ce la vie. I was asking John Anderson about this year's Easter course.

<u>Morning:</u> **30 minutes squash with Davie Reid**

<u>Afternoon:</u> **6 x 150 yards from lane 5 or 6 to make me work hard; all between 16 and 17 seconds; Gym/weights session**

11th March, 1973 It was another lovely day. I was running quite well and spent the whole day at Meadowbank. I did my training session with Dave Bedford today; there can't be many novice 16 years olds get the chance to train with a world record holder. He's actually a really great down to earth bloke. However, Coach Walker says I'm to run the 400 metres this year; I'm not sure how I feel about that, but I guess he knows best. I came home to Porty and sat in front of the coal fire all evening reading the *Sunday Post* and the *Sunday Express*.

<u>Morning:</u> **3 x 600 metres (6 minutes recovery) 94; 92; 94 seconds**

<u>Afternoon:</u> **5 x 300 metres at 3/4s speed**

1975 This cold and throat and temperature is getting worse; it's a bugger with the British Junior Indoor Championships approaching. I'll need to take around five days off training to get over it.

1978 After breakfast I collected my Athletics Weekly, but not much in it-full of cross country results. I ran a good session although I was slightly behind Paul and Norrie throughout. Afterwards, Paul and I enjoyed a set of tennis before I went home. At teatime I ran five miles around Portobello Park and Golf Course; there was a continuous light drizzle. Back home, as the light began to fade, I enjoyed looking out at the raindrops falling onto the pond; for whatever reason it took me back several years to when I used to borrow Dougie Blades' racer and go for solitary contemplative wee cycle rides from Oxgangs up to Redford. I always liked to just freewheel around the streets and houses reflecting on life and to where the future might lead. After a luxurious hot bath I picked up Lorraine Morris and we met Paul and *Diana the goddess of love and hunting* at the west end before heading out to Morningside and the Dominion Cinema to watch *Looking For Mr Goodbar.* I didn't enjoy it at all-how to destroy yourself. Afterwards we had a delicious Chinese meal and a lot of fun at the Mei Kwei Restaurant. I dropped Paul and then *Diana* off. At Mountcastle Lorraine and I sat in the car debating communism versus capitalism until 1.45 a.m. A score draw.

Afternoon (12.30 p.m.): 700 metres 99 seconds; 600m 84 secs; 500m 69 secs; 400m 54 secs

Evening (5.00 p.m.): 40 minutes steady run

12th March, 1973 The start of a new week at Thomas Graham & Sons. I thought it was going to be a scorcher of a day, but it remained mild. Work wasn't too bad and passed relatively quickly; I was out playing footie in the yard with the warehousemen; I played well and we won 26-11. Gaga gave me a lift to Meadowbank. I was running well and got a new personal best. I think Coach Walker got a bit of a shock at how well I'm progressing; I beat both Willie Sinclair and Duncan Baker over the 400 metres; they're two of the favourites for the Scottish Youth and Scottish Boys titles'

Coach Walker was definitely surprised that I beat Sinclair. I think there's more to come!

Evening: 500 metres 73 seconds (10 minutes recovery); 400m 53.9-a personal best! (10 mins rec); 300m 39.1 secs

1975 My cold is even worse.

13th March, 1973 I wasn't running too well this evening. I should have been trying much harder and gone with John Scott. From now on I'm definitely going to make a great big effort to stay with him and to beat him. He isn't invincible; I've just built up this image.

Evening: 500 metres 76.0 seconds; 4 x 150 yards 17 secs

1974 I fancy taking the *Simone de Beauvoir Philosophy Queen* out to see *Love Story*, but I'm not sure whether she would go out with someone like me. Paul and I have a poor reputation as the dregs of athletics society.

Evening: 15 fast 100 metres indoors with a walk back recovery

Before Bed: Arm-action; calf-raises; press-ups; sit-ups; squats

1975 I'm feeling hellish; my cold is worse and there's only a week until we travel to Cosford. I phoned Coach Walker to give him an update. I had some Arcaris ice cream from Portobello for my throat and also some *Redoxon* vitamin C.

1978 After studying all day on the spur of the moment I decided to drive from Broughty Ferry to Edinburgh to watch *Star Wars*. Impetuous? Who, moi? Derek and Tom decided to come too and managed to contact their girlfriends in Stirling and Edinburgh. It turned into a great wee adventure.

We picked up *Diana the goddess of love and hunting* at 7.40 p.m. at Silverknowes and headed into the Odeon Cinema at South Clerk Street where we met up with Fiona and Penny. The film was enjoyable and afterwards we all went out to Currie to Tom's house for supper. On the way back to Dundee we just managed to get some petrol at the Maybury Roundabout before it closed-whew! I was tired on the drive back and was glad to get to my bed. However, a lovely fun evening in great company and all the better for doing something on the hoof rather than planned. Derek and Tom are really lovely guys.

14th March, 1973 Crikey, I know I said yesterday that it would be a new me when training with John Scott, but I think I surprised everyone tonight! Last week Coach Walker was scratching his head when I beat Willie Sinclair when running a personal best of 53.9 seconds which totally came out of the blue; well tonight he was probably gobsmacked when I ran 52.2 seconds! I guess he was right when he told me last month that I wasn't to run the half mile, but the quarter instead. He must know something after all!

Evening: 2 x 400 metres (8 minutes recovery) (1) 60.0 seconds-I wasn't warmed up properly; (2) 52.2 secs-a personal best

1974 I got thrown out Coach Walker's group AGAIN for letting Ted and Stuart in the concourse doors for nothing. He really gets on my wick sometimes. He's probably done it tons of times himself.

Evening: 2 x 4 x 150 metres (2-4 minutes' walk back recovery; 10 mins between sets) I was running pretty well, from lane 2 (1) 16; 17; 16; 16 seconds (2) 16.5; 16; 16.9; 16.9 secs; I've got a cross country race coming up against the British ATC on 30th March

1977 *Diana the goddess of love and hunting* and I spent the day in Peebleshire; we had a light lunch in Peebles and then went down to Stobo to where Paul and I used to go camping in the summer when we were boys. We toured the area looking at some lovely old houses and then sat in the car having fun completing a crossword puzzle together. Coach Walker told me he had been speaking to someone at Moray House about me going there to study-that would work out quite well. I felt a bit low at training but pushed on quite hard.

Evening: 8 x 300 metres (walk 100 metres recovery) 42; 42; 41; 41; 43; 43; 43; 43 seconds

15th March, 1973 I'm glad that my boss Roy Wallace wasn't in at work today; somehow it made for a more enjoyable day for us all; once again I was running well in training. I was surprised Coach Walker didn't say much about last evening's startling 400 metres in training as I know he was shocked at how much I've improved, however he did say that the way I'm running he's considering giving me a run in the Edinburgh Athletic Club British League team in the 4 x 400 metres relay. Crikey, last season I could hardly get in the youth team.

Evening: 8 x 200 metres (2 minutes 30 seconds recovery) 25-27 secs

1975 Having been off with a very bad cold all week I ventured up to Meadowbank and did a light session; hopefully I'll have fully recovered for next weekend's British Junior Indoor Championships; an easy afternoon watching Scotland get beaten 7-6 by England in a very close match at Twickenham. In the evening Ann Clarkson phoned me.

Morning: 6 x 60 metres technique runs

16th March 1978 It was lovely wakening up in my own room. I spent the day studying and also pondering whether I should go out to this training camp in Spain. I reluctantly decided against it as I just can't afford it. I had been really looking forward to running the long clock that Coach Walker had scheduled for us; I'd wanted to really test myself out against Paul; Norrie and Adrian and had intended to put the foot down a bit just to see whether I could shake them up for a change. However, the weather was so God-awful I knew Coach Walker would change the session; which he did. After training he gave me some ultra-sound.

Evening: 10 x 200 metres (walk/jog recovery) 26-28 seconds

17th March, 1974 With the British Junior Indoor Championships fast approaching, we were meant to have time-trials today but there was a howling gale and the rain was pouring down. After the 300 metres Coach Walker wasn't exactly pleased and I had an argument with him. I think I've definitely finished with him now. Mind you I couldn't blame him after that performance-it was pretty shit. As I splashed through the puddles I was only going through the motions. Afterwards Paul and I enjoyed a good game of table tennis and a bit of a lark and a laugh, especially over my misfortunes. He manages to stay on Walker's good side better than me; aye he's a bit cannier. Mind you if Coach Walker spots him hanging aboot wie me he'll be out on his ear too! Like the weather, doom 'n gloom. I'll have to come up with yet another rescue package; I suspect my only way back is to get a surprise medal at next weekend's championships, but with an official best of 52.0 seconds I might be pushing it a bit against the 48 second Englanders.

Morning: 10 x 40 metres technique; 5 x 30 metres from blocks; I was less than half a metre down on Drew Hislop

Afternoon: 300 metres D. Harley 36.0; K. McMillan 40.2; Hoffmann 40.3 seconds 2 x 4 x 40 metres fast; hour table tennis

18th March, 1974 Can you believe it, a few days before my first British Junior Indoor Championships and I awoke with a very raw and sore throat, so no Thomas Graham & Sons for me. I went out to Dr Motley. I've definitely finished with Coach Walker although he's allowing me to train with the group until Cosford.

Evening: 300 metres 36.0 seconds; I had to run wide to get round people (10 minutes recovery); 3 x 200m (5 mins rec) in at least 23.7; 23.5; 24 secs; the second 200 metres felt the fastest run of my life; I just seemed to be floating along; Coach Walker didn't give me my times, only Keith Ridley's, but I was ahead of him

Before bed: Arm-action; calf raises; press-ups; sit-ups; squats

1975 My hamstring is really bad and giving me gyp. After coming back from the physio I spent the whole morning on the phone to people. Paul ran badly at the World Cross Country Championships in Morocco-he was fifth last; still it's all experience for him. I also phoned Coach Walker. After cashing my ten pounds cheque from the SAAAs I bought a couple of cardigans and a tee shirt that's far too small for me. In the evening I ran a hard session.

Evening: 3 x 2 x 26 seconds runs (1 minute recovery) covering around 210 metres with first reps at 24 secs pace; because of my hamstring I was just striding

Before bed: Arm-action; press-ups; sit-ups; mobility

1978 Norman and I ran an excellent session, very much the best I've felt all winter; I'm really starting to flow along. I ran Norrie home and looked briefly into Safeway to see *Diana the goddess of love and hunting*; the shop was hell of a busy; a frustrating study afternoon which I took out on an evening run. *Diana* phoned me during Kojak-*Would I be coming up to Lorna's 21st? Yes, I guess so*...we sorted things out, at least a bit...she stayed overnight.

Morning (10.30 a.m.): 8 x 200 metres (3 minutes recovery) 24 seconds; I felt the best I've been all winter; starting to run with rhythm, at speed and within myself too!

Evening (7.00 p.m.): 4 miles run

19th March, 1973 I got my Athletics Weekly this morning making for a good start to the week at Thomas Graham & Sons. All morning I beavered away on the lines and pricing invoices and the time passed quickly; come lunchtime Scott Wallace and I took a wee tootle along to Morningside and the Hung Lam Chinese Restaurant for one of their five bob specials. It made for a good break. Spring is fast approaching; the daffodils are out; the weather is getting milder and the birds busier. It's always the most optimistic time of the year. However, the afternoon was miserable and the office clock seemed to stand still. Scott's dad was waiting for him outside the showroom door on Balcarres Street at five o'clock so it meant I got a lift up to Cochrane's Garage and thus just a gentle stroll down to the Kings Buildings and a 42 bus home. In the evening I went training; I didn't really feel like running tonight, but continued with the good form and improvements I've been making recently. My 16 year old love-life is barren; it would be good to go out with some girls to add a little sparkle to my life.

Evening: 2 x 400 metres 56 and 59 seconds; 2 x 300m 42 and 44 secs; 2 x 200m 28 and 27 secs (5 minutes recovery); 4 x 100m (walk back recovery) 12.2; 12.2; 13.1; 12.2 secs; not bad times considering I just did not feel like running tonight

1974 I was about to head off to work, but after breakfast Nana said I should stay away from Graham's as my throat is still very sore. Mid-morning I walked down to Portobello Library and took out two books on athletics as I'm now trying to coach myself. In the afternoon Mum phoned to say Dad was in the Andrew Duncan Clinic (for alcoholics) so Gaga and I travelled out to Morningside to collect his clothes and we returned them to Nana Hoffmann's at Dean Park Street, Stockbridge. I felt very sorry for her; I think my life's going badly, but what about hers? Because of the rapidly approaching British Junior Indoor Championships I was keen to train in the evening and I did my own session. However, when Paul was timing me Coach Walker told him to stop otherwise he'd be out on his ear too; what a rotter! When I got home from Meadowbank I felt pretty low and downhearted, but when I think about it I'm very lucky when I think about poor Mrs Snowdon or Nana Hoffmann. I think that come this summer I'll try to escape over the gates of Thomas Graham & Sons and make an effort to study and transform my life; I could even go to evening classes.

Evening: 600 metres 87.0 seconds which is actually a personal best (15 minutes recovery); 3 x 4 x 50m back to back at 3/4s speed (30 secs rec; 2 minutes between the sets); I'm really easing off now

1978 I dropped Nana and Aunt Heather off at Waverley

Station as they are off on a bus trip today. *Diana* and I looked into the Art Exhibition to collect Josephine's paintings but it seemed to be closed. Despite the wind and the rain we did a session down at Gullane. I took Brian Scott; Norrie; and *Diana*. It was a lovely run down the east coast and I enjoyed their company. The session was good although I picked up a few cuts on my legs from the marram grass. On the way back to Edinburgh we stopped off as usual at Lucas at Musselburgh to enjoy an ice cream with all the others. Coach Walker's group sessions are always fun with a great group of people-very happy days. After a hot shower at Meadowbank *Diana* and I managed to collect Josephine's unsold paintings. I thought how beautiful Edinburgh looked on this quiet wet Sunday afternoon. I studied for a few hours and then *Diana* and I walked around the Figgate Pond-just to celebrate British Summertime. After dropping her off at Silverknowes by the sea, on the way home I picked up a small Chinese carry out.

Morning: **Gullane sand session including 6 miles of running**

1978 I dropped Nana and Aunt Heather off at Waverley Station as they are off on a bus trip today. *Diana* and I looked into the Art Exhibition to collect Josephine's paintings but it seemed to be closed. Despite the wind and the rain we did a session down at Gullane. I took Brian Scott; Norrie; and *Diana*. It was a lovely run down the east coast and I enjoyed their company. The session was good although I picked up a few cuts on my legs from the marram grass. On the way back to Edinburgh we stopped off as usual at Lucas at Musselburgh to enjoy an ice cream with all the others. Coach Walker's group sessions are always fun with a great group of people-very happy days. After a hot shower at Meadowbank *Diana* and I managed to collect Josephine's unsold paintings. I thought how beautiful Edinburgh looked on this quiet wet Sunday afternoon. I studied for a few hours and then *Diana* and I walked around the Figgate Pond-just to celebrate British Summertime. After dropping her off at Silverknowes by the sea, on the way home I picked up a small Chinese carry out.

Morning: Gullane sand session including 6 miles of running

20th March, 1974 Paul; Ian Ogilvie and I did a streak at Meadowbank. Afterwards I was talking away with Petrina Cox and the *Simone de Beauvoir Philosophy Queen*.

Evening: Fast 200 metres 23.0 seconds; I feel I could have run around 22.7 secs if I hadn't been so tight! 2 x 150 yards 15.9 and 15.6 secs; then a streak!

1975 Fantastic news, I got my stolen spikes back.

1976 Coach Walker is never overly happy about me doubling up at championships, so I thought I'd take it a stage further and decided to go for three events at today's Scottish Indoor Championships; it's often back-fired on me, but not today-the triple crown!

1976 Scottish Indoor Championships Perth:

SAAAs Junior 50 metres heat 1st; final 1st 6.22 seconds

SAAAs Junior 300 metres heat 1st 37 secs; final 1st 37.7 secs

SAAAs Senior 600 metres heat 1st 88 secs; final 1st 80.5 secs (championships record)

1978 I sat outside the church facing the main street in Dundee and read the History of the American Economy; the sunshine on my pow; the fresh air; and watching the street life are a good tonic for the soul; a few hours of Accounts and then an easy run with Derek and Tom. We had a lot of fun playing with the lie detector.

Evening (9.00 p.m.): 5 miles run

Thaw

'...Over the land freckled with snow half-thawed
The speculating rooks at their nest cawed
And saw from elm-tops, delicate as flower of grass,
What below we could not see, Winter pass'

Phillip Edward Thomas

EDINBURGH CORPORATION 031-661 5351
MEADOWBANK SPORTS CENTRE
.... JUNIOR Membership
NAME   PETER HOFFMANN
ADDRESS 6 OXGANGS AVENUE
         EDINBURGH EH13 9JA

Issued subject to Conditions of Membership. Copies are available on demand.
THIS CARD IS NOT TRANSFERABLE.
Expires Last Day of .... AUG 1972

A life-changing moment

Gaga and Nana with Alison and Fiona Blades; Paul
Forbes, Peter and Iain Hoffmann, Stobo, 1972

The author's parents on honeymoon, Isle Mull, 1955

David Jenkins, Edinburgh Highland Games, 1971

Paul and Peter, Oxgangs, 1972, fooling about; as usual

And again!

Coach Walker, Meadowbank Sports Centre (The
Herald, Steve Cox)

Norman Gregor

Adrian Weatherhead

Peter and Paul, Meadowbank Sports Centre, 1972

Roger Jenkins (Photograph, Ed Lacey)

Diana the goddess of love and hunting

The only known photograph of the author and Pixie
Mia Farrow together; Musselburgh Highland Games,
1973

Pixie Mia Farrow lookalike

Peter Hoffmann winning the European Junior
Championships semi-final, Athens, 1975

A who's who-the Edinburgh team leaving for Munich,
1975

Edinburgh reception from the City Fathers for
Olympians Chris Black; Helen Golden; Stuart
Fitzsimmons; and Peter Hoffmann

Pat and Ronnie Browne (Daily Record photograph)

Peter Hoffmann, August 1976

Trial for Scotland team, 1978; effectively a dead-heat
between Peter and Paul although I was given the
verdict; photo by Keith Ridley

'The look!' Last session before facing the Jenkins', 1978

Peter Hoffmann winning 1978 Scottish Championships
400 meters ahead of Roger and David Jenkins

Paul and Peter, winter 1978, Meadowbank; photo
courtesy of training partner, John Scott

A pensive Paul Forbes and Peter Hoffmann lining up to
face Sebastian Coe, UK Championships, 1978

**Approaching the bell, Paul Forbes and Sebastian Coe,
UK Championships, 1978**

Hoffmann closing down on Coe, but alas too late; UK
Championships, 1978

Sebastian Coe winning the controversial 800 final, ahead of Peter Hoffmann.

Mike Street

part in that match, too, winning the 1500 in fine style, but such is the resolve and endurance of this

The author next to a portrait of Eric Liddell, 2015

Peter and Paul, Jamestown, Strathpeffer, 2015

Peter; Paul; and Adrian Weatherhead,
Starbucks, Holy Corner, Edinburgh, 2016

The Author (Image by Peter Jolly)

'A great photo of long-time friend (50 years and counting), Peter Hoffmann as he's caught off guard by the paparazzi in the bustling burgh of Strathpeffer, somewhere north of Inverness. Quite how the news hounds found him is something of a mystery and to catch him coming out of the lavy with his new book in his hand is simply beyond mere chance. Note how Hoffmann's left hand teases the photographer by cunningly concealing the face of his comrade on the book cover. Selflessly, protecting his friend from the harsh glare of publicity. (I'm not sure what he's doing with his right hand but it's none of my business)

A Life in a Day in a Year, by Peter Hoffmann, a stocking filler if ever I saw one (and I've known a few).

Well worth a read; I know; I was there.'

Paul Forbes

The Song of the Ungirt Runners

'...And we run because we like it
Through the broad bright land'

Charles Hamilton Sorley

Spring

21st March, 1978 I felt miserable out running this morning. Mrs Neve's husband starts at 7.00 a.m. this week so I wasn't sure whether he'd go out ahead of me; he did, which meant I could sneak the hot water on. So, no cold bath this morning-luxury! I studied in the library all morning and then managed to contact a Glasgow travel agents and have booked a flight out to Spain. It's only £73; it's a shame I'm unable to go for two weeks which would have cost £108. Derek and Nigel took me out for lunch to The Bistro for a rump steak. After Accounts I picked up some Maths books then went to the gym. Tom had just finished a weights session. After my circuit I ran a miserable, solitary session down at Riverside. I got back in time for dinner. Tom and Derek have gone out to the pictures; meanwhile I studied Maths for several hours. *Diana the goddess of love and hunting* telephoned to say she'd got her hair cut-urchin-style; I think I'll like it. I made myself an omelette then off to bed to sit and read up on the Russian Economy until 10.00 p.m.-as one does! So went the day.

Morning (6.30 a.m.): 3 miles run; circuit arm-action; knee-raises; sit-ups; squat-jumps; squat-thrusts

Afternoon (4.00 p.m.): Gym circuit; 4 x 6 x 120 metres back to back (20 seconds recovery; 2 minutes 30 secs between sets)

22nd March, 1975 I didn't feel great, but won my first British title. It was a very close race against last year's AAA's champion, Brian Jones. I stumbled out my blocks which almost proved to be costly, but I just managed to catch him on the line. I should have won the double-the 200 metres and 400 metres. I was pretty scunnered to draw lane one in the final of the 200 metres. It's just impossible to win from there. The first bend is so tight I was having to contort myself and hold back just to keep upright before launching myself down the back straight. I was catching the guy William May all the way; another couple of metres and I would have been past him. We were given the same time, but he got the nod. If I'd had his lane, I would have won it easily by half a second. Still, a gold and a silver is a good haul; six races in 20 hours and I still feel fresh and ready to run again! On the way home from Wolverhampton to Edinburgh I ended up feeling a bit tipsy. Davie Reid gave me a drink of some *orange*. God knows what it was laced with. Kim sat on my knee for a while; you would have thought a bus seat would have been comfier! We arrived back in Edinburgh at 4.30 a.m. in the morning; Bob Sinclair was very good and gave me a lift home. Coach Walker's given me a rest day!

1975 AAAs Junior Indoor Championships

400 metres 1st 49.5 seconds (I just managed to beat Jones)

200 metres: Heat 1st 23.2 secs; Semi-final 1st 23.2 secs; Final 2nd 22.8 secs (same time as the winner; I drew lane 1 and the bend was just too tight; it's about time they seeded the 200 metres for lane draws)

23rd **March, 1974** When we got up this morning we discovered our clapped out bus had a flat tyre. It's no wonder it travelled all the way down from Scotland yesterday at only 40 mph! Anyway, the long and short of it was we all had to walk a mile down to the railway station carting our bags and belongings to take the train out to Cosford. Not the best of preparations for delicate flower athletes who like to be pampered. I surprised myself against the more fancied Englanders by making the final as the fastest loser. Having made the final I desperately wanted to come away with my first AAAs medal and surprised everyone by getting the bronze. I guess we're never happy as afterwards I immediately realised I could and should actually have got the silver. However, going into the championship with my lowly 52.0 seconds outdoor best from winning last summer's Scottish Youth Championship compared to the likes of Brian Jones and Phil Grimshaw who have won several AAAs and English Schools' titles between them and run around 48 seconds, I went into the race aiming to ensure I came away with a medal. I was cautious and sensible. However, in doing that, I came with such a flourish at the end I almost went past Grimshaw, running the same time as him. If I'd run for the silver I could have beaten him. I don't think I've quite realised how much I've improved. My time in the final of 50.2 seconds is a new personal best indoors and outdoors so I'm not dissatisfied.

To round the day off nicely Paul managed to come away with a bronze medal too. There was really three races going on in the half mile. There was a real burn-up resulting in a U.K. Junior record when Wayne Tarquini just passed Tony Dyke, with both recording 1 minute 52.6 seconds. Paul did well to run 1.57.8. Our risk of going down to the prestigious AAAs as first year juniors paid off; we could have raced instead at Perth in the Scottish Indoor Championships and had an easier time of it. Getting a medal at this level and in a pretty good time has given me a lot of motivation for the future; I'm starting to think I could be quite good. My next goal is to get back into Coach Walker's group. I could tell he was secretly pleased that I'd medalled, but he also told me I should have got the silver. Of course it's easy to be wise in retrospect. I like both the English lads, Brian Jones and Phil Grimshaw. They're bright, intelligent, highly personable and friendly lads as well as old rivals. Phil's at Manchester Grammar School whilst Brian is aiming to go to Oxford next year. Despite being a lowly cost clerk at Thomas Graham & Sons it's good to feel I've been welcomed into such elite company.

1974 AAAs Junior Indoor Championships

Morning: 400 metres Semi-final 2nd (50.7 seconds personal best); unlike last night I felt great at the end of the race and just missed catching Grimshaw; I made the final as the fastest loser

Afternoon: 400 metres Final 1, B. Jones (Liv P) 49.1; 2, P. Grimshaw (Sale) 50.4; 3, P. Hoffmann (Edin) 50.4 (personal best); I could have got the silver if I'd run a bit harder

24th March, 1973 Although it was a Saturday I went into work early and left late morning to join Coach Walker's group at Gullane. I really enjoyed the session and it's a nice counter to life at Thomas Graham & Sons. As we head into spring and with the light stretching out, driving down the east coast through the lovely East Lothian villages of Longniddry and Aberlady is such a refreshing change; plus the training is hard and bringing me on; and it's good fun being part of a group of people who have become such good friends. And of course, the morning is nicely rounded off with a Lucas ice cream at Musselburgh. Happy weekends, if not happy weekdays.

Morning: 1.5 hours Gullane Sands session

1974 We made the long overnight journey back from Cosford in the clapped out bus. Dave Hislop and I were walking around a quiet Glasgow at 6.30 a.m. on a Sunday morning whilst awaiting the Glasgow girls being picked up by their parents. Back in the capital I took Scrubs and Derek Innes home for breakfast. I did a relaxed session at Meadowbank. However, I was barking away and the cough was so bad that David Jenkins came over and advised me to go to bed for four days. Later in the day the cough got worse and I felt so unwell that I travelled out to Oxgangs to see the doctor. He says I've got bronchitis and gave me a penicillin injection. I passed out. Quite a weekend, but worth running to get that first AAAs medal.

Morning: 6 x 150 yards relaxed (3 minutes recovery) 16.0; 16.2; 15.9; 16.7; 16.5; 16.3 seconds

1977 At lunchtime I ran a brilliant hill session up on Arthurs Seat. I felt like a machine. In the afternoon I completed an essay and then in the evening joined the middle distance guys. I gave Susan Rettie a lift home in the Spitfire to Brighton Crescent. I'm taking her down to the Gala Sevens, but I feel guilty as it is upsetting *Diana the goddess of love and hunting*. Anyway, Susan and I are just pals. A pair of Adidas spikes arrived in the post today.

Afternoon (1.00 p.m.): 10 Arthurs Seat 20 seconds hill runs; I was running like clockwork; on the first six runs I was just bouncing up the hill!

Evening (7.00 p.m.): 8 x 400 metres (1 minute recovery) 61; 61; 63; 63; 62; 61; 62; 62 seconds; my legs felt heavy before we started; I ran with the top guys all the way; I don't think many other quarter milers would last that session

A light exists in Spring

'A light exists in spring
Not present on the year
At any other period
When March is scarcely here…'

Emily Dickinson

1978 A lovely fresh, sunny spring day. I took Jo and Aunt Heather out for a wee tootle down to the Borderlands. We stopped off for a delicious Cauldwell's ice cream at Innerleithen and then on to Melrose. On the return journey, what a pain, but also a laugh too. The windscreen wipers on Dad's car wouldn't go off; having run out of windscreen fluid, to prevent the blades scraping the windscreen, I pushed the wipers outwards. As we drove through Penicuik two outstretched arms were swaying from side to side across the top of the bonnet, like a man kissing a woman's breasts; we didn't half get some queer looks from passers-by!

Pat Browne sent me complimentary tickets and in the evening I picked up Lorraine, Paul and *Diana* and we went along to see the Corries concert which as ever was very enjoyable. After a meal at the Mei Kwei Chinese Restaurant in Morningside we all went down to Brighton Crescent for Drew Kennedy's party in his converted basement. Ronnie Browne was along and we had a good chat together. He was very interested in Paul and my ambitions for the Commonwealth Games; he's a good guy.

25th March, 1974 After collapsing last night I stayed at Oxgangs and lay on the sofa all day. Gaga picked me up at four o'clock. In the evening I looked into Meadowbank to pick up an application form for a scholarship pass. Paul reckons I've a good chance of getting back into Coach Walker's group.

26th March, 1975 I ran a very good and very hard session with Roger and Stewart McCallum. Later, I gave Kim a lift home.

Evening: 200; 300; 400; 400; 300; 200 metres (walk 200 metres recovery); Roger was sick; Stewart packed up with 50 metres to go; a very hard session; the lactic acid was incredible-loved it!

1977 Always a good start to get my Athletics Weekly. Paul and I put in a good double session today; the first one at Meadowbank. My sister Anne came along. It's a pity she doesn't have the time to train properly as she could be good. The three of us had lunch at 45 Durham Road before Paul and I travelled down to Gullane together in the Triumph Spitfire to knock fuck out of each other on the sand dunes, followed by a long hot soak in the bath afterwards. In the evening *Diana the goddess of love and hunting* took poor me out for a meal; a very nice evening. It rained throughout the night.

Afternoon (12.30 p.m.): 8 x 300 metres (2 minutes recovery) 39; 41; 40; 40; 39; 39; 41; 41 seconds

Afternoon (3.00 p.m.): Gullane 3 miles run; 16 x sand dune hill runs; with Paul-we worked VERY HARD!

1978 This Easter morning I had Radio Forth on in the background having awoken from a strange dream. I was high up on Arthurs Seat looking down on children playing in the valley below. I walked, barefoot, to a church service which was being held out in the open air-a bit like the old

Covenanters. I could make out George Sinclair the Edinburgh Southern Harriers coach; Helen Golden the sprinter; and Norrie Gregor and his girlfriend Shirley, who were all in attendance!

Easter Away

'…Like a magnet, drawing me in
Wanting to whisper something to me
I'd like to listen. But can't
Easter's a strange time. And the world is whizzing
And to stop. And maybe find out
That you were only a dream.'

Peter Hoffmann

From the imaginative to reality. I ran another decent session, although my legs were tired. Later I re-arranged my bedroom bringing in the large old squishy armchair. Will and I nipped down to Musselburgh for an ice cream. I gave him two pounds towards his car insurance; Mum and Iain did the same. I like seeing Will happy and the wee contributions gave him a boost. Whilst we were down at Musselburgh Mum phoned to say Iain's wife Kim is pregnant and would I come out; they're only 16-17 years old, but what can you do, other than give them a baby-care book! On the way back from Oxgangs to Portobello I got a nasty fright from another car driver; it was my own fault; I just wasn't paying attention and instead was in a *dwam*, sorting out the world and putting it to right. I was very lucky to escape unharmed. *Diana the goddess of love and hunting* was down. We sat and watched *Love Story*, laying back on the sofa; sometimes it's great to have her down; sometimes I'd rather be on my own; this evening it was the latter.

Afternoon (12.00 p.m.): 4 x 600 metres differentials (6 minutes recovery) 300m (41 seconds)-100m (30 secs)-200m (26 secs)

27ᵗʰ March 1973 As I had a lot of work to do the morning at Thomas Graham & Sons passed quickly. At lunchtime I played football out in the yard with all the warehouse lads; Derek was losing the head a bit-my class was just too much for him. I should pack up the running and join a club and see if I could be picked up, but I enjoy the running too much. Roy was clocking out my card so I'll get a wee bit of overtime. He and Andrew Curran have been advising me to write for other jobs. They've got my best interest at heart; they advise Scottish & Newcastle Breweries as a good company to apply to. In the evening a nice wee session at Meadowbank; of the two Anns I'm leaning towards the charms of Johnstone rather than Sowersby.

Evening: 2 x 4 x 100 metres sprint-slow-sprint

1976 I didn't feel particularly good at training.

Morning: 4 x 300 metres (10 minutes recovery) 34.2; 34.8; 34.8; 35.2 seconds; it was very windy, cold and damp so I ran two bends rather than two straights; I didn't feel great

1978 I ran four miles with the dog around Portobello Park and Golf Course. It was a miserable morning out-raining, cold and windy. After a light breakfast *Diana the goddess of love and hunting* and I looked into Safeways before going up to Meadowbank. Coach Walker has got us jobs working all week running an athletics course for the kids during the Schools' Easter Holidays. We enjoyed ourselves, although hard work on my wimpish legs. I'd forgotten how tired

Roger and I used to feel when we did the job in previous years. I now remember why we used to sit down whenever possible to referee; we're such prima donnas! After lunch I lay down for an hour and a half and thereafter studied for the rest of the afternoon. It rained continuously, with some intermittent downpours. Before tea I took Will's car up to Swann's Newsagent's for an Edinburgh Evening News. For once his car is going sweetly. I was thinking how much I love home and feel tranquil and at peace. A light tea, more studying, then I ventured up to Meadowbank for a track session. Home; brown bread and honey and more studying. So went the day.

Afterthought: As I was driving home from Meadowbank I thought how lovely it would have been to be going back instead to a flat with the lovely *Diana* waiting for me. Oh well...

<u>**Morning (8.00 a.m.):**</u> **4 miles steady run; home circuit**

<u>**Morning (9.30 a.m.):**</u> **3 runs up Meadowbank steps; 1 each leg hopping**

<u>**Evening (6.30 p.m.):**</u> **150; 170; 190; 200; 200; 190; 170; 150 metres speed endurance clock; general circuit work**

28th March, 1978 We managed to take the children outside today; *Diana the goddess of love and hunting* took half of them for long jump whilst I took the others for high jump. The weather couldn't make up its mind all day, a mix of sun and rain; it was the latter when we trained, however the whole squad was kept going by the sight of Alison Lumsden's charms and physical attributes!

<u>**Afternoon (12.00 p.m.):**</u> **Gym circuit**

Evening (7.00 p.m.): 20 x 110 metres with jog back recovery

29th March, 1973 I spoke to Davie Rogan the manager and he says I can have my summer week holiday on 8th April so that I can join John Anderson's Easter Course. It should be brilliant with Dave Jenkins, Don Halliday etc. plus the likes of Sheila Carey and Dave Moorcroft who are all travelling up from Coventry. Paul and I are fair looking forward to it.

30th March, 1974 A beautiful day. I ran in the cross country out at Turnhouse against the British ATC. I'll clearly never be a navigator because I ran off course and ended up running six miles rather than four. A pity, because I was lying in fourth place at the time. In the afternoon I went to Easter Road to watch a cracker of a match: Hibs 3 St. Johnstone 3. To round the day off nicely I had 1st; 2nd; and 4th in the Grand National. In the evening Scott Brodie picked me up and we joined the usual crew for a few drinks and a Chinese meal.

Morning: Cross-country v British A.T.C.; it was meant to be 4 miles but I ended up running 6 miles

31st March, 1975 I felt a bit out of sorts, but after an afternoon session felt a lot better. Afterwards I took *Pixie Mia Farrow lookalike* home for tea.

Afternoon: 6 x 30 metres (walk back recovery; first two with tracksuit on) 4.0; 4.0; 3.9; 3.8; 3.9; 3.8 seconds-10.7 secs 100 metres pace; 6 x 30m rolling start 3.2; 3.1; 3.0; 3.0; 3.0; 3.4 (relaxed); 6 x 60m technique runs

Evening: 4 x 100 metres (50m technique/50m flat out; 4 x 110m (40m flat out; 30m relaxed; 40m flat out); gym circuit

Before Bed: Arm-action; press-ups; sit-ups; mobility

1977 I ran a pretty hard session and then gave Susan Rettie a lift home; I'm meeting her at 1.30 p.m. on Saturday.

Evening: 8 x 300 metres (30-45 seconds recovery) 42 seconds until last two-treading water in 46 secs-very hard!

1978 I exchanged some pounds for pesetas. I was up at Coach Walker's house all evening planning the early season; we had an excellent chat.

The West Wind

'It's a warm wind, the west wind, full of birds' cries;
I never hear the west wind but tears are in my eyes.
For it comes from the west lands, the old brown hills,
And April's in the west wind, and daffodils.'

John Masefield

1st April, 1978 When I awoke it was raining and stayed that way all day long. Given it was cold and wet I ran a fair session including 64 seconds for the 500 metres. It was okay as I could easily have converted it into a 78 seconds 600 metres; I kind of lost interest in the rest of the session-50 seconds for the quarter; a 35 seconds 300 metres and a 25 seconds 200 metres. Later on I managed a little packing before I head off to Estepona, Spain tomorrow. I've been reflecting and decided I need to adopt a *Cyclops'* philosophy-train hard; race hard; study hard; pass my exams; make money. I guess the earlier objectives are more a Stoic philosophy.

Morning: 500 metres 64 seconds; 400m 50 secs; 300m 35 secs; 200m 25 secs

2nd April, 1978, Estepona, Spain Jo was on the warpath at around 5.30 a.m. I had a sleepy breakfast at 6.00 a.m. before going out to Edinburgh Airport with Will; Jo and *Diana the goddess of love and hunting.* I went into the international departure at 8.30 a.m. only to hear an announcement that because of a Spanish air traffic controllers' strike we wouldn't be taking off until 1.00 p.m. and we couldn't leave the area. I managed to signal the public telephone number through the glass pane to *Diana* so she phoned every hour on the hour. I was surprised to see John Wilson from my year who was flying out to Malaga too; I enjoyed chatting with him. Despite the cramped conditions on board I managed to study for most of the journey. I took a taxi from Malaga Airport to the Seghers Club, Estepona-it set me back 2000 pesetas (146 to the pound). On arrival I was surprised to see a British squad of sprinters there. I had my evening meal with Faye Nixon and Michelle Probert; we had a lot of fun! Outside there is the most delicious aroma. It's a very sweet scent which pervades the air around the villas. Despite being so early in the year the cicadas are chirping away constantly. I spent a few hours studying some Economics.

Evening: Arm-action; knee raises; press-ups; sit-ups; squat-jumps; mobility

3rd April, 1978 Seghers Club, Estepona After travelling out from Edinburgh yesterday I slept well and came down to breakfast at the clubhouse at 8.30 a.m. for a bowl of cornflakes, coffee, bread and jam; I love the creamy continental milk they serve up. Afterwards a short browse in the little shop which sells ceramics and other serendipities; one or two nice pieces, but at exorbitant, inflated prices; of course this is a resort targeted at the rich, if not the famous. I studied a little Economics then wandered down to the running track, which is basically just a very long straight. It was still and already warm, with the sun climbing high in the sky. It was surprisingly busy-mainly Bill Marlowe with the British girls' relay squad, including Sonia Lannaman. I ran a fairly good session. Coach Walker's Irish coach/friend is here too with a party of athletes. I may be able to get a lift with them later in the week as they intend to visit the full sized track in Malaga and are intending hiring a car. A pleasant lunch with an interesting combination of meat, egg and pineapple in a mayonnaise sauce; on the surface it shouldn't have worked, but somehow it did. I sat out in the sun and got a pile of Economics chapters completed; I'm really satisfied about that and feel I've got a really good grasp of the course which is encouraging this far out from the diet of exams in June. By five o'clock it was only slightly cooler, but I ran a steady five miles on the dusty roads out toward a small village in the opposite direction to Estepona. It's a great feeling being out running in just a pair of shorts. It made me wonder how training in warmer climes throughout a winter would bring me on. When I got back I did a light circuit amongst some giant Scandinavians and then finished off with an invigorating length of the pool, the water, ice cold. Before dinner some more Economics, a shower and then I smartened up for the evening meal. Several of the other athletes were getting a bit high spirited, whilst I retired at a reasonably early hour. I feel to do anything else would be contrary to what this is about. Boring old me!

Missing You

You're missing.
I'm missing
You
Tonight
And you
Are you. Too
Missing me
Tonight?
This night
Not right. Missing you
But right. Too. Tonight
For I might
Not. Have missed you.
And missed.
Missing you.
(So) Tonight
I don't fight
Missing you. Right
And
Tonight
Miss. I miss you.

Peter Hoffmann

When I got back to my room I felt surprisingly lonely; and yet in many ways I'm a loner. I'm off to sleep; to ease my passage I intend to dream about *Diana the goddess of love and hunting*. So went the day. *Bon soir* or should that be *buenas noches dulces sueños...*

Morning (10.30 a.m.): **12 x 120 metres good rhythm and pace with a walk back recovery; good to be running in just a pair of shorts**

Evening (5.00 p.m.): 5 miles steady run; gym circuit

4th April, 1973 Yahoo! it's not long till my week's holiday from Thomas Graham & Sons and the start of John Anderson's Easter Course. I'm having lunch tomorrow with Iain and Les.

1978 Seghers Club, Estepona I didn't get up until 9.00 a.m. I twisted and turned in bed until 2.00 a.m. It was either the warmth, which I'm unused to, or spending some time in the sun yesterday. However, when I did get to sleep it seemed to be one pleasant dream after another. Surprisingly there was a steady drizzle for much of the day. I was just starting to warm up when Coach Walker's friend Harry and his wife Pam asked if I fancied joining them to go to the track in Malaga? Unfortunately we took a hell of a long time to find the stadium and by the time I arrived there I felt hungry and lethargic. I felt so jaded I had to push myself just to warm up to do a session on my own. So, all things considered I was glad to have done something. It was a hazardous drive back to Estepona. Harry's not the best of drivers. For much of the journey he was distracted telling me about all the problems in Irish athletics. I was surprised to find it was six o'clock when we got back; I'd lost all track of time. I went straight out and ran five miles; I felt a little tired and halfway through I stopped by a little stream for a few minutes. In the evening, a lovely meal in good company with Bill Marlowe, Mary Stewart etc. There was some sparkling conversation and I was in good form. I enjoyed myself. I strolled back to my room at 9.30 p.m. and did an hour of Economics. I would have liked to have done more studying today but it was just the way it panned out. However, over the next few days I'll be based at the Seghers Club so I'm aiming to complete the Economics programme which I've set myself. I don't feel so lonely this evening. Off to bed once again with the Russian Economy, paper and pen.

Afternoon (3.00 p.m.): Malaga 3 x 600 metres (12 minutes recovery) 85; 84; 84 seconds

Evening (6.30 p.m.): 5 miles (2.5m-5 minutes stopover-2.5m)

Before Bed (10.30 p.m.): Arm-action; knee-raises; press-ups; sit-ups; squat jumps

5th April, 1975 My final season as a junior augurs well as shown by today's double session. In the morning I did some pure sprints with George McNeil. He's quite phenomenal. I have no doubt if he had been able to race in the Olympics in 1972 it would have been between him and Valery Borzov for the gold medal in the 100 metres. I'm sprinting really well just now. Earlier in February I won the Scottish 50 metres title and in today's session I was running 10.5 speed. I've been bettering Drew McMaster and others in training too and I was really pleased with today's session. So that's the context. Well, George was taking 2 metres off me over 30 metres! Two metres! It was incredible to witness and be part of the session. The only thing I could compare it with was watching Dave Jenkins a few years back when he trained with John Anderson and we used to watch him running 19 seconds for rolling 200 metre runs or his flying 300 metres repetitions. Ironically, if David he'd gone for the 200 metres in Munich, Scotland might have won the gold in both sprints! After running with George in the morning I ran a second good session at lunchtime, but this time with Roger and David Jenkins. On a lovely spring day what could be better? Afterwards Robert Sinclair came down to the house and we watched L'Escargot win the Grand National.

Thereafter Paul joined us and we went to see *The Three Musketeers* followed by a Chinese; a good day.

Morning: 4 x 30 metres in 3.7/3.8 seconds; George (McNeil) was taking 2 metres off me and I was flying! 2 x 4 x 30m with running starts all in 2.8/2.9 secs; all runs with an easy walk back recovery

Lunchtime: 500 metres Dave Jenkins 63.6 seconds; Hoffmann 64.0 secs; Roger Jenkins 65.5 secs; 400m Hoffmann 49.8 secs; Dave 50.0 secs; Roger was 20 metres back; 300m Hoffmann 35.0 secs; Dave 35.1 secs; Roger 35.3 secs

I felt very much in control and able to handle anything Dave threw at me, never mind Roger; a good session and a good day's work; augurs well for the season ahead

1978 Seghers Club, Estepona Once again another poor night's sleep; it would be breaking the Trade Description Act to call it sleep. I twisted and turned constantly. I got up at 9.00 am. It was raining and never stopped all day; I bet it's sunny back home at Meadowbank! I met Paul and Frank Dick at breakfast. They'd arrived late last night. I ran a track session in the rain and after a delicious buffet meal went back to my room to study. At tea-time I did some weights and then went out for a run; I bumped into Mary Stewart so ran five miles with her. I struggled a wee bit; we were probably running around 6 minute mile pace. She's very, very fit just now. After a bath I went down for a meal; it wasn't so good this evening, although the beef burger and mushrooms were fine, as was the gateaux. I was sitting next to Bill Marlowe and was bemused at Frank trying to glean as much information out of him about the upcoming Technical

Director's post, but of course in the nicest possible way! Tapio Kaunlenan, the Estepona Sports Director was there too; he's an interesting guy; quiet, but confident and a helpful person. He enjoys Frank's company and Frank regularly drip feeds interesting and fascinating little snippets into the conversation. He's a source of knowledge; he's shrewd. It was a free masterclass; if I were so inclined. At 9.30 p.m. I came back to my room. It was hard to do so as everyone else is down at the bar. A bit like Monday evening, I'm longing for *Diana the goddess of love's* arms.

Morning (11.00 a.m.): 2 x 4 x 240 metres (120m turnaround) with 45 seconds recovery; good rhythm and hard on the lungs

Afternoon (4.30 p.m.): Gym circuit; lots of stretching on the inside leg-a great new find which may help with stride length

Afternoon (5.15 p.m.): 5 mile run with Mary Stewart in 30 minutes

6th **April 1975** I felt sorry for Ross Hepburn; he was telling me about his struggle with his exams; he's probably in a similar position to me from a few years ago.

Evening (5.00 p.m.): 2 x 4 x 200 metres (2 minutes' walk/jog recovery; 10 minutes between sets) 24 seconds

Evening (6.30 p.m.): Gym circuit

7th **April, 1974** Gaga's car wouldn't start this morning so I had to get the bus to Meadowbank. In the morning I trained with Drew McMaster and then joined John Anderson's squad in the afternoon; afterwards some table tennis, a good blether with Stuart Togher and back home to enjoy a film with Gaga, *Jack of Diamonds*. I gave Gaga £5.50 towards the paper bill from Swann's Newsagent, Milton Road West. It's not just for the newspapers because we also get the *Amateur Gardener* for Josephine and another big outlay is all the comics-*The Hornet*, *The Hotspur* and *The Victor*, but it's money well spent as we love reading them. Of a soft spring afternoon if we hear the paperboy, we jostle each other down the hall to get first read; what a laugh we have; I'm 17 and he's 70 years of age!

Morning: **8 x 30 metres out of blocks with Drew McMaster; I was beating him on more runs than he was beating me (no flyers!); 5 minutes rest then I joined Arthur Orr and Dave Wilson 3 x 4 x 60m back to back with decreasing recovery 25; 20; 15 seconds recovery and 90 secs between sets; I was running ahead of them both**

Afternoon: **3 x 4 x 150m (90 secs rec; 5 mins between sets); I was going well beating Gus McKenzie and Roger Jenkins on a lot of runs; weights session**

Before Bed: **Arm-action; press-ups; sit-ups; squat-jumps**

1976 For a wee change I trained with Drew McMaster and the rest of Wilson Young's squad; I was just playing with them!

Evening: **2 x 3 x 60-20-60 metres**

1978 Seghers Club, Estepona Biding my time to get a lift into the track in Malaga I didn't do a track session this morning. However, frustratingly it never came off.

Eventually I just went out for an easy run along the beach with Paul in the direction of Estepona. It rained and absolutely pissed down. At one stage we had to leap across a twelve wide river of sewage which was flowing straight in to the Mediterranean. We stopped off at the harbour. It was the most charming scene; handsome, rugged and tanned fishermen with pipes in mouth and each one wearing a jaunty cap; they were full of character; all it needed was a painter to capture the moment. In direct contrast, across the harbour on a separate quay lay all the luxury yachts. After the evening meal we enjoyed a drink and a beef burger at *El Rancho*.

Afternoon: 3 miles run

8th April, 1977 An Eros day with *Diana the goddess of love and hunting* and she stayed overnight too. *Roots* began on the box tonight-absolutely brilliant. I'm looking forward to discussing it with Roger.

1978 Seghers Club, Estepona The weather was much brighter. I ran a pure sprints session with Cameron Sharp. It was the first time in months that I've run flat out. Cameron was absolutely flying, but considering I've been focusing on half mile work I was pleasantly happy at just how close I was to him. Frank had hired a car (in his name), but couldn't be arsed driving Paul and me into Malaga after lunch to do a track session. Instead, he said to just take the car ourselves, which was a bit dodgy given we weren't entitled to drive the vehicle or insured. Things were going swimmingly until we were in the heart of busy Marbella. To our dismay I managed to stall the car at a busy set of traffic lights and after that it was pandemonium. We couldn't get the fucker to start again. A long tail back of traffic built up behind us. Drivers were blaring their horns, leaning out windows shaking their fists.

Paul gave them the V sign which certainly didn't help things. Panic stations. We could see a policeman in the distance wondering what the fuck was going on. I could just picture him asking to see our documentation! Paul leapt out and pushed the car into a side street where we tried to do a jump start. FAIL! I tried a second time. SUCCESS! I did a *Uie* and we drove straight back as fast as we could to the Seghers Club. When we arrived back Frank was lounging back sunning himself astonished to see us back so soon. Paul and I went off to play power tennis for a couple of hours, then went down to the beach to cool down. The last I saw of him was drifting off in a dodgy canoe in the direction of North Africa doing a Largs' Jimmy Johnston! Ach well, one down, two to go; all I've to bother about now is getting rid of Coe and Ovett! In the evening a meal; then El Rancho for a beef burger with Jim Brown and Alistair Hutton. Early to bed.

Morning (11.00 a.m.): 2 x 100; 75; 50; 25 metres flat out with Cameron Sharp; he was flying; I was within touching distance; my hamstrings were sore afterwards as I haven't done any pure speed work for months

Evening (6.00 p.m.): 2 hours tennis with Paul

Apple Blossom

'The first blossom was the best blossom
For the child who never had seen an orchard…'

Louis MacNeice

9th April, 1973 It was a beautiful spring morning, getting the John Anderson Easter Course off to a perfect start. I walked down to Duddingston Crossroads and Mr Drever gave me a lift out to Riccarton. I was really excited about joining John's international group for the Easter Course. Now that I've broken twelve seconds for the 100 metres I felt more confident; John was pleased to hear about me running 11.4/23.4 yesterday and said he wasn't surprised and there's much more to come! Brilliant! It turned into a good day's training; after the morning session we had a good laugh playing on the trampoline and some table tennis too. I like the Riccarton set-up. In the evening we did a session at Meadowbank. Paul was told not to run, but he did so and stupidly pulled a muscle. The classy Anne Johnstone was down this evening; oh and Dougie McLean got a new second hand car. If that's not a contradiction!

Morning (Riccarton): 6 technique 60 metres; 3 x 3 x 100m back to back; trampolining/table tennis

Evening (Meadowbank): Clock 2 x 160m; 180m; 195m and 1 x 200m; weights session

1975 Considering I've picked up yet another cold I ran a good session with Roger and George McNeil.

Afternoon: 4 x 300 metres (20 minutes recovery)

(1) Roger Jenkins 35.4 seconds; George McNeil 35.8 secs; Hoffmann 35.9 secs (2) Jenkins 35.5 secs; Hoffmann 35.5 secs (3) Hoffmann 34.8 secs; Jenkins 35.0 secs (4) Hoffmann 34.4 secs (200m 22.0 secs); Jenkins 35.4 secs

1977 *Diana the goddess of love and hunting* took the bus to work at Safeways, Davidsons Mains; I got off at Meadowbank and ran a good session with Roger. Afterwards he gave me a lift back home to Durham Road and joined us for lunch. Josephine was charmed by him; he was admiring some of her paintings and particularly liked the one of the Montague Bridge at Dalkeith. In the afternoon Will and I hired the ramp at Texaco and drained and replaced the car oil. *Diana* was back down in the evening.

Morning: 4 x 300 metres (10 minutes recovery) 35.4; 33.9; 35.1; 35.5 seconds; an excellent session with Roger Jenkins

1978 Seghers Club, Estepona I wandered down for my last breakfast here. As I was up early there were only a dozen people about. After packing my bags there was a bit of a quandary at reception over the bill. They said it was 14,000 pesetas; I said no, it should only be 7,500 pesetas. Anyway, the long and short of it is that it went on Frank's bill; it serves him right for not having an agreement set out in black and white. I didn't think I was going to make it to Malaga Airport never mind arrive there on time. The Irish coach is a maniac behind the wheel. It wasn't helped by their decathlete forgetting his passport; we had to do an about turn on the highway which ended up delaying us for ages, whilst he hunted high and low for it. My flight to Edinburgh left at 3.30 p.m.; that was a lot better than the athletes returning to Dublin; Bristol; Manchester etc. Their flights were all delayed for hours. The flight home was boring. It wasn't helped as I didn't feel like studying and most unusual for me, I didn't have a book in my pocket; that must be a first. The only distraction was a pleasant chicken dinner. I was really looking forward to arriving home in the capital and Nana; Gaga and *Diana the goddess of love and hunting* were all there to greet me at Edinburgh Airport. On a soft spring afternoon it was an easy drive home to Durham Road where a freshly baked rhubarb tart awaited me on the table; our next door neighbour, Miss Hopkins, had handed the rhubarb in as a present. The household was happy with the little serendipities I'd brought back; *Diana* decided to stay over. We went for a wee stroll with the dog down to the Figgate Park, just getting in before the rain started. We settled down in front of the coal fire to watch *The Cincinnati Kid*. Bon soir. Spring is here.

Blackbird

'He comes on chosen evenings,
My blackbird bountiful, and sings
Over the gardens of the town
Just at the hour the sun goes down...'

John Drinkwater

10ᵗʰ April, 1973 Another glorious start to the day with the sun shining on the breakfast table. And what a contrast to the usual grey Dickensian working world of Thomas Graham & Sons. It's great not having to go into work this week and to be able to fully enjoy John Anderson's Easter Course. I'm just soaking it all up. It's a great feeling being a welcome part of the group. I could get quite used to such a life focusing on athletics. It must be a great life for lots of John's athletes like the Jenkins', Dave Wilson, Dave Moorcroft, Gus McKenzie, Ruth Watt etc. who are all students as well as athletes. They all seem to have such a great life, combining sport and study and having the time to be able to be part of this week. I want to be part of that culture in future, but given they're all champion athletes and well qualified and I'm a lowly cost clerk with two O levels and won nothing I'm not quite sure how I might transform my life to become like them.

Follow Your Bliss

'Follow your bliss. If you do follow your bliss, you put yourself on a kind of track that has been there all the while waiting for you, and the life you ought to be living is the one you are living. When you can see that, you begin to meet people who are in the field of your bliss, and they open the doors to you. I say, follow your bliss and don't be afraid, and doors will open where you didn't know they were going to be. If you follow your bliss, doors will open for you that wouldn't have opened for anyone else."

Joseph Campbell

Over a sunny breakfast I enjoyed the moment and the daydream. And having taken the week off from work, in a funny way I feel I've become like them even if it's only for a pretend week. I took the bus up to Meadowbank. Everyone gradually arrives; already Paul and I feel an integral part of the group. Wee conversations are going on and it's really interesting being a fly on the wall hearing them talk about their future plans; what they're aiming for in athletics and life and their thoughts on training. I'm just soaking up the experience. People like Don Halliday, David Wilson and David Jenkins are great characters with a bagful of international experience, intelligence and are often quite forthright with their views-some more so than others.
I was running really well and part of that is to do with being highly motivated. And whilst I'm a long way short of the top male athletes and the brilliant junior athletes like Roger Jenkins and Gus McKenzie, I'm certainly able to run well against the international women athletes like Ruth Watt and Liz Sutherland. The only sour note was Paul and I have been told by R.M. that we've got to pay him £25 for his stopwatch which went missing. I don't know what the fuck happened to it. It was definitely lying around the Meadowbank Cafe

window table area where we were sitting. But the next thing we knew it just disappeared. It was a complete mystery and I honestly don't know what happened to it. He of course thinks Paul and I have nicked it, but he doesn't really understand our mentality; he's just way off beam. Perhaps if he were less nosey asking us about what our fathers do for a living and what school they went to and concentrated more on where he'd laid the watch it wouldn't have come to this. But it's left a bad taste. He thinks we're just a pair of ruffians from Oxgangs who would do something like that. And yet nothing could be further from the truth. Yes, we get up to all sorts of daft things, but to steal something from a fellow athlete is so removed from our values and mentality that it just bugs me.

Anyway, on a much happier note, in between the morning and afternoon sessions it was great hanging about with all of John's squad. I feel I'm learning so much from them. I mean crikey, there's four Olympians from Munich here-Sheila Carey; Halliday; Wilson and Jenkins. There's lots of little things to pick up on too; how they warm up; their competitive mentality and the banter that goes on too. It's just so inspirational; I'm loving being here. John makes us feel such an integral part of the whole group too. He takes as big an interest in Paul and me as he does with his own athletes. He seems to have time for everyone. The good weather is helping too. All in all, it was no wonder I got another personal best as I'm very keen to impress everyone; it was a big one too; not only was it the first time I've broken 38 seconds for 300 metres, but I actually broke 37 seconds! I'm looking forward to running my first 400 metres race. Later, Coach Walker gave Ann Dunnigan, Paul and me a lift out to Broomhouse. I'm staying at Paul's tonight. We sat and watched the John Wayne film, *Flame of the Barbary Coast*, but it was rubbish. We listened to Radio Luxembourg and talked for a few hours before going off to sleep. A great day!

Morning: Speed-clock 3 x 60; 2 x 100; 1 x 150; 2 x 100; 3 x 60 metres with a slow walk back recovery

Afternoon: 2 x 300 metres (1) No time (2) 36.8 seconds; a personal best

1975 Paul said it was one of the funniest things he'd seen. An unhelpful bus driver took off from the bus stop just as Ann Sowersby, Paul and I arrived; I pressed the outside handle; the doors swung open and I nonchalantly waved my bus pass at him and swanned on; well it was like something from a *Carry-On* film, because the next thing they witnessed was me being thrown off the bus, followed ten seconds later by my training bag. Paul was lying on the ground helpless with laughter; I wisnae happy.

Morning: 500 metres (65 seconds); 400m (49 secs); 300m (37 secs); 200m (24 secs) (10 minutes recovery); not great-my legs were still heavy from yesterday's session

1978 I wasn't able to do much today; my last session in Spain with Cameron Sharp has left my hamstrings feeling very tight. Mum was saying Iain gets married a week on Saturday at West Maitland Street. I managed a wee run up to Meadowbank to get some ultra-sound from Coach Walker. Denis Davidson gave me a rub at 3.00 p.m.-very good of him at such notice. At 4.00 p.m. I went in to see Helen Blades at the Royal Infirmary; she's dying of cancer; the news came as a shock. Despite having to see so many visitors, she was delighted to see me. Knowing I wouldn't see her again, as I was leaving I kissed her; she hugged me tight and tried to hold back her tears. It was very sad. She was such a big influence on me when I was growing up at The Stair. She had such a magnetic personality; the nearest person I could compare her to is John Anderson. You always wanted to help her out; when I received the slightest modicum of praise from Helen I would be on cloud 9 for the rest of the week. I'll never forget how one sunny summer's afternoon when Helen; Marion; Mum and lots of the kids were out in our back garden and I was a wee boy showing off by sprinting round and round the block, she said I'd run in the Commonwealth Games one day and how her eldest daughter, Liz, quite rightly, but sniffily said, *Don't be silly Mummy*. Well, let's prove Helen right! Helen's passing is going to leave an enormous gap in the lives of her six girls and Douglas. Afterwards, I gave one of her visitors a lift back to Craiglockhart. She was a pleasant middle class woman, but was trying to pair me off with her daughter. Iain showed me his quadrophonic stereo-whatever that is!

Mid-day: 2 miles run to Meadowbank; 2 miles home; felt rubbish

Evening (8.00 p.m.): Gym circuit

11ᵗʰ April, 1973 Paul and I got up at 9.15 a.m. to head off for day 3 of the Easter Course. We met Ann Dunnigan on the bus and then Ann Sowersby also got on and joined us. Once again I was running well. We also had a good game of table tennis. Later on Duncan and I went for a bottle of juice, did some weights; then I had a talk with Coach Walker. That's the first time I've had a proper discussion with him. Athletes like Ann Dunnigan have always been the main focus, but I think he realises I'm quite committed now and that I could do well at the Scottish Youth Championships. A shower and then home. I've decided to tell that R.M. he should just go to the police about his stopwatch. Oh, he now says that Paul and I are to only give him £20-just over two weeks' wages from Tommy Grahams. I hadnae realised the watch was gold plated!

Morning: **6 block starts; 2 x 50 metres technique; 2 x 50m flat out**

Afternoon: **Power Clock 3 x 100 metres; 2 x 150m; 1 x 300m; 2 x 150m; 1 x 100m; the session included a 16.3 and 16.4 seconds 150m and 36.9 secs for the 300m**

Evening: **Weights session**

1976 I've been going out with the *Simone de Beauvoir Philosopher Queen* for over a month now and we're getting on surprisingly well. I'm up at her house regularly; I'm made to feel very welcome and I already feel part of the family. It's a warm, loving, animated and fun household with a lot going on as she has a sister and two brothers. It's a good place to be. Her mum is absolutely lovely and like her daughter highly intelligent. The dad's an intellectual-honestly, he really is and he asks my views on all sorts of things. He's glad that I like reading so much and has come to the conclusion that I'm an autodidact! He's passed copies of William Burroughs' *The Naked Lunch* and Joseph Heller's *Catch 22* into my hands and other such challenging books. Once I've read the tomes he wants me to join him at the pub to discuss them. He's interesting to chat to, but usually tootles off to the pub around 9.00 p.m. Meanwhile, I've got another cold. But it was the E.A.C. Club Championships so I turned out and ran a poor quarter. There's only two months until the Olympic Trials and I'm going to work very, very hard before my next race down south in London.

E.A.C. Club Championships:

400 metres 1st 49.1 seconds; felt whacked at the end

<u>Before Bed:</u> **Arm-action; press-ups; sit-ups; squats**

12th April, 1973 I couldn't sleep, so I got up at 8.00 a.m. It's day 4 of the Easter Course and as we were only doing one session today I didn't wander up to Meadowbank Sports Centre until around lunchtime. We ended up doing a light session. Afterwards we all piled up to the Commonwealth Pool for a dip and a bit fun. Scott Brodie gave Duncan Baker, Paul and me a lift. With the weather being so great this week it was good to be able to cool off. Tomorrow's the last day of the course and we've going to have some time trials and then in the evening we're all going out to a Chinese Restaurant at Bruntsfield to finish the week off in style. It's strange how Paul and I haven't won anything compared to a lot of good athletes of our age at Meadowbank and in Edinburgh Southern Harriers, yet we're now rubbing shoulders and on good speaking terms with the likes of Britain's best athlete, David Jenkins. I feel it's changed my mentality a wee bit. I feel more confident, but I have to be careful not to be arrogant too, as I haven't achieved anything yet; but I've got the bit between my teeth. I want to become as good as some of these athletes. I think Paul feels the same way too; he and Ann Dunnigan have been putting in some good sessions with Sheila Carey and Dave Moorcroft, who's a hard worker.

<u>Lunchtime:</u> 3 x 4 x 150 metres (90 seconds recovery) controlled 3/4 speed; swim at the Commonwealth Pool

1975 It was an absolutely foul day-wet, cold and very windy. It was the E.A.C. Club Championships, the first races of the new season. Despite the weather and with no competition I manged to run a 400 metres personal best and more importantly a European Junior Championship qualifying standard. Radio Forth were along and I was interviewed on and off all day, offering them my pearls of wisdom! I also got a mention on the telly at tea-time. In the evening six of us including Paul went to see *Freebie and the Bean*; it was okay. We raced a boy in a Rover, had a Chinky meal and then had a laugh at Arthurs Seat with a couple caught en flagrante-what a laugh, what a scene.

Edinburgh Athletic Club Championships:

100 metres 11.1 seconds (p.b.); 200m 1st 22.6 secs; 400m 1st 48.3 secs (p.b. and European Junior Qualifying Standard); a wet, cold, windy day; the wind was against in the home straight

1978 I had a bad headache throughout the night until the last few hours before I arose. *Diana the goddess of love and hunting* and I went down to Portobello for a brown loaf. It was a beautiful sunny day, but cold. We drove through the Meadows to Demarco's Café and sat at a table with a tramp-a man of the road. He was full of character. We bought him a coffee and a bacon roll. He told us he'd been down at Hawick yesterday. When I asked him if he picked up many colds he answered *Not really; I just have one all the time!* His story and tales reminded me of the young John Buchan's Peebleshire vignettes in either *Grey Weather* or *Scholar Gypsies*.

After lunch *Diana* and I lay on my bed and giggled for much of the afternoon. She gave my chin a shave with Iain's razor. I studied some Accounts for a few hours, whilst *Diana* helped Grandma Jo mow the lawn-the first cut of the season. While I studied she sat looking through the scrapbooks Josephine keeps of my running and also reading my diaries: *I like them, but I hope they're not going to be published—especially about the lovemaking! Don't worry, they'll be edited and you'll have a pseudonym; how does Diana the goddess of love and hunting sound? I like it!* At 8.00 p.m. I went out for a run. It just about ended in a fight. A guy purposely walked into my path and started swearing at me. I stood my ground for twenty seconds then he backed down and walked off shouting again trying to maintain his pride; what are some people like! Back home for a bath, wash my hair and some telly before running *Diana* back home to Silverknowes by the sea.

Evening (8.00 p.m.): 5 miles run, last two miles Fartlek; runs/hops up and down Meadowbank steps

13th April, 1973 I went up to Meadowbank for the time trials, but didn't run too well. I was a wee bit tired from training each day, plus there was a really annoying and irritating wind blowing against us. It's perhaps a good sign, but I'm clearly getting fussy on the job, given that until last weekend at Grangemouth I'd never even broken 12 seconds. In the evening I met Duncan Baker outside Meadowbank Stadium and we travelled up to Bruntsfield to join John Anderson and everyone at the Yangste River Chinese Restaurant for a meal; it's Dad's friend, Ben, who owns and runs it; he used to work at Edinburgh first Chinese Restaurant, *The Bamboo*, at South Queensferry Street. Afterwards we all walked up to the Bruntsfield Hotel. It's been a fabulous week and if we weren't already enthusiastic enough, it's really fired Paul and my appetite for athletics; we're on board the train! Later on, some of us went down to 54 East Claremont Street to Coach Walker's. I got a taxi home just after 1.00 a.m.

Afternoon: **100 metres 11.5 seconds; 300m 37.6 secs; against the wind; I'd hoped to sign off with a real flourish to really impress John Anderson and Coach Walker, but it wasn't quite there today**

1976 Yet another cold; I'm on penicillin all week; it will be just slightly different for Jenks out in California.

The West Wind

> '...*Will ye not come home, brother? Ye have been long away,*
> *It's April, and blossom time, and white is the may;*
> *And bright is the sun brother, fire to a man's brain,*
> *To hear the wild bees and see the merry spring again...*'

John Masefield

1977 I've been in bed by ten o'clock this week which means I awake just before seven.

1978 *Diana the goddess of love and hunting* stayed over.

Evening (7.00 p.m.): **6 x 400 metres (3 minutes recovery) 56; 56; 54; 57; 58; 58 seconds**

14th April, 1974 This morning I trained at Meadowbank with Drew McMaster; Dave Coombe; and Robert Denham. In the afternoon Iain; Nana; Gaga; Heather and I went down to Stobo, Peebleshire and revisited the farmer's field beside the River Tweed where we camped two years ago. Iain and I went swimming in the river, but I ended up cutting my foot. I've actually ripped it. To help my driving I drove down and Gaga drove us back to Portobello, via Oxgangs, where we dropped Iain off. A good and rather interesting film on in the evening, *Guess Who's Coming To Dinner*. Although the premise was inter-racial marriage, it was more of a love story.

Morning: 2 x 3 x 130 metres from blocks; flat out 60m-ease 20m-flat out 50m; I was either alongside them or ahead on each repetition

1975 It poured with rain all day. There were excellent write-ups in several newspapers about my performances at Saturday's club championships, mainly saying it was extraordinary to come out and run a personal best European qualifying time with little opposition on such a wild inclement day etc. laced with my inanities and inability to accept a compliment. I'm dismissive of my performance. Later I phoned Dad to see if he might buy me a pair of spikes. I had tea out and then picked Paul up.

Evening: 300 metres 35.4 seconds; so relaxed and strong at the end (6 minutes recovery); 200m 21.6 secs (10 mins rec); 2 x 150m (walk back rec; 10 mins rec) 15.5; 15.7 secs; 4 x 100m relaxed with tracksuit on

Before Bed: Arm-action; press-ups; sit-ups; mobility

15th April, 1973 After the John Anderson Easter Course it was back to normality, but with a new zest for athletics. Gaga ran me up to Meadowbank. I ran a really tough session. Paul and I were supposed to go to Aberdeen but it would have cost us too much money. It was a very hot day. In the afternoon we lay about on the high jump mat having a laugh with the *Simone de Beauvoir Philosophy Queen* and Petrina Cox. I stayed the evening at Paul's at Broomhouse; we sat up talking and laughing until midnight.

Morning: 5 x 300 metres (5; 7; 9; 11 minutes recovery)
40; 41; 39; 40; 38.5 seconds

Afternoon: 6 x 50m with easy walk back recovery 6.7;
6.5; 6.4; 6.3; 6.3; 6.2 secs; Weights session

16th April, 1973 I don't go back to work until tomorrow so I
had a long lie in at Paul's until 10.30 a.m. Just before
lunchtime I left Broomhouse and went out to Oxgangs. It
was another lovely day, in fact it was really hot. Mike Hanlon
is home on leave from the Navy, before going off to the
Mediterranean. In the afternoon we got all the old crew out
for a great game of football. Whilst speed and endurance
were always an asset, having been training for the past year
or so, I'm able to even more effortlessly slip the ball past
players and just leave them for dead.

With me being away from Oxgangs and Mike having joined
the Navy we're the first two boys from The Stair to leave
school, I wonder if that's the last game we'll all ever play
together? In my quiet philosophic moments I've occasionally
reflected on the concepts of first and lasts. Football was
always one of them. Sometimes I would idly day-dream as to
when will we all be together for the last game of football up
at The Field? Afterwards a few of us sat out on the old shed
roof, which was lovely and hot; we sat and played cards and
talked on a dreamy afternoon like *Tom Sawyer; Huckleberry
Finn* and a thousand other sets of boys over the centuries.
It's funny how serendipity comes into play, turning the
ordinary into the extraordinary. None of today was planned.
If I hadn't decided to come up to Oxgangs, then I wouldn't
have seen Mike and so on; and how one thing leads to
another. Like life itself. I reflected on this at teatime as I took
the number 4 bus down to Meadowbank and ran a good
session. I fancy one or two of the Edinburgh Southern

Harriers girls. Later I was up at Dougie McLean's house studying yesterday's results.

Afternoon: Football

Evening: 2 x 5 x 150 yards (3 minutes' recovery and 10 mins between sets); all in 16-17 seconds

1975 I met Dad at St James Centre. He bought me a pair of *Adidas Spider* spikes. I'm delighted to be back in business again. At lunchtime Mum met us both for lunch at the John Lewis Restaurant; it was good fun and nice to have the three of us back together again and in such a positive way too. In the evening I trained with Roger.

Evening: 6 x 300 metres with walk back recovery 37-40 seconds; 12 laps consisting of jog a lap alternating a lap with two hard 100 metres straights

1978 On awakening I immediately looked out the window to check the weather; it was dry and still, so I knew I could run the planned for session. *Diana the goddess of love and hunting* and I drove the car up for the Sunday papers then took the dog to Portobello Park. My favourite type of a morning. After breakfast I read some Economics for an hour before going up to Meadowbank to run a fair session. After a delicious steak dinner (courtesy of Iain) I wrote up my journal and then ran an easy 3 miles. *Diana* gave my legs a massage; a steak sandwich for tea and then it was off to Dundee. En-route I dropped *Diana* off at the West End; she'd decided she was going to take a wee tootle out to Morningside on the 41 bus. I found the drive up relaxing; it's a good time for reflection and considering the future. When I arrived at our digs I didn't get much of a welcome from our land-lady's sultry 16 year old daughter, Laura; she basically just opened

the door. And that's it; you're on your own. Being penniless I couldn't even afford to go out for a ginger beer and lime. I spent a couple of hours on Economics before bed.
Diana called which was thoughtful of her, however due to a faulty telephone box she wasn't on for long. I lay abed for an hour reading the Sunday Times.

Afternoon (12.00 p.m.): **800 metres 1 minute 54 seconds; 600m 81.6 secs; 400m 49.7 secs; my front thighs felt a bit tired after the half mile**

Afternoon (4.00 p.m.): **Easy 3 miles run**

17th April, 1973 Well, after living in the dream world of John Anderson's course last week and rubbing shoulders with some of the sport's superstars and how they live I was brought back down to earth with a bang as I returned to the boring blacking factory of Tommy Graham's. At least I've gone back on a Tuesday so that will shorten the week a touch, however it was a very boring day. There's also been a few changes since I was here last. In the evening I was running very poorly. I'm really keen to get a girl-friend. I feel it would transform my life for the good. Dougie's new second hand car wasn't running too well.

Evening: 2 x 5 x 150m (90 seconds' recovery and 8 minutes between sets) in 18-19 seconds; absolute rubbish; weights session

1975 I had to sit in the doctors' waiting room for two hours. In the evening I had on a rather classy outfit, including my new Adidas Spider spikes; it made me reflect on one of the Pros' maxims, *Feel good, run good.*

Evening: 5 x 300 metres (5 minutes recovery) 40; 38; 38; 38; 38 seconds; very relaxed, although I was a bit stiff from last evening

18th April, 1978 I really enjoyed my early morning run around Broughty Ferry, all helped by being able to run in just shorts and a tee shirt. Derek and I drove into Dundee; I studied in the library for an hour before sitting my Economics exam. I've done enough to pass. Derek and I joined Nigel Snow for lunch at Kidds-always good fun, although I felt guilty about eating the lovely gateaux. In the Accounts tutorial we went over the term exam paper and got out early at 2.30 p.m. As I hadn't managed to get through to Coach Walker to get Stuart Hogg's number to arrange to train with Drew Harley at Glenrothes I just decided to travel down to Edinburgh to train instead. It occurs to me that I don't think anyone else trains with such a wide and varied range of athletes. One day it's pure sprints with Drew Hislop or Drew McMaster and then it's a miler's session with Adrian Weatherhead. I enjoy the challenge of taking them on over their speciality area and trying to get the better of them. I'm always positive; if I train with the sprinters I just tell myself I've more endurance; if it's a middle distance workout I tell myself I'm quicker and therefore able to keep up as I'm expending less effort. When Derek heard of my plans he jumped in the car and came with me. We had tea at Grandma Jo's at Portobello and then I took him up to Meadowbank to show him around. He was impressed with the facilities. He stood with Coach Walker and watched me run a fair session on my own; one which will probably do me a bit of good. En-route back to Dundee we stopped off at Davidsons Mains for a drink with *Diana* before we wolfed it back to Broughty Ferry. We arrived back at our Broughty Ferry digs at 10.30 p.m. Fair play to our landlady, Anita, who prepared a meal for us; it was really very good of her, although a bit too *carbohydraty*. Although she's as tough as old boots I think she warms to what I'm trying to achieve, especially aiming for a place at the Commonwealth Games.

Morning (6.30 a.m.): 4 miles steady run

Evening (7.30 p.m.): 2 x 4 x 200 metres 23 seconds (2 minutes recovery; 10 mins between sets)

19th April, 1973 I was in at Thomas Graham & Sons early this morning. Our latest recruit to the long line of cost clerks, young and old, is fat and bearded Angus. He started working in the Cost Department a few weeks back. He strikes me as being a young-old foggie; but as I don't exactly know what a foggie is. He's around 30 years old, but dresses in an olde worlde way in a tweed jacket. He could easily pass for being a decade older. He struck me as being the church type, but this morning he arrived at the office with a pile of nude magazines. No one was complaining, although church going old Tommy Drummond pursed his lips, disapprovingly. It struck me as an odd thing to do; slightly misjudged. The warehouse is full of magazines so it's nothing novel, but given he's only been here for a few weeks. Anyway, what he has done is set himself up for Roy's merciless rapier wit. Thus far Roy's gone gently on him, just slowly feeling out the lie of the land, but by the afternoon poor Angus was toast. Roy was off on a rift and Angus's wit is as slow as his cumbersome movements. Anyway, it provided a bit of light relief. Like Mutley I sniggered in the corner. I got sixteen shillings taken off in tax so I didn't join the lunchtime crew at the Chinese Restaurant. In the evening I was running a little bit better, but not perfectly. I chickened out of asking Anne Johnston for a game of tennis.

Evening: 8 x 60 metres

20th April, 1973 Good Friday I was in at work quite early this morning. Driving through Arthurs Seat at 7.15 a.m. Gaga and I saw Dave Jenkins out running on the grass below Pollock Hall, which was pretty unusual to see. Come lunchtime a few of us went out to the *China Night Restaurant*; I was in Roy's car; in his lighter moments he's a good laugh and at heart he's a nice guy. I was thinking I'll have to visit Nana Hoffmann more often. I enjoyed the film *Song for Bernadette* and the story of Lourdes-*Pray for me Bernadette*-powerful stuff for Easter. When Anne got back from the mineral club Gaga brought in some St Andrews chips, but they were unusually poor. Oh, Gaga needs to get something done to the car. Again!

1974 Anne and I sat about talking for a couple of hours before I went up to watch the Edinburgh Southern Harriers Club Championships. Come two o'clock Coach Walker gave me a lift home to pick up my athletics kit and we drove out to Peffermill. I ran a good 200 metres. Afterwards I took D.W home for tea. Scott picked me up and we went to the dance at the Minto Hotel; it was very good. I ended up getting off with a pretty girl called Aileen Gordon; she wants me to give her a ring on Monday evening. Meanwhile Paul and D.W. came back to stay the night. Well that was an experience and a half! The three of us shared the same double bed. Well fuck me, I'd only been asleep half an hour when I awoke with a start with D.W.'s arm and leg draped and wrapped snake-like around me. I sat bolt up-right with my hair standing on end like Oor Wullie and shook him off. I went through to the loo; ten seconds later Paul follows me through and says *The bastard had his hand on my fucking knob!* Well the pair of us just collapsed in to paroxysms of laughter; we were squealing away. I thought my sides were going to split and wake up the rest of the household! Anyway, we ended up grabbing a duvet and went through to the living room for the rest of the night. There has always been this on-going joke about D.W. but I'd always taken it with a pinch of salt. We won't forget that one in a while. Oh, and that's the last time D.W.'s invited back for the night!

Afternoon: 200 metres at Peffermill 1st Roger Jenkins 23.5 seconds 2nd Hoffmann 24.1 secs 3rd Charles Luxon 24.5 secs; a terrible track and a strong wind against the whole way; ironically I felt I ran well against Britain's top junior 200/400 metres athlete

1975 Having stayed at Robert Sinclair's last night at Goldenacre I went down to Meadowbank and ran an extraordinarily good session with Dave and Roger Jenkins. Afterwards I sat around Meadowbank all afternoon chatting to various people before giving Anne; Iain and Lucy a lift home to Oxgangs. I spent the evening at Coach Walker's house agreeing that come August we should be aiming for a European Junior gold medal in Athens. I dropped Coach off at Waverley Station.

Morning: 500 metres Dave Jenkins 62.2 seconds; Hoffmann 63.1 secs (p.b.); Roger Jenkins 63.1 secs; 400m 48.6 secs (ran in lane 3 down the last 100m as I moved onto Dave's shoulder); Dave 48.6 secs; Roger 48.8 secs; 300m 34.4 secs; Dave 34.4 secs; Roger 35.5 secs

21st April, 1975 The Edinburgh Holiday. I spent the morning reading. I wandered up to Meadowbank at lunchtime and ran a good session with a very powerful group of athletes-George McNeil; Roger Jenkins and Graham Malcolm. I'm beginning to surprise myself at just how quick I've become over pure sprints. At teatime I also ended up doing a wee session with John Anderson. I spent several hours in the Meadowbank Cafe chatting to a variety of people including Audrey Smith my Hunters Tryst Primary School girl-friend. She's a professional dancer appearing on the Andy Stewart shows at Hogmanay etc. She's still as lovely, in all senses of the word-a gentle girl with just an innate loveliness to her.

Afternoon (1.30 p.m.): 6 x 50 metres flat out; George McNeil was first on each run, but I was a strong second ahead of Roger Jenkins and Graham Malcolm-pleasing as they are 10.5 seconds guys

Afternoon (2.00 p.m.): 2 x 4 x 200m (90 seconds recovery) all in 24 secs; very relaxed, easily handling Roger

Evening (5.00 p.m.): Starting practice from blocks with John Anderson

22nd **April, 1974** It was a long morning at Thomas Graham & Sons, but the afternoon passed quickly. I joined the middle distance guys this evening and ran a really good session managing to stay with them the whole way. I telephoned Aileen Gordon and got on quite well with her; she's quite small; we are going to see *The Sting* on Sunday. She says she might come down to Meadowbank to see me racing on Friday. I must remember to phone Mum at the Scottish Office tomorrow to see if she could buy me a new pair of trousers.

Evening: 8 x 300 metres (2 minutes' recovery) average of 42 seconds

Before Bed: Arm-action; press-ups; sit-ups; squats

1976 After being at the physio, Roger phoned. We ran a light session. *Pixie Mia Farrow lookalike* (who has been out of my life since December) was at Meadowbank this evening. She looked beautiful.

She Walks In Beauty

'She walks in beauty, like the night
Of cloudless climes and starry skies,
And all that's best of dark and bright
Meets in her aspect and her eyes…'

Lord Byron

I got to bed at 10.00 p.m. tonight. Good boy!

Evening: 5 x 200 metres (jog 2 minutes recovery) 24 seconds; I ran in my tracksuit

Before Bed: Arm-action; press-ups; situps; (9.15 hours sleep)

23rd April, 1973 Boy was it some day at work at Thomas Graham & Sons. Scott came back from his week off. I stayed in at lunchtime to help out with the workload. Roy was up to his usual nonsense and I confronted him about it. Well, the line of cost clerks were aghast; they kept their heads down; their mouths agape and their ears open. It almost ended in a fight as Roy wanted to go boxing, but I stormed off to cool down. It took an age traversing Edinburgh and I got back to Porty at 6.00 p.m. for a quick dinner; en-route to the Edinburgh Mineral Club, Betty dropped me off at Meadowbank. I was running well. I quite fancy the *Simone de Beauvoir Philosophy Queen*. Dougie gave me a lift home. I've picked up a chill so may stay off work tomorrow.

Evening: 9 x 150 metres (jog/walk recovery); quite fast in 17-18 seconds

1978 I was up around 8.00 am. It was a lovely morning. *Diana* and I collected the papers and took the dog to Portobello Park. After breakfast I lounged around reading the papers before going up to Meadowbank. I wasn't going to run, trusting that my indoor performances would get me into the Scotland team, but Coach Walker said no, I had to run as I've no outdoor pedigree for selection for the half mile. I relented and decided to race Paul. It was a nerve wracking, tension filled race. I just managed to win it on the line in a personal best time of 1 minute 50 seconds. We were both given the exact same time and the photo-finish couldn't separate us, although I was given the nod. I was delighted, but a bit annoyed with my tactics as I gave Paul 15 yards at 600 metres, but ran a sub 24 seconds last 200. A good crowd of people watched the race unfold including Denis Davidson who was impressed with my run. It should now earn me selection for the Greece v Wales v Luxembourg v Scotland match in Athens next month. Afterwards I picked up the Portobello crew and we went out to Oxgangs for Iain's do; Mum made a fantastic job on the food front. Les Ramage and Doreen were there as was Anne's boyfriend Ian Cropley. Iain took care of Will giving him a bottle of whisky; he's really very good to Willie. At eight o'clock I drove *Diana* out to Silverknowes where she picked up her training gear and books. We went out for an easy 3 miles walk/jog. It was a lovely warm evening.

Afternoon (2.30 p.m.): 800 metres 1st 1 minute 50.2 seconds; a personal best; bad tactically; Paul was still 6 meters up on me with 100m to go; just won it on the tape

Evening (9.00 p.m.): 3 miles jogging

24th April, 1973 Having caught a chill I stayed off work. I lounged around watching a very funny Bobby Darin and Sandra Dee film, *That Funny Feeling*. I felt a bit better and decided to go up to Meadowbank earlier than normal to do a weights session, before joining Coach Walker's squad. During the track session, of a sudden my legs turned to jelly. I still don't have a girl-friend which would improve life no end; I live in hope. I got in at 9.45 p.m. and am sitting listening to the *Top 30*.

Evening: Weights session; 8 x 300 metres (3 minutes recovery) 43; 43; 43; 44; 46; 46; 46; 46 seconds; the gym session really shattered me so I had to fight to finish the last four 300s

1976 I ran a strong session with Roger.

Morning: 500 metres 66.3 seconds; 400m 48.1 secs (Roger 48.6 secs); 300m 34.4 secs; 200m 22.2 secs (15 minutes recovery); a very good session as the weather was cold, wet and windy

25th April, 1973 After the flare up with Roy on Monday I went back to work today. It wasn't as bad as I thought it might be; perhaps he'd done some self-reflection because we were back to our generally good working relationship. Scott's Dad picked us up outside the showroom so I was home at a reasonable time before going up to Meadowbank to run a good session. I've decided to go the dance at Watsonians Rugby Club on Friday. Alan Bowes' sister is lovely, but out of my class.

Evening: 300 metres 41 seconds; 200m 26 secs; 2 x 150m 16-17 secs; 2 x 100m; 4 x 60m with a short walk back recovery

26ᵗʰ April, 1974 With thinking about going out tonight the day at work dragged. Gaga gave me a lift to Meadowbank and I ran a very hard session with Norman Gregor, before Gaga dropped me at the ABC where I met Aileen Gordon to go to see *The Sting*. She wasn't as pretty as I'd recalled through the mizz of alchohol, but she was lovely company and it was a nice evening out; she says she's coming to Meadowbank on Sunday to watch me race.

Evening: 6 x 200 metres at 90% effort; walk back recovery; Norman and I were absolutely shattered seeing stars!

1976 A very hard session.

Evening: 4 x 2 x 200 metres (30 seconds recovery; 5-10 minutes between sets); I was sick as a dog afterwards

27ᵗʰ April, 1973 Gaga's car started okay so I got out to Morningside and into work early. I'm unsure if I'll go to this dance this evening, especially as I didn't go out to buy a new pair of loons. Anyway, I tossed a coin and ended up going, with Scott and Dougie picking me up at 8.00 p.m. We went to the Waverley Bar then out to Watsonians Rugby Club. The dance was good fun. A very squashed car on the way back home with a much older woman and an innocent 16 year old young lad and a bit of, sort of, you know! Bon soir.

28ᵗʰ April, 1974 What weather for running in! There was a howling gale and it rained all day-absolutely wild, miserable and cold. I won my race in a good time. Mum and John came down to watch me run; it's the first time Mum's ever seen me racing; I think she quite enjoyed it. George Sutherland gave me a lift home. I'm going to bed early as I don't feel too well; a bit dizzy.

<u>Scottish League:</u> 400 metres 1st 50.0 seconds; a personal best; the weather was terrible with a howling gale; 4 x 400m relay 1st split approximately 50 secs

29th April 1975 I was just beaten in the dip in a 100 metres time trial by Scott Brodie and Drew McMaster; we were all given the same time; I was pretty disappointed and was on the phone to Coach Walker for an hour afterwards telling him so; he told me I'm expecting to beat everyone whether it's McMaster over a 100 or Paul over a half mile and to just except I'm running well and to focus instead on the European Junior 400 metres.

<u>Afternoon (4.30 p.m.):</u> 100 metres time trial McMaster; Brodie; Hoffmann all in 10.8 seconds; thereafter I ran 3 x 3 x 120m in 13-14 secs

The Waste Land

*'April is the cruellest month, breeding
lilacs out of the dead land, mixing
memory and desire, stirring
dull roots with spring rain…'*

T. S. Eliot

30th April, 1978 I'm glad not to be racing today; the weather is shocking with heavy rain, very windy and blooming cold too. I instead ran a session on my own-a 600 metres. All things considered I was pleased with it. Afterwards I sat in the Meadowbank lounge all afternoon with *Diana the goddess of love and hunting;* Gavin Miller joined us. After phoning her Mum. *Diana* was upset. She was saying to her what a poor mother she was and how she might just end it all.

Diana phoned her back and had a long conversation and says she sounded much better. Late afternoon I went for a run around Arthurs Seat; it was absolutely freezing. Heather had baked a chocolate cake and in the evening I enjoyed a couple of slices. Late on *Diana* and I went for a wee jog together; later she rang her mum to ensure she was okay.

Morning (10.30 a.m.): **600 metres 80.4 seconds; on my own; cold, wet and windy; actually the quickest run of the winter**

Afternoon (4.30 p.m.): **4 miles**

Evening (9.00 p.m.): **Easy 2.5 miles jog with Diana**

1st May, 1973 A fine May morning. When Gaga and I drove through Arthurs Seat there were still some people about who had been washing their faces in the morning dew-a long standing Edinburgh tradition. On the walk to work I bought *The Hornet* comic at Bairds Newsagent's where I used to work and then strolled up Morningside Drive and down through Morningside Park and on to Graham's at Balcarres Street. As I was working hard, the morning flew by. At tea-time Angus gave Scott and me a lift to Mayfield. Once home I watched a John Wayne film called *The Flying Seabees* before going for a run round Portobello Golf Course.

Evening: **30 minutes Fartlek; I reckon I covered between 4.5 and 6 miles**

2nd May, 1978 I was up at 5.30 a.m. this morning thinking it was 6.30 a.m. I had Derek dancing around as I threatened to pour the cold contents of his hot water bottle over him. We then crept through to awaken Tom. Back to bed till 6.45 a.m. then out for a run. I put in a good morning on the studying front, a curry lunch with the boys at Kidds then we went out looking for an engagement ring for Tom; £36-what a waste of money! Back into a warm library for 90 minutes of Sociology before driving down to Glenrothes to train with Drew Harley and Roy Buchanan; Stuart Hogg supervised the session. It's a good feeling knowing I'm handling such a good sprinter as Drew yet knowing I'm actually half-miling. Having this speed reserve gives me a lot of confidence. Afterwards Drew and Ann invited me back for a meal. I really didn't have the time, but driving back to Broughty Ferry I was thinking how great it is that because of athletics I could go anywhere in Britain and know people. *Diana the goddess of love and hunting* phoned at 8.00 p.m. Mrs Neve served up my first non-pastry based meal-great, I just wish I'd mentioned it to her 6 months ago and I'd be a couple of pounds lighter. We all had a couple of drinks at Jolly's before retiring to read up on the Russian economy.

Morning (6.30 a.m.): 3 miles steady

Afternoon (5.30 p.m.): 6 x 150 metres (7 minutes recovery) with Drew Harley

3rd May, **1976** I flew out to Athens.

4th May, 1975 I was running extraordinarily well, just floating along; the warm weather helped, but an annoying wind against in the home straight

Morning: 500 metres 63.1 seconds; 400m 48.7 secs; 300m 34.6 secs; 200m 22.5 secs

5th May, 1976 I'm part of a select group of British athletes including Adrian Weatherhead, Ian Stewart etc. invited out to Athens to an invitational meeting. It's nine months since I was last here. The weather has been hot for the past few days. As usual all the distance guys have been out pounding the streets, with most of them trying to avoid Stewart! I ran relatively poorly, going out slowly and finishing with too much under the bonnet.

Evening: Athens Invitation 400 metres

1. Joe Chivers, 47.8 seconds; 2. Hoffmann 48.4 secs (24.5/23.9 secs!)

6th May, 1973 I ran my first official 400 metres race today and won it; and also a leg in the relay. Mike Williams won the A race for Pitreavie; he's likely to be my main rival at the Scottish Youth Championships next month, but I feel quite confident. On the way back I stopped off at Meadowbank for a wee while, before going home to watch Hitchcock's film, *The Birds*. I've got a terrible cold.

Scottish Young Athletes League, Pitreavie

400 metres B 1st 52.9 seconds (official personal best);

400m in the relay-approximately 55 secs

1974 Oh no, it's Monday. It was a long, boring day at Thomas Graham & Sons. Travelling across the city after work I was absolutely shattered. But, great news! Paul and I have been selected to run for Scotland in a match in two weeks' time. We're on our way!

Evening: **2 x 300 metres (15 minutes recovery) 35.2; 35.5 seconds with Stewart McCallum**

1978 A morning of studying before running a good session at Meadowbank. After an aerotone bath at Portobello Baths I came back to watch (John) Robson run a very good 800 metres. I'm thinking of doubling up and racing him in three weeks' time at the East of Scotland Championships, although Coach Walker doesn't approve of me running two events.

Morning: **5 x 300 metres with walk 100m recovery 38; 38; 41; 38; 38 seconds; that's my limit VO2-wise. Weight 145lbs**

7th May, 1973 After a pleasant weekend on the athletics front it was back to that Monday morning feeling as I trecked along Balcarres Street and back to work. The morning passed quite quickly. At lunchtime I went out with Roy for a haircut; what a bloody mess! In the evening I was running quite well. Coach Walker gave me a bit of a telling off about yesterday at the Scottish Young Athletes' meeting at Pitreavie even though I ran a personal best of 52.9 seconds and it was my debut. He said I should have insisted on running against Mike Williams in the A race. However, I'm confident I'll beat him at the Scottish Youth Championships. Anyway, despite that, he's told both Paul and me we're in the E.A.C. team for the British League match at Wimbledon this weekend. Exciting times. Last summer I couldn't get in to the youth team; now it's straight in to the senior team. It's great that Paul's going too. We should get a laugh with the likes of the hammer thrower Willie Robertson etc.

Evening: **Technique runs followed by 3 x 100 metres flat out; I was ahead of Derek Smith on each run**

1978 I studied from 8.00 a.m. for a few hours before going up to Meadowbank to run the time trial Coach Walker had scheduled. Given there was a very cold wind I thought it was a superb run; also I didn't feel great at all. I just wasn't flowing the way I do at my best. It was a hard distance to judge (700 metres). I've taken a couple of things from it. First, I was strong at the end. And second, I can crush my personal best of 1 minute 50 seconds. I'm looking forward to my second serious 800 metres race, a week today in Athens. Paul gave me £20 which was a welcome boost. *Diana* wrote out my last essay of coursework and then I ran an easy and enjoyable four miles over Portobello Golf course; being a Saturday tea-time there were only one or two golfers out. The trees surrounding the park are in full bloom. The sunshine transforms life in Edinburgh.

Lovliest Of Trees, The Cherry Now

*'Loveliest of trees, the cherry now
Is hung with bloom along the bough…'*

A.E. Houseman

As I floated across the bouncy turf I reflected on how well life is going on the athletics, study and love-life fronts as well as enjoying life with Will and Josephine. Happy days. It's important to enjoy the moment, but without tempting the gods.

Afternoon (12.30 p.m.): 700 metres 93.2 seconds (400m approximately 51 secs) Cold and windy; really pleased; 4 x 200m (walk back recovery) 26secs

Afternoon (5.00 p.m.): 4 miles steady

Evening (9.00 p.m.): 2 miles jog/walk with Diana

8th May, 1974 The weather was so lovely I stayed off work. I met Paul and we went in to Lilywhites to look at their range of spikes. As usual we don't have a penny to rub together, so all we could do was drool over them and dream of what might be. Afterwards we took a wee tootle in to Princes Street Gardens and had a game of putting. Thereafter we wandered down to Meadowbank and chanced our hand going in to see the manager, Andy Bull, to ask if we could get a job for the summer holidays. Although he's reprimanded us a few times over the years he's got a bit of a soft spot for us; he probably sees us as likeable rogues. The day ended on a sour note as I had a big argument with Coach Walker in the evening.

Evening: 500 metres 65.0 seconds (p.b.) I went through the quarter in 51.9 secs; it was very windy; I ran it badly; followed by 5 x 80m flat out, all between 8.7 and 9.0 secs

1976 I made my own way out to West London Stadium to meet up with the E.A.C. team for the British League Division 1 match. Paul made a tremendous breakthrough in the 800 metres running down Pete Browne (who ran for Britain against East Germany last weekend) getting a big personal best of 1 minute 48.8 seconds. I ran well and almost caught Glen Cohen on the line; he's the UK's second best quarter miler, so it was quite encouraging.

British League 100 metres 4th 11.0 seconds; 400m 1. Cohen 47.6 secs 2. Hoffmann 47.7 secs; 4 x 100m relay; 4 x 400m relay (48.3 secs split)

1978 A rather lovely and different day. Josephine was away up town to see Heather into the hospital. It was such a soft, warm May day, spur of the moment, Will and I drove down to Stobo in Peebleshire, to where Paul and I used to camp when we were boys. I settled down for a few hours with my back against a tree and sat reading John Kenneth Galbraith's *The Great Crash*. It was glorious sitting out; John Buchan would have done this as a student when he was up in the Borders on holiday from Oxford 80 years previously. It was sunny without a cloud in the sky; the only sounds, the birds in full voice interspersed with the gentle ripple and plashing of the River Tweed. Cows grazed happily in an adjacent field. Grandpa Willie settled back and read his Daily Express whilst the dog nuzzled up beside him. A Scottish version of Adlestrop.

Adlestrop

Yes, I remember Adlestrop-
The name, because one afternoon
Of heat the express-train drew up there
Unwontedly. It was late June

The steam hissed. Someone cleared his throat.
No one left and no one came
On the bare platform. What I saw
Was Adlestrop-only the name

And willows, willow-herb, and grass,
And meadowsweet, and haycocks dry,
No whit less still and lonely fair
Than the high cloudlets in the sky.

And for that minute a blackbird song
Close by, and round him, mistier,
Farther and farther, all the birds
Of Oxfordshire and Gloucestershire.

Edward Thomas

At mid-day we wandered down to Eddleston for a pub lunch at the Horseshoe Inn. Will enjoyed fish 'n chips whilst I had a curry soup and some scampi. Once back to Portobello I sat out in the greenhouse all afternoon studying, before going for a massage at Denis Davidson's and then down to the track to run a few swift 150s. A lovely day; often when you do something spur of the moment it's more enjoyable; and especially good to have spent quality time with Gaga.

<u>Evening: 4 x 150 metres</u>

9th **May, 1978** If anything the weather was even better than yesterday; there wasn't even a light zephyr, not a cloud in the sky and the sun was beating down. The day was so fine Josephine packed her paint box and along with Grandpa Willie we took another wee tootle down to Stobo, Peebleshire.

Josephine spent the morning by the side of the River Tweed, painting with the pastoral woodland looking at its sylvan best. Will sat and read his newspaper whilst the dog strolled about; its paws were so muddy I had to throw her in the river-at least that's my excuse. As I have an exam in Dundee tomorrow I studied for several hours and also sunbathed too. We stopped off for an ice cream in Peebles before heading back to Portobello for lunch. Mum and my sister Anne were down. Mid-afternoon I had an aerotone bath and swam a few lengths of Portobello Baths, followed by an excellent track session. It's my last before racing for Scotland in Athens in five days' time in a second head to head with Paul. *Diana the goddess of love and hunting* and I met up at Demarcos at Tollcross for a coke float before enjoying a light Chinese meal at the Ping On in Stockbridge. These are good days.

Morning (8.00 a.m.): 3 miles

Evening (7.00 p.m.): 6 x 200 metres (3 minutes recovery) 23 seconds; just floating along; very controlled and relaxed; I'm now starting to feel the benefits of the good work over the winter and spring, but I've Paul to face on Sunday, along with other international half-milers; I'm confident of breaking the 1.50 barrier

10th **May, 1978** I was up at 6.45 a.m. to drive up to Dundee for the Economic Development exam. I'd picked Tom up as he was sitting it too and Grandpa Willie came along for the trip. Afterwards, Will and I went for a coffee at Kidds and drove back to Edinburgh for 2.30 p.m. It was good to take Will out and he enjoyed his day. After lunch I popped up to Edinburgh to get some Greek drachmas for the trip to Athens. Denis gave me a rub; as ever he was in good form saying all the right things about how well he thinks I'll run. Back to Porty to watch Liverpool win the European Cup followed by an excellent Play of the week-Terence Rattigan's The Winslow Boy.

11ᵗʰ May, 1973 No work today as Paul and I are away for our first trip to Englandshire; he phoned at 10.30 a.m. and we met up at mid-day. The bus left at 3.00 p.m. mopping up all the office workers; at 16 years of age we're the youngest on the E.A.C. team by a good bit, so we get our legs pulled by the likes of the hammer-thrower Willie Robertson, but we're able to give as good as we get, at least until he gets a hold of us! It was a long journey down, but I enjoyed playing cards which passed some of the time. En-route we stopped off at a transport cafe, but the prices were just ridiculous and way above my budget. We didn't arrive at Leicester until quite late joining the others for a pint and some chips before we hit the deck.

1978 I was up early to give Jo a lift up to the Edinburgh Sketching Club before meeting *Diana the goddess of love and hunting* at Waverley Station to take the airport bus out to Turnhouse to fly down to London. I met Roger down there as well as David; I haven't seen Roger for ages so it was good to catch up; he's enjoying life. He's wintered in Paris, partly to improve his French and also to be guided by Jean-Claude Nallet, the former European champion at 400m hurdles. He's beginning a banking career with Barclays and on the way to his first million! On the flight out to Athens I was talking with Stewart McCallum; he's excellent company. On landing, as usual, you're hit by the heat and the smell of air fuel. It's a heady mix and immediately sets off a hint of adrenalin and the firing up of the senses that I'm here on a mission. At Athens Airport there was the usual hassle and it took an age for our luggage to come through. I was fortunate-guys like Stewart Atkins lost their kit, including spikes. That's never happened to me. Years ago, Roger gave me a good tip on my first race abroad to always carry my spikes, vest and shorts as part of my personal hand luggage. Whilst sitting around I wrote a letter and posted it off to *Diana*. Late evening a few of us sat out at an open air cafeteria and enjoyed a small snack before eventually retiring to bed at 2.00 a.m. I'm rooming with Stewart Atkins and Andy Kerr.

12th May, 1978 Athens This morning, before the temperature climbed up to 25 degrees or so I ran an easy three miles going out and back to the stadium and the adjacent warm-up track. Having raced here in 1975 and 1976 everything came back to me immediately. A team meeting was held there at 10.00 a.m. By then the temperature was picking up and it was really quite hot. In the afternoon, Roger, David and I went down to the track; Roger ran well over some hurdles, however Dave hurt his leg attempting the same-stupid bugger! On the way back to our hotel we picked up some ice at the Olympic Hotel so hopefully it will help aid his recovery. In the evening we went out together to a local fishermen's restaurant; it was an interesting experience and the fish was good. A few of the girls tagged along. We finished off the evening sitting outside enjoying a slice of gateaux and coffee. Before bed I telephoned *Diana the goddess of love and hunting*.

Morning (8.00 a.m.): 3 miles easy run

Morning (10.00 a.m.): Light jogging and stretching

13th May, 1978 Athens I slept well. The couple of small beers last night did the trick nicely. For a second day running there was a Scotland team meeting at mid-day up at the stadium. Roger and I sat out in the sun for an hour, Roger writing, me reading, the world completely unaware of the reflective Edinburgher Samuel Pepys.

I went back to my room for an hour's siesta; however and most annoyingly just as I was drifting off to sleep I was awakened by phone calls from Ewan Murray and then Lawrie Smith. I always find it difficult to be more than civil to the former. Since we were kids Paul and I have never liked him; we always found him to be a bit of a weasel and more interested in how officials were looked after. I recall us being treated as second class citizens on trains and over meal expenses and representative vests. It's reciprocated of course, because he doesn't like Paul or me; we were always too rebellious, radically challenging the status quo. I suspect if he ever had the opportunity to wield the knife he would. Anyway, whilst I'm running so well there's little that he can do.

In the evening Stewart Atkins, Andrew Kerr and a few others went out for a coffee and a slice of gateaux. Tomorrow's the big day-my second serious 800 metres race. After last month's 1 minute 50 seconds I'm confident of running faster, but nervous too. Mentally I've been steeling myself to the task. I'm very motivated and desperate to be selected for the half mile at the Commonwealth Games; my primary motivation is Grandpa Willie. More than anything I want to run well for him. The half is different from the quarter as during the race itself I've so much more time to think, so, around the 500 metres mark to help spur me on I've been using daft little mantras...*First to the tape-first to the tape; never give in-never give in*; alongside *You're running this for Will* etc.

14th May, 1975 I went up to Lizars for the interview for the driving job, but I've no chance of getting it. The application forms for Borough Road College arrived today; they're keen for me to come down and study P.E. In the afternoon I walked along to the garage to get new clutch parts for Gaga's car. Having been off for several days with a sore hamstring I went up to Meadowbank to do my first session this week. I beat McMaster twice in trials over 100 metres; things are looking promising for the international junior season ahead.

Evening: 2 x 100 metres time-trials 1st Hoffmann 10.7 seconds (p.b.) and 10.8 secs; McMaster was 2nd on each run

1977 Love in the morning rather than the mist; lunch at St Andrews Restaurant and then on to a summer fete where *Diana the goddess of love and hunting* and I bought an olde worlde bagatelle set; we played it all evening until ten o'clock-great fun.

Afternoon (4.00 p.m.): Squash

1978 Athens Well the big day has come around. In the morning I ran up to the stadium and then back down to the hotel. My hamstring has been giving me a little bit gyp, so I put some ice on it. I spent the afternoon in my room, but because of all the adrenalin couldn't sleep at all. I always hate these hours before a race. You want to think ahead to the race, but you also want to put it out of your mind too. You want to rest, but all the time your heart-rate is up and you are burning nervous energy. It's always difficult to strike that fine balance. If you weren't nervous you wouldn't run well. And as ever, the fact that I'm getting so nervous means I must think I can run well. It's also the tension of trying to make the Scotland Commonwealth Games team for Edmonton.

At 4.00 p.m. I wrote out several postcards for the folks back home then had an omelette and three slices of brown bread and honey. Before leaving for the warm-up track I had a warm shower. The blooming timetable was running three-quarters of an hour late which meant it was a real pain trying to keep warmed up, but not overdoing it; it only added to the tension. I'm someone who likes to go at the planned time; I hate hanging around, which of course only prolongs the agony; let's get it over and done with. The tension was unbearable, however I ran fantastically well to win the race in a big personal best time of one minute forty seven point nine seconds which will surely get me into the Scotland team for Edmonton. The mental relief afterwards was just immense.

When I say I ran well, I raced very poorly. Going down the back straight I was last of the eight man field; somehow I extricated myself from the adverse situation, ran wide on the bend and chased the leaders down the home straight, just pipping Paul on the line. He ran a personal best too which should get him into the Scotland team for Canada, which is great. Afterwards I could hardly wait to phone Coach Walker. Yesterday I hadn't broken one minute fifty; now I've dipped inside one minute forty eight seconds and didn't feel tired at the end. After the relay I managed to get through to East Claremont Street; Coach Walker was delighted. In the late evening we went to a fancy night club in the shadow of the Acropolis. They served up some lovely grub and some great music too; although I was whacked, it was a great evening with some smashing fun and laughs. A good day. A good evening. And good times in both senses of the word.

<u>**Morning (10.00 a.m.):**</u> **2 miles jog**

<u>**Greece v Luxembourg v Wales v Scotland**</u>

800 metres 1. Hoffmann 1.47.9 (p.b.); 2. Paul Forbes 1.48.0

4 x 400m relay 1. Scotland (Hoffmann 48.0 secs)

From *The Scotsman*, 15th May, 1978 Report from Sandy Sutherland

'...The 800 was a Scottish monopoly with the Edinburgh Athletic Club colleagues providing another thrilling race, almost a repeat of the trial last month. Paul Forbes, winner of this race in last year's match, took the pace and Peter Hoffmann again seemed content to lie at the back. But Hoffmann, who afterwards said his hamstring muscles were tight from the long wait-the programme ran an hour late-was nearly 15 metres down with 300 metres left yet again produced an incredible finish to catch his training partner right on the line...'

15th May, 1973 It was a lovely day, with the sun out. Bob Taylor, the Heating Manager gave me a lift along Balcarres Street to work. In the afternoon I spent the whole time hunting down invoices which had gone astray. After work Angus gave Scot and me a lift. After a mad dash I just caught the 42 bus at the Kings Buildings and back home to Porty. Gaga gave me a lift up to Meadowbank. David Jenkins gave me a telling off about my 400 metres at Wimbledon. It was only my second race and I did 52.4 seconds but he's told me to up my game. I actually felt quite flattered that out of all the dozens of kids at Meadowbank he should take the time to come over and speak to little old me; particularly as he can appear to be quite aloof. It's quite motivating. On another happy note, I see there's a couple of E.A.C. girls who fancy me!

Evening: **100 metres time trial 11.4 seconds; short, very fast clock 60; 80; 100; 120; 100; 80; 60m with a walk back recovery**

1974 A key date in life. Having worked at Dickensian Thomas Graham & Sons for almost two years now since being unceremoniously turfed out of Boroughmuir in September, 1972 with only two O Levels to my name and thereafter enduring the mind-numbing *ennui* of life at the blacking factory I've taken a very positive step. I went out to Telford College Annexe for an interview. I got on okay and they've accepted me to undertake a few Highers. Although I've got paltry qualifications I convinced them not only of my serious intent and motivation, but that I'm better than I appear on paper and that I'm especially well read; I threw in the odd line-I'm an autodidact etc., which raised a bemused look.

I'm excited about the prospect of student life and think I can do it. Hanging about with the likes of Roger Jenkins, Norrie Gregor, Adrian etc. has made me realise they're no brighter than me; it's just that I'm going to have to take a more unconventional route. I'm more mature now and self-aware that if you've got a wee bit of ability, are highly motivated and apply yourself then the world's your oyster. And I want to turn my life around. Sometimes in dull, quiet moments at my work bench at Balcarres Street I compose mini CVs which say 4 Highers and 7 O Levels and think, gosh, how great would that be? I realise I have to leave Graham's. I know what I want in life. I want to become more academic. I want to become a great athlete. And I want a girl-friend. The major issue is how I'm going to make it all happen, particularly financially, although I've got some loose ideas. If Mum could buy me a bus pass each month that would solve all my travel issues. Travelling from Porty to Telford will involve several bus trips each day, not to mention going up and down to Meadowbank for training each evening. Dad's more settled now and earning a good salary as a Chief Officer working abroad. If I could get an allowance of £25 each month from him then I think I could just get by; I'm currently paying Josephine £3 each week for my digs. I've got my scholarship card from Edinburgh District Council which gets me in to Meadowbank free and Coach Walker is brilliant the way he gives up his time not to mention always dipping his hand in to his pocket for two bob when I'm looking for an ice cold can of Lilt or Fanta when I'm gasping after a hard training session! Imagining how things might be, makes me very excited; it's given me a real buzz. And whilst I fantasise like Billy Liar and even be quite bemused about my highfalutin ideas, there's a strong kernel there that I believe I can make it all happen; it's not like when I was at Boroughmuir School.

It was such a beautiful sunny and warm day Paul and I watched the Jordanhill College Sportsday at Meadowbank. In the evening I went back to the doctor about my bronchitis which has got even worse; he gave me antibiotics. On the way home from Oxgangs to Porty I went in to see the Meadowbank manager, Mr Bull, about a summer holiday job; another positive wee step. So, a poor day on the athletics front, but perhaps a rich day to look back on one day; the day my future took a turn for the better..

16th May, 1975 I awoke with a bad cold so stayed in all day. I was looking at the European Junior rankings in this week's Athletics Weekly; although I don't appear in them I found them to be quite pleasing as I know I can improve significantly on my official best of 48.3 seconds. A chap called Henryk Galant from Poland is top with 47.3 seconds. In the evening I gave Coach Walker a tinkle and we had a good chat about what might be possible.

17th May, 1973 I took my training bag to work. It was a quick day. Roy dropped me off at Oxgangs for my tea, before I went up to Pentland Community Centre to meet the rest of the team to travel out to Fernieside for the Edinburgh Boys Clubs' Championships. Paul won the 800 and 1500 metres; Duncan Baker was there and won the 100 and 200 metres in the younger age group. I won the 200 and 400 metres; my first titles since winning the Interscholastics Championships 100 yards when I was at Hunters Tryst Primary School. On the way home to Portobello, Duncan and I had an argument with a bus inspector. I didn't get home until 11.30 p.m. and had some coke. I've now added a couple of wee shields to the two medals I've won.

1973 Edinburgh Boys Clubs' Championships

Evening: 200 metres and 400 metres; I won both titles

18th May, 1973 A lovely sunny day, so much so I bought a couple of ice poles. Now I'm flavour of the month again and Roy's favourite cost clerk he took me home to Lasswade for lunch. He has a lovely wife and the view from their house is super. In the afternoon I bought some Post Office savings stamps before meeting Gaga for a lift home from Waughs the Butchers; he gave John a lift too-he also works in the shop. As ever, Star Trek was excellent, The Way To Eden and the start of a new It's A Knockout series meant for a good television evening; Stuart Hall and Eddie Waring always make me laugh! My sister Anne is staying; when she got back from the mineral club with Jo and Heather we went down to St Andrews Restaurant for a fish supper.

19th May 1975 As it's the Edinburgh Holiday Nana and co. were away for the day. Paul phoned and came down to Porty for lunch. What a fucking laugh we had throwing water around. After a game of putting down at the lovely Rosefield Park we had some ice cream from Arcaris then went to the fun-fair; I won a yo-yo.

Evening: Gym circuit

1977 I ran a good session which has given me some confidence; my leg was less sore on the second repetition. Afterwards Denis gave me a long massage. Later on I had a Chinese meal with Susan Rettie. Despite the late hour it was soft and warm; I stood out and chatted with old John Binnie from across Durham Road; he was enjoying an evening pipe. I like chatting to him and hearing his tales of long ago.

Afternoon (2.00 p.m.): 2 x 300 metres (1) 34.1 seconds; (2) 34.4 secs; I set Davie Reid up 20 metres

1978 I spent the morning studying before swimming a few lengths of Portobello Baths. It was another glorious day. Sandy and Liz Sutherland live adjacent to the baths at Bellfield Street and I dropped by for half an hour; to an extent Sandy is at the heart of our sport; it's like a hub and spokes model. I sometimes think what a force for good the Sutherlands are in the Edinburgh and Scottish athletics community. Duncan Mckechnie was also there; I'm very fond of Duncan-he's one of the good guys and a bit like

Sandy, always excellent company. Dad picked me up at 2.00 p.m. and dropped me off at Meadowbank; we had a salad, before the E.A.C. team bus left for Liverpool. *Diana the goddess of love and hunting came* down for the trip. We had an excellent card game going and it was generally a good trip down other than Ross Hepburn blaring out punk music from the back of the bus! We joined the team at a nearby hotel for a meal before retiring early for the night.

20th May, 1978 We awoke to the sun shining in to the room and a petrol tanker parked outside our hotel window. They took a while to serve up breakfast; thereafter we left for Kirkby Stadium; it was good to arrive early. For lunch I just had a few slices of brown bread and honey. I won the 200 metres very easily; given I've been doing half mile training I was surprised at how well I was running, including both relays. On the way back *Diana the goddess of love and hunting* and I enjoyed an omelette at 1971 prices, much to the chagrin and dismay of the waitress. Someone must have removed the outer current price list, leaving the original one in its stead!

British League Division 3:

200 metres 1st 22.2 seconds
4 x 100m relay 1st 42.6 secs
4 x 400m 1st 3.17.3 (48.3 secs tactical last leg)

Going Down Hill On A Bicycle: A Boy's Song

'...Dart, with heedful mind;
The air goes by in a wind.

Swifter and yet more swift,
Till the heart with a mighty lift
Makes the lungs laugh, the throat cry:-
'O bird, see: see, bird I fly...'

Henry Charles Beeching

21st May, 1975 After lunch I popped up to Meadowbank; I was running well against George McNeil. After tea I watched the Lothian Schools' races-Derek Innes ran well. I spent much of the time chatting with Meg Ritchie. Sandy Sutherland gave me a lift home, as he did earlier in the week.

Afternoon: Trained with George McNeil 4 x 50 metres; I was given a 2m start; 6 x 50m this time starting level with George; standing starts; very encouraging on the second set-felt I was flying!

1977 It was disappointing to have travelled all this way to wake up this morning to discover there was a gale blowing which ruined any opportunity of a good time. Anyway, I managed to beat Sale's Carl Hamilton in a respectable time. In the evening Norman Gregor and I joined Ian Stewart for a few drinks and a chat. As ever Stewart was straight talking, but I enjoyed his company. You could learn a lot from him, particularly if I move up to the half mile. He has Adrian's grit, but a harsher more overt manner. On the bus trip home I played cards throughout the night. Ironically, after yesterday's adverse weather, the outlook along the Biggar Road at 6.00 a.m. was quite stunning. It was a beautiful sunny morn with a soft light cast across the countryside; the old stone built houses glowed-it all looked quite magical. I think I'd be happy living in this part of the world. I hit the sack at 7.00 a.m. and didn't arise until 1.00 p.m.

British League

400 metres 1. Hoffmann 48.7 seconds; 2. C. Hamilton (Sale) 48.8 secs

4 x 400m relay E.A.C. (J. Scott; S. Laing; P.Hoffmann (48.2); N. Gregor) 3rd

1978 I had a light breakfast of a couple of boiled eggs. Despite having had three races yesterday and travelling back from Liverpool late at night I went up to the track at lunchtime to train with Paul. It was a glorious day-typical-it always is for the women's East v West match. I ran what I regard as my best ever session. Not necessarily time wise, but I base that comment on the way I was feeling and handling the session. I was completely in control and just floated along with no effort, always feeling there was another gear there if I needed it.

Whilst everything was being set up the Meadowbank staff kept the inside two lanes free from hurdles. We had the track to ourselves other than athletes and officials slowly gathering for the meeting. Coach Walker was away, but Adrian (he's injured) kindly came down to hold the watch for us. Following the Pros' advice-look good, feel good, run good! Paul and I wore identical outfits-white Kenyan vests, green Adidas shorts and white baseball caps. We alternated a 300 metres apiece at the front with each other moving up to ease ourselves through the line together. I thought we looked just great. In some respects it was the pinnacle of all we've worked hard for over the past seven years. And yet those watching would have thought our successes were effortless. Even Adrian was stunned at the quality of the session and afterwards told us to go away for five days as he was concerned we'd leave it all on the training track! I didn't stay on for the meeting and instead spent the afternoon studying and then ran four miles in the early evening.

Afternoon (12.30 p.m.): 3 x 600 metres (10 minutes' recovery) 79.3; 79.9; 77.5 seconds; a lovely day with a slight breeze; a remarkable session

Evening (6.00 p.m.): 4 mile steady run

22nd May, 1975 Really great news! The British Board phoned me up this morning to invite me to run at the British Games at Crystal Palace, London a week on Saturday. I gave Coach Walker a tinkle immediately afterwards. Come the evening I wasn't running too well.

Evening: 3 x 300 metres (25 minutes recovery) 34.4; 35.2; 34.6 seconds

23rd May, 1974 I returned to Graham's this morning and had a long talk with the manager, Davie Rogan. Although it kicked off about my regular absences and the prospect of the sack it turned into a positive meeting and a positive outcome. I was entirely open with him that I'm keen to make something of my life and that I have to move on. He was surprisingly reasonable and ended up being quite supportive; we both accept my days at Balcarres Street are numbered and coming to an end. And whilst athletics is getting in the way, he's now aware that I'm not going to sit about with two O levels to my name in a dead-end job, where there is little opportunity of advancement. So, we've agreed I'll leave but at a time of my choosing. Fair play to Davie Rogan. And I still received my full pay too! My legs are still pretty tight, but just runnable.

Evening: **2 x 200 metres (2 minutes recovery) 24 seconds; (10 mins rec) 2 x 150 yards (2 mins rec) 16 secs; (rest) 8 x 60m**

1975 B.E.A. phoned me this morning about my trip to London next week for the British Games so I went up to their office at Hanover Street to book my flight. After lunch I went up to Meadowbank and ran a terrible session. Coach Walker had an interview today for the Assistant Manager's post at Meadowbank; fingers crossed for him. Gaga and I went out to Oxgangs; Iain came down to Porty with us and chopped the hedge.

Afternoon: **500 metres 66 seconds (51.5 through 400m); 2 x 200m (30 secs recovery) 22.9/27.3; 4 x 150m (jog 50 recovery); a very disappointing session**

1976 I ran a solid session before settling back to watch the women's East v West match. I had lunch with *Pixie Mia Farrow lookalike*. I've hardly seen her this year. She's more beautiful than ever. She was encouraging me to make the Olympic team; I said it wasn't looking promising. In the evening the *Simone de Beauvoir Philosophy Queen* and I went to Inverleith Park and then back to her home to watch an enjoyable Tom Courtenay film, Otley, followed by England v Brazil with the Canarinhos scoring in the last minute.

The sunlight on the garden

'The sunlight on the garden
Hardens and grows cold,
We cannot cage the minute
Within its nets of gold,
When all is told
We cannot beg for pardon.

Our freedom as free lances
Advances towards its end;
The earth compels, upon it
Sonnets and birds descend;
And soon, my friend,
We shall have no time for dances.

The sky was good for flying
Defying the church bells
And every evil iron
Siren and what it tells:
The earth compels,
We are dying, Egypt, dying

And not expecting pardon,
Hardened in heart anew,
But glad to have sat under
Thunder and rain with you,
And grateful too
For sunlight on the garden.'

Louis MacNeice

Morning: 3 x 300 metres (15 minutes recovery) 34.4; 34.3; 34.5 seconds

24th May, 1973 A lovely start to the morning. I bumped into the lovely *Pixie Mia Farrow lookalike* on her way to Mary Erskine School. Marion forgot to bring me in my tape recorder so that was a tad disappointing. I was running quite well except my knee is a bit sore. I enjoyed the charms of Mandy McLean-from a distance, of course; she wouldn't pass the time of day with the likes of little old me.

Evening: 2 x 4 x 60 metres very fast

1978 I watched the Phillips' Night Of Athletics which was pretty poor, but (John) Robson's devastating kick scared me. Apart from the Kenyan, Wilson Waigwa, down the home-straight he blew everyone away, including Rod Dixon. He also ran 1.47.8 last season which is quicker than my best time in Athens. Am I taking on too much on Saturday by doubling up against him immediately after the 400 metres final? We'll find out!

Afternoon (3.00 p.m.): 4 miles steady run

25th May, 1974 It was great to awaken to such a beautiful morning, with no wind and the sun shining down. I was quite excited about competing in the East Districts Championships at Meadowbank. Without winning anything I made a major breakthrough. I broke 50 seconds for the first time; later on I was astonished at my 200 metres time as my previous best from last year was only 23.4 seconds. It was a great day all round and I really enjoyed myself; the regular hard work is paying off and I feel a million dollars! Afterwards Paul came back to Porty for tea and then we joined Davie Reid up town to see a rubbish film. On the way home I bumped in to Dave Coombe-a lovely bloke.

1974 East Districts Championships

Senior 400 metres

Heat 53.2 seconds
Final 2. Hoffmann 49.8 secs (p.b.)

Junior 200 metres

Heat 23.8 secs

Final 1. G. Malcolm 21.5 secs; 2. R. Jenkins 21.8; 3. A. Harley 21.8; 4. Hoffmann 22.2 secs! (p.b.) Crikey, I don't know where that came from, but imagine running that and only finishing fourth!

4 x 100m Relay 1. E.A.C. 42.4 secs; 2. E.S.H. 42.4 I ran the last leg

26th May, 1973 Early this morning we heard that my great-grandfather, Pumpa, has had a stroke. He's 91 years old so it's perhaps not surprising and yet he seemed fine two nights before when he was down for a wee visit. I went up early to collect my Athletics Weekly but it wasn't in-always a disappointment. The magazine is an integral part of the journey I'm on with my athletics. Paul's not interested it at all, but I find it inspiring to read the profiles of good international athletes or about my superior peers in Englandshire and the results home and abroad. It improves my knowledge about training principles. I feel it helps me lift my horizon from just Scotland and to keep aiming higher and higher. Later in the morning I went up to run at the East District Championships; there was no Youth 400 metres so I ran the 200 metres, making the final and equalling my best time. However, late afternoon I ran a stoater of a 400 metres leg for E.A.C in the medley relay.

1973 East Districts Championships

Youth 200 metres 4. Hoffmann 23.4 seconds; equals my p.b.

Youth 400/200/200/400 metres Medley Relay 1. E.A.C. (51.0 secs split)

1975 Coach Walker has officially been offered the Assistant Manager's post at Meadowbank. I'm pleased for him; having him based there is going to be a tremendous boon to us all, knowing we can call on his services at a moment's notice. I ran another good session with the Pro, Jimmy Smith, who's preparing to compete in the 3M Pro Track and Field Stars circus which is coming to Meadowbank. I like Jimmy-he's a lovely bloke; I like his coach too, old Alf Nicol who's a real character.

Evening: 3 x 2 x 200 metres (30 seconds recovery; 10-15 minutes between sets) (1) 21.7/25.2 secs (2) 22.2/26.0 secs (3) 23.1/25.1 secs

27th May, 1976 A disastrous race at Gateshead finishing second last behind the likes of Cohen; Marlow; Aukett and Chivers. I felt awful. I have no idea why I'm running so poorly; a few months ago I would have been unhappy with that time as part of a training session. What makes it so galling and disheartening is I have no idea why I'm running so poorly. With only two weeks until the Olympic Trials things are looking bleak…

Gateshead Superspike International

400 metres 7. Hoffmann 49.4 seconds

1978 Once again it was a lovely sunny, warm day with only a light breeze for the East District Championships; they always seem to strike it lucky for these championships, certainly since I've been going along. I spent an easy morning at home, before venturing up to Meadowbank. Much to Coach Walker's consternation I doubled up, with only a five minutes lap jog separating the final of the 400 metres and the 800 metres. In my own mind I set the championships ablaze winning both the quarter and the half. I did just enough to win the 400 metres from Ken Glass then carried on jogging for a lap before tackling John Robson in the half. He went out hard, but I just sat on him. Around the 500 metres mark I was feeling the effects of the previous three races, but I got an encouraging shout from John Scott and others which helped to spur me on. As we hit the home straight I moved wide to out-kick Robson. What was pleasing was it was more of a strength kick-not my usual zippy sprint finish. Dad, young Roddy and *Diana the goddess of love and hunting* were down watching, so it turned it in to a pretty special day which we could all share in. Coach Walker was relieved and smiling at the end, especially with selection for the Commonwealth Games only a week away. Meanwhile Paul ran well in Belfast last evening-a 1.49.6 to Steve Ovett's 1.49.

1978 East District Championships

800 metres Heat 1. Hoffmann 1.57

400m Heat

400m Final 1. Hoffmann 48.7 seconds

800m Final 1. Hoffmann 1.49.2 (Championship Record) 2. Robson 1.49.4

Postscript: A bit surprising to see it's still a championship record 40 years later!

28th May, 1973 On my way to pick up my Hornet comic from Bairds at Morningside Drive I saw *Pixie Mia Farrow lookalike* on her way to Mary Erskine School. My heart soars whenever I see her. Is it possible to get a lovelier start to the working week? That's a rhetorical question. The work day flew by. At the end of play I was quite lucky getting a lift home all the way from Morningside to Portobello from old Jimmy Wilson. Although he has a quick temper, Jimmy's a classy wee fellow. He's a very dapper dresser and friendly with a wee bit of class; for years you can understand why he was Graham & Sons representative. He's got a neat little Triumph Herald which goes along with his image; the car is a replacement for the Ford Cortina company car he used to have. He's done better in life than Grandpa Willie; he owns his own house; has a better car; and earns his corn in an easier way too; since he's retired he's now working beside us part-time in in the Costing Department. His health is much better than Will's too. In the evening Gaga gave me a lift out to Saughton to run in the Scottish Young Athletes' League. I won the 200 metres in a not bad time. Later, Eric Fisher was very good giving me a lift all the way home via Coach Walker's house where we dropped by for a chat.

Scottish Young Athletes' League

200 metres B Race 1. Hoffmann 23.6 seconds

4 x 100m Relay 1. E.A.C. 46.8 secs

29th May, 1978 It's a beautiful morning out; 1978's turning in to a lovely summer. I spent the morning studying for my upcoming exams. Norman Gregor phoned me. He's really got his work cut out; he will have to run low 51s to be selected for the Commonwealth Games. Early afternoon I took the dog to Portobello Park for a run about and then watched the Inter-Counties; not much to worry about there. After a rub at Denis's I met *Diana the goddess of love and hunting* at Demarcos for coffee and ice cream. In the evening I did some speedwork; I felt a bit sluggish, but it will come round quickly-it always does. Late on I watched the second part of The Godfather; it's magnificent. I lay and read before going off to sleep. Josephine just won't back down over *Diana*; so I guess I'll just have to.

Evening (6.00 p.m.): 6 x 150 metres

30th May, 1977 Yesterday whilst giving Dougie Flett a lift along London Road I was booked for speeding; for some stupid reason I always assumed with the road being so wide and with two lanes it had a 40 mph speed limit. Given I was in the Triumph Spitfire there was more than an element of *schadenfreude* when the policemen issued the ticket; anyway I had to go into the police station today with the documentation. On a happier note a good session at Meadowbank.

Evening: 4 x 200 metres (7 minutes recovery) 22.2; 21.7; 21.8; 22.3 seconds

1978 Given I'm pretty assured of my place in the Scotland Commonwealth Games team at 800 metres I've decided to contest the 400 metres at this weekend's Scottish Championships. It will give Paul a clear run at the half too.

With David, Roger and me all having won the title twice it's all to play for. All week the press have been building the race up as the race of the championships and it's been getting coverage in the papers, radio and television; STV is filming the event too. And today there was a photographer along snapping away at my every move at our training session. So, with such a sprint race coming up I'm trying to bring some speed around; I know I'll be strong against David and Roger down the home straight, but if I hope to win I'll need to be close to them at 300-certainly within 10 metres.

I ran a couple of hurdles with Alan Sumner and Norman Gregor. I went back home. Brian Meek from the Daily Express was on the phone asking me about the race and what my thoughts were. On the basis that David or Roger might read the article I made sure I came across as being positive; no point in giving them a psychological advantage. Later on I did a light session before going in to the Meadowbank physio; she was a very enthusiastic type.

Afternoon (1.00 pm.): **2 x 200 metres**

Evening (6.00 p.m.): **2 x 80 metres; 300 metres 34.8 seconds**

31st May, 1975 A very easy London morning before wandering down to Crystal Palace for the British Games. I met Coach Walker at the restaurant for a coffee and a chat. In the afternoon I made a big breakthrough winning the 400 metres breaking 48 seconds for the first time and also beating Bob Benn who has been one of the U.K'.s best Juniors for years. Later I ran a 200 metres and got another official p.b. Coach Walker and I flew back to Edinburgh and he gave me a lift home. A successful mission and it will bring me to the notice of the selectors for the European Junior Championships.

British Games
400 metres 1. Hoffmann 47.8 seconds (electrical timing 47.6-23.2/24.4 secs!) 2. B. Benn 48.2 secs
200m 4. Hoffmann 21.81 secs

1978 I studied all morning; in the 11 o'clock post there was a letter to say I've been selected to run for Great Britain against East Germany in the 800 metres. I'm partnering Sebastian Coe so I'm hoping for a personal best and a European qualifying time. I felt terrible for today's session-stiff and sore; it's probably with doing some speed-work the past few days as the countdown toward the Scottish Championships continues; the race may come a bit too soon for me. Afterwards, Denis gave me a great rub so that helped a little.

Evening: 2 x 200 metres; 150m; disappointingly slow

1st June, 1977 In the afternoon there were a few photographers at Meadowbank taking pictures to promote the upcoming G.B v Russia match which British Meat is sponsoring; the company hosted a reception afterwards. The weather was fine so late afternoon Davie; Paul; Lorraine; *Diana the goddess of love and hunting* and I went down to Stobo and swam in the River Tweed.

Afternoon: 6 x 60 metres from blocks; giving Paul and Davie Reid 2 metres

2nd June, 1975 After the weekend's exploits I've a sore abductor muscle so in the morning I visited Davie Campbell the physio at Duddingston Road. Talk about a change in the weather-it was snowing! At Meadowbank I had a slight argument with Coach Walker; but on a happier note, after my performance on Saturday I've been selected for the British senior team for the first time for the match in Dresden, East Germany. In the evening I went along to Kim's party; it was superb-great fun. I ended up running Jackie; Lynn; Paul; Fiona; Rab and the lovely *Pixie Mia farrow lookalike* home.

Evening: 2 x 4 x 150 metres 16 seconds (walk 250m recovery)

1978 Another lovely day, however as the day progressed a wind came up. First thing I took Dad's car out to Carnie's for a service; he left for Japan yesterday. I studied all morning; a break for a salad lunch, more studying and then back out to Corstorphine to collect the Opel Kadette. In the evening I went up to Meadowbank to run my heat at the Scottish Championships. Although I qualified comfortably it felt faster; clearly the half mile training has taken the edge off things speed-wise. Both the Jenkins' and Andy Kerr looked more impressive than me. Afterwards *Diana the goddess of love and hunting*, her wee brother and I went out to the Mei Kwei Restaurant for some Chinese food. It was a good call as it helped me to relax after the adrenalin created from racing. Later I watched half of the World Cup match between Argentina and Hungary. Back into the gladiatorial arena tomorrow to face David and Roger.

1978 Scottish Championships

400 metres heat 1. Hoffmann 49.7 seconds; it was windy and felt harder

3rd June, 1975 Coach Walker is still working at Heriot Watt University until he starts at Meadowbank. Now that I'm starting to get invites to race abroad we decided it was time to get a full passport, so I went out to the labs at Riccarton and Coach took some passport photographs. Come the evening a good session.

Evening: 2 x 4 x 200 metres (2-3 minutes recovery; 15 minutes between sets) 23; 23; 23; 23; 23; 23; 22; 24 seconds

1976 Having mostly given up any hope of running well at the Olympic Trials I've continued working hard, mainly with Roger. Yesterday I ran 8 x 100 metres in 11.5 seconds with a jog 100 recovery and dropped him. Today we'd planned to do a morning and afternoon session to help replicate two races at the Trials. Unfortunately for Roger he wasn't able to run in the afternoon as he has a slight niggle. I'm slightly more optimistic than I was a week ago. It was a lovely morning for the 500 metres and despite the early hour I ran well. I sat in on Roger to 400 metres then went past him very smoothly down the last 100 metres; I definitely had at least a second in hand. Perhaps we were overly-ambitious as after the evening session I felt a slight pull too.

Morning (9.45 a.m.): 500 metres 62.5 seconds (p.b.); we went through 400m in 49.7 seconds; I easily maintained that pace

Evening (6.00 p.m.): 300 metres 34.4 secs; on my own, so quite good

1978 I had a very easy morning; a little studying and a gentle walk in Portobello Park, half thinking about the afternoon's final, half putting it out of my mind. I went back home and had plenty of brown bread and honey then went up to Meadowbank. It was another lovely day with a slight breeze.

With it being the Commonwealth Games Trials the place was absolutely buzzing with excitement; a lot of people were looking forward to the 400 metres final. I felt less pressure than many others and more relaxed than normal. Not being the favourite I felt I had nothing to lose. On times this year both the Jenkins' and Kerr were the favourites for the medals in the quarter; also as I think I'm an automatic selection for the half mile I just wasn't as nervous as usual;

meanwhile Paul should have a clear road in the 800 metres to confirm his place alongside me in Edmonton.

Although it was a hot day I still warmed up in my blue Adidas wet suit; when racing I like to be warmer than usual, plus if you'll excuse the contradiction, it's a pretty cool outfit!

I felt good doing my strides and was excited about the race-looking forward to it rather than being worried; it was almost as if not having to run twice around the track came as such a bonus that I was taking the quarter in my stride. There was a big crowd there; partly because of the importance of the occasion, but helped too by the good weather, with several spectators sitting out with their tops off.

Before the race a lot of people wished me well. I ran a practice start round the bend and felt good. As I strolled back to the start there was a little bit of extra motivation; *Pixie Mia Farrow lookalike* was down to spectate. I hadn't seen her for ages. She was standing behind the fence between the track and the cafe. I looked at her and caught her eye; she smiled and waved. I thought, *Here's a great opportunity to show off in front of her-let's grab the chance!*

I'd drawn lane 3 which is a good lane, but with David Jenkins outside of me I decided to resist the temptation to go out too hard; I'd decided to aim for even paced splits. Roger was inside of me so I was also aware of him chasing me down too.

I got out the blocks very well and relaxed down the back straight, but perhaps letting too much of a gap open up; Roger moved past me after only a 100 metres, but I didn't panic, instead I just maintained my pace allowing him to move ahead, patiently biding my time.

He'd built up a big lead at 300 metres but when I put the foot down there was a great response there, especially compared to everyone else; although in reality they were probably just slowing down, with me maintaining the pace.

I moved past David 50 metres out; I thought I'd left just too much to catch Roger, but drove on nipping the verdict on the line, just when he thought he'd won the race!

The response from the whole of Meadowbank was delight at with my victory; I don't know if it was the surprise or the excitement of the close finish, but I've never felt so popular, with lots of people congratulating me, seeming to be genuinely pleased. Another wee bonus was I equalled the Scottish Native Record. A further bonus was that I didn't feel that tired; the lactic acid generated was relatively fine and minimal. I'd more or less fully recovered within minutes of the race.

When I got home the household was delighted and quite animated. I travelled out to Oxgangs to see Mum and the family; they had watched the race unfold on telly. Mum said she's never seen Grandpa Willie so pleased and happy, especially at defeating David Jenkins whose presence has loomed over the household for years.

Afterwards and once back home to Portobello I went out late on for an easy 4 miles run on a quiet Portobello Golf Course; however, with it being a soft summer's evening there were one or two wee groups out still playing golf. After all the excitement of the day it was good to take some quiet time out to reflect on what had just gone before and to truly savour the moment. Such days don't come along often in life. I'm aware of just how special an occasion today was and I wanted to truly re-imagine the day and capture the moment. And whilst I'm naturally delighted for myself, what's more important is the joy it's brought to many others in my life.

After beating Dave Jenkins over a quarter mile in some respects there's a certain poignancy too. In a way it feels to me that if not the end of a journey it's certainly the end of a chapter in my life. Seven years ago as a schoolboy I watched David win the 1971 European Championships in Helsinki. His fantastic win there so motivated me that I went out and organised our very own local championships on the track at Redford Barracks and around 40 local kids from around Oxgangs turned out. It also provided the motivation for me to go along to Meadowbank and begin training. So it's been a long road from when I took these first faltering steps; there was no way I ever thought I might beat him over a quarter mile of distance run.

There's also a further natural conclusion there too as it's the only time David, Roger and I have all raced one another at the Scottish Championships. We'd all previously won the title twice, so I feel my third win brings the curtain down on these seven years of our dominance. We may never all race each other again over the quarter mile.

Later on I sat in and relaxed watching Scotland get beaten 3-1 by Peru-a disaster. Talking of disasters. Paul was beaten by Terry Young. I've said a little prayer for him that the selectors take it as a small blip; Young's perhaps fallen in to a no-mans' land as he ran a big personal best, but only 1.49.4 Whereas Paul ran it from the front going through 400 metres in 52.2 seconds and blew up allowing Young to make up a lot of ground in the last 150 metres. Paul was just too brave for his own good. The team is announced tomorrow so it will be a nervous 24 hours for Paul, but I'm sure he'll be selected.

1978 Scottish Championships

400 metres 1. Hoffmann 47.1 seconds (equals Scottish Native Record); 2. R. Jenkins 47.2 secs; 3. D. Jenkins

Evening (7.30 p.m.): 4 miles steady

Before Bed: Press-ups; squats; sit-ups

4th June, 1978 The morning after the night before, I was still feeling on a bit of a high after yesterday's victory over David and Roger at the Scottish. The newspapers were full of reports on the race; it was the main headline: *'Hoffmann shock for the Jenkins brothers'* or *'Peter Hoffmann, the boy with the fantastic finish, created the shock of the day...Hoffmann's time...equalling his own Scottish native record...'* etc. There were also some good photographs too, mainly of the dramatic finish.

I managed to set it all aside and studied all morning before going up to Meadowbank to get on with some bread 'n butter work on my own as Coach Walker was attending the team selection meeting. After my session it was great to hear from Coach Walker that Paul has been selected for the Commonwealth Games Scotland team for Edmonton, as have I. Coach Walker said I was one of the very first picks after Chris Black in the hammer. The only issue was whether I wanted to run the quarter or the half; he was quite surprised, but put them right that it was the 800 metres I was going for. The good weather continues apace so in the afternoon Lorraine (Morris); Paul; *Diana the goddess of love and hunting*; and I drove down to Stobo, Peebleshire for a dip in the River Tweed.

Whilst I wrote last evening that I felt the circle had been rounded regarding the journey I'd been on with Dave and Roger Jenkins, feeling it had reached its natural conclusion, now that I'm focusing on the half mile, I contrasted that observation with Paul and my journey together. It's completely different as there's a more optimistic and youthful note at play. And whilst I feel our selection for the Commonwealth Games team is the pinnacle of our journey so far, from us first coming along to Meadowbank together as kids back in 1971 to train under the auspices of Coach Walker, that it's still a staging post; albeit an important and key one. And whilst it's satisfying for us, I'm more pleased for Coach Walker; it's a small reward for the vision and all the hard work and commitment he's put in standing outside with his stopwatch, no matter the season or the vagaries of the weather conditions. I wonder what the odds would have been that two kids from working class Oxgangs, growing up only 50 yards apart would be selected for the Scottish team in the same event for the same Games. It couldn't have happened without Coach Walker and is a validation of his training philosophy.

It's great that alongside both Jenkins' a significant number of the athletes he's worked with are in the team; out of the main squad I'm just sorry that Norman Gregor hasn't been selected; and it's a pity Adrian Weatherhead has been injured because for much of the winter he was roughing the two of us up. I'm sure he was capable of a 3.55 mile. Whilst we were down at Stobo we bumped in to Iain and his wife Kim. It's a small world. Late afternoon we travelled home. I had a steak dinner before going out in the evening to Portobello Golf Course for an easy relaxed 4 miles run. Happy days.

Afternoon (12.00 p.m.): 3 x 600 metres (10 minutes recovery) 84 seconds

Evening (7.00 p.m.): 4 miles run

5th June, 1978 I was awake before Aunt Heather called me at 6.00 a.m. I had a bad night's sleep. I tossed and turned and intermittently dozed; not the best preparation for this morning's exam. I guess it was the mix of the weekend's excitement; spending yesterday in the sun at Stobo and worrying about the Mathematics exam, which is the killer subject that leads to most students being turfed out of the course. Will ran me up to Waverley Station for the Dundee train. The Maths paper lived up to its name and was indeed a killer, however I'm optimistic that I've passed it. I got the one o'clock train back to Edinburgh. I'm a bit tired. Will picked me up at the station. After a bite to eat I looked in to Coach Walker's to discuss whether I should run for Britain against East Germany on Sunday, especially given I've exams all week. In the evening I warmed up, but decided against running the 1500 metres at the Northern Trophy; a good call methinks. Whilst I've got a winning streak of 14 races in a row it was less to do with that, more that I just felt tired and a bit weary, both physically and mentally; a good call. Some sensational news emerging from Argentina; Willie Johnston is being sent home from the World Cup after admitting to taking drugs. It was the main news. I feel very sorry for him and also his family.

Evening: Warm up jog; stretching and strides

6th June, 1975 I phoned Bob Sinclair first thing and in the afternoon we did an illegal session, climbing over the fence at Meadowbank which was closed for the day. Earlier in the day I'd got a call from the British Board-Would I race in Belgrade, Yugolsavia next Wednesday? It was a pleasant surprise. I think they feel I have some potential for the European Junior Championships. In the evening I took my old Hunters Tryst Primary School girlfriend, Audrey Smith to a dance, but she had to leave early; later I gave Bob and Dave Hislop a lift home

Afternoon: 3 x 4 x 60 metres; I gave Bob 4 metres and beat him on each run!

1978 Up again at 6.00 a.m. Will dropped me off for the dawn Dundee train. I had a coffee at Kidds for some last minute preparation and then into the hall for the Accounts paper. I was pushed for time and was writing right up to the very last second! I think I've scraped a pass. Back in Edinburgh I felt pretty rough as I jogged three miles, however in the evening I ran a fairly good session with Norman and Paul. Early to bed this evening.

Afternoon (3.00 p.m.): 3 miles run

Evening (7.15 p.m.): 6 x 300 metres (90 seconds recovery) 39 seconds; circuit work

7th June, 1973 Another lovely day; it helps on the journey along the tree lined Morningside streets to be no longer facing the vicissitudes of the cold and bitter wind and instead be enveloped by a warm and pleasant zephyr; however I'm then back inside for much of the day, although I alleviated that with a game of footie at lunchtime out in the yard with the warehouse boys.

The Ice Cart

Perched on my city office-stool
I watched with envy while a cool
And lucky carter handled ice…
And I was wandering in a trice
Far from the grey and grimy heat
Of that intolerable street…'

Wilfrid Wilson Gibson

In the evening I was running fabulously well-I was going like a rocket! I see Mandy McLean is still going about with Alan Waters. A pity. Still there's the *Simone de Beauvoir Philosophy Queen* and a host of other lovely Edinburgh Southern Harriers flowers in the garden. I had to wait ages on a 5 bus this evening.

Evening: 300 metres 37.0 seconds; 3 x 200m in 24.0 secs; 4 x 100m 11.6; 11.7; 12.1; 11.9 secs

1975 I wasn't feeling very good this morning, but ran an excellent session. Puma sent me some pairs of spikes, trainers and a bag. So, along with yesterday's call about Belgrade and my selection for the British senior team in East Germany things are starting to come together. In the evening Coach Walker; Kay; Robert; Iain; Lucy and *Pixie Mia Farrow lookalike* and I went through to the bowling alley at Glenrothes. What a fun evening, made all the more better for *Pixie* being along.

When You Are Old

'…How many loved your moments of glad grace;
And loved your beauty with love false or true,
But one man loved the pilgrim soul in you,
And loved the sorrows of your changing face…'

William Butler Yeats

Morning: 4 x 300 metres (10 minutes recovery) 35.3; 35.4; 35.5; 35.6 seconds

1978 Just like yesterday, up at 6.00 a.m. for the early morning train to Dundee. It was Sociology and Psychology this morning; the former went particularly well; the latter, a decent pass. I managed to extricate myself from the exam hall at 11.55 a.m. and made a mad dash to catch the mid-day London train, so I was back in to the capital by a quarter to two. I went out to Portobello Park and ran a gentle three miles to clear my head. There were various wee groups of golfers out; I always like to see them; somehow it makes the world seem all right. I was famished afterwards and devoured a couple of bowls of porridge. In the evening Coach Walker had me do a couple of runs; we're still discussing and finding our way forward regarding what to do on the half mile; whereas quarter mile training came more naturally.

Afternoon (3.00 p.m.): 3 miles steady run

Evening (7.00 p.m.): 1000 metres 100m fast stride/100m stride last 200m flat out; 500m 67.5 secs; it was very windy

8th June, 1976 The Olympic Trials are only a few days away; I'm not quite in the dark place I was two weeks ago, but it's still looking bleak. Roger will be in London earlier than me as he's staying at his folks' home in Croydon. Although it was a hit last year, I'll look back on these days and associate the period with the warmth of the summer of 1976 and the Typically Tropical track Barbados. It has been getting significant airplay and seems to always be on whilst we're warming up. When it comes on the radio Roger immediately leaps up to perform a zany dance…*Hey!, we're going to Barbados…Woh I'm going to Barbados, Woh, backa to the palm trees Woh, I'm going to see my girl-friend Woh, in the sunny Caribbean Sea…*

Afternoon: 4 x 150 yards (2 minutes recovery) 14.5-15 seconds; 4 x 120m (3 mins rec)

1978 I'm getting used to these 6.00 a.m. starts and the train to Dundee. It's already warm and pleasant out. But it's the light which makes the biggest difference of all. Seeing the paperboys out on their rounds always gives me a wee fillip. I studied all the way up on the train; had a coffee at Kidds then wrote thirteen pages in the Economic Development paper. I was pleased; it went well and I feel I've passed. Back home to Edinburgh and I went out immediately to run in Portobello Park; then down for an aerotone bath at Porty Baths which left me a little drained, before running a light track session at Meadowbank. I felt a bit rough-not running very well at all. Back home for an hour's study and then lights out. So went the day.

9th June, 1975 I telephoned the British Board about my upcoming race in Belgrade. They seem to be laid back and rather disorganised, especially as it's being held behind the *Iron Curtain* in Yugoslavia. Anyway I guess they must know best and I didn't want to appear pushy at this early stage in my career. I did a good rhythm session in the afternoon giving Stewart of Bonnyrigg 3 metres over 60 metres and won all bar one run. In the evening I strolled about Meadowbank chatting to various people.

Afternoon: **2 x 4 x 60 metres (good recovery; 15 minutes between sets); all runs between 6.7 and 6.9 seconds**

1976 Another bleak update on my preparation for the Olympic Trials in two days' time. I ran a poor 200 metres and then had to curtail the session with a groin strain; and I can't even blame the *Simone de Beauvoir Philosophy Queen!* Dispiriting, to put it mildly...

Morning: **200 metres 22.2 seconds; cold and windy day; knackered groin**

1978 On the train journey to Dundee I looked over my Economics. It's the last exam and I may have failed it. It was a really unbalanced paper-two mathematical problems made up 55% of the paper which threw me a bit. Typical McGillivray. Much as I admire his intellect, is that any real way to examine a year of economic theory? Anyway, I'm hoping all the hard work I did in Spain may pull me through to a pass mark in the second part of the paper. I managed to just catch the mid-day train; Will picked me up at Waverley and I was home for lunch by two o'clock. Iain phoned me half way through. Denis gave me a massage; as ever he was in ebullient form; thereafter back home for a delicious (Josephine) macaroni tea and then we headed out to Turnhouse Airport to fly down to London for the East Germany match. Spur of the moment I asked *Diana the goddess of love and hunting* if she fancied coming down to London with me! She had nothing with her, but it's easy to buy a toothbrush and pair of knickers; before she could pause for breath we were on board the eight o'clock flight and then the train out to Crystal Palace and a taxi to the Queen's Hotel. I managed to get her a room; even better it was a large one with three beds so I just camped down there for the evening and will stay there all weekend. It's lovely to have her down with me, especially as I've not seen her all week because of my exams and just how frenetic life has been. Of course her folks aren't happy. But it's fun being so spontaneous; we're young; we're in love; we're destined to be together and it's something we'll look back on one day and be glad that we did.

10ᵗʰ June, 1975 Well I wasn't far wrong with yesterday's observation about the laxity of the British Board. I came back from signing on the dole at Portobello to find Nana in a real panic. I was on the phone to their office in London all morning and was basically just being mucked around. It now turns out I'm not to fly out to Yugoslavia until tomorrow. Every cloud has a silver lining and all that; I went up to Meadowbank. *Pixie Mia Farrow lookalike* was there, but unable to train because of her ankle. Making one of my better moves in life I took her down to Musselburgh instead for a game of pitch 'n putt. It's the first time we've been out alone together since I took her out 15 months ago to the cinema to see It's Only A Paper Moon. We had a lovely evening and got on so well together with lots of fun and laughter; she won by three holes which tells you everything! I'm off to sleep now to dream about her.

1978 24 hours until the big day and tomorrow's U.K v G.D.R 800 metres. At nine o'clock I went out to some local park-land and did some light jogging and stretching. Thereafter *Diana the goddess of love and hunting* and I had a fun morning in the local London community. We took a wee tootle to pick up some newspapers; at a second hand bookshop I bought a book for Josephine; and also a knight in shining armour from an olde worlde shop selling serendipities. Back at the Queen's Hotel I joined the team meeting then went back to our room and lay down for an hour before going down to watch day one of the international. Unfortunately the weather took a turn for the worse-a bit sour, with a cold wind. Pascoe had a good win as did Steve Ovett against Jurgen Straub in the 1500 metres; I had a brief chat with Ovett. Whilst sitting in the stand *Diana* and I enjoyed some strawberries and cream-very genteel. In the evening we went out with Coach Walker who's travelled down to watch me run, as well as his father in law, Tom Drever. It's strange having Tom watching me running for Britain when I think back to me being a young boy and how after training at Meadowbank him dropping me off at Duddingston Crossroads to walk back home to Durham Road. He's always gruff, straight talking, but has my best interest at heart. After a drink (soft for me!) we went back to our rooms; what a laugh *Diana* and I had tickling each other!

11th June, 1974 After last year's breakthrough as a youth athlete I feel I'm coming on hand over fist just now. I ran a great session with Norman Gregor running with him all the way. We were both absolutely shattered, with splitting headaches and feeling sick. My legs were packed with lactic acid. Apart from that, I loved it!

Evening: 4 x 200 metres (3 minutes' recover) 23.3; 23.5; 23.9; 25.0 seconds; (15 minutes recovery) then 2 x 200m 22.8! and 23.2 secs; (8 mins rec) 6 x 60m back to back

Before Bed: Arm-action; press-ups; sit-ups

1975 Gaga ran me out to Turnhouse Airport. When I reached London there was a message saying I wasn't to bother going out to Belgrade and instead I was to get in touch with Alan Pascoe to get a run at Crystal Palace in the AAAs v Borough Road College meet. At four o'clock I telephoned Coach Walker to bring him up to speed on what was happening then had a Chinese carry out; well that was a big mistake as I felt unwell afterwards. However, by the time the race came around in the late evening I was okay and ran a personal best of 47.43 seconds which will rocket me up the European Junior rankings. I immediately jogged back to the Queen's Hotel to watch the race on the telly and then phoned Coach Walker. Given all the hassle, he was quite pleased-another stepping stone and all's well that ends well.

AAAs v Borough Road College 400 metres 1. S. Chepkwony (Kenya) 45.9 seconds (best of 45.1); 2. Hoffmann 47.43 secs; 3. B. Benn 47.8

1976 I arrived in London with no great hopes for the Olympic Trials, but once again the importance of the occasion seemed to bring out the best in me. It was more or less identical to last year's European Junior semi-final where I again ran a very controlled semi-final in 47.6 seconds to qualify for the final. I've no idea where that came from. Two weeks ago I ran 49 seconds and was whacked at the end; this evening I was just floating along with little effort and felt I had a lot left at the end. I let David go, but was able to easily control the likes of Jim Aukett, Brian Jones and Steve Scutt. Of a sudden my hopes of making the team for Montreal have risen once again.

1976 Olympic Trials Crystal Palace, London

400 metres Semi-Final 1. D. Jenkins 46.72 seconds 2. Hoffmann 47.60 secs

1978 I was unimpressed with the hotel's breakfast-pretty substandard. *Diana the goddess of love and hunting* and I took a wee stroll down to collect the Sunday newspapers. The weather had improved and the sun was out. I spent the morning reading and watching a little television. Gavin Miller came in and disturbed us; I tholed him for half an hour before moving him on. I had some brown bread and honey and then walked down to Crystal Palace. I sat in the physio room for a couple of hours with my feet up before going out to warm up. Ovett came over and spoke to me and warned me about how good Straub is. I felt okay whilst jogging and even better when I did my strides. Earlier in the week Sebastian Coe had pulled out and a Dave Warren is replacing him. I was clearly going to be nervous, but I was happy with it just being a four man field; I knew I'd have to stay relatively closely in contact and there wouldn't be so many people to go past. The Germans took the race out; I sat at the back and went through the quarter in 54.1 seconds. As we entered the back straight at 500 metres I sensed there was a risk of Warren becoming detached so moved past him. Beyer followed by Straub had opened a gap at 200 metres so I began to put the foot down a little. Entering the home straight Beyer had opened a further gap; Straub is very strong and I had to move wide to go past him; I then started chasing Beyer down the home-straight; it got a reaction from the crowd. Although I closed right down on him, I couldn't quite get passed.

After the race there were three immediate reactions. First, because of my inexperience (only my fourth serious 800 metres) I was confused when I saw the electronic clock; it read 106.3. I thought what the fuck does that mean? It took a while to realise it was 1 minute 46 seconds! Second, I couldn't get over just how strong Beyer was; it struck me how robotic he seemed. His strength was very apparent; he's the first athlete to withstand my kick this season. And third, although it was fifteen being unlucky and losing my winning streak, it was also encouraging too; I didn't feel bad at all-there's definitely a 1.44 in my legs this season.

I joined Coach Walker; Tom Drever; Linford Christie's coach Ron Rodden (who's a good friend of Coaches Walker's) and *Diana* too. They were fine about my run; Coach was joking that he'd assured Rodden beforehand that I intended to go out fast and when they saw me bending over in a crouch start with my hand on the line, they thought, Oh, hear he goes! only for me to immediately settle back in last place.

Nelson Fairlie gave *Diana* and me a lift to East Croydon Station where we got a train out to Gatwick. We bumped into Betty Steedman at the airport. *Diana* and I enjoyed some delicious scones, jam and cream, followed by a meal on the flight. Before we knew it we were back home. *Diana* had really enjoyed herself. I was whacked, but mission accomplished. A month ago I hadn't broken 1.50; now I'm only a second slower than Ovett. Oh, and Scotland beat Holland 3-2 at the World Cup in Argentina. So went the day. And the weekend.

UK v D.D.R. (East Germany)

800 metres 1. O. Beyer 2. Hoffmann 1.46.61 (p.b.) 3. J. Straub 1.47.0 4. D. Warren 1.49.6

Athletics Weekly

'An international breakthrough also for Peter Hoffmann who has clearly found his event in the 800. Last at the bell in 54.1, with Olaf Beyer in 53.0, the 21 year old Scot was still the best part of 10m down on the leader at 600 but a dynamic final 200 covered in 25.7 carried him through to second in a glittering 1:46.6. Before this season he hadn't run faster than 1:53.0!'

Postscript: Looking back, although this was a loaded field, I did not feel out of my depth; however each of these athletes thereafter moved on to greater success. Warren ran in the 1980 Olympic 800 metres final alongside Coe and Ovett; whilst Jurgen Straub took the Olympic silver medal in the 1500 metres behind Coe, but ahead of Ovett.

Meanwhile, Olaf Beyer finished the 1978 season ranked as the number one 800 metres athlete in the world. To the surprise of many he defeated Coe and Ovett at the European Championships. In only my fourth proper race at the half mile I ended up getting as close to him that season as anyone. I wasn't surprised at his victory in Prague. I'd felt he was unnaturally strong. Many years later when the Berlin wall came down and there was access to Stassi files, it was revealed that Beyer had been a part of the country's mass sports drugs programme.

12ᵗʰ June, 1973 Last evening after racing at Longniddry I enjoyed speaking with *Pixie Mia Farrow lookalike* in the Meadowbank cafeteria; this morning on my way in to work I saw her at Morningside on her way to Mary Erskine's School; my cup runneth over...

Evening: 6 x 150 metres (3 minutes recovery) Fast!

1975 Colin O'Neil very kindly gave me a lift out to Heathrow Airport. He's a lovely guy; athletics is full of such individuals. Unfortunately I had to wait three hours for a flight home to Edinburgh, but took advantage of the gorgeous weather and lay out sunbathing on the rooftop gardens. Nana and Gaga collected me at Turnhouse Airport. They enjoy the wee car run out from Portobello and had watched last night's race on the telly. It's lovely the way they get some pleasure and return for all they do for me. They're such an integral part of my athletics journey; in many ways it's really a team approach. In the evening I ran a good light session with Graham Malcolm. *Pixie Mia Farrow lookalike* was down; she too had watched the race. I gave her the Phillips T-shirt which I'd won as a prize; it's analogous to the proud hunter bringing home the spoil!

Evening: 2 x 4 x 60 metres; taking 2 metres off Graham Malcolm; 4 100m strides with Ann Clarkson

1976 As the clock counted down to the Olympic Trials 400 metres final there was a sublime mix of fear and confidence. My head and everything else was in a much better place than two weeks ago. I felt good as I warmed up on the area adjacent to the track. David and Roger of course were there; we spoke intermittently but mostly wanted to just inhabit a world of our own. Just before I'd gone out to begin my warm up I was allocated my lane draw-lane 8; FOR FUCK'S SAKE! What a great disappointment.

It was the worst possible draw of the eight athletes and it meant I would have to run blind. My forte has always been to run off people; just to slot in behind them and run in as relaxed a manner as possible. Whenever I run from the front I feel tense. I never relax and always run more slowly than I'm capable of; plus I seem to use up more energy too. I had forty minutes to get my head around the bad news. Out with that I felt good and quite positive after last night's run.

Half an hour later we got the call and filed out to the start to get our blocks ready. I always associate that walk with a condemned man going to his death. Normally I always feel a dual nervousness; I'm nervous of the race, but I'm also nervous about the pain.

It was a lovely day and there was a big crowd spectating. Once we reached the start I looked up to the top of the stand. I could see the journalists Sandy Sutherland (The Scotsman) and Brian Meek (Scottish Daily Express) talking together. They'd just seen the lane draw. I thought I bet they're thinking well David's fine; Roger may well book a place on the team, but given he's got the outside lane young Hoffmann's had it. It was a pivotal moment. I thought to myself, well let's show them just how wrong you can be. And let's try to box clever; yes I'll be running blind for 200 metres, but let's allow David to go past and then see if I can't lock on to him and the others around the bend.

Vitai Lampada

'...And it's not for the sake of a ribboned coat,
Or the selfish hope of a season's fame,
But his captain's hand on his shoulder smote
'Play up! play up! and play the game!'

Sir Henry Newbolt

The gun sounded and I took off. Before I knew it I was half way down the back-straight; *Keep calm and relaxed now, you know how important this race is-it's what you've been training for all winter, not to mention for years.* I disciplined myself to follow my race plan; as some of the field moved past on my inside I tried to maintain my form. As I came off 300 metres I could see there was a lot to do, but was frightened to look across. I ran all the way through the tape, closing rapidly on Bennett over the last fifteen metres, but not quite knowing where I was and frustratingly finishing with something still in the tank, but knowing I couldn't be critical of myself either; to have gone out too hard would have been disastrous; it was better to be cautious. The result came up-CRIKEY! fourth in a personal best of 46.76 seconds. .

My immediate thought was *Yes, I'm on the aeroplane to Montreal!* My second reaction was *Bugger, only 5/100ths behind Ainslie Bennett-that could be costly.*

After the race Ronnie and Pat Browne came down from the stand to congratulate me; unknown to me they'd flown down to watch, but didn't want to let me know in case it made me more nervous; they were absolutely delighted. Poor Roger was last, a second behind me. Out with the 500 metres race, it's only the second time I've ever beaten him. I felt sorry for him knowing just how hard we'd trained together over the past few winters and everything we'd put ourselves through and endured. Later in the evening he'd gone back to the family home in Croydon and cried himself to sleep listening to Neil Diamond's live album, Hot August Night.

Because I'd finished with something in hand and alongside the excitement of what I'd done allied to the adrenalin I ran in a scratch all Scottish 4 x 100m relay team. We beat two of the British teams including the 'A' team narrowly losing out to the 'B' team when Drew Hislop just couldn't hold on. I ran a blinder of a first leg. Coach Walker often puts me on that leg for the club; I don't know what it is but I always run well and handed us over in the lead against Les Piggott and Mike McFarlane. With no baton practice we managed to run the second fastest time ever by a Scottish team after the Scotland quartet at the Edinburgh Commonwealth Games in 1970.

I joined the large Scottish contingent on the late evening flight back to Edinburgh. Willie and Josephine were there to collect me and were delighted. I played things down, but fingers crossed for selection. The team will be announced on Monday.

1976 Olympic Trials

400 metres

1. D. Jenkins 45.50; 2. Cohen 46.11; 3. A. Bennett 46.71; 4. Hoffmann 46.76 8. R. Jenkins 47.63

4 x 100m relay

1. G.B. 'B' Team (Hill; Hoyte; Matthews; Cole) 40.22 secs
2. Scottish Team (Hoffmann; Wells; McMaster; Hislop) 40.41
3. G.B. 'A' Team (Piggott; S. Green; Roberts; Cornaby) 40.48
4. G.B. 'D' Team (McFarlane; Monk; Moven; Bonsor) 40.79

1978 With my exams out the way I began my summer job placement with Edinburgh Corporation's Recreation Department. Bob Sinclair has been very helping in securing me the job. Over coffee at St James Centre I met Alan Duns the head of the department; he sounds okay and has assured me there's no problem getting time off for my athletics this summer. I spent the afternoon at Craiglockhart Sports

Centre with the manager, Jim McKechnie, who gave me the general background on how the centre is run. After the excitement of yesterday's 800 metres against East Germany I had to put up with all the post-mortems about my run and tactics. *Diana the goddess of love and hunting* gave me money towards my overdraft as I'd payed for her flight to London.

Evening (7.30 p.m.): **3 x 600 metres differential runs 300 metres 40 seconds; stride 100m; 200m in 27 secs**

13th June, 1973 Some pleasant relief from the usual *ennui* of life at Balcarres Street; the Galashiels branch of Thomas Graham & Sons is understaffed so Joe Rendall our company rep. ran Tommy Drummond and me down to the Borders to help out in their office. The drive through the early morning Borders landscape made for a different and rather pleasant start to the day; the downside was the smallness of the office-we were like mice tucked up in a nest or chickens cooped up; and old Tommy isn't the best of company; he's a very sober type. Come lunchtime I escaped its confines and went to the local Wimpy Bar. I was surprised at how late in the day we were kept there (5.00 p.m.); a Mr Jackson gave us a lift back to Edinburgh. By the time I arrived at Meadowbank for my session I was shattered! Afterwards I was talking at the bus-stop with the lovely Jan McCall. I'm back at Galashiels tomorrow and Friday; by then I suspect the novelty will have worn off.

Evening: 150-200 metres clock (8 runs-first 4 good; second 4 rubbish!)

1976 Unsurprisingly, after yesterday's Olympic Trials 400 metres race and the relay leg, my legs were very tired today, however I turned out for the club in the Pye Gold Cup heat at Meadowbank. I faced Hugh Robertson in the 200 metres and with an early season 21.5 second under his belt and a victory in the 100 metres today he's a solid performer, so all things considered I was happy with the win. I also ran both relays too.

Pye Gold Cup Heat

200 metres 1. Hoffmann 21.9 seconds 2. H. Robertson (Fife) 22.3 secs

4 x 100m Relay 1. E.A.C.

4 x 400m Relay 1. E.A.C.

High Flight (An Airman's Ecstasy)

Oh, I have slipped the surly bonds of earth
And danced the skies on laughter-silvered wings;
Sunward I've climbed and joined the tumbling mirth
Of sun-split clouds-and done a hundred things
You have not dreamed of; wheeled and soared and swung
High in the sun-lit silence. Hovering there
I've chased the shouting wind along, and flung
My eager craft through footless halls of air;
Up, up the long, delirious, burning blue
I've topped the wind-swept heights with easy grace,
Where never lark nor eagle flew;
And while, with silent lifting mind I've trod
The high untrespassed sanctity of space,
Put out my hand, and touched the face of God.

John Gillespie Magee

14ᵗʰ June, 1976 The world, at least my wee world went slightly mad this morning. Ironically, when the news broke, I was sitting in of all places the doctor's surgery (injured after racing on Saturday and Sunday). The receptionist came through and announced to the packed waiting room that I'd just been selected for the Olympic team! Grandma Jo had phoned up the surgery with the news. Like Lazarus it seemed to bring many of the patients to life as they came up to congratulate me. Dr Motley is always happy, but he seemed particularly so this morning at my good news and was genuinely delighted. He was also regaling me with tales of his own career in American Football, as well as saying how if I ever wanted to go to Oklahoma University, he could arrange a scholarship for me. He's also going to arrange for a collection to be taken at the surgery.

Well after that it was all a bit of a blur.

I looked in to 6/2 Oxgangs Avenue to give Mum the good news. The press had been on the phone to Porty all morning, indeed the phone never stopped ringing all day; Josephine did her best to field the calls. In the afternoon I met various photographers up at Meadowbank where I some 'practice starts'. Brian Meek from the Daily Express was on the blower and Harry Pincot wants to do a profile for Friday's Scotsman as well as a myriad of other newspapers. Come the evening when I was out at Meadowbank, Grandpa Willie was delighted to get a congratulatory call from Dunky Wright the famous marathon runner; I've never met Dunky, but he was one of Will's heroes.

When I had some time to reflect afterwards it seems incredible to think I only ran my first 400 metres three years ago. Although I'm delighted, part of me has just taken it in my stride, as if it were the natural order of things and yet I was in a pretty dark place two weeks ago. More than anything, what's given me the greatest pleasure is the joy it's given to a lot of people out there who have been part of the journey and the story so far. Obviously my grandparents, Will and Josephine; it was the former who really set me off on this path two years ago when I wrote in my journal that I had to make this team as Gaga would be unlikely to be alive come Moscow. I'm pleased for Coach Walker too, yet like me, we've both been pretty low key accepting it as a staging post along the way; we've both got Moscow at the back of our minds; Montreal's just a bonus, crazy as that sounds! I didn't train today, but that's because I'm injured. My left foot is so swollen after a weekend of racing that I can't get it in to my shoe; given how frenetic the day has been, probably a blessing in disguise.

Rather than so went the day, instead, a day I'm unlikely to forget; who needs a journal!

15ᵗʰ June, 1974 Roger had turned down selection because of the grass track, so Norman and I represented Scotland at Bearsden today. Unbelievably, having just broken 50 seconds for the first time last month I ran a sub-49! Wait till Roger hears what he missed!

Scotland v N. Ireland v Midland Counties (Bearsden Highland Games)

400 metres 1. N Gregor 47.9 seconds; 2. Hoffmann 48.8 secs; a personal best and on a grass track!

1975 I was in a bad mood this morning and feeling rather sorry for myself after yesterday's disastrous British League trip to Manchester where I'd run generally poorly. The track at Sale was awful; my 100 was okay; the quarter was a disaster; we got disqualified in the 4 x 100m relay and I ran so-so on the 4 x 400m relay leg. I sat in Holyrood Park for a while doing some reflecting then went up to Meadowbank to run in the Invitation 100 metres and also 600 metres. I ran well, comprehensively beating McMaster and a good field in the sprint, then beating Paul over 600 metres. I must be doing something right when I'm taking out the U.K.'s best juniors over the sprint and middle distance. Alongside the races I was chatting with the *Mary Rand lookalike from the south-west*; Shona and Fay; isn't it amazing how one's demeanour can improve from the morning to the afternoon! In the evening I went up to Coach Walker's house for a chat about the mixed weekend and the season ahead; in particular the upcoming European Junior Championships in August. I didn't leave until ten to one in the morning-Kay, Bill and family make me feel too welcome!

Invitation 100 metres **1. Hoffmann 10.8 seconds 2. A. McMaster 11.0 secs 3. G. Malcolm 11.0 secs**

Invitation 600 metres: 1. Hoffmann 84.4 secs 2. P. Forbes; I just sat in on everyone and outkicked them easily down the home straight

1976 I featured in many newspaper headlines e.g. 'The trails of Hoffmann lead him to Montreal'; these sub-editors are clever. Amongst a large mail for me this morning, there were notes from C.K. Lipton and Frank Dick:

Dear Peter,

Many congratulations! Who knows? There could be some great personal achievement at Montreal. I am very happy for you.
Keep in touch.
Sincerely,

C.K. Lipton

Dear Peter,

Just a few lines to record my heartfelt congratulations on your selection for Montreal. It seems no time at all since you were a little lad trying his first 400-yet here you are, an Olympian. It says a great deal for your commitment and personal talent, and I'd like to thank you for representing such a great source of inspiration to young athletes in Scotland and generally Edinburgh in particular. I wish you all the success you deserve.
Sincerely yours.

Frank Dick

1978 After yesterday's lovely day, the weather was grim today-cool and blustery. However, it was an absolute joy to be out on Portobello Golf Course where I was just flowing easily and effortlessly over the bouncy turf. I felt great physically and mentally. When it all comes together like that it's the most wonderful sensation in the world. Part of me takes it for granted, but realise much of it's clearly down to all the hard work and application over the past six years-it doesn't just happen! And yet when these rare moments come along I don't think in these terms at all. I'm living solely in the moment and just assume it's the natural state of affairs. A naive part of me feels I'll always feel like today, whether it's next year or even forever! Whereas the rational part knows I could wake up tomorrow, next week or next year and it's all gone. But right now I feel a million dollars and as if anything might be possible. Throw Jenkins, Forbes, Coe or Ovett at me right now and I could run with them. From that esoteric and sublime state of heavenly affairs, back down to planet Earth. I went in to my summer job at York Place to work laboriously on statistics on family memberships at the council's leisure centres.

<u>Morning (7.00 a.m.):</u> **4 miles-just flowing along; arm-action; squats; sit-ups**

<u>Evening (7.00 p.m.):</u> **8 x 200 metres (2 minutes recovery) 25 seconds; arm-action; sit-ups**

Weight 143 lbs

16th June, 1973 Great news! Paul phoned me up to say he'd won the Scottish Schools 1000 metres Steeplechase title. All his hard work over the past year has paid off. I'm hoping I can match him and win my first Scottish title in two weeks' time at the Scottish Youth Championships at Grangemouth; fingers crossed! Paul chose the right event with the likes of Jim Fleming and Mark Watt in the 800 and 1500 metres who are pretty dominant.

1975 In the evening along with some E.A.C. colleagues I picked up some of the Harvard-Yale guys. We've got a chap called Lance staying over; I haven't taken to him; there's something insincere about the guy, but Grandma Jo is happy, so all's good. *Pixie Mia Farrow lookalike* and I took him and his pal out for a meal; on the way back to Meadowbank we had a great laugh.

Evening: 380 metres time-trial 1. Hoffmann 44.9 seconds; 2. Jimmy Smith (Pro) 45.4 secs; a pleasing run

1976 There was a fabulous congratulations card with love from *Pixie Mia Farrow lookalike* in this morning's post. I too didn't need the trampette! On the back of the card was there was a wee note from her too:

Dear Peter,

I was on the point of jumping on the trampette when Elaine Davidson told me you'd made the team and after that I didn't need anything to give me elevation because I was so happy for you. I phoned but you weren't in so I thought I'd send the card.

I am really, really pleased and as you have worked hard despite setbacks (cough) and I hope that you take Montreal by storm.

Yours Pixie x

1978 Mid-evening I picked up Paul; Drew McMaster and Elaine Davidson at Meadowbank; we drove down to the Peebles Hydro Hotel for the Scotland Commonwealth Games team get-together. We arrived around ten o'clock. There was a very casual team meeting; afterwards Paul and I had some fish 'n chips and a game of billiards before hitting the sack

Morning (7.00 a.m.): 3 miles steady run

17th June, 1973 Paul and I ran for Edinburgh Boys Clubs in the Scottish Boys Clubs' Championships at Grangemouth. After yesterday's Schools' win Paul came unstuck and didn't run well, but I won the 200 and 400 metres titles, as well as helping Edinburgh win the relay. Although I've won my first Scottish titles today, in my heart of hearts I know it's only second division stuff. I'll only consider myself a national champion if I win the Scottish Youth title in two weeks' time. I'm hoping Paul will still make the Scottish team for British Boys Clubs' Championships next month in Englandshire.

Scottish Boys Clubs' Championships

400 metres 1. Hoffmann 53.5 seconds (new championship record)

200 metres 1. Hoffmann 23.7 secs (new championship record)

1975 With last night's time-trial 380 metres thrown in, tonight was really my fourth day in a row of racing. I had a brief chat with Coach Walker beforehand then ran a controlled race holding off Brian Gordon. Coach is so busy with everything revolving around him that afterwards I gave Kay and the kids a lift back home to East Claremont Street in his car.

SAAA's v Harvard/Yale v R.A.F. v Scottish Universities

400 metres 1. Hoffmann 48.1 seconds 2. B. Gordon 48.6 secs; cold, windy; I didn't feel that good

18th June, 1975 I'm heading off to East Germany tomorrow with the British senior team for the first time. I met Mum up town and she gave me some money to buy a new shirt for the trip. In the afternoon I did some speed-work with Les Piggott and Scott Brodie; Piggott is an interesting and enigmatic individual. He's quiet, but confident and self-assured with definite views on the world. Later on I met *Pixie Mia Farrow lookalike* at Meadowbank to watch the 3M PRO meeting. It was an interesting experience and the spectacle was presented with flair and razzmatazz compared to the amateur fayre, but many of the great athletes on parade are past their best. Ben Jipcho ran well over two miles; George McNeil was third, but not really running at his best; I've been training recently with Jimmy Smith and helping him out, but was disappointed with his run in the quarter. Afterwards *Pixie* and I went to Helen Golden's party; *Pixie* went off with X which pissed me off no end, spoiling the evening. C'est la vie.

Afternoon: 60; 80; 60; 80 metres (3-10 minutes' recovery) followed by 6 x 50m with Les Piggot and Scot Brodie

1978 After breakfasting at the Peebles Hydro I left the hotel at 9.30 a.m. I took my luggage out to the car. Early Sunday morning it was lovely to hear the sweet sound of the church bells calling the local townspeople to worship; the sound carrying crystal clear across the valley. How right someone was when they said As clear as a bell.

In Summertime on Bredon

'...The bells would ring to call her
In valleys miles away:
'Come all to church, good people:
God people, come and pray.'

A. E. Houseman

The road back to Edinburgh was very quiet; it was glorious driving through the tree-landscaped Borders countryside. Dad's car felt as sweet as a nut to drive and it effortlessly glided through the sweeping bends. June is the bonniest month and the trees are light green, fresh and full; the season of hope and beauty. It only took me twenty minutes to get back to the capital. At lunchtime I looked in to a quiet Meadowbank and cruised through an easy, but encouraging session on my own. As Josephine and Heather are away, in the afternoon *Diana the goddess of love and hunting* and I took Will down to North Berwick. The grand weather had brought the crowds out. We stopped at Yellowcraigs Beach and I ran on the sands and took an invigorating dip in the Forth. Come the evening I took *Diana* to see Saturday Night Fever. I thought it was poor. We had a meal at the Mei Kwei Restaurant in Morningside.

The days are flying by with little time to reflect.

<u>Afternoon (12.00 p.m.);</u> 3 x 500 metres 65.9; 66.6; 64.9 seconds; on my own; cruising; followed by 60; 80; 100 metres

19th June, 1973 I was running quite well this evening; afterwards I was talking with Norman Gregor. He's a great lad always bolstering my confidence, saying I'll win the Scottish Youth title. Walking down Durham Road I almost got in to a fight with a hard man-the odd juxtaposition of leafy middle class Duddingston and Niddrie.

<u>Evening:</u> 300 metres 36.9 seconds; 200m 23.4 secs; 150m 16.2 secs; 100m 11.6 secs (15 minutes recovery)

1976 There was a lovely card from the Rosses in the post written by my cousin, David: it meant a lot because it was the Rosses who first took me along to Meadowbank in 1971 and introduced me to Coach Walker:

Dear Peter,

You've possibly been showered with letters from everyone vaguely connected with you. Although no-one really has the right to stand back and say "Oh, very good!" may we, sincerely say, Well done on Saturday's race and your selection for the Montreal squad; we're very glad for you that the work is paying off. Everyone is quite thrilled and happy about your selection and Aunt Jo's newspaper cuttings collection now probably rivals the Central Libraries' newspaper archives after your latest coverage.

You certainly gave the clock a hammering on Saturday. I (David) missed the actual race on the T.V. as I was in England (I'm sorry to say) but the second by second account I received when I got home (including the swearing concerning a certain Mr Jenkins) was very impressive.

I hope it isn't getting too heavy along there with the inevitable advice and pressure and may everything go okay with you.

Good wishes-the Ross camp.

20th June, 1975 It was panic stations this morning. Coach Walker's car wouldn't start, but Liz Sutherland came to the rescue and gave me a lift up to Waverley Station. Coach and I took a taxi out to Turnhouse Airport. There's a strong Edinburgh contingent in the U.K. team including Helen Golden; Meg Ritchie; Gus McKenzie; Roger and Adrian which makes it easier to fit in to the team. I enjoyed the flight out to Dresden; we were treated royally on board and they served up a fine meal. In the evening I wandered down to the track; it's very good and looks fast. Later on I joined the Daily Telegraph journalist James Coote, Frank Dick and a few others for a coffee and some orange juice. I'm rooming with the good English sprinter Chris Monk who won the Europa Cup 200 metres two years ago in Edinburgh. He's an unusual bloke-quite hyper-quite different, but pleasant all the same. Denis Davidson, the physio, has this theory that sprinters are nervy, twitchy types, living on their nerves, whereas distance runners are the opposite-his theory stands up here, but I'm unsure where that places me on the firmament! It's so hot I had a cold shower before bed.

1977 Having been off with yet another cold, this time for a week, I ran a middle distance session on my own. I felt terrible for over an hour afterwards; it was like a lactic acid factory down there. The side of athletics the public don't see!

<u>Evening:</u> 6 x 300 metres (3 minutes recovery) 38; 38; 38; 39; 40; 40 seconds

1978 After training at Meadowbank, *Diana the goddess of love and hunting* burst in to tears; she told me she'd got the sack from her wee part time job at Safeways. She'd been contemplating stealing ten pounds. She was foolish, but she's young and fortunately hadn't actually done it. I took her out for a drink to comfort her. There are no ramifications.

<u>Morning (8.00 a.m.):</u> 4 miles

<u>Evening (7.00 p.m.):</u> 4 x 600 metres differentials (5 minutes recovery) 300m 41 secs; stride 100m; 200m 27 secs

Will Ye Go, Lassie, Go?

'Oh, the summertime is coming
And the trees are sweetly blooming
And the wild mountain thyme
Grows around the blooming heather
Will ye go lassie, go?'

Summertime

'Summertime, and the livin' is easy...'

DuBose Heyward; Ira Gershwin; George Gershwin

Summer

21ˢᵗ June, 1975 Dresden, East Germany A quick shower before going down to breakfast and then along to the British team meeting. I went for a wee stroll around some local shops. It's very hot out; I was surprised at just how warm it is on the continent at mid-summer. I bought a couple of pairs of shorts at a sport shop. After lunch I lay down in my room; the usual mix of being excited and frightened about the race ahead, but looking forward to it too; but also trying to put it out of mind. Although I lie back and rest, I never sleep.

Another shower-something cool, before going down to the track. I felt good and ran my second fastest ever time and so acquitted myself. It's also helped to consolidate my position in the European Junior rankings. However, whilst watching the main competition between the U.K. v D.D.R. I had what I thought was a revelationary moment. As I reflected about today's race, I didn't like the fact I wasn't as fast as the Germans over a 200 metres. What an advantage that must be knowing you're quicker than everyone else over half distance. It's made me reach the conclusion that I'm definitely going to move up to the half mile one day to get that competitive advantage and race confidence. In the evening I went out for an ice cream and coke with Roger; Bob Benn; Steve Ovett; Ian Stewart; Mary Stewart; and Lesley Kiernan-within the team it's a good group to be a part of.

East Germany v United Kingdom Invitation 400 metres:

J. Aukett 47.28 seconds; Hoffmann 47.66; Benn 47.73

22nd June, 1973 Because of a strike there are no Scottish newspapers out today. A grindingly slow day at Graham's as we pass mid-summer, but still it's a Friday. Lightening the day, I played yard football at lunchtime and enjoyed Roy taking the crap out of fellow manager, Andrew Curran. He was off on one of his rifts-he can be quite funny. In the early evening Paul and I had a good game of tennis at Meadowbank. We saw Mr Walker & co. there. Stuart Gillies gave me a lift; we passed the lovely Porty schoolgirls, Jan McCall and Lorraine Morris.

1974 A mixed day. I competed in my first Scottish Senior Championships and quite enjoyed myself, but threw away a place on the Scotland team for Oslo which pissed me off. In the late morning I went up to Meadowbank and won my heat. Afterwards I came home for a bite of lunch and a wee sleep, before going back up for the final. It's quite a surreal feeling being able to come back home in between races. I guess it's one of the advantages of living with Will and Jo and only two miles away from Meadowbank-a single bus ride on the 5 or 44 and a wee walk down Durham Road. It's a completely different preparation compared to those athletes who have travelled from throughout Scotland; it's also a slightly strange separating the day and the races out in this way. I got a medal finishing third. I was never going to win it against Roger Jenkins who's head and shoulders above everyone else, but I would have liked to have beaten Brian Gordon. I felt I could have run better tactically-more positively. That said, on a dull, windy day I probably did quite well, it's just that I'm setting high standards for myself. There was a cracking 800 metres blanket finish between Fromm of East Germany and Frank Clement and Dave McMeekin. Norman won the 400 metres hurdles and Adrian won his first Scottish title, but in the steeplechase.

Afterwards Paul came down to stay the night; we had a Chinese meal for our supper.

1974 Scottish Championships

400 metres Heat 1. Hoffmann 49.7 seconds

400 metres Final 1. R. Jenkins 47.7 secs 2. B. Gordon 48.5 secs 3. Hoffmann 48.9 secs; I think I had a couple of tenths to spare

1978 I tagged along with Mike Wilson and Rich Kenney including a visit to meet the Craigmillar Festival Society. It was a real eye-opener. They're well organised, got substantial funding and a prominent place at the political table; but more than that they're doing a fine job improving community well-being making the area a better place to live. We broke off for lunch at the University Arms at Peffermill before going back to the Jack Kane Centre for a couple of hours. I always love going past the olde worlde big Mitchellhill's Healthy Life biscuit factory sign on the Peffermill Road; it takes me right back to being a wee boy and Grandpa Willie taking us for ice cream at Lucas en-route to our Sunday dinner. Come the evening, despite the wet and windy weather I ran a solid session. An early night with The Boys From Brazil!

Morning (7.30 a.m.): 4 miles

Evening (8.00 p.m.): 1000 metres 2 minutes 28 seconds; 600m 84 secs; 300m 36 secs (15 and 10 mins rec)

23rd June, 1974 After getting a bronze medal in yesterday's Scottish Senior Championships I pushed on in training and ran my best ever session. It's great training with Norrie

Gregor who's bringing me on no end. Afterwards Norman invited me up to his flat at Bruntsfield for Sunday tea.

Morning: **4 x 350 metres (15 minutes recovery) 42.0; 42.0; 41.8; 40.8 seconds; very pleasing; I seem to be getting better by the day!**

1975, Dresden The morning after the night before! On the return flight to London I thought I was bound to be sick. I had a very sore head. I sat next to Andrea Lynch and she kept my mind off things. From London a group of us including Adrian got an afternoon flight back to Edinburgh. Nana and Gaga met me at Turnhouse; we were able to give Meg Ritchie a lift back to Musselburgh. Thereafter, straight back into the way of things in the evening with a session at Meadowbank.

Evening: **3 x 3 x 150 metres (walk back recovery); fast and relaxed-the seventh run 14.8 seconds! (5 mins rest) 4 x 60m**

1976 Coach Walker telephoned to say there's a storm brewing over my decision to travel out to Estepona, Spain with Frank Dick and a few of the other Scottish athletes selected for the Olympic team. I went up to Meadowbank and remained there until 4.00 p.m. going over all the ramifications; the press were on the phone etc. It seems the SAAAs is up in arms that we all won't be competing at the Scottish Championships; there's talk of them preventing us going. Huh! It's the first time they've ever shown any interest in me! In between I ran a session; went home for a snooze; hit a few golf balls with Iain; then gave the *Simone de Beauvoir Philosophy Queen* and her sister a lift home.

Afternoon: 2 x 3 x 200 metres (20 seconds recovery) (15 minutes between sets) (1) 24; 26; 28 seconds (2) 25; 26; 26 secs

1977 Mid-afternoon Roger and I ran some 200s; then to Dennis's for a rub; then back to Roger's flat at Thirlestane Road where he rattled up some dinner.

Afternoon (3.00 p.m.): 2 x 200 metres 22.5; 22.3 seconds

24th June, 1974 Two big pieces of news. First, Paul's got a job at Thomas Graham & Sons at £16.50 a week. I'd recommended him. Funny that he'll be starting as I'm leaving-revolving doors. And second, FABULOUS NEWS!- I'm in the Scotland senior team to go to Oslo-my first trip abroad. I'm really excited! After being disappointed to finish third on Saturday I thought I'd blown my chances. I'm partnering Roger Jenkins in the 400 metres and I'm also in the relay team too.

Evening: 7 x acceleration 300 metres; I wasn't feeling that good

1976 I hit a few golf balls in the morning and watched Wimbledon in the afternoon; I could see Bjorn Borg win the title for the first time. Frank Dick has asked me to write a couple of thank you letters to the sponsors of our trip to Spain, so I picked up pen and paper. After training I gave the *Simone de Beauvoir Queen of Philosophy* a lift home; as I'm heading off to Spain tomorrow (despite the SAAAs protestations), we took a slight detour en-route!

Evening: 300 metres 33.8 seconds (15 minutes recovery) 2 x 200m 22.1 and 22.8 secs (8 mins rec) 4 x 100m 10.9 secs

To A Mouse

'...The best-laid schemes o' mice an' men
Gang aft agley,
An lea'e us nought but grief an' pain,
For promis'd joy!...'

Robert Burns

1978 Some grapefruit for breakfast then a relaxed session at Meadowbank. I collected *Diana the goddess of love and hunting* at the West End and we drove down to Peebles for our picnic. Unfortunately, the best laid schemes of mice and men-it was raining! We watched the professional Peebles Highland Games and we won a good bit of money on the sprint which enabled us to go out to the Three Inns. However, we had a fall out-my fault, with me rather pettily walking off. It involves deeper things rather than what came across on the surface-the self-imposed pressure I'm putting on myself to win the Commonwealth Games gold medal; my self-imposed impossibly high standards of self-discipline; athletics; diet; money and career etc. and not using *Diana* as my touchstone. When I got home I went out and ran four miles in Portobello Park. *Diana*, honey, if you ever read this diary entry, I love you more than anything-okay!

Afternoon (12.00 p.m.): 6 x 300 metres (2 minutes recovery) 41 seconds

Evening (9.00 p.m.): 4 miles

25th June, 1973 It's the start of the week and the countdown to my first Scottish Youth Championships. Gaga ran me all the way along Balcarres Street to Grahams' front door. At lunchtime I went along to Morningside to get a haircut. I didn't half get a crop! Betty gave me a lift up to Meadowbank. She's got a new Morris Maxi. I was running not badly this evening. I gave everyone a good laugh with my hair. Dougie gave me a lift home. We're putting up a girl from Leicester on Friday evening. I now wish I hadn't got my hair cut.

Evening: 600 metres 88.2 seconds (personal best); 6 x 150m (2 minutes recovery) 16-18 secs

1974 My letter invite for Oslo arrived in the post. As I was having my tea at Oxgangs I took the letter out to show Anne and Iain. After we'd eaten we went down to visit Mum at the Astley Ainslie Hospital; she looked very pale.

Evening: 4 x 150 metres (walk 250m recovery)

1976 Frank Dick picked me up at Haymarket and we drove through to Myra Nimmo's where we had a coffee before collecting Christine McMeekin. Because of the furore over the trip there were journalists and photographers waiting for us at Glasgow Airport. Rather than having photies of us scurrying away to Spain, we decided to accommodate them. London Airport was roasting and having to hang around there until 10.00 p.m. was really quite unpleasant. Tapio picked us up at Malaga Airport. I'm rooming with Frank. A long day, but I slept well.

Postscript I was of course nicely set up by the press when the photographer threw me a sombrero type hat shouting *Hey! Peter put this on for one of the photos-it will look good.* Naively I accommodated him and put it on not realising it gave off a subtle I don't fucking care! two fingers message to the SAAAs! I can now just imagine them spluttering over their cornflakes, thereafter not being able to get the song Y VIVA ESPANA out of their heads all day!

1977 I felt terrible after a 50 seconds heat at the Scottish Championships and considered pulling out. So much so, I drove from Meadowbank up to the Commonwealth Pool for a sauna and a relaxing lie down! Just over an hour before the final I thought, I'll warm-up and make a decision on how I feel. I decided to race. Approaching the 300 metres point I was down on Roger and Andy Kerr; Roger pulled a hamstring; I pushed on down the home straight and eased past Kerr to win in 47.7 seconds. A funny old race. Later in the evening Roger; Paul; Lo-Lo (Lorraine Morris); *Diana the goddess of love and hunting* and I went for a drink.

1977 Scottish <u>Championships</u>

11.00 a.m. 400 metres Heat 1. Hoffmann 50.0 seconds

4.00 p.m. 400m Final 1. Hoffmann 47.7 secs

26th June, 1976 Estepona, Spain I slept so well and long I ended up missing breakfast. I lay out on a sunbed close by the sea sunbathing for part of the time sipping coke with ice and lemon. After a pleasant lunch I did some gentle swimming in the pool. In the early evening when the temperature had dropped a little Frank drove us out to the local polo fields where I ran a few 200s. In the evening, dinner and a drink; Frank's excellent company with a fund of good tales.

<u>Evening</u>: 4 x 200 metres

27th June, 1973 Pumpa died at 7.00 a.m. this morning. I think he was 91 years old. Nana wasn't so effected as she was about Wee Nana's death which hit her hard. Life is so strange-after that kind of a shocking start to the day, life goes on. Gaga was very good; even though he wasn't working today at Waugh & Son he gave me a lift from Porty right out to the front door of Graham's. And come the end of the day I was chauffeur driven again as Angus gave Scott and me a lift to the 42 bus stop at the Kings Buildings. Once home Nana had my usual meal on the table-fried potatoes, meat, apple sauce and peas and a glass of orange squash. It's brilliant-I've hardly sat down and it appears on the table as if by magic! On the way up to Meadowbank I bought Gaga a couple of gallons of petrol at the Texaco Garage, Willowbrae. My preparations for the Scottish Youth Championships countdown are going well and I'm cautiously optimistic about winning my first title; on Monday evening the session included a p.b. for 600 metres of 88.0 seconds; last night I did a p.b. 500 metres of 68.0 seconds. This evening I was running averagely, but okay. Afterwards I sat up in the cafe talking with Paul and Duncan Baker; I didn't like what Coach Walker said about me. Back home I watched the Wimbledon highlights; there were no shocks.

Evening: 4 x 200 metres (7 minutes recovery) 23; 23; 24; 23 seconds

1978 I spent much of today working out of York Place; it's a great holiday job although I put in a lot of good work too on the council's summer holiday playscheme. I worked out of Rich Vinnicombe's office, but also got out and about with Robert Sinclair including a visit to Meadowbank. Come the end of the day a wee rest before going up to Meadowbank. It was a foul evening-absolutely pouring down and blowing a hooley. Given the weather and front-running I was pleased with my run; front running ain't my forte so I was pleased to run the fastest leg for the team although it was really just a stride. A pity about the weather and the lack of real competition as we had a very powerful team out there tonight with Adrian; Norman and Paul which would take out any club team in Britain, perhaps even the world!

E.A.C v Pennsylvania/Cornell Universities v Scottish Universities

4 x 800 metres 1. E.A.C. (Hoffmann; Gregor; Weatherhead; Forbes) 7 minutes 33 seconds (Hoffmann 1.51.5)

28th June, 1973 A very hot Thursday which was exaggerated within the confines of Thomas Graham & Sons' airless and windowless office. However, I at least managed to get out at lunchtime to play yard football with the warehouse lads. And even better, that's me off work now for five whole days. My preparations continue to go well for my first appearance at the Scottish Youth Championships. Gaga dropped me off at Meadowbank and I was running not badly again. Scott Brodie gave me a lift home and he's going to give me a lift through to Grangemouth on Saturday for the championships. It was good to be able to put my feet up and enjoy Match of the Day from Wimbledon

Evening: 2 x 300 metres (1) 36.8 seconds (equals my p.b.) (2) 39.3 secs; against a very strong wind; 6 x 60m flat out

1974 It's the Scottish Junior Championships tomorrow at Meadowbank. Paul came down to stay the night.

1975 I wandered up nice and early for the Scottish Senior Championships. The good news was they got a sunny day for them. Sometimes it comes off, sometimes it doesn't-today was the latter. I tried to double up, but didn't quite manage to pull it off in a blanket finish in the 200 metres with Drew Harley and Drew McMaster-a good result for the juniors! I wasn't disappointed and felt I might have won the race if I had not run two quarters beforehand. But for me what was more interesting was what actually happened to me in the 200 metres final-something that has never occurred before-my legs, literally gave way about five metres from the line. It was the oddest sensation, although I still managed to fall over the line and claim a medal. During the afternoon Alison Brown was over talking to me-she's a nice girl. At tea-time Coach Walker gave me a lift home. Later I went up town; neither Bob Sinclair nor Davie Reid turned up which was okay as I didn't really feel like going out. Late on I bumped in to Stuart Togher and Paul Buxton in the St Andrews Restaurant.

1975 Scottish Senior Championships

200 metres heat 1. Hoffmann 22.5 seconds

400m heat 1. Hoffmann 49.7 secs

400m final 1. Hoffmann 48.7 secs

200m final 1. Harley 22.0 secs 2. McMaster 22.2 secs 3. Hoffmann 22.2 secs

1976 Estepona, Spain Frank drove Christine McMeekin and me to the rubcor track in Malaga. It was sweltering and with the long drive and heat I fell asleep. When I awoke I felt shit. I was so lethargic I needed to force myself to even warm up, so all things considered I was happy with the session. I spent the afternoon either sleeping or in the pool-even when it was raining; it's a surreal experience swimming in the rain-that odd juxtaposition of water around you as well as it falling upon your head. I read before bed, but unsurprisingly didn't sleep well.

29th June, 1973 I got my Athletics Weekly this morning. After breakfast, mid-morning we headed out to Dalkeith for Pumpa's funeral. The extended family including Ronnie Browne, Andy Ross et al were all there and my cousin David as well as many old Dalkeith worthies who would have been familiar with his blacksmith's work. When the coffin was being lowered into the ground there was a downpour and the rain came tumbling down. With my imagination I thought *What's that all about-a sign from the heavens!* We were back to Porty by lunchtime; I phoned Scott to agree our departure time for tomorrow's Scottish Championships at Grangemouth. Thereafter I watched Wimbledon before going off for a wee sleep. Anne's staying over. We had our Friday evening treat of a St Andrews fish supper, all enhanced with a brilliant episode of Spy Trap; with its complex story lines about The Department, it's intriguing stuff.

1974 As Paul had been staying overnight we headed up to Meadowbank for the Scottish Junior Championships. I don't know what was up with me, but I felt awful-very weak and tired. Anyway, I won my second Scottish title-perhaps more on the basis of reputation, where I suspect my rivals had conceded defeat beforehand; meanwhile Paul was second in the half and picked up a silver medal. Afterwards the two of us joined the big crew at the Waverley Bar, but I was home by 11.00 p.m.

1974 Scottish Junior Championships

(2.00 p.m.) 400 metres Heat 1. Hoffmann 53.0 seconds

(3.05 p.m.) 400 metres Final 1. Hoffmann 49.3 secs 2. I. Murray (Garscube) 50.7 secs

1976 Seghers Club Estepona, Spain A much easier and more relaxed day. I ran a speed session on the club's straight track; it was a light session-I feel my speed, certainly going by the times, is in a good place. Afterwards, it was great fun playing with a canoe on the Mediterranean. Come the evening Myra; Christine; Frank and I went to an enjoyable fancy dress party. I really enjoyed myself-jiving away!

Morning: 6 x 60 metres; all in 6.7-6.8 seconds

1977 Another bad cold. We were willing Virginia Wade to qualify for the women's final at Wimbledon, which she eventually did taking Chris Evert down.

1978 As we were running some 600s this evening I just ran an easy three miles first thing. The summer holiday job with the council is going well; Robert Sinclair and I took some equipment out to a playscheme at Ratho; on the way back to York Place we checked out how the schemes at Currie and Balerno were going. It's really the perfect wee number for us; come the evening a solid enough session.

Morning (8.00 a.m.): 3 miles steady run

Evening: 4 x 600 metres (6 minutes recovery) 85; 83; 84; 83 seconds

30th June, 1973 Scott Brodie gave me a lift through to Grangemouth to run in my first Scottish Championships. I couldn't believe it-I WON!

I was nervous before the final and ran a cautious race. I ran with everyone including the Scottish Schools silver medallist, Ken McMillan (George Heriot's School) until 300 metres; it was a great feeling when I put the foot down to find myself easily moving ahead of the field. Beforehand, I was quite bemused by MacMillan enjoying a fag; an interesting double-bluff which is wasted on a lad from Oxgangs-I was always going to treat him seriously! I phoned Nana and Gaga to give them the good news. I was on cloud 9 afterwards. It was just a great feeling. For the first time in years I feel I've achieved something. To be known as a Scottish champion feels just brilliant. Mr Groundwater kindly gave me a lift all the way home. For the whole journey I felt encased in a warm glow; on arrival at Durham Road I was almost expecting the flags to be out!

Scottish Youth Championships 1973:

400 metres 1. Hoffmann 52.0 seconds

1974 The family are going to buy me a blazer; grey trousers and new shoes for my first trip with Scotland to Oslo, Norway.

Morning: 4 x 3 x 50 metres with flying starts

1976 Seghers Club, Estepona, Spain Having been sharing a room with Frank all week I've got to know him much better. He's an interesting mix and very likeable, but I think (understandably) he struggles to get that balance between being your pal and a professional athletics coach. He's not an intellectual, but highly intelligent and shrewd; he's someone who makes the most of his abilities. He's ambitious and knows what he wants and where he wants to go. He works hard and prioritises and devotes time to those areas which are important to him. He's an achiever and wants to fulfil his potential and leave a mark. Peppered with the addition of motivation makes for a powerful mixture. Working on his own initiative and essentially as his own boss, albeit to a committee, means to a large extent he can pursue his own agenda, enabling him to concentrate on his research and writing; someone else in the post would tackle the job differently.

In some respects there's a purist dimension there too, but he's also materialistic and would probably like to continue this work lifestyle but be earning more money. He likes his Alfa Romeo, but would probably prefer something better. He's got a reputation as a bit of a ladies man; as well as his looks he's good company and a fund of amusing tales. I laughed at his one about the needle, thread and eyeball; also how when he was a student at Loughborough when they'd been abroad on a student trip they'd smuggled cheap watches back in to the country. Anticipating the customs' officials searching through their suitcases they had streaked their underwear with Bisto and carefully arranged them at the top of the suitcase. When the officials duly requested them to open their suit-cases, the officials paused when they noticed the 'soiled and streaked' underpants and just said 'Thank you sir-that'll be fine.' and waved them through!

In the afternoon I shocked and amused the party by getting my hair dyed. It was supposed to turn out blonde, but has turned out a ghastly shade of orange; it's the stuff of nightmares! The evening meal was lovely including an exquisite desert, but I left early as the ghastly English high jumper, Val Harrison, was getting on my proverbials and I didn't want to end up being rude to her. She's spent the whole trip moaning and complaining about seemingly everything.

I came back to my room and wrote a letter to the effervescent and highly intelligent Helen Barnett who I've been corresponding with weekly for the past year or so. Sitting here on the balcony writing my journal I'm looking out to the Mediterranean where I can see two lights from two small fishing boats out in the bay (Bahia de Estepona). On a late evening, with the sweet aroma of the exotic flowers and the chirping of cicadas I'm enjoying these fruits of my athletics labours-not that I'd ever been working for such a bonus. But I'm grateful to Frank for facilitating this trip and arranging the sponsorship.

1st July, 1973 It somehow seems appropriate to be awakening on my seventeenth birthday as the Scottish Champion; with my shiny gold medal sitting by my bedside I really didn't need any cards or presents to celebrate. I was keen to get straight back in to training, but when I went up to Meadowbank the only athletes there were Paul and Dougie McLean. The place was empty. I noticed Drew McMaster hovering about. It's good to become a fellow national champion, but I'm a bit short of his level...yet! Paul came back to Porty for his Sunday dinner and stayed all afternoon. Mrs Elliot (Josephine's sister) phoned up; I guess to discuss what happens now that the funeral has been held. We watched the East Germany v UK v Bulgaria international; Jenkins was absolutely rubbish!

Morning: 12 laps sprinting the straights and walking the bends then vice versa

1974 An eighteenth birthday to remember; not in a party sense-I would never host a party for myself; it's just not my scene. But a lovely day in my small world. I'm on holiday, so it kicked off with a visit to Davie Campbell the physio at Duddingston Road; I've a slight groin strain. Back home, Gaga had picked up his Scottish Daily Express; Brian Meek had given me a great write up. I don't really feel I deserve it as I'm still pretty second rate. Mum had received £20 from John's mum and she gave me £15 of it which was **really great** of her. So, armed with all that cash Gaga, Paul and I went in to town in search of a blazer, grey trousers and shoes. Success! I may be the crappest athlete on the Scotland team to Oslo, but I'll look very smart. I also picked up a new pair of Adidas training shoes. After lunch at Porty, Paul and I played pitch 'n putt before going up to Meadowbank where I ran a brilliant session.

Evening: 2 x 3 x 200 metres (2 minutes' recovery; 15 mins between sets) all between 21.4 and 23.0 seconds; slight rolling start

Before Bed: Arm-action; press-ups; sit-ups; 9.45 hours sleep

1975 There were quite a few birthday cards in the post this morning, including one from *Pixie Mia Farrow lookalike*. I was actually supposed to be taking her out, but she's got a hospital appointment. As a wee break in training I did a hurdles session; I quite enjoyed it and thought I was reasonable. The *Mary Rand lookalike from the south-west* is through for a few days and we're going out tomorrow evening.

Evening: 8 x 130 metres over 3 foot hurdles; 60m; 100m; 300m (35.0 seconds)

1976 Seghers Club, Estepona, Spain A very relaxed day mainly spent reading and sunbathing, with a light session thrown in. The group (Christine; Myra; Frank et al) celebrated my birthday with a cake and a bottle of champagne which was very good of them all; we were entertained by the artist Frederick; none of us got to bed until 1.30 a.m. The *Simone de Beauvoir Philosophy Queen* sent me an amusing birthday card, which was thoughtful of her; she's a bright girl. It takes its place in the journal alongside the witty note on a paper-bag which she'd sent me earlier in the week. It's illuminating how she's more open and expressive on paper including sending her love; it made my day.

1977 Virginia Wade won Wimbledon-I'll take that as my birthday pressie! Delightful stuff. And as Dan Maskell said *'Oh! well played, Miss Wade!'* Diana the goddess of love and hunting was at her granny's funeral today; I diplomatically stayed away. In the evening we went out for a few drinks and a meal.

1978 Birthday cards and pressies to start the day and then up to Meadowbank to run a good session with Paul; Norman; and John Scott. It was good fun having a core part of the winter group back out together-the first time for a wee while. If it's just Paul and me there's a tendency to knock fuck out of each other! I lazed about all afternoon reading before going out to run a flowing five miles on Portobello Golf Course-I enjoyed that. Afterwards *Diana* and I went to Blackford Pond; I held the umbrella over her whilst she fed a brood of ducks; happy days and great to be in love. Along with Norman we'd been invited round to Gavin Miller's for a film show; it was an okay evening but he'd made a poor job of filming some of my races.

Afternoon (1.00 p.m.): **light circuit; fast 60 metres; 2 x 500m (72, 68 seconds) 100m jog 300m (41 secs); 4 x 100m**

Evening (5.00 p.m.): **5-6 miles**

2nd July, 1973 Sheer luxury being on holiday from Thomas Graham & Sons for a few days. I took a wee tootle up town to buy a jumper with my birthday money from Nana and Gaga and then travelled out to Oxgangs. Iain only got up when I knocked on the door. It was such a lovely hot day I sat out on the back shed roof with Iain and Les; shortly afterwards Paul joined us. A very pleasant way to spend a summer's afternoon-just like old times. Later I went down to Meadowbank to train, but came back to Oxgangs to stay the night. Iain and I were playing at boxing.

Evening: 300 metres 40.0 seconds; 2 x 200m 26 secs; 3 x 150m 18 secs; 4 x 100m 11.9; 11.3 (p.b.); 11.7; 11.7 secs

3rd July, 1973 Having stayed over at Oxgangs last night I lay in bed until 10.00 a.m. when Paul awoke the household; he'd cycled up from Broomhouse. Later on I went down to Waugh & Son, Butchers at Morningside to meet Gaga to get a lift back home to Porty. I felt very tired so just took it very easy at training. I'm fed up too. A mix of feeling whacked, but perhaps after the high of winning the Scottish Youth title I'm just coming back down to planet Earth. And not helped by it being the last day of my mini-break and returning tomorrow to the grind and toil of Thomas Graham & Sons, Builders & Plumbers Merchants.

Evening: 10 x 60 metres; very easy...I was feeling tired

4th July, 1973 I went back to work today. Fair play to my boss, Roy Wallace, but he took me out for my lunch to celebrate me winning the Scottish. He's always good company. As I've observed before there's a very good side to Roy; perhaps he's just a 1970s example of a Jekyll and Hyde Edinburgher; the doppelganger! Come the end of the work day, the usual mad-cap dash across town involving bus (41)-run a mile from Blackford-bus (42)-sprint up Durham Road and home for dinner, before running a good session at Meadowbank. Being a Wednesday it was an Edinburgh Southern Harriers' girl's night, so I enjoyed their charms, mainly from a distance including the red headed Fay Robertson. I had an argument with Derek Smith; I feel there's some frisson between us. There's been a mixed reaction to me winning the Scottish-it's not all positive, but mainly it is. But I'm conscious of down-playing it if it's ever mentioned. Anyway, in my own mind I'm wanting to win much bigger things and to leave this level behind immediately. Although it's mid-summer I'm already looking forward to getting stuck in this winter. I don't have work or a career to look forward to, but I've got Meadowbank and my athletics.

Evening: 6 x 150 metres (3 minutes' recovery)

5ᵗʰ July, 1973 Roy told me to bring my gold medal in to work today. Come lunchtime the two of us went out to the International; they always serve up a grand supper. We got our pay rises today-I got a couple of quid taking my wages up to £11 a week, however Fred McBride only got 64 pence and he's told us all he's leaving. Although Roy was very funny, he's a bit of a bastard too, because he was winding Fred up, saying it reflected his performance, not to mention his absenteeism record. With a sly dig to me he said Fred wasn't really gold medal material. It's true though-he's hardly ever here. Anyway, if he does leave it could open the door for Paul to come and work at Thomas Graham & Sons which would make work much more enjoyable for me. I got the same bus home as Gus McKenzie who was heading back to Musselburgh. I stopped off for a fish supper and then home for the Wimbledon highlights; Jan Kodes knocked out Roger Taylor-a bit of a surprise, at least to me.

Evening: 200 metres 24.5 seconds; 2 x 150m 16.5 secs; 3 x 100m 11.9; 11.7; 11.5 secs; 60m 6.9 secs-possibly a flyer, but a quick time!

1975 We arrived at Crystal Palace at just after mid-day. I made my debut over 400 metres hurdles and won the race in the second fastest time by a British Junior this season. Afterwards I was asked by John Le Masurier whether I'd consider running for the British Junior team in the event, but I said no. I couldn't quite get to grips with the stride pattern and really just ended up jumping over the hurdles then running in between. In training earlier in the week I'd actually felt quite smooth over the barriers. I like John Le Mas; Josephine loves his silky voice; whenever she speaks to him on the phone, it brightens up her day no end! Thereafter, I ran a solid 200 metres for the club too. I didn't fancy the long trip up the road on the club bus so I took a flight back to Edinburgh with Coach Walker; he gave me a lift home to Portobello. The great thing with British Caledonian Airways is you just turn up, take a seat and pay on board-it's just like getting on a bus!

British League, Crystal Palace:

400 metres hurdles 1. Hoffmann 54.2 seconds

200 metres 1. Hoffmann 21.8 secs

1978 I had just completed my morning run and was freshening up when the doorbell rang. I dashed down the hall, half-hoping it might be my exam results, wanting to get them out of the way, one way or another. Sure enough there was a letter from Dundee stuck in the letter box. This is it! I opened it up and I went wild-I've passed all my exams-YAHOO! That's me through to second year. I told Josephine and then because *Diana the goddess of love and hunting* is persona non grata I dashed up to the phone box to give her the good news too. She was delighted. I also phoned Coach Walker at Meadowbank. At lunchtime I did a wee run and then went out to Oxgangs to let Mum know. She too was delighted. In the evening another wee run followed by a physio's appointment at Denis's and an easy night in reading. I've decided I'm going to take some of the second year course work reading material with me to Canada.

Morning (8.00 a.m.): 4 miles

Afternoon (1.00 p.m.): 3 miles

Evening (6.00 p.m.): 4 miles

6th July, 1977 A very relaxing day. Roger picked me up at ten o'clock; we stopped by the launderette, a meal at St Andrews Restaurant at lunchtime; a Lucas ice cream at Musselburgh, then he drove us down to Gullane in his white Ford Escort estate. When I say his, it's actually his Dad's; rather than taking a salary increase from B.P. he just takes a new car instead and gives it to Rodge to drive around in; I think he preferred the previous maroon Mini; alongside the Thirlestane Road flat, how the other half lives! We spent the afternoon sunbathing, swimming in the sea and running a few 60s in the surf. Come tea-time we went round to Denis's for a rub. When I got home *Diana the goddess of love and hunting* was there making me a new pair of shorts. Afterwards, we had a couple of drinks stopping off via a cornfield; we enjoy our nature!

Wish upon a star

'...The two of us staring
At the stars in the sky
Making wishes on comets
And things that fly by

...We're out in the cornfield
In my old Chevy truck
Planning out life's direction
On a stroke of good luck

Questions unanswered
Questions not asked
Some are worth knowing
Some left in the past
Go in with eyes open
Your life will be grand
Just give it your damndest
And go lead the band...'

Roger Turner

<u>Afternoon:</u> 60 metres runs in the surf; sun on my back

7th July, 1974 First thing, Iain gave me a good massage, but it didn't prevent me running poorly in training. Afterwards I had another massage, this time at the physio's. In the evening I watched West Germany beat Holland 2-1 to win the World Cup-not the result most neutrals wanted. I've packed my bags for Norway-my first trip abroad. Exciting times.

8th July, 1974 A wet start. We took the train from Waverley Station to Glasgow before flying out to Copenhagen. Like the rest of the team I bought some duty free whisky. It was the first time I'd flown; a strange thing happened on the flight; one of my ears started to bleed. I was sitting with Roger and he gave me some cotton wool and also a sweet encouraging me to swallow because of the air pressure. Without exiting the plane we flew from Copenhagen on to Oslo. In the land of the midnight sun, the city looked beautiful.

The track is great-just six lanes. I've got my blocks fixed just right. A pleasant evening with the team. I enjoyed a drink I've never seen before called Seven-Up. Because we're so far north there's very little darkness. Scott Brodie didn't come to bed until 2.00 a.m.

1975 No holiday job today as the Duke of Edinburgh is in town. Roger and I ran a really good session in the morning before going down to Portobello Baths for an aerotone bath to help us recover. Earlier on I'd called off representing the senior Great Britain team in the A match in France. The travel arrangements including trains and busses and the length of the trip were just ridiculous. Although I'm still a junior athlete I'm already getting fussy about what I want or don't want to do. However, I've been told in no uncertain terms that if I turn down the invitation it will do me 'Irreparable damage'! So, I've been given an ultimatum!

Morning: 3 x 300 metres (11 minutes recovery) 35.1; 34.4; 34.1 seconds; legs are still sore and heavy from Sunday's football

9th July, 1974 Oslo After breakfast, along with the pole-vaulter, Dick Williamson, we walked down to the adjacent lake. On a beautiful summer's morn in the northlands it looked quite beguiling and it was lovely to see small family groups out enjoying themselves. When I started on this athletics journey just over eighteen months ago, little did I think I'd reach international representation, never mind so soon. Getting an opportunity to travel abroad for the first time and to broaden my horizon wasn't really a spin off that I had ever considered, yet here I am.

After a light lunch I lay down in my room to prepare myself for my first international race in the evening. It's something I guess I'll have to get used to; part of me was thinking nervously about the race ahead and the pain I always associate with the quarter mile-there's a double nervousness at play there-the competition and knowing I'm going to have to hurt myself; but at the same time I'm trying to put it out of my mind too, to avoid draining myself beforehand. Late afternoon we travelled down to the legendary Bislet Stadium-not a bad place to make my international debut. There were a lot of Norwegians helping out, including a girl called Bjorg Larsen, who quite captivated me; I hope she comes along to watch again tomorrow.

I finished sixth and last, but didn't disgrace myself. I was the youngest in the race and once again broke 50 seconds for the third time in a row. Roger went crazy, blasting through 300 metres in about 33 seconds; I went out too fast, going through in 33.8 seconds which was a p.b. and of course ended up treading water down the home straight, as did Roger, who faded from first to third! Still, very enjoyable and I gave it a go.

Norway v Bulgaria v Scotland, Bislet Stadium, Oslo

400 metres

1. M. Danov Bulgaria 47.6 seconds
2. R. Tjore Norway 47.8 secs
3. R. Jenkins Scotland 48.1 secs
4. J. Naevdal 48.7 secs
5. K. Khristov 48.9 secs
6. P. Hoffmann 49.1 secs

1978 A relaxed family breakfast at Porty and a relaxed lunchtime session with Paul at Meadowbank. Although breezy, at last a gloriously warm summer's day. In the afternoon I watched the Phillips' Gateshead Games; Wells ran a great 100 metres in 10.29 seconds to equal the U.K. record. Sebastian Coe was quite impressive beating the Americans including Don Paige. I'm quite looking forward to racing Coe next weekend, but I'm conscious of how hard he goes out over the first lap. Late afternoon I ran for the club in the 4 x 400 metres relay and managed to get us disqualified for barging...hmmn! A very enjoyable evening with Gavin Miller and *Diana the goddess of love and hunting* at the Roxburgh Hotel.

Afternoon (12.00 p.m.): 600 metres 84 seconds; 4 x 200m 23 secs

Afternoon (5.00 p.m.): 4 x 400 metres relay leg- disqualified

10th July, 1974 Oslo God, what a change in the weather; it was absolutely pouring down and Thor the god of thunder roaring in the background. Because the weather was so bad Roger, Norman and I sat inside and played cards. I've been shocked at the cost of living here; it's like three times the price of back home. Going on the maxim that you can take the boy out of Oxgangs, but not Oxgangs out of the boy, I went round half the team offering to buy their whisky and fags off them at double what they'd paid, then sold it on to some Norwegians at an excellent profit. I thought it was a win-win-win especially as the Scots can still buy duty free before they head back home to Scotland, however X made a nasty comment to me; to be honest, I can't stand him.

Late afternoon we went back down to the Bislet Stadium for day two of the international match. The beautiful Norwegian girl, Bjorg, from the evening before was there. She came over and sat down beside me. We talked away; she spent most of the evening smiling at me. I asked her out and she agreed, however, disappointingly she wasn't allowed. I walked her home. I'm definitely going to write to her. She's so beautiful. With me also running in the relay I'd been given two prizes of attractive silver spoon mementos, so I gave her one of them. Although we finished third in the relay I ran well; my official split was 47.4 seconds-WOW! considering I hadn't broken 50 seconds until last month things are coming on. We ran a Scottish record too, so all in all I haven't disgraced myself, well apart from on the entrepreneurial front!

Norway v Bulgaria v Scotland

4 x 400 metres relay

1. Bulgaria 3.11.5
2. Norway 3.12.1
3. Scotland (McCallum; Gregor; Hoffmann; Jenkins) 3.12.4

1975 At lunchtime I gave Roger a lift out to the airport. In the afternoon I played indoor football with the Meadowbank managers; Coach Walker wasn't pleased, particularly as I ended up injuring myself, so there's no way I could even run in the France v Great Britain match, even if I wanted to. Anyway, it's all in flux and a bit of a balls up on the arrangements front. Reluctantly I took a wander up to Thomas Cook to collect my London train ticket; they had no knowledge of it, so I ended up going out to Turnhouse and flew down to London. I've a sore leg; had a Chinky; and just phoned Coach Walker.

Afternoon: **Hour indoor football**

1978 I picked up the Commonwealth Games kit from Aitken & Niven at George Street. I must say they've done a hell of a good job; whilst it doesn't compete with the giant Olympic suitcase full of Santa goodies, there were only a couple of dud pieces-like the suitcase itself, especially if you were to leave it out in the rain. A tiring afternoon driving around the Edinburgh parks ensuring the play schemes were running smoothly left me a bit whacked. After tea, Gavin Miller dropped by-ostensibly about the possibility of *Diana the goddess of love and hunting* travelling out to Canada, but it would never work because of the start of her nursing studies. In the evening *Diana* and I went out for a walk along the banks of the River Almond.

Morning (7.00 a.m.): 3 miles

Evening (7.00 p.m.): 4 miles

11ᵗʰ July, 1975 As the trip to France has fallen through for various reasons I travelled out to the airport and flew back to Turnhouse. The rest of the day involved work; reading, television and fish 'n chips for dinner. Gaga had to have Ming our Pekingese dog put down. It was very sad, but for the best.

12ᵗʰ July, 1974 The combination of feeling very tired this morning and my days at Graham's coming to an end made me just decide to stay off work. I gave Paul a ring and we met up for a game of tennis. Afterwards I went to Davie Campbell the physio-he said my legs are in great condition. I phoned Coach Walker about tomorrow's arrangements to go down to the Duns Highland Games. Early to bed.

1977 Susan Rettie phoned me and we played tennis at Rosefield Park all afternoon. With attending St Margaret's School in Edinburgh with all their courts she's an excellent player; she's great fun to be with and a quite beautiful girl.

Miss Joan Hunter Dunn

'Miss J. Hunter Dunn, Miss J. Hunter Dunn,
Furnish'd and burnish'd by Aldershot sun,
What strenuous singles we played after tea,
We in the tournament - you against me!

Love-thirty, love-forty, oh! weakness of joy,
The speed of a swallow, the grace of a boy,
With carefullest carelessness, gaily you won,
I am weak from your loveliness, Joan Hunter Dunn...'

John Betjeman

Afterwards we enjoyed a Lucas Ice Cream and she walked me up the hill to Durham Road. I ended up being too late for my appointment with Dennis, so I just did some easy strides before looking in to see him later. I had a glimpse of RUN CHEETAH RUN! Afterwards I met *Diana the goddess of love and hunting* for some chips; afterwards we stopped for ten minutes down the coast.

<u>Afternoon (3.00 p.m.):</u> 1.5 hours tennis

Evening (7.00 p.m.): 6 x 90 metres

13ᵗʰ July, 1974 I met Coach Walker; Paul; Mark Wilson and Kim Roberts at mid-day to travel down to Duns. Well fuck me!, that was a car-ride we'll never forget. It was like something out of Wacky Races-a real white knuckle job. There were times when Coach Walker couldn't see the road in front of him as we swept around bends and on other occasions we were literally sailing through the air without a pilot's licence as we sped over several hill summits. I know this is Jim Clark territory, but even old Jim would have been left in the dust! I don't know if it was just the shock, but Paul and I were laughing hysterically as we gripped on to anything in the car that didn't move. In between Paul was turning the air blue, which made me laugh all the more... *'For Christ's sake Bill!...'* to put it mildly.

Somehow we got there in one piece, but had probably used up all our adrenalin, before getting to the starting line. Despite the handicaps (with us being selected to run for Scotland they didn't do Paul and me any favours with the handicapping), I still managed to pick up four prizes-a cutlery set, a silver dish etc. The announcer was grateful for us showing face and acknowledged and thanked us over the tannoy. We never usually run at Highland Games, but I think Coach Walker has an old association with them, so he'd told the organisers we'd run today; it was a wee change from training-July's always quiet. Afterwards, we came back to the capital at a slightly more sedate speed, but not much. Coach dropped Paul and me at Portobello. After tea, I decided not to go out dancing.

Duns Highland Games:

100 metres 2. Hoffmann

200m (off 7 metres) 1. Hoffmann 22.5 seconds

800m 2. Hoffmann

Relay 1. Our composite E.A.C. team

14th July, 1976 We left London to fly out to Montreal today-exciting times; I thought I should capture the moment with my camera so on the bus taking us out to Heathrow. Steve Ovett and Brendan Foster were sitting adjacent so were the main focus of my lens.

1977 I went up to the Royal Infirmary and it seems I'm allergic to pollen etc. Will; Jo; and Aunt Heather dropped me off at Turnhouse; I managed to buy a British Caledonian voucher for Paul. A pleasant wee flight and then the usual traverse across London town to the Queens Hotel arriving late-around 11.00 p.m. I'm rooming with Bob Danville and Dave West. We fly out to Nice tomorrow at a slightly more civilised hour for the international against France.

1978 I awoke quite early so it made for a very long day before running in the U.K. Championships heat in the evening. However, it's a complete luxury to be at home with the venue, Meadowbank, only two miles away. After breakfast I took a wee tootle out to Oxgangs to see Mum and Anne; we sat and chatted and played some good L.P.s including Francois Hardy.

I drove back to Porty for lunch and then lay down for a few hours. In some respects you're never quite sure whether taking a slightly unorthodox approach to race days i.e. resting does you any good. It's completely different to how you go about your normal day when you still end up running solid training sessions. There's almost an argument to continue with your normal pattern, not that many of us would ever do that when there's the chance to put your feet up.

I went up to Meadowbank at 4.00 p.m. to take in the scene and had an omelette. Dave Jenkins, John Scott and Gavin Miller were about so I had wee blethers with them. I drove back home; it's great only being a ten minutes' drive away. It's like I'm able to separate that world, putting it on a shelf to rest, before coming back to pick it up again; quite surreal really. Once back home I sat beside the goldfish pool with my feet up; it was dreamily relaxing-perhaps too much so, as I was finding it slightly easier than normal to keep the nerves at bay. But again that surreal feeling of separation; I suppose I could just as easily sit here and not bother going up to race at all; it's as if that world doesn't really exist-it's an imaginary other world; and all that truly exists is the here and now-my little world, with me sitting here, by the side of a garden pool with the dog and cat beside me, occasionally wandering off around the garden sniffing and exploring their own little worlds, before returning to brush themselves against me. Anyway, having mulled over that reflection, tempting as it was-after all who wants to hurt themselves?-who wants to put themselves through the stress; the nerves; and the pain? Certainly not me, yet off I went; it was time to go; it was time to do the business.

Having run the fastest time in the world this year it was unsurprising to see Sebastian Coe win the first heat, but I was impressed too at Paul's positivity; journalists and others under-rate how brilliant he is. Yes, at times he can be inconsistent and be up and down, but he can be exceptionally gritty at times too. He's much harder than me; then again everyone out there is; I'm soft as shite! I just have to make the best of what I have-talent; motivation and discipline. Anyway, I won the second heat, in the fastest time of the evening, but running rather riskily! That said, it wasn't an evening for running quickly-the usual overcast Meadowbank weather by the time we came to race, which was quite late on. In the evening *Diana the goddess of love and hunting* and I went out for a drink at the Two Inns; I had a pint of beer and felt quite light-headed! I feel if I keep relatively close to Coe tomorrow I can beat him, but the key issue is whether the usual negativity kicks in and I'm too cautious and conservative. Out with heats it's only going to be my fifth proper 800 metres race. I really should have done what was our original intention to have moved up last year to take the rough edges off and get the experience. But as Roger astutely wrote to me last September I avoided it going back to the safety of the quarter mile. Anyway, let's see what tomorrow brings. I read before going off to sleep.

1978 UK Championships 800 metres

Heat One 1. S. Coe 1.51.03 2. P. Forbes 1.51.40

Heat Two 1. Hoffmann 1.50.70 2. L. Nicholson 1.50.74 3. R. Harrison 1.50.78 4. P. Browne 1.50.83

Glasgow Herald

'...The most exciting moment was saved to the very end when Peter Hoffmann once again gave his supporters the jitters by leaving his sprint incredibly late in his 800 metres heat.

The Edinburgh man moved out of last position with just metres left, and coming into the final straight it looked as if he was not gaining at all on a leading bunch of five, with four to qualify, Hoffmann gradually pulled level however to win literally with his last stride in 1 min. 50.7 secs. the fastest time of the evening.

His Scottish team mate, Paul Forbes chose a safe route by leading from the bell in the other heat, and only British record holder Sebastian Coe could catch him, the Sheffield man winning in 1 min 51 secs...'

The Scotsman Report by Sandy Sutherland

'...Peter Hoffmann (Edinburgh AC) must delight in giving his coach, Bill Walker, palpitations. Hoffmann, known for his delaying tactics, seemed to have overdone it at last night's Kraft UK National Championships. With 250 metres to go he was still last of the ten man field and only passed the bunch of runners contesting the lead in the last few strides to win by the tiniest of margins...'

15th July, 1974 Paul started work today at Thomas Graham & Sons, whereas I'm getting my books in two weeks' time, so there'll only be a short period of Forbes 'n Hoffmann havoc at the blacking factory. I wonder what kind of books they give me? It poured with rain all day; I'm unsure what sign that is from the gods! I'm pleased for Paul sake that he's got his first job and that I've been able to help him to get the post. He's working upstairs in Ian Slater's department. Meanwhile, I'm also pleased for myself, to be getting out and moving on to start on a new path in life. Next month I'm going back to study at Telford College. I'm taking a couple of Highers and O levels, but this time, unlike school, I'm very motivated, plus I know I can do it. These are the two major differences; for some reason I no longer doubt myself; I'm brighter than I've given myself credit for and I know I'll apply myself and work assiduously. I think that's the big lesson that athletics has taught me since I began working at

Graham's in September, 1972. Going on to win the Scottish Youth and then Junior titles has made me realise you only get back what you put in.

Since leaving Boroughmuir two years ago and starting working at Graham's has proven to be a very harsh lesson in life and at times it's been quite dispiriting. The nature of the work was not for me and there were no prospects either. After only a few weeks in post I realised what a ghastly mistake I'd made, and I came to regret skiving school for half the time and then leaving Burrie with solitary O Levels in Arithmetic and History. It's been soul-destroying coming in at 8.00 am. each day knowing that I was cooped up inside in a window-less office with nine hours in front of me each day and with no real autonomy. And whilst sometimes seeing *Pixie Mia Farrow lookalike* either heading off to Mary Erskine School in the morning or occasionally in the evening returning home always raised my spirits, it was also a kick in the teeth and reminded me of the contrast with our lives. She was bright and vivacious and out there doing something very positive with her life, whilst for all purposes I was like the young Charles Dickens over a century before and at a similar age, with no prospects in life, heading back and forth each day to and from the blacking factory; it was like the 20th century meeting the 19th century. I've never said how miserable I've been here, always putting on a brave face to Mum and others; even in agreeing a way forward with her support I've sold it or spun it that it's for positive reasons. However, the reality was that I'd quickly mastered pricing interminable invoices within a few weeks and it wasn't stretching me at all. Ultimately, it's only been my athletics that has assuaged life here. Of course it's not been all been entirely bad. I've grown up a bit and I've matured and am slightly more world-wisely. Also, I like many of the people here, particularly Willie Fernie and I'll miss our wee lunchtime games of chess. I've also enjoyed the wee social outings to the Silver Bowl Chinese Restaurant at Comiston Road for the three-course specials and also to the International Restaurant. I've become good pals with Scott Wallace, but he's left now too, to better his life.

Along the way there have been many laughs and Roy's a funny and witty guy. In particular I've had some tremendous laughs with him and it's hard to pick out the best amongst them. I won't forget my first week. I'd paid a visit to the gents' loo and was sitting quite contently in cubicle number 1 contemplating life as one does; of a sudden, from the cubicle next to me (cubicle number 2) I heard someone groan out; Eh, what's that about?; then, a foot appeared under the adjacent wall into my cubicle; what the fuck! I didn't say anything and held my breath-what the fuck was going on here; then a minute later there was a much deeper groan and the foot suddenly became a shin; I held my breath; I was completely mesmerised as I stared intently down at this trouser-ed leg only an inch from my own foot so much so I was forgetting to breathe; Christ did that mean the guy's opposite leg was intruding in to cubicle number 3? Was he completely splayed out? I was so mesmerised-I couldn't move; the tension became unbearable-what would happen next? Of a sudden the intense silence was broken by the most FUCKING LOUD cry out, followed by the most God Almighty enormous long-drawn out groan and a further cry of intense pain; the next thing I knew the whole fucking leg appeared on top of my foot. I hopped off the lavy seat with my breeks half-way down my legs-Christ I thought, that poor guy's got some constipation! I was going to shout through to enquire if he was all right, but decided no and instead I couldn't get my arse wiped quickly enough before scarpering back through to the office. Fuck me, what kind of a house of horrors had an innocent young sixteen year old landed up in! I sat down with beads of sweat running down my pow to try to focus on my work. A few minutes later Roy walks in to the room, rubs his hands and announces to one and all with a wee wink in my direction and a scratch of his arse 'Ah, that feels much better!' My introduction to the inimitable Roy Wallace!

But no, overall, I've generally hated it here. Balcarres Street has been a miserable wind tunnel, particularly when summer turned to autumn; in the winter, whilst it's been nice to get in to the warmth, one emerges in to the darkness at five o'clock. Neither will I miss the long travail across town-dashing up through Morningside Graveyard to get the 41 bus, but I will miss the wee bar of Needlers' chocolate orange that I treated myself too to sustain me en-route. Neither will I miss running up Blackford Avenue and down West Mains Road to catch the 42 bus at the Kings Buildings to dash in and wolf down my dinner before going training. I never had the money, but often I recall when I emerged from Grahams' door, how I regularly looked at a little Reliant Bond Bug parked in Balcarrres Street and with my imagination day dreamed that it was mine. It was basically a two seater, but on three wheels. I'd fantasise about buying one of my own and how wonderful it would be at the end of the day to be able to make my own way across town and drive back home in comfort and out of inclement weather, all cosy and dry to head back home in relative comfort to Durham Road, Porty.

I'll miss travelling out each morning with Grandpa Willie to his wee part-time morning job at Waugh & Son, Butchers at Morningside Road. And him parking the car at Nile Grove whilst I sat and read his Daily Express before walking along to Grahams to begin work. We've enjoyed each other's company and travelling together has eased both our passages.

Turning the negative in to the positive, in combating the *ennui* at work has allowed me much time to go off on flights of fancy and to think and to dream and to plan about how life might be. It's given the luxury of time to properly reflect on and consider what I really want to do with my life. Having to work all day whilst my peers have been at school and university has made me realise, that yes, I want some of that life too. Even just simple things like training with students on Wednesday half days has an enormous appeal to it, rather than being hunched over this work-bench, so much so it sends an adrenalin shot through my veins, making some of the miserable days much more bearable as I lived in an imaginary world of my own making.

The mix of being away from my friends and family at Oxgangs, combined with life at Graham's has also made me realise just how important Meadowbank has become in my life; not only for athletics, but as the focus of my social life too. Anyway, come August an exciting new world awaits me. I think I can do it-in fact I know I can do it and make it work; and much of that is due to the support to follow my bliss from Mum and Dad, as well as the ongoing support from Nana and Gaga.

One other small change is Gaga is going to have to box clever for first read of The Hornet! Up until now he's been mostly in without me about when the paper-boy delivers it on a Monday afternoon-now he's going to have to fight for first read! The good news on that front is that Wilson is back in the comic from next week in a new adventure. Of course out with Jenkins, Wilson's my real hero!

A lovely dinner, whilst reading The Hornet and the added bonus of some lovely Lucas ice cream-a real treat. In the evening I watched the Schools' International; with being booted out of Boroughmuir I've never been able to enjoy that great honour. I thought Ann Clarkson was great-a super run and I told her so; she just needs a little more confidence and she could become really very good indeed. On a less happy note, the father-figure of Edinburgh Athletic Club, Bert Sinclair, died this evening. It came as quite a shock. Even when you're young, the death of someone you know halts you in your tracks. Nothing's for ever; and all the more reason to seize the day and the future too.

1977 A small group of us flew out on the 10.00 a.m. flight to Nice to join the rest of the Great Britain team. And very civilised it was too as we joined the jet-set! Brian Hewson was the official overseeing us; the other two athletes were Drew McMaster and Steve Wymark. Travelling with Drew is always an experience. As Grandma Jo would say, all Drew's eggs have double yolks. Yet, despite him being so over-the-top, in a strange way I warm to him. I'm aware I'm very much in the minority there. His athletics is his raison d'etre-there's no real hinterland there. Despite all his apparent success in life, there's something which always slightly saddens me about him-I'm unsure what the right word is to properly capture and describe him-it's not pathetic or pitiable, but I always feel a certain poignancy or sadness when I'm in his company. For short periods of time, he's actually enjoyable company, but then it grates a little and wears thin. Gaga always compares him to a wee bantam cockerel strutting about the farmyard with his chest stuck out; whenever he hears him being interviewed on Radio Scotland in the morning and he talks about his rivalry with Allen Wells, it always delights Grandpa Willie, making his morning boiled egg and toast all the more enjoyable! He's unpopular with most of the Meadowbank crowd, although some of that is perhaps down to jealousy. Perhaps because I'm at a similar level to him with mighty aspirations on what I might achieve over the half mile, I've never ever felt that way towards him. Also, I know I can match him running wise; whenever we occasionally train together we've been on a par. He's always been fine whenever we've been thrown together in to each other's company; and although the conversation is always about him, I feel he has a certain respect for me, particularly with me running over a further distance that involves a degree of pain and fortitude. The biggest thing I have to avoid is taking the piss out of him; there have been occasions when Paul's been there that I've used him as a foil to get group laughs-it's partly passed Drew by, but Paul is very aware of what I'm doing, mischievously encouraging me to deploy some dry wit. It's not *Schadenfreude* at all, because as I say, when I've done it and drawn him out, it's sailed over his head; I've tried to limit it, trying to get the right balance between anyone of us taking the Mickey out of one another, but not taking it tae far!

A complete counterpoint to Drew is Brian Hewson who is an absolute gem. He's a lovely, gentle, caring and all round decent, good guy and incredibly modest with it, given what he's achieved in athletics. I think most of the team are completely unaware of what a great athlete he was; I'm only aware of his pedigree because I've devoured the sport's literature and read *Flying Feet*; but he was good enough to have been the Olympic champion if circumstances had been different. As ever, **Ecclesiastes 9.1** comes to mind: *'I returned, and saw under the sun, that the race is not to the swift, nor the battle to the strong, neither yet bread to the wise, nor yet riches to men of understanding, nor yet favour to men of skill; but time and chance happeneth to them all.'*

The flight to Nice was smooth and it was pleasant touching down in the warmth and sunny south amongst the rich and famous. After unpacking, Drew and I wandered down to the Promenades des Anglais and the beach to enjoy the sights, in all senses of the word! After a meal with the team and some games of pool many of the team went out for an evening stroll along the promenade; it was slightly cooler and dark, but lovely to out; what a contrast to Porty Prom! As it was such a gentle and pleasant evening we sat out at a café, had some cokes and enjoyed many good laughs. This is a much more relaxed and laid back trip than I'm used to; Dresden in '75 had it, but only after the competition was over. As none of us were tired and we knew if we retired too early we'd only twist and turn we stayed out surprisingly late. I didn't get back to my room until 2.00 a.m.; young Wymark wasn't amused.

1978 A surprisingly good sleep, not awakening until 8.30 a.m.-perhaps that single beer last evening did the trick; especially as I don't really drink at all. The first thing I did was to put on some training gear and went out and did an easy jog around Portobello Golf Course, followed by a light breakfast. I picked up the newspapers-The Glasgow Herald and The Scotsman focused on my last minute tactics in the heats. I was keen to pick up an Athletics Weekly, but had to make a wee detour by Menzies to get one. It was encouraging to read I'm ranked in the top 5 in the **Leading Contenders For Edmonton.**

The weather out is warm, but unfortunately it's pretty windy. A relaxed morning, mainly reading, with the TV on in the background. Come lunchtime, Josephine and Heather arrived back from Edinburgh and had picked up the usual fish order from Croan's on the High Street, so I had a light lunch of white fish, potatoes and veg.

I went up to Meadowbank-probably a little too early, hanging around for too long. I like to be neat and precise-not rushing things, but not spending too much time on the job in hand either. I felt super-charged-just too much adrenalin, mainly because I knew Sebastian Coe would take the final out quickly. Should I go with him or should I stay back?

As I warmed up I contemplated the two alternatives. Even when I went to the start line I still didn't quite know what my tactics might be. Looking afterwards at the television coverage and photographs I can see my nervousness and indecision.

The gun sounded and I ran swiftly for 30 metres before easing down. Meanwhile, Paul was the opposite and ran very positively from the gun, immediately settling on Coe's shoulder from the gun as they went through the first lap in 51.9 seconds; fair play to him!

Easing down so quickly was a big mistake and I settled down in the comfort of the main field and catastrophically got completely entangled for the first 500 metres. Meanwhile, Coe and Paul were extending the gap at the front; it was very frustrating knowing I couldn't get after them.

At 300 metres the field was 'miles down' on Coe and Forbes. By the time I'd extricated myself I was at the 200 metres point; in my heart of hearts I knew I'd given the leaders far too much ground and that I was never going to make it up. So much so, I didn't even kick; I kind of just went through the motions and instead just gradually lifted the pace. I moved wide on the bend and glided past Paul and flowed home in a very controlled manner to the tape. By the end I was actually surprised at how much I'd closed Coe down-in fact another 15 metres and I think I'd have gone past him.

Afterwards I felt a bit depressed. I wasn't even tired at the end-very, very frustrating, but fortune favours the brave and Coe got his just deserts and took the laurels.

I felt slightly less down after a very positive chat with Duncan McKechnie and Coach Walker who both rammed home the message and hoped that I've learnt my lesson. What cheered me up no end was when a message came down to say that David Coleman the BBC commentator wanted to meet with me in Andy Bull's office and to come and speak to him.

On the replay of the commentary he absolutely lambasted me...*Tactically, Hoffmann really is a disaster... and then at the 200 metres point of the race ...Well if Hoffmann wants to beat Coe, he better get on his bike!* etc. That comment is going to take a bit of living down. Coleman hauled me over the coals and was very critical, but also very supportive too. He said that I must learn from this race, because You've got the talent and the ability to go all the way, but you can't give athletes of Coe's class 20 metres with 200 to go-they just ain't going to come back to you, fast as you may be. In the evening Coach Walker; his wife Kay; daughter, Debbie; *Diana the goddess of love and hunting* and I had a lovely Chinese meal out at Morningside.

1978 United Kingdom Championships

1. Coe 1.47.1 2. Hoffmann 1.48.3 3. Forbes 1.49.1 Very windy.

Athletics Weekly

800: 'An easy, assured victory for Sebastian Coe in 1:47.1 after leading through 200 splits of 25.5, 26.4, 27.0, and 28.2.

The drama came later when it was announced that he had been disqualified for breaking prematurely from his (outside) lane, but after a protest to the jury of Appeal, who watched a video recording of the race, Coe was reinstated. Peter Hoffmann, as usual, laid far too much off the pace-he was 15m down on Coe, in 5th place, with 200 to go-and there was no way he was going to make all that up in the closing stages against a runner of Coe's calibre. Hoffmann could have a great future in this event (he has run 1;46.6 in this his first serious season at 800) but when up against top class rivals he must endeavour to stay in contact with the leaders on the first lap. Dave Wottle was a law unto himself.'

16th July, 1973 Staying at Oxgangs this week made for a nice wee tootle on a summer's morning down to Morningside on my favourite bus, the number 16, The novelty made the working day at Graham's somehow more pleasant and bearable. Angus was back to work, but Scott didn't arrive-perhaps the mere thought of returning to the Hard Times of Dickensia was just too brutal a thought for the poor lad!

What am I like, but I somehow got the photostat machine all mixed up-PANIC STATIONS! I'm pretty clueless.

Oh, I saw Jonathon Taylor at lunchtime-he's left school too and training as a heating engineer-good for him; but how the hell did I arrive where I am after being selected to go to Burrie five years ago...hmmm. What brightened up today was Paul had his interview so he looked in to the office afterwards; and he's also been selected for the Scottish Boys Clubs' team for the trip to Birminghamshire for the British, so we'll be able to travel down together. Whilst it makes going in to work easier in the morning, the down side is that in the evening I had to travel all the way in the 4 bus back to Oxgangs from Meadowbank and didn't get back until 10.00 p.m.

Evening: 3 x 4 x 150 metres 17-18 seconds (short recovery; 5 minutes between sets)

1976 Montreal There was a dress rehearsal down at the Olympic Stadium; it was so hot and close, that we heard that dozens of people had fainted so they're intending to issue 14,000 salt tablets to avoid a repeat tomorrow. Also, that after the torrential downpour when the weather broke, the stadium roof leaked like a sieve. I'm unsurprised because we got caught in the rain when we were walking back to the Olympic Village from the training track. I have never, ever seen rain like it. I got absolutely drenched. If you can imagine standing up fully clothed under the most powerful bathroom shower, then multiply that by ten and it will give you some idea of what it was like. My training gear was saturated through. It was something else to experience. Coach John Anderson held the watch for me in training. Because he's only got a limited coaching pass and access to the facilities and the trip is costing him a small fortune, afterwards I took out a tray to him with a three course meal on it and passed it out through the gate.

Afternoon: 2 x 300 metres (1) 33.4 seconds (2) 33.1 secs

1977 Nice Having retired to bed at 2.00 a.m. I slept okay and then spent a very easy day, essentially just lazing around the pool-side; doing a little swimming; eating; and having a game of pool. In the evening I ran solidly, in my best time of a fallow year. I was fourth, but not far behind Jean Claude-Nallet, the former European Champion; also I was the first Brit ahead of Wymark and Alan Bell. The track proved to be very slow for the sprints. Adrian ran solidly in the 1500 metres and was in the mix at the end. Afterwards I decided to walk back to the hotel with a few others as my warm down; it was quite delicious just to dive straight back in to the cool, refreshing coolness of the water of the hotel swimming pool...how the other half live!

France v UK

400 metres 1. Nallet 46.93 seconds 4. Hoffmann 47.36 secs

1978 The morning after the night before, but it felt great to be awakening with no nerves this morning, after the tension of the previous two days' racing at the UK Championships. In the morning I ran a very easy session. Come the evening five of us went round to the bookmaker, Pilmar Smith's house; being a wealthy athletics fan he had video-taped yesterday's racing on the BBC. When I saw the video tape I was astonished-I was 25 metres down on Coe and Paul at 300 metres out-I had no idea I was so far down! Lesson learnt! Late on, as the temperature dropped and the light faded I ran three miles round an empty Portobello Golf Course.

Morning (11.00 a.m.): 6 x 200 metres (2 minutes recovery) 25 seconds

Evening) 10.00 p.m.): 3 miles

17th July, 1976 Olympic Village, Montreal We've all settled in pretty well at our flat, especially considering there are nine of us in it with three to a room. I'm sharing with Frank Clement. I don't really know Frank that well, but have gradually become more acquainted. It's no wonder Steve Ovett has decided he's going to move in to a local hotel to have a room to himself. That said, the flats are brand new and will be sold on immediately afterwards so they are of a high standard. A couple of doors along the first floor landing from us are some of the swimmers including Edinburgh's Alan McClatchey whom I've met at some functions. Having got used to wandering around the village and seeing many of the planet's most famous athletes wandering around-Olga Korbut and Nadia Comenichi the gymnasts and Valery Borzov the reigning Olympic sprint champion, to name but a few, it was an oddly mixed day. In the morning it had kicked off with many of the Africans boycotting the Games and it was poignant seeing the likes of Filbert Bayi and Mike Boit walking forlornly through the village with their bags packed and their hopes, dreams and aspirations dashed and cruelly killed off, as they began their long journey home. The boycott is over New Zealand's sporting ties with South Africa and yet, perversely, I saw some of the great New Zealand athletes shaking hands and hugging many of the Africans, with both sides genuinely feeling for one another-quite surreal really.

The sadness of the morning was replaced in the afternoon with the excitement of many of us gathering for the Opening Ceremony. It was a long, tiring affair in the heat with a few occasional chances to sit down. I was in the row directly behind Princess Anne, so that was interesting; she's surprisingly tall-around my height of 5 foot 10 inches, at least with her heels on. I got a number of photies of her. Once inside the magnificent modernistic stadium with 73,000 onlookers and billions watching around the world, the Canadian Air Force-The Snowbirds, flew spectacularly overhead, before Princess Anne's Maw performed the opening ceremony; she was looking rather classy and low key in a pink coat with white hat and gloves-all very tasteful. The rest of the immediate family were there too. It felt rather special to be a part of the occasion, knowing Nana, Gaga and the rest of the family would all be looking out for me on the box, 3,000 miles away across the Atlantic Ocean. The Canadian national anthem, Oh Canada is a very lovely piece.

1977 Nice A repeat of yesterday, lazing around the hotel pool-side. With the hot sun and dream-like surroundings I could almost imagine being part of the jet-set life here in the south of France, instead of being an impoverished student back home. Come the cool of the evening the British team travelled to the stadium for day two of the athletics international against France. Although it's a year since I went out with the *Simone de Beauvoir Philosophy Queen* dropping her gently when *Diana the goddess of love and hunting* introduced herself to me when I got back from Montreal last year, it was good to see *Simone* get a British vest and to acquit herself well in the 100 metres hurdles race. I meanwhile ran respectably on the last leg of the 4 x 400 metres relay but was handed the baton miles down so just strolled round. In the evening there was a pretty wild, fun and high jinks party going on. I enjoyed a couple of glasses of wine; many of the athletes ended up in the pool in their evening wear-Lorna Booth the hurdler topless! A few had too much to drink and there was a bit of a dust-up between Bob Danville the hurdler and Keith Stock, the pole-vaulter. I wasn't feeling too chirpy-the combination of the sun; the race; and the wine so went to bed at an early hour. Feeling ill I wish *Diana* was here to look after me.

France v United Kingdom

4 x 400 metres relay 1. France 3:10.2 UK 3:11.7 (46.9 seconds leg)

18th July, 1976 Montreal Geoff Capes is in one of the other bedrooms; he's feart of flying so to get to Montreal he sailed across the Atlantic on a big liner. We were sitting playing chess with a crowd of athletes watching; I knew the Bishop's Opening was on and I could win the game within a few moves-Should I go for it, which might be a little humiliating for big Geoff? I did and after realising what had just happened to him he was fine; he roared with laughter and with a bemused look, shook his head! The village is surprisingly large. One thing I wasn't expecting is there's a three hole golf course-amazing! I had an enjoyable knock-about of half a dozen holes in the afternoon with two British judo medallists from the 1972 Munich Olympic Games, Brian Jacks and Dave Starbrook; both good lads.

I like the feel of the warm-up track and have been putting in some quick sessions. I sit down there quite happily watching some good athletes come and go; perhaps the most interesting is the American 400 meters hurdler, Edwin Moses. He's a very classy athlete to watch-tall, lithe, rangy and a bouncy, quite powerful sort of a runner; he's a stylish dresser too-there's a touch of the artist to him with the colourful beads round his neck. On the Games front itself the news has been dominated by Nadia Comaneci's sensational perfect 10 score.

<u>Morning</u>: 300 metres 33.1 seconds
.

1978 I'm absolutely scunnered; I awoke this morning feeling wiped out with a temperature and a very sore throat. I don't know where the fuck I picked that up, but it's completely floored me. Most worrying is we're due to fly out to Canada for the Commonwealth Games in a few days' time. Of all the times, but is it really unexpected given the lost weeks every year since I started training five years ago. The worrying thing is how very slow I am at shaking these infections off-it usually takes me around ten days. I phoned the doctor but couldn't get an appointment until later. I ended up going in to work at my summer holiday job with Edinburgh Corporation; that was a big mistake as I felt pretty rough. I've been given some antibiotics-oxytetracycline and also a throat spray. I sat in feeling miserable. Later on, *Diana the goddess of love and hunting* dropped by to see me.

19th July, 1976 Montreal When you awake, each day is exciting; there's an interesting mix of feeling you are on holiday-almost in a holiday camp, but something more akin to a high class training camp with the structure of a session to put in to your day's diary, but after that the world is your oasis. I've gone in to the city a couple of times with the two pole-vaulters, Brian Hooper and Jeff Gutteridge. Keith Stock didn't make the team, but the three of them are very much Jack-the-lad street boys. They're quite good fun and I get on fine with them, but what I dislike is there's an immature insincerity to them too-I'm happy to spend a few hours in their company, but would tire of them easily too. Gutteridge is only nineteen and along with Daley Thompson and me we're the youngest in the team. Coming from a working class Oxgangs background my antennae switches easily between the mores of the street and that of the middle classes e.g. the Jenkins'. The pair of them work as a pair in their interactions with others; there's a sense of a shared superiority-they're taking the piss, showing a feigned interest in others, which I don't like to see. Anyway, it's been handy to share a taxi with them and we've got in to the habit of shouting out PACER! every time we see one of the cult American cars go by. We absolutely love them; they're futuristic, highly rounded with an extraordinary amount of glass and for a small car easily accommodate four people. We've seen nothing like them back in the U.K. and we squeal with delight each time one goes by. We're now such connoisseurs that we're beginning to appreciate the more unusual colour schemes and models which we see.

Where Brian and Jeff have been useful is in sussing out all the different sports good manufacturers' reps. Today we were at the hotel of the Japanese company, Tiger and have been given a bing of stuff-shoes; spikes; clothing etc. I absolutely love my yellow Tiger Paw spikes-I wore them at training and not only are they great to run in, but they look absolutely amazing. By getting in to the companies early on has been to our advantage-what with Adidas and Puma as well I'm seriously worried at getting all my luggage home! I'll need an extra trolley because I've got boxes and boxes of stuff. On the Olympic Games front it was great to see David Wilkie get another silver medal to match 1972, but this time in the 100 metres breaststroke; there were loud cheers emanating from the flat a couple of doors down. However, there was sensational news coming out about a Russian Modern Pentathlete, Boris Onischenko, who was found to have been caught out flagrantly cheating. Evidently he had tampered with his weapon so that a hit light flashed up when he hadn't made any contact with his opponent at all. Ironically, it was Britain's Jim Fox who caught him out. All very strange and rather sad to hear, but no doubt the press and world's media will love it.

Afternoon: 300 metres 33.4 seconds; 200m 21.4 secs; 100m 10.6 secs

1978 With this fluey-cold there was no way I could go in to work. I had a high temperature, sore throat and was quite lethargic. I sat back, took the antibiotics and felt very sorry for myself. What's made it so depressing and especially disappointing is that Coach Walker and I had put together a hard schedule for the remaining few days before I fly out to Canada. Today we had made all the advance arrangements for me to try to run an even pace 1 minute 44 seconds half mile time trial where I just sat in all the way. John was going to take me through in 52 seconds with others then taking the pace at 400, 300 and 200 metres out. I'd really been looking forward to seeing what I was capable of, especially given the world record is 1 minute 43.5 seconds. Later on Gavin Miller dropped by to see me; he was actually quite good company.

20th July, 1973 Having been to Englandshire back in May with the club, I'm a bit more streetwise about the motorway cafe prices; so to help keep costs down, when Iain and I went along to The Store (St Cuthbert's Co-operative) at Oxgangs, I stocked up on a lot of food and drink for the journey south. Paul and I joined the rest of the Scottish Boys Clubs' team to head down to Birmingham for the British Boys Clubs' Championships. It rained for much of the journey. To pass the time we played cards. The blinking exhaust was half off so we had to stop en-route to get it fixed; it seems to be a thing with the Boys Clubs that they only seem to use old shiter busses! We didn't arrive at our hotel until after midnight; we played a few games of darts before hitting the sack. I'm rooming with Paul. I'm looking forward to tomorrow and think I can do quite well.

1976 Montreal After breakfast a few of us went to see the film, Rollerball. On Roger's recommendation I'd seen it before; a world in the distant future-2018-with a globally, violent sport; is it that really any different from the Olympics now! Discuss. From there, a wee stroll around some of the shops, which are relatively up-market; they're hoping to make as much off the tourists as possible, making hay whilst the sun shines. I had a relaxed and restful afternoon. There's a library of Agatha Christie novels and I'm making my way through the ones featuring Hercule Poirot.

Once the weather cooled a little, late afternoon, I ran another good session with the American 200 metres sprinter, Mark Lutz. John Anderson took the session; Lutz and I ran a 300 metres time-trial dead-heating in 33.1 seconds. I was speaking with Frank Dick; he's recommended a very good course for me at St Andrews University; he says he could get me on to it as he has close links with the Director Archie Strachan. I'm due to start at Loughborough University in September; given that's Frank's alma mater, the fact he's suggested I stay in Scotland means I should perhaps have a wee rethink.

Afternoon (5.00 p.m.): **300 metres 33.1 seconds; 6 x 100 metres (5 minutes recovery) all in sub 11 secs**

21ˢᵗ July, 1973 Birmingham In the morning Paul and I took a short wee walk round some of the local shops before heading out to the stadium. I ran quite well in the preliminary rounds and then won the 400 metres final as well as taking a third place in the 200 metres too. Alongside winning the Scottish Youth title overall it's been a successful first season; and although it's second division stuff, it's great to win something at British level; I'm not quite ready for the likes of the AAAs Youth Championships, but this is a good staging post. Travelling back on the bus to Scotland I was thinking how much I'm looking forward to training this winter, to try and get better and better. We stopped off for a comfort break and Paul managed to bugger up a pinball machine-what's he like!!!

British Boys Clubs' Championships:

200 metres 3. Hoffmann 24.0 seconds

400 metres 1. Hoffmann 52.6 secs

1975 I'm enjoying working at Meadowbank on the summer holiday play-scheme programme with Roger. The afternoon was particularly fun. In between we ran a good session, although my upper thighs are sore. A sci-fi evening with Star Trek followed by an interesting film, The Man With The X-Ray Eyes.

Afternoon (12.30 p.m.): 2 x 3 x 120 metres (3 minutes recovery; 10 mins between sets) (1) 12.6; 12.4; 12.4 seconds (2) 12.2; 12.2; 12.6 seconds

1976 Montreal I enjoyed a long lie this morning before strolling down for breakfast with the hurdler, Berwyn Price. The food hall is always fascinating; it's open 24 hours a day and you always see someone interesting. Afterwards I took a wee tootle down to the training track, but just to spectate. Because of the massacre at the last Olympics in 1972 at Munich the athletes' village is enclosed by a high fence and we have to go through security at the entrance/exit. But out with that it's fairly relaxed and large crowds of the public gather wanting to exchange or buy badges off us. Several Americans want to buy my tracksuit and have offered me $100 dollars for it. The tracksuits are crap, plus I've two of them, so I'm contemplating selling one. I enjoyed the morning, watching the Cuban, Juantorena run an impressive 600 metres; I think he could pull a surprise in the half. Late morning I played chess with the American based steeple-chaser, Tony Staynings. After lunch I slept and then ran an excellent session; I'm running as well as ever just now. After tea, I took advantage of the facilities on tap and had a good massage and then some American telly.

Afternoon (4.00 p.m.): 4 x 200 metres (10 minutes recovery) 21.8; 21.6; 21.8; 21.4 seconds

22nd July, 1976 Montreal One of the daft things we've been doing in the large sitting room is having wrestling matches-mad really. I was impressed at how well young Daley Thompson the decathlete acquitted himself against the hammer thrower Chris Black. I fought the steeple-chaser Tony Staynings; blimey! I hadn't realised just how exhausting and strength sapping wrestling is. Each day, larger and larger crowds have been gathering at the gates; it's now not just the athletes swapping badges, but the public too. Indeed there's a roaring trade going on.

1978 I'm still floored with this bug which made for a rather low-key, maudlin approach to packing my suitcases for Edmonton, pitter-pattering around the house. Willie gave me a lift up to Meadowbank. I was supposed to be seeing Coach Walker regarding my training programme across in Canada, but that went by the by as everyone seemed to be wanting a piece of him and he was doing this and that. *Diana* was down, making a scene! Coach Walker gave Paul; Margot and Allen Wells; and me a lift through to Glasgow to the BBC film studios. We arrived too late to see the film, however the BBC showed my races against Beyer and also Coe privately. Thereafter, as Allen and I are regarded as Scotland's best hopes for a medal on the track we went off to do an interview with Ron Marshall for BBC Radio Scotland. Late on there was a dinner reception for the whole team. I managed to give *Diana* a call. Unbelievably Gavin Miller made an appearance; it quite spooked me; he's as mad as a box of frogs!

23ʳᵈ July, 1976 Montreal The athletics started today. The 400 metres hurdles heats were on; Ed Moses looked a different class from everyone else. Pascoe was in the same heat, but Moses just breezed away from him. It was fascinating watching Valeriy Borzov in the 100 metres; he's not expected to do anything given the past few years, but he's such an enigma, I couldn't take my eyes off him. Whilst he didn't win either of his two races, he qualified okay looking across at the opposition; is he playing mind games with the American and Caribbean athletes or is it just a double-bluff? We'll see tomorrow. Although I'm biased the 800 metres is shaping up to be THE event of the Games; there's a fantastic field. Both Frank (Clement) and Ovett qualified in first place, but they've got their work cut out.

1978 Given this dose I was a bit stupid but I went out this morning and ran four miles. Probably just panic at being off ill from training all week and knowing I'll lose another few days travelling out to Canada. Another example of just how thick I am, but I managed to get lost in the streets of Glasgow too, eventually finding my way back to Queen Margaret Hall. The team bus left for Prestwick at 11.30 a.m. We were there for a while so I had a meal and telephoned *Diana the goddess of love and hunting* before we took off at four o'clock for the seven and a half hours flight to Edmonton. I didn't sleep at all-read; chatted and had a couple of meals. Arriving at Edmonton was a pain; it took an absolute age for the team to be processed through customs alongside picking up our identification, including being photographed etc. Further bureaucracy awaited us at the Games Village, before Paul and I were eventually allocated our room and getting to bed. The temperature has been in the 80s all day, so that didn't help; I predict a restless night ahead, particularly as I don't feel great.

24ᵗʰ July, 1976 Montreal What a great way to spend a Saturday; John Anderson supervised a good training session in the morning and then I strolled down to the Olympic Stadium to watch day two of the athletics; what a life! In the semi-finals of the Men's 400 metres hurdles, Moses stretched his legs a little more easing to an American record, but there's much more to come. It's a pity John Aki-Bua is part of the African boycott; he was reputedly in 47.5 form which is faster than the world record. Undoubtedly, if Moses gets his stride pattern right, he can blow the world record away. Pascoe looked but a shadow of himself, just scraping through in 50 seconds. From my angle it's good as he shouldn't really be considered for the relay team. Sitting up in the stand in great seats is fantastic. There's some interesting fans here too; Mick Jagger was sitting just along from us; he's a track and field fan and I know he runs every day; his dad is or was a P.E. teacher. The athletics got better and better. Borzov qualified again without winning, but once again was his enigmatic self, glancing around. The half mile semis were great to watch; they really got my heart racing. Juantorena is a cool guy and just strolled round, with Van Damme, Ovett and Singh just behind. Everyone's warmed to the Indian and the brave way he takes the races out. The second semi was very hot too with Wolhuter; Grippo; Susanj and Wulbeck; it's going to be some final-I can hardly wait. I'm glad I'm waiting until 1980 to run the 800-it might be a tad easier by then! Later on, the men's 100 metres final closed the day's proceedings. Crawford took the gold and Borzov took the bronze. I was initially disappointed, but all things considered it was a great performance by him and the first time he's been beaten in a major championships.

As Quarrie took the silver it deprived the Americans of any medal at all. A good day of athletics and fantastic to be here watching it live.

<u>Morning:</u> **100 metres 10.6 seconds; 150m 15.9 secs; 200 metres 21.2 secs; 150m 15.8 secs; 100m 10.7 secs**

1978 Edmonton After a sleepless night I was up around 7.00 a.m. Paul and I went out and ran a steady 4-5 miles in a beautiful park with a man-made lake. The rest of the day was spent finding our way around the Games Village. The food is pretty good. In the afternoon a few of us took a wee tootle down to the stadium. It's impressive, although I'm unsure whether the track looks very fast; it looks a wee bit heavy going. In the evening I'm able to follow one of my favourite programmes, Star Trek, before retiring for the evening; boy do I feel tired.

<u>Morning:</u> **4.5 miles steady run**

25th July, 1975 Whilst picking up my pay at Meadowbank, Nana phoned in a bit of a panic. Brian Burgess and I travelled through by train to Glasgow. We met the two athletics officials, my old nemesis, Ewan Murray and Eddie Taylor before we set off for Liverpool by car. At a motorway café e-route we bumped in to Drew Harley's coach, Stuart Hogg. Murray refused to allow Paul Buxton and me to have a snack at 3.00 p.m. You could just imagine the atmosphere, especially with a large hungry bear of a thrower! I've fallen out with Murray before. In the evening a few of us went out for a Chinese meal, followed by a relaxed evening in watching the television before tomorrow's AAAs Junior Championships; unfortunately the atmosphere at the team meeting was *ELECTRIC!* Murray just rubs everybody up the wrong way. Ironically, last year I was much happier travelling down with Dave Hislop and not being a part of the official Scottish team-crazy! Because I've been running so well in training I've decided to double up in the 200 and 400 metres. I'm going so well I feel quite confident, even though the opposition in the 200 metres with McMaster and Harley is good. We were all on the line together at the Scottish Senior Championships and that was after two 400 metres; this time it's before the quarter and I've been flying in training, running quicker than ever.

1976, Montreal After breakfast I took a wee tootle down to the golf course and did some driving practice off the tee. Good fun; I'm definitely going to play some golf in future. When she's been off-duty Lucy and I have been seeing each other most days and more so on her days off too! We've enjoyed strolling around; going for coffee and just sitting out talking. She's taken me into the city on a couple of occasions too. Me being me, to quote Jackson Browne, I'm crazy about her and of course fallen head over heels in love with her. Later, a good training session and thereafter down to the track for Day 3; I could hardly wait! My heart was racing at the prospect of the 800 metres final. Once again we got great seats and Mick Jagger was just along from us again.

As they lined up for the half mile, my heart was in my mouth; the field was just outstanding. Whilst I understand why they run the first 300 metres in lanes it seems a bit unwieldy and I felt sorry for Steve (Ovett) in lane 8. Because he couldn't see any of the opposition, as soon as I saw him run a fast 100 metres diagonal from 300 metres to the bell to catch up, expanding a significant amount of energy for effectively nothing meant there was no way he could win.

They went out so quickly, Singh wasn't in the lead this time, but passing the bell he had the impudence to go past Juantorena! Singh's a lovely runner; out with Ovett easily the best stylist in the field, but it was a mistake to do that; still, I loved his chutzpah! By 500 metres Juantorena was back in front again powerfully striding down the back straight going through 600 metres in 77.1 seconds. With a 100 metres to go, just for a moment Wolhuter came on to his shoulder, but the Cuban was impressively strong down the home-straight; for once, strong as a horse is the appropriate term; we quickly realised it was a world record. It's the best race I've ever seen and ever likely to see. Fair play to Ovett for finishing fifth as everything went against him and it would have been easy to have finished further back.

We were just getting our breath back and heart-rate down when the athletes emerged for the 400 metres hurdles final. When I see them all down there with 70,000 people in the stand I can empathise with the terror they must be feeling. The nearest I've experienced was last November at Parkhead in the 500 metres against Pascoe et al in front of 55,000 people. Stressful stuff. It's easy to crumble. Easy to become negative. It takes someone special to go out on their shield, so fair play to Pascoe; he's a shadow of himself, but he went out with all guns blazing, fading badly down the home-stretch to finish in last place in 51.3 seconds. A year ago, he would have medalled. Moses was pure class; he just kept striding out with that effortless bouncy stride winning by as much as my hero David Hemery in Mexico. Great stuff. Afterwards we all headed back, drooling over Juantorena. Once again I took a three-course meal on a tray and slipped it out to John (Anderson); it's the very least I can do. In the evening I had a massage, then relaxed, reading Hercule Poirot.

Morning: **8 x 60 metres**

1978, Edmonton I slept like a top last night, so much so I never heard Paul come in during the early hours. When I got up I was surprised to hear from him that along with a few other athletes he's to be reprimanded! Fucking hell! Evidently, the dawn patrol must have caught him, although I'm unsure how. A joke's been going around the camp, that like Mr Creep at Greytowers (Winker Watson, The Dandy comic) that perhaps management has access to a master key and they come round inspecting the athletes' rooms after dark when we're all asleep! Anyway, Paul told me that last night he was basically swinging from the chandeliers and dancing atop of the bar at a night club having had a good bevy, entertaining all and sundry. When I turned the local radio on, I was pretty surprised to hear them confirm his tale; it's a big story in the media, with Paul featuring most prominently of all. Well fuck me! After breakfast, you would have thought it had been me on the piss, because when we went down to run a track session, I was off the pace. It was my first track session for over a week and I just haven't recovered from this dose. I was really struggling on the second 600; the 120s were equally disappointing; I would normally blow away middle distance runners over that distance and be able to run with sprinters like McMaster; but it just wasn't there. After lunch Paul and I had a set of tennis; it's about the only thing I'm good at just now! It was an enjoyable wee game and the weather is very warm.

I phoned *Diana the goddess of love and hunting*. It was great to hear her voice-$9 for three minutes and worth every cent. Directly afterwards I did a gentle run in just my shorts in the parkland and then wandered down to watch the first of the warm-up meets with McMaster just beating Cameron Sharp over 200 metres, with both athletes recording 21.2 seconds-about what I should be running, but I'm flat and miles off that kind of pace. Later in the evening a group of us were chatting in Frank Clement's room. Allen Wells is very uptight; I think it's probably all the pressure he's under and it's getting to him.

Morning (10.00 a.m.): 2 x 600 metres (15 minutes recovery) 82 seconds-struggling-FFS! 3 x 120m

30 mins tennis with Paul

Afternoon (4.00 p.m.): 3-4 miles steady run

26th July, 1973 It looked like being another lovely day. Gaga dropped me off at Milton Road and Dougie Mclean gave me a lift. I helped out at Meadowbank; it was quite good fun firing the starters gun doing the starts. I trained with Roger Jenkins, but I wasn't running too well. He's a brilliant runner; I'm miles behind him and could never be as good. I managed to slip in to the water at the steeplechase so got soaked! My hamstring is hurting me a bit. Later on Dougie ran me home.

Evening: 800 metres 2 minutes 13 seconds; 4 x 300 m (10 minutes recovery) 39; 38.4; 38.6; 39.4 secs; 200m 24.0 secs; 100m (off 5m) 10.8 secs

1974 En-route to work I bumped in to Paul. Today was the end of an era for me and a very harsh lesson in life after I'd endured two years at Thomas Graham & Sons, Builders & Plumbers Merchants, Balcarres Street, Edinburgh. I was glad to walk out the door at 5.00 p.m. for the very last time and not once did I take a backward glance.

For two long years it's been day after day of *ennui*. Within a week of leaving school back in September 1972 and starting here I knew I'd made the biggest mistake of my 16 year old life and have bitterly regretted skiving school for the previous two years. How I've hated walking along the wind tunnel that calls itself Balcarres Street on wet 'n windy autumn mornings with the rain teeming down; on bitter winter mornings, arriving at the back door to clock in my time-card; and on spring and summer mornings when I should have been enjoying life, instead of feeling life was ticking away slowly like the second hand of the office clock.

My life felt it was ebbing away like the sands trickling down an hourglass. Most days have been long and I've had hundreds of hours for self-reflection to dream about a new, different, exciting and fulfilling future. I want to make something of myself and my life and I want to be happy. As I've written many times before in this journal I've felt a kinship to young Charles Dickens knowing that he too had to go through something similar at the blacking factory.

I don't want to ever forget this period and how I've felt, because I need to use it to spur me on. And whilst it's taken two years out of my life and set me back two years, there's something very positive to be taken out of it too. There's a growing maturity. I've proven to myself that by getting my sleeves rolled up that I can reach a pretty high level in athletics. The lessons I've learnt there can be equally applied on the academic front. A wee bit of talent; a goal; the accompanying motivation and the discipline to study day in day out can take you a long way. And, I'm not going to be like a normal 18 year old laid back student. My new philosophy in life is Festina Lente-to make haste slowly. As I start out on this new journey I appreciate all the support I'm going to get from Mum and Dad and the ongoing support from Nana and Gaga as well as Coach Walker. Let's make it happen-Let the dice fly high!

In the evening it was day one of the U.K. v Czechoslovakia match. Paul and I were helping out but got a telling off for not wearing our tracksuits-rebels to the end! The weather was atypically Meadowbank-crap, cold and windy. However, Helen Golden ran an absolute cracker of a 200 metres in 22.97 seconds-I take my hat off to her, or at least my headband. In the evening we went to a dance at George Watsons but it wasn't very good at all.

1975 Having been running very well in training over the past few weeks, it was really disappointing to wake up feeling quite unwell. I'm not sure if it was food poisoning or what, but I had the worst headache ever. I lay in bed all morning, before we travelled down to the stadium at 1.00 p.m. Because I'm running so well, I still managed to breeze through the heat and semi-final and thought I could still win the 200 metres. Directly after the semi-final I was speaking to Stuart Hogg who although he coaches Drew Harley said I was just cruising and playing with the field and that I would win the final. I told him how awful I was feeling. As the afternoon wore on I felt the headache progressively worsening and feeling pretty sick. I asked Stuart whether he thought it okay for me to take some paracetamol and I took a couple of tablets but it made no difference. Come the final I just felt crap and the conditions were pretty poor too-a strong wind against us all the way. I was disappointed with the outcome. I came down thinking that with perfect conditions I could run close to 21 seconds as I've been flying recently in training against Graham Malcolm, who's a 21.5

seconds man. Anyway I finished a close up third. It was amazing to see four Scots in the first five; Brian Dickson should have made it five out of six! I've got all the races filmed so it will be interesting to see the deterioration in my races; irritating, because I should have got relatively stronger as the rounds progressed; instead I ran slower in the final compared to the semi-final.

I'm hoping to get some sleep before tomorrow's 400 metres, as selection for the European Junior will depend upon it, despite me having a fast time in the bank. However, I'm feeling absolutely terrible with a violent headache. Before bed, Stuart Hogg was very good and gave me a massage. On a much happier note Paul stunned everyone, apart from probably me, by winning the 800 metres, upsetting the favourite Malcolm Edwards as well as Gary Cook and Chris Van Rees. He went past Van Rees at 500 metres and none of them could get past him down the home-straight. A great run and he'll be a surprise choice on the plane to Athens. Robson was knocked out in his 1500 metres heat, with Coe winning the final.

AAAs Junior Championships, Kirkby, Liverpool

2.15 p.m. 200 metres Heat 1. Hoffmann 22.4 seconds-against the wind

3.25 p.m. 200m Semi-Final 1. Harley 22.0 secs 2. Hoffmann 22.0-I was just cruising

5.10 p.m. 200m Final 1. Harley 21.9 2. McMaster 22.0 3. Hoffmann 22.2 secs

1976, Montreal I met Lucy again this morning and we spoke for a while before she had to push on with some work. Brendan Foster took the bronze in the 10,000 metres, our first medal. It was a gutsy, disciplined run as he got dropped six laps out. On another day he might have won it; past halfway, every so often a few yards gap opened up which he had to keep closing; he never looked comfortable; to my mind he just looked slightly out of sorts. Wee Tony Staynings charged through for fourth, not very far behind Foster. I wonder how Ian Stewart would have got on if he'd been selected. Whilst he won, I wasn't overly impressed with Viren. Part of the issue for Brendan is his lower torso-his legs seem much bigger and chunkier than the lithe Finn's.

Dave Jenkins qualified for the semi-final after running two rounds of the 400 metres today, but Glen Cohen got knocked out. I would have liked to have been out there. Not only were the times slow, but I would have thrived on two races in the one day. Whilst I was pleased to see Don Quarrie win the 200 metres, Jenkins might have been better focusing on this event in Munich and here. I reckon he would have taken the gold medal today if he hadn't left John (Anderson) and begun focusing on slower work, instead of pure speed-work; not that I would say that to him. Hopefully I'm proven wrong and it comes together, but Juantorena looks a bit of handful, especially once he gets going.

1978, Edmonton A good breakfast with Frank Dick this morning, before going out for fifteen minutes just to stretch my legs. After lunch I gave Cameron Sharp an absolute pasting on the draughts board, before taking an hour's kip. We went down to the main stadium to train; gee! was it hot; it was like a frying pan. The bends feel a little tight, but the track is probably slightly quicker than I thought. Because I've been struggling so much I decided to just train on my own. Striding out I felt a little happier, but with no watch on the session or company to compare myself with, who can tell. It was great to get back to the Games Village where Cameron and I went off to the pool for a great swim; oh the luxury, as my hot pow hit the cool water. There was steam coming off the water! In the evening Frank Clement; Lawrie Spence; John Robson; Jim Dingwall and I went to see *Grease*. That scene with John Travolta and Olivia Newton-John-WOW!

Morning (10.00 a.m.): **2 miles run**

Afternoon (4.00 p.m.): **3 x 175 metres; 2 x 175m; stride 400m**

27th July, 1975 If it hadn't been the AAAs Junior Championships and the fact I needed to run to ensure selection for the European Junior Championships next month I would have pulled out yesterday before the 200 metres.

I had a restless night and I'm still unwell, so the prospect of running the 400 metres today felt like an even more tortuous exercise in masochism. Despite more paracetamol, my headache didn't subside at all and I tried to nurse myself along as best as possible in both senses of the word

I ran a controlled heat, running very quickly through 300 metres, building up a big lead and then eased right down to qualify. In the final I thought Bugger it! and tried to bluff it, flying through 300 metres with a good lead on Brian Jones, but he's a strong lad and there's been little between us all season and he went past me around 30 metres out.

Full credit to Brian; we've had some good races and he's highly ranked in Europe too with his 47.3 seconds-he's at number seven, with me eighth. Although we're big rivals and clear of everyone else, Brian and I get on well. He's a lovely Liverpool lad and I'm fond of him. He starts at Cambridge University in the autumn, so he's outstanding in both fields-athletics and academia.

All in all I've actually performed solidly, but I'm unsure what the selectors will make of it all. I know I shouldn't have doubled up, but given how well I've been running in training I really felt I could do it. Ce la vie, a silver and a bronze, but they weigh less than gold. Ironically, if I'd have run the 400 metres hurdles based on my single debut at the event I'd have won it. Once back home to Porty I'll study the film of the race later. All this doubling and tripling up at Championships is probably madness but I find it difficult to resist the temptation. Over this weekend, that's five events I feel I could have medalled at the AAAs Junior-the 100m; 200m; 400m; 800m; and 400m hurdles too.

On a happier note Duncan McKechnie gave me a lift back to Edinburgh which was perfect; I really enjoy his company; he's a very interesting bloke and a treasure trove on the history of Scottish athletics; I felt I was sitting in a private seminar. It was fascinating hearing about some of the good athletes from the 1960s; I hadn't realised how good half-milers such as Duncan Middleton; Graeme Grant; and Mike Maclean all were as well as the coach Stuart Togher's brother, Justin who was an excellent sprinter. It took my mind completely off my lowly silver and bronze medals over the weekend. Oh, and on top of that I've passed all my exams so I'm now the proud owner of several Highers; the decision to leave Tommy Graham's Builders & Plumbers Merchants has been vindicated. I'll do some more this year and be able to go to yooni next year, 1976; I'll only be a couple of years behind everyone else.

1975 AAAs Junior Championships

400 metres Heat 2. Hoffmann 49.2 seconds-easing down

400 metres Final 2. Hoffmann 47.8 secs

Athletics Weekly '...The 400m was an excellent race, as local hero Brian Jones was running against Peter Hoffmann, who had not been sure of running the final as he had a slight injury (actually unwell) and was in the lead at 200. Jones accelerated down the straight and with about 25m to go he went ahead to finish in 47.3, to take 0.8 off his personal best, and to equal the championship best, set by the Jenkins brothers. Hoffmann relaxed to finish with 47.8.'

1976, Montreal There was a telegram for me this morning, from the Scottish Young Athletes League congratulating me and sending best wishes. Setting modesty aside, it's a vindication of what they set up a few years ago to give kids like myself the opportunity to compete for Edinburgh Athletic Club against other kids from other local clubs in athletics competitions. It was a very thoughtful gesture-I wonder who sent it?

1978, Edmonton After breakfast Paul and I took one of the Games Village cars down-town to the Sheraton Hotel to see the Adidas reps about getting some equipment. He's phoning England, so we'll see what comes through, but for my money I reckon he thought we might be a couple of Scottish chancers! We drove back to the track and I thought I might try something a little quicker-my first such session for several weeks. The track felt quite fast, but my running was pretty iffy and my legs pretty tight. The last two runs may have been a bit quicker.

Back for a spot of lunch and a snooze, before going down to the South-Side track to train. I now know something's not quite right with me; my running is way below par. It's odd. I'm the lightest weight I've been. We get weighed each morning and the Scottish swimming coach who was recording the stats this morning was saying to me how thin I was. I did a session with Paul, Frank Clement and John Robson. It's one where I should fly-right up my street where

I should run them in 37 seconds. Instead I struggled to run 42 seconds-schoolboy stuff; in particular the last two runs were grim. Robson gave us all a bit of a hammering and yet his session was one I wouldn't have even remarked upon at Meadowbank in the middle of winter.

To cool down and relax I took a wee dip and swim afterwards, before the whole team had to go to a reception hosted by the Scottish Edmonton Society. It was a good meal and our table had by far the biggest laughs, especially during the speeches; I was going off on some rifts which had Paul helpless with laughter. Paul was absolutely steaming. In between laughing I had to help carry him back in a vertical position and put him to bed, hopefully without raising the suspicions of George Hunter; Uncle Tom Cobley and all. It was a wee bit of a challenge as en-route he was telling everyone who might listen to him-particularly those wearing skirts, that he had the biggest tadger in the whole Games Village and that it was SO LARGE it was now officially known as The Monkey's Tail! I might have to handcuff him down to make sure he's still in bed when the dawn patrol carry out their secret torchlight searches! He's asleep now, dreaming like a bairn; meanwhile I'm laying back in bed reading a biography of Lewis Carroll Fragments of a Looking Glass by a French intellectual, Jean Gattégno. An interesting contrast!

Morning (10.00 a.m.): 3 x 120 metres; 2 x 40-20-40m; 600m

Afternoon (4.00 p.m.): 2 x 4 x 300m (90 seconds recovery; 6 minutes between sets) 41-42 seconds I was struggling on the last two

28th **July, 1975** After the weekend away to the AAAs Junior Championships at Liverpool and feeling unwell, it was good to have a relaxed day back home. It's just occurred to me that between us, Paul and I picked up a full set of medals-his gold and my silver and bronze-not a bad haul. Along with Iain, the three of us went down to Stobo with Gaga and had a dip in the River Tweed. Both Paul and Iain had a wee shot of driving the car. Come the evening a light session.

Evening: 5 x 150m (3 minutes recovery) 15-16 seconds; some pull-ups; dips; step-ups in warm-up

1976, Montreal Dave Jenkins split the Americans to finish second in his semi-final, but to my mind he just isn't the same athlete since he left John Anderson three years ago; I hope I'm proven wrong. Juantorena won the first one. He's quite zany. The gun fires; he pauses; stands up; then flies for 300 metres then takes his foot off the gas. The men's 5000 metres is going to be a cracker; a pity Brendan (Foster) had to run so quickly to qualify. In the evening the Groundwaters invited me across to a supper party being held at their hotel It's lovely the way the family use such championships to build their family holidays around. It felt quite surreal to be talking to Arthur and Jackie 3,000 miles across the Atlantic Ocean-the very same Arthur who gave me a lift home to Portobello after winning the Scottish Youth Championship three years ago at Grangemouth. They were all in good form.

1978, Edmonton With racing tonight I took things very easy. In the morning I played five pin bowling with Ian Gilmour and just won in a close game. Canada is the only country where the game is played. I slept for a few hours in the afternoon. I got up around four o'clock and had a couple of cups of coffee. I ran a very controlled 1000 metres-the first time I've raced two and half laps, although I've run it once in training. It's quite an awkward distance to run; I don't know if I could drag my legs over a mile though! I felt somewhat ambivalent afterwards. Having missed training over the previous weeks with this infection it was probably silly to race especially over a distance that doesn't really suit me. I basically just felt one paced. On the other hand it's something under my belt. Afterwards I joined a few others at the cinema to watch Straight Time; it was so poor that after an hour I walked out and went back to play draughts with Cameron Sharp and watch some television.

Edmonton Warm Up Meeting 1000 metres 2:24:8

29th July, 1973 Despite getting back from yesterday's British League match at Nottingham at 5.00 a.m. this morning I got up at 9.45 a.m. I ran the second leg of the 4 x 400 metres relay and did 51.6 seconds. It was a good day, from the moment the pole-vaulter, Arthur Orr awoke me, till tea-time when we won the match by 30 points; Coach Walker was pleased. Others probably sensibly took the day off, but I was keen to train and ended up doing two sessions; not a bad way to spend a Sunday. I was running well including a new personal best for a 300 metres. I'm getting better and better. Brian Kerr is off with Pat. Scott ran me home. I intend to stay off Graham's tomorrow although my conscience is bothering me.

Morning: 5 x 300 metres (5 minutes recovery) 42; 43; 40; 43; 39 seconds (20 mins rest) 300m 36.0 secs p.b.

Afternoon: Fast clock 40; 60; 80; 100; 80; 60; 40; 40 metres I was moving really well!

1976, Montreal I'll have to hire my own private flight back as I've garnered in so much equipment from Adidas; Puma; and Onitsuka Tiger. Training's been going well, although there are now fewer athletes to be seen down there, but it's been fun with John Anderson holding a watch, with me thereafter bringing him out a three course meal-a good reciprocal arrangement. I've also been spending time with Lucy about the Games Village and in to Montreal too. I had mixed emotions watching the 400 metres final. As expected, Juantorena won the 400 metres-a fabulous achievement, but he had to work to get there. I felt sorry for David Jenkins, who finished seventh. But he's a shadow of himself. The Athletics Weekly guys Mel Watman; Jon Wigley; and Cliff Temple were suggesting Jenks should consider the half mile, but they're WAY OFF BEAM! They've no real comprehension whatsoever. Knowing David as I do there's no way he could ever run the half. What he should have done is gone in the opposite direction and he could have won the 200 metres! Meanwhile, it was good to see my occasional training partner from John's Easter Courses, Dave Moorcroft, qualify easily in the 1500 metres.

I've been told by Arthur Gold he wants Pascoe to run in the heats of the relay tomorrow. I was pretty scunnered given I'm flying just now and would fancy my chances against Alan. Gold's living in the past; even I know how well Alan ran four years ago in '72; Gold's concerned at how young I am; I was all for having some fierce words with him. I know Jenkins is supportive, but John Anderson encouraged me not to say anything in case it prejudices me getting a run later-not like John to be so diplomatic! I took his advice on board, reluctantly; especially as I know the team can get a silver medal as we can definitely beat the likes of the Germans and Poles.

1977 I did a little work on the garden pond before leaving on the Edinburgh Athletic Club bus for tomorrow's British League match. It was enjoyable playing cards especially as I won £11, including £8 on one game of shoot pontoon-that's the game! The meeting is in London, so we stopped en-route to stay overnight at the County Hotel, Walsall. Paul was steamboats and had us all in fits of laughter! He was rooming with me; is that the short or the long straw! Around ten o'clock I phoned *Diana the goddess of love and hunting.*

1978, Edmonton After last evening's 1000 metres I was out early and ran four miles around the park-land and the lakeside. Despite my poor form it was lovely to be out. Paul and I thereafter borrowed one of the Games Village cars and drove downtown to pick up a bagful of gear from the Adidas rep. After a wee lunch we took a tootle over to the Runners World shop; unfortunately the Tiger rep was out 'n about, which was a pity. I telephoned Diana; it cost me $19! I've passed my Higher Economics. I just took it for fun. But on a much happier note she's passed her Anatomy and Physiology Higher and got a comp. O level for Biology; it's a pity she didn't get her two Highers but she'll be able to get in to nursing. I was delighted to hear my sister Anne got 5 O levels-I'll get her a big present to celebrate the good news-it shows you what Firhill can do. We did a little relay practice followed by some great fun in the swimming pool, particularly on the rope swing with Paul; Frank Clement; Nat Muir; Alistair Hutton etc. In the evening I went along with Frank Dick and Cameron Sharp to see King Kong. It was terrible! I get on well with Cameron; he's a likeable guy; quite serious, but with a gentle sense of humour.

Morning: 4 miles

30th July, 1975 I've been taking the kids on the athletics course all week, but found it to be a bit boring this afternoon. The build up towards the European Junior Championships continues; I did a very hard session this evening, so much so I was away with the fairies afterwards, feeling awful. On a happier note I was chatting away with *Pixie Mia Farrow lookalike.* In the cafe I was talking with Norman Donnachie. He's a good guy; a Borough Road man.

Evening: 6 x 300 metres (4 minutes recovery) 37.4; 37.9 42.5; 35.3; 37; ? Afterwards, 45 minutes of agony; some pull-ups; dips; step-ups in warm-up

1976, Montreal

Hoffmann unlikely to compete
Report from Sandy Sutherland, The Scotsman

'Peter Hoffmann (Edinburgh), the European Junior Silver medallist last year, is currently in the best form of his life. Yet he looks like joining a fairly long list of people who have gone to an Olympics without actually taking part. Perhaps he can take comfort from from the fact that one of those, John Sherwood, came back to take a Bronze medal the next time....'I have twice run 33.2 sec for 300 metres recently, easily my best' Peter said, 'and I reckon I could run in the low 46s for the full distance...But even the inclusion of Pascoe and Cohen on current evidence is contentious...'

Fucking hell, the 4 x 400 metres relay team never got the baton round in their heat. No-one seems to know what happened; Bennett and Cohen got us off to a good start but Pascoe was treading water 60 metres out; we couldn't tell whether the baton slipped from his hand; whether he just ground to a halt and threw the baton down or whether it was knocked from his hand. Anyway we're out. It's UNBELIEVABLE as apart from the Americans there's no one there; I was pretty pissed off and wish I'd been out there running. Anyway, I immediately started to think about Moscow in four years' time.

On a brighter note Dave Moorcroft and Frank Clement qualified for the 1500 metres final; Ovett didn't, but I think he chose the wrong event; the half mile was loaded; he should have focused on this instead. The 5,000 metres final was out of this world. At the bell I thought Ian Stewart was going to win it-in fact the old Stewart would have but he faded badly 250 metres out, partly because he'd been aiming for the 10,000 metres but wasn't picked for that event. I've simply no idea how Viren won, but he was aided by his main rivals all running wide on the bend, playing in to his hands. An extraordinary race that no one there could ever forget; just a privilege to be there; it eased a little of the pain of the relay fiasco.

1978, Edmonton I awoke this morning to discover no sign of Paul and his mattress was undisturbed. Strange. Most odd. On the way to breakfast an unusually serious Frank Dick approached me and asked if I'd seen Paul Forbes. I played a bit dumb, mumbling that he's probably along in Ian Gilmour's room. I went back to our room and noticed there was a note asking Paul to report to the management; I'd missed it earlier, but clearly after us joking about them having a key to our rooms the buggers really do-the dawn patrol! Heading back down to breakfast I bumped in to Paul and John Robson. They had been out all night. Anyway that was the start of a furore which went on all day, going back and forward.

The athletics officials and George Hunter etc. were all for sending Paul home; it was only the direct intervention of Peter Heatley who prevented that from happening. Of course it's an absolute gift for the media, because pre the start of the Games they're always on the hunt for a story and the radio, television and newspaper reporters were having an absolute field day, especially as the rumours are that Paul and John spent the night in the girls' quarters. The rumour going around is that the way Paul sneaked past security was dressed in a discarded doctor's white coat...you could just imagine, 'Ahem, Dr Forbes here...just to inspect one or two of the girls!' Fuck me, it reminds me of the film Carry On Doctor with Paul with his stethoscope sticking out...don't go there Peter! I know Lorraine enjoys her supplement from Paul, but this time he's been far too generous! Anyway, I better save these riffs up for later to cheer him up when the shit hits the fan!

What helped a little in escaping the heat and light was taking a wee trip in the afternoon out to an Indian Reservation-they of course had already heard the tales about Scottish athletes-presumably by Indian smoke signal; they were most disappointed he wasn't along-there was a long line waiting to get his autograph! It turns out the tribe is vastly wealthy; as of today they have $34 million dollars to share amongst 4,400 of the tribe. In the evening I went to see Kung Foo At The Movies. Meanwhile, poor Paul has been grounded-you have to laugh. I sneaked him up some buns to eat-some small crumbs of comfort, if you'll forgive the pun. Fuck me! it's like Winker Watson and his gang at Greyfriars or something out of Dickens! Evidently the story has already hit the headlines back home.

Morning: 4 miles steady run

31st July, 1976, Montreal A lovely start to the day; there was a telegram from *Pixie Mia Farrow lookalike* wishing me good luck. But unlike last year's one in Athens before the final of the European Junior 400 metres, with the relay team having been knocked out yesterday, it tasted dry as dust. Even more so after watching today's final, with a medal going in 3:02:0-a bit of a sickner. The only thing I got out of it was I swapped vests with Benny Brown one of the American runners who I've become friendly with. Like me he qualified fourth in the US Olympic Trials, but of course, unlike me, he ran today. Their system is much more straightforward-they just run the first four from the trials; today I wished I'd been an American, but I was pleased to see him so happy. I admired Walker's win in the 1500 metres; Frank was frustratingly close to a medal.

1977 The Edinburgh Athletic Club team bus arrived back from London at 7.00 a.m. Once home I was surprised to see *Diana the goddess of love and hunting* wasn't there. At 10.00 a.m. her mum phoned to say *Diana* had burnt her eye in an accident with her hair tongs last evening and everything that happened. Jeez! I got a taxi out to Silverknowes to see her. I stayed all day. She slept for most of the time. Her mum ran me home. It's been a year since we started seeing each other; I don't know what I'd do without her.

1978, Edmonton Paul and I ventured down to breakfast. With all the publicity and the prior wild stories Paul had been spreading throughout the Games Village about his tadger, he's now of course a celebrity. Anyway, a group us were enjoying our bowls of cornflakes when a very large, buxom female shot-putter approached our table. In a loud friendly voice she said she was looking for 'The Monkey's Tail'. We of course all looked in Paul's direction. Paul looks up from his cornflakes and replies in between spoonfuls of Kelloggs 'Aye that'll be me' he says with a wink. She looked him straight in the eye and with a smirk says 'I think I'd like a taste of it.' 'Well then' he replies, 'You better stand well fucking back!'

Of course the table evaporated with laughter and I'm rolling about the cafeteria floor with my sides sore with laughter. I shouldn't encourage him. After breakfast we took a car downtown to see the Tiger Onitsuka representative and I got myself very nicely kitted out indeed. At first he tried to limit what I might get, but I took a hard line with him. After he saw my curriculum vitae including OG (Olympic Games) and that I'm one of the favourites for a medal he soon changed his tune. Poor Paul was left to a few crumbs from the table!

We got back to the village just in time for lunch; I was starving. An easy afternoon as I'm supposed to be racing this evening. As it turned out I couldn't as my left hamstring was very niggly. What a last few weeks; off with an infection for over a week; some worryingly crap track sessions; a one-paced 1000 metres and now I can't run. Frustrating or what. Although I felt tired I couldn't sleep-probably the unused adrenalin from pulling out of racing. Paul was the same but the opposite; given all the hassle he rather impressively put all his worries behind him and won the half mile in 1:49:8 taking out some well-known names. However, with the adrenaline and given it's just after ten o'clock and therefore five hours too early for him, he was struggling too. The local night clubs would have been quiet without him!

Evening: Warm-up and some strides

1st August, 1976, Montreal It somehow felt appropriate that the closing ceremony should be held on a Sunday allowing for a fresh start tomorrow when we fly back home across the Atlantic Ocean. It was quite exuberant and fun to be a part of, but there was a sense of poignancy too as I watched the white-suited athletes stand out against the dark sky (it was 9.30 p.m.) and fold up the Olympic flag. It won't see the light of day for another four years when much of the world will be a very different place for all of us here. Various nations' flags blew in the gentle breeze and I thought of what might have been, but also much more of what's to come and Moscow, 1980 when I'll run the 800 metres. It was a strange experience back at the Games Village; there was much partying throughout the night, but many of the athletes had already left Montreal, so vast swathes of the accommodation were lying empty; it was as if there had been some great catastrophe with pockets of light and joy contrasted against quiet, dark spots.

'Only in the agony of parting do we look into the depths of love.'

George Eliot

I spent the whole evening and night in Lucy's arms. Come the morning I won't ever see her again. It seems strange, but for now I'm capturing the memory, indeed all the memories in my mind's eye.

Au Revoir Canada.

1978, Edmonton First thing this morning I looked in to see the physio about these niggles, before going off to run four miles slowly around the track. Back for a shower and over lunch, Roger Jenkins recommended that I visit the Medical Centre. What a wise move. I was there for over an hour and the girls had the most amazing technology and machinery; the girl who treated me really knew her stuff. My leg feels better already.

Earlier, at two o'clock I'd phoned Coach Walker's office at Meadowbank. *Diana the goddess of love and hunting* was there and she's settled in well at the Nurses Halls of Residence; the room is fine and she's having to complete dozens of forms. Paul's featured in an amusing Giles cartoon in the Daily Express. Seven athletes are bent over in the start position and the starter has his gun raised, however there's a delay whilst an athlete in a Scotland vest is getting a last minute squeeze, hug and a kiss from a buxom blonde; you have tae laugh! I lay in bed but couldn't sleep.

<u>Morning:</u> Easy 4 miles jog

2nd August, 1974 Dave Hislop and I got the 9.30 a.m. train down to London. I picked up The Scotsman; my name was in it. A long journey; we didn't arrive at our hotel until 5.30 pm. We watched the first part of Ironside then tootled off to bed at 10.15 p.m. An exciting day ahead tomorrow.

1976, Montreal We left Canada to head back to London. I've got so much stuff it's uncanny. It was a bit of a panic trying to keep up with Chris Black as we changed terminals at Heathrow to fly to Edinburgh as I had two trolleys-that's how bad, or good it is-boxfuls of shoes etc.

1978, Edmonton After this morning's team meeting I headed straight down to the Medical Centre to get some heat packs on my legs, back and shoulders. Paul received the most wonderful supportive letter on beautiful embossed paper from an old retired Canadian High Court judge-a Judge Forbes, mischievously congratulating him on keeping the clan name to the fore and how much he approved of his success with the women and wishing him all success at the Games! Paul pinned it up on our landing noticeboard. At 11.00 a.m. I looked into the restaurant for coffee, bread and honey. It was nice to see three pieces of mail awaiting me from *Diana the goddess of love and hunting;* Grandma Jo and Coach Walker. Coach's letter was excellent; it's just I'm unlikely to do justice to his words; last month I felt I could have, but my running form just seems to be mysteriously running through my fingers like sand from an hourglass.

Some extracts from his letter below:

'...I believe it's very warm over there which must be a good and positive sign for you. I am sure if you concentrate on winning the 800 metres final you will find it easier than you expect, as long as you make it easier on yourself by keeping in contact when your body is fresh. You are fully aware that you can out-kick anyone if you come in to the home-straight with them. You have been in very good shape all season and you will have lost nothing from this short illness. I think you had more problems before you left for the European Junior...I have always been confident of your ability to produce something special on the big occasion and this time I feel more confident than usual. I think your only problem is that you do not fully realise how much potential you have and this inhibits your running. I have been confident since 1974 that you were capable of winning gold in Moscow and I now think you've

finished your 800 metres apprenticeship and are ready to take on the world. ...Do your <u>best</u> and that will be good enough.

Good Luck, Bill

In the evening I ran a 600 metres at one of the Edmonton Warm-up Meetings. There's something far wrong. I finished seventh in 79.3 seconds, way behind Glen Grant; even Steve Cram was just in front. I should be running at least 74 seconds, so I'm five seconds behind where I was three weeks ago back in Edinburgh. When we got back, Paul's letter had been removed from the board. Later on, Paul woke me up again; he's been phoning Britain at one o'clock each morning and sets his alarm each night to awaken himself.

Edmonton Warm-Up Meeting

600 metres 1. Norris (NZ) 77.7 seconds 7. Hoffmann 79.3 secs

6 x 100m back to back; 6 x 100m strides

3rd August, 1974 I lay in bed most of the morning reading the newspapers and watching a wee bit T.V. before Dave Hislop and I went down to Crystal Palace for the AAAs Junior Championships. It's slightly intimidating facing all these big Englanders, especially when you're just a wee first year junior. I spoke briefly to Roger Jenkins who of course is the big favourite. He flew down earlier in the week to stay with his folks at Croydon. I got through my heat (50.4 seconds) and my semi-final too; I feel confident of being in the first four tomorrow. Later I phoned the Forbes household three times. Dave and I had some fish 'n chips before an early bed.

1974 AAAs Junior Championships

4.20 p.m. Heat 1. M. Clarke 50.3 2. Hoffmann 50.4 seconds

5.35 p.m. Semi-Final 1. C. Van Rees 49.3 2. B. Jones 49.4 3. Hoffmann 49.4 4. R. Ashton 49.5

1976 I went up to Meadowbank to put in my first training session back on home soil. It was difficult to do much as people were coming up to speak to me all evening asking about Montreal. An Edinburgh Southern Harrier called *Diana the goddess of love and hunting* came over to speak to me. I've never seen her before. I was quite taken by her. She was saying she's going to watch Friday's Coke Meet at Meadowbank. I said I could get her some comps; we've arranged to meet for a coffee on Friday morning at the McVitie-Guest Restaurant at Charlotte Street.

Evening: 3 x 300 metres (5 minutes recovery) 38; 38; 35 seconds

1978, Edmonton After a good breakfast I ran a slightly better session; I felt more controlled; I hope my form suddenly comes back come the day of the races. The opening ceremony was terrible; perhaps because I've experienced the Olympic one two years ago I've seen it all before. We spent much of the time out in the baking heat, taking photographs and hanging around. Standing out in the sun dressed in our official kit with the temperature in the 80s couldn't have been good for some of the more elderly members of the Scottish team, especially as we were hanging around for hours. I had Josephine's letter in my blazer pocket and sat down and read it. I thought how sweet and charming it was-a letter from a grandmother to a grandson.

Dear Peter,

How nice it was to hear your voice; I hope by the time you get this letter you'll be in good shape again and over your cold and injury. Another parcel came from Adidas so I opened them both. The big one was a beautiful big blue bag and inside one red T shirt; one blue T shirt; a top (towelling) with hood in blue; and a beautiful pale blue training tracksuit; and a pair of TRX blue shoes. The other parcel had one pair of blue TRX shoes and one pair of spikes in green. Everything is really lovely.

The weather has been cold and wet-we had thunder yesterday morning. We had Jill (Fox-Terrier) to the vet this morning and we've to take her back on Friday, maybe to get her stitches out. She's had a bad time of it but is on the mend now. Your grandfather went out to see Iain this morning and got some tripe for Jill; we haven't heard from Iain all week, indeed since a week past Sunday. Your grandfather is to see him on Friday.

The cat spends most of the time on your bed and the rest of the time at the fish; the pool looks fine. Heather and I got new glasses on Monday and went and had a look at a silver exhibition at the Tappit Hen at the High Street.

Pat & Ronnie Browne are having a house warming party on the 19th August. They've invited Heather but she won't be going. I've been picking lavender in the garden; I've never had so much; it's lovely and I must make lavender bags for Xmas.

I believe the food is marvellous at Edmonton-steak for breakfast they keep saying on the T.V.; we shall watch tomorrow night and see if we see you in the parade.

Mima up in Bensons (grocery shop) is always asking for you; she still goes out every morn for a run; she was wringing her hands this morning when I told her you had injured yourself.

Your grandfather is sitting sleeping on the chair with his hat on. Jill is lying in front of the electric fire on the black carpet. I wish I had something nice to tell you but I haven't.

I think it's great that the Queen & Prince Phillip are opening the games. I shall be thinking about you all the time and wishing you well; in fact everybody does-Heather shouted 'Best of luck!' when you were on the phone.

I hope this letter doesn't take too long to get to you.

Love Jo

I shall write one more letter next week. J.

Afterwards I went back to the Medical Centre; by the time the Games start I shouldn't have any injury problems. Another enjoyable episode of Star Trek before going to my room to write a long letter to *Diana*.

Morning: 3 x 200 metres (30 seconds recovery) 24.8; 25.9; 25.0 seconds; 2 x 120m

4th August, 1974 What a morning; when I got up London was wet-pouring with rain and very windy. It was disappointing, because knowing I couldn't win or anything I was hoping to come away with a personal best, so that ruined any such hopes. I finished fourth in the final, only 0.1 behind my best time. Despite it being a loaded race, at first I was disappointed, but not any longer because I'm in the British Junior team-FABULOUS! Dave Hislop and I took the long overnight train back to Edinburgh arriving at 5.00 a.m. His brother, Drew Hislop picked us up at Waverley Station.

1974 AAAs Junior Championships:

3.25 p.m. 1. R. Jenkins 47.3 seconds (equals David's cbp)
>**2. C. Van Rees 48.3**
>**3. B. Jones 48.3**
>**4. Hoffmann 48.9**
>**5. M. Clark 49.0**
>**6. R. Ashton 49.2**

I'm in the G.B. Junior Team; great-I'm on cloud 9!

1975 With less than three weeks to go until the European Junior Championships I ran my best ever session. Thereafter to the physio for a rub and home to watch The Man Who Haunted Himself. Enjoyable stuff-the doppelganger at work, once again.

Evening: 3 x 300 metres (20 minutes recovery) 33.9; 33.5; 33.6 seconds WOW! GREAT SESSION!

1978, Edmonton A relaxing Scottish team day. We were driven about an hour's bus ride out to some of the lakes and spent a lovely day being warmly looked after by ex-Scottish pats. The weather was glorious and I spent a lot of time swimming in the lake and enjoying the barbecues being cooked up for us all; they also served up some quite delicious Ukrainian food too. The weather was glorious. Later on I was given a trip on a speedboat-hair-raising stuff. How many people of my age get the chance to play about in the waters of a Canadian lake! We didn't get back until five o'clock, just in time for a light session as the temperature cooled slightly.

5th August, 1975 A pretty easy morning working with the kids at Meadowbank. In the evening I was speaking to *Pixie Mia Farrow lookalike;* she's really great. Sandy Sutherland gave me a lift home.

Evening: **4 x 200 metres relaxed 22.4; 22.2; 23.1; 23.5 seconds**

1978, Edmonton Paul and I took a taxi downtown to do some shopping and spent around three hours there. I bought a T shirt for Iain. I felt pretty miserable for the rest of the day. I'm just not feeling right and very tired. Normally when big races are approaching I get really excited because I know I'm in with a chance and I'm living on the edge just knowing I can snatch something, no matter. I don't feel that way just now at all and am unexpectedly deflated and flat. It's not like me at all. Late on I manged to go for a jog. I felt better for that, at least mentally.

4 miles jog

6th August, 1974 Coach Walker is delighted I've been selected for the British Junior Team. I did a double session and my legs felt shattered come the evening. Gus McKenzie gave me a lift home.

Morning: **Gym Session**

Evening: **300 metres 35.6 seconds (legs shattered); 4 x 150m**

Before Bed: **Arm-action; press-ups; sit-ups**

1975 I had a good chat with Coach Walker about the European Junior Championships. We ended up sitting in his car until 12.30 a.m. and having to push his car to start it!

1976 I met Diana the goddess of love and hunting for the second time and our first 'date' at McVities-Guest Restaurant for a coffee and chocolate eclair. I immediately regretted ordering the cake as it was very sticky and the cream was going everywhere which exaggerated how I felt-awkward! A good lesson. Me, being me, despite quite fancying her, after I gave her the complimentary tickets for this evening's meeting, well, I couldn't get away quickly enough, although I would have liked to have stayed! She probably thinks I'm uninterested in her and was only giving her the tickets out of the goodness of my heart! It was a foul day-wet 'n windy. I probably shouldn't have trained last night and rested instead, but all things considered, at the Coke Meet this the evening I ran the exact same time as Glen Cohen and actually beat Ainsley Bennett who were of course half the Montreal relay team.

1976 Coke Meet: 400 metres Hoffmann 47.62 seconds (G. Cohen 47.62; A. Bennett 48.18 secs)

1978, Edmonton The Games proper finally got started today so that gives a better and more interesting structure to each day. After breakfast Paul and I went down to the stadium to watch the heats of the 100 metres and the 400 metres amongst other events. Come the afternoon I finished reading a biography of Churchill. After lunch back to the stadium to see some fancy running in the second round of the quarter, with Roger making an exit and David only scraping through as a fastest loser. Both of them looked very tense and jerky; neither were smooth or relaxed. Both of them look different runners from a few years ago-heavier and more muscular. Having beaten them both at the Scottish, perhaps the quarter might have been an easier bet than the half. A relaxed evening-a small beer and a snack with Paul; hopefully it will help me sleep.

4 miles steady run

7th August, 1978, Edmonton As I'm competing tomorrow I did no exercise at all and had a very easy day. I didn't even bother going down to watch Allen Wells in the 100 metres. An easy evening in front of the box and a game of draughts.

8th August, 1973 A wet 'n miserable day. First thing I was out to Oxgangs then in to Graham's for a very boring day. Last year I was a schoolboy enjoying *me hols*-now I'm incarcerated and paying heavily for playing truant. Less than a year in to the job surely this can't be my life for the next half century. To relieve the *ennui* I tidied up my desk; it looks not bad and gave me a wee bit of pleasure. Gaga gave me a lift up to Meadowbank and also 10p. I was wearing my new yellow jumper, but it didn't help the running any-I was running absolutely rubbishly. On a much happier note, in the evening Paul stunned everyone by winning the Berwick Law Race; he flew down the hill sailing past a bunch of astonished athletes; the trophy's almost as big as him!

1975 A group of Scots took the train down to Birmingham for the Great Britain v France Junior international. Because of a train crash it didn't arrive at New Street until 6.15 p.m. In the evening Malcolm Edwards; Gary Cook; Chris Sly; Paul and I went out to get a carry out-Chinese, not beer! Drew McMaster is room sharing with me-they must assume I get on better with him than Paul-you could take that either way!

1976 My first local races after coming back from Montreal; a relaxed outing, but I flew my leg in the 4 x 100m relay.

Pye Gold Cup Semi-Final

100 metres 1. D. Hislop 2. Hoffmann

400m 1. Hoffmann 49.3 secs

4 x 100m relay 1. E.A.C. Ran the first leg handing over a BIG lead-I just love running that first bend, often surprising the pure sprinters!

4 x 400m relay

1978, Edmonton A bitterly, bitterly disappointing day, so much so it's difficult to put pen to paper. Paul's so much better at taking things on the chin than me. We set the alarm for 6.30 a.m. and wandered down to the restaurant for a solid breakfast, with lots of carbohydrates. We took the 9.00 a.m. bus down to the stadium. The English coach John Le Masurier passed over his copy of the *Athletics Weekly*. Their two pundits were predicting the bronze medal for me. A month ago I might have said *Huh!* But not today.

Athletics Weekly 800: 'Third in the 1972 Olympic, 2nd in the 1974 Commonwealth, deprived of his chance for Olympic glory in 1976 and 2nd to Juantorena in that monumental World Cup duel last summer: there would be no more popular winner or deserving winner than Mike Boit...while the Briton with the best prospects is Peter Hoffmann-who could do very well indeed if he doesn't leave himself with too much to do in the last 200....**(Mel Watman) 1, Higham: 2, Maina; 3, Hoffmann. (Stan Greenberg) 1, Higham; 2, Boit; 3, Hoffmann**...'

I scraped through my heat, but did not feel well; I'm just completely flat with no energy; I'm just going through the motions. On the way back to the Games Village the bus was involved in an emergency stop and along with several other athletes I was sent bouncing and sprawling across the floor. Paul and I had some lunch, a massage, and a sleep and then headed back down. Apart from feeling completely flat again, I didn't help myself with my tactics; but the me of June or July when I was chasing Beyer or Coe down the home-straight would have just cruised past everyone. It felt pretty miserable to be knocked out and in such a very poor time. What's rubbing salt in to the wounds is this is a championship for the grabbing.

Glasgow Herald report by Doug Gillon: '...Scotland's big let-down of the day came in the men's 800 metres. Peter Hoffmann and Paul Forbes were both eliminated in the semi-final. It was the usual sorry tale from Hoffmann. After seeming to have laid the bogey of his rear-running tactics with a comfortable third place in a sensible first round race he was back to his diabolical worst and was comprehensively cut out, finishing fifth in 1 min 50.1 sec. But the blackest spot was reserved for Forbes. He was lying second at the bell, which was reached in 55.4 sec by the leader Mike Boit (Kenya) but going up the back straight the pace hotted up. Forbes's head fell and he was dropped by the pack like a hot potato trailing in last and finishing in just over 1:57 – a time well within the capacity of an average runner of many Scottish clubs...'

Very late at night I had a major argument with Frank Dick-he was awaiting to discuss the race at one o'clock in the morning-unbelievable!

1978 Commonwealth Games

11.00 a.m. 800 metres Heat 2. 1. J. Higham (Aus) 1:48.9 2. C. Szwed (Eng) 1:49.1 3. Hoffmann 1:49.1 4. G. Grant (Wales) 1:49.3

4.00 p.m. 800m Semi-Final 1. S. Newman (Jam) 1:48.83 2. Grant 1:49.25 3. C. Darval (Aus) 1.49.26 4. P. Lemashon (Ken) 1.49.93 5. Hoffmann 1.50.1 6. Szwed 1.50.89 7. D Wournel (Can) 1.50.89 J. Maina (Ken) disq

9th August, 1974, Madrid I went up to Learmonth Terrace to the Jenkins' family home. His mum, Vera, gave Roger and me a lift out to Turnhouse to catch our flight to London to meet up with the British Junior team; Roger gave me some cotton wool for my ears and both the London and the ongoing flight out to Madrid went well. As we stepped off the plane in Madrid, boy did the heat hit me; the temperature was boiling. We went down to the track to do some relay practice. Back at the hotel we were all given our Great Britain kit; it's fantastic; it's like Christmas in the summer. An 18 year old's dream. I'm just so happy to get my first British vest and tracksuit; we also got Adidas shoes and shorts too-you've got to hand it to them-it's first class. It's really great, but I didn't get a badge. Late evening Chris Van Rees; Richard Slaney; Roger and I sat out on a balcony talking. I had a terrible sleep; it was just so hot.

1975 A very easy morning; some breakfast and the team meeting. It's a really hot day-not like Birmingham at all. En-route to the meeting there was quite an amusing incident with some of the more boisterous members of the British Junior team when a plastic bag full of water was dropped from on high and hit both Mark Hatton the hurdler and the team official, Brian Hewson, absolutely soaking them. Afterwards I lay down and then went down to race. Although I only finished third behind Jones and Van Rees I definitely haven't given up hope of doing well at the European Junior Championships; I went out hard and was leading all the way until 30 metres to go. My form is beginning to come through. In the evening there was a big water fight going on. A bunch of us took a taxi into town; I was ribbing McMaster a bit at night. Oh, I also did a wee steady run.

UK v Spain v France Junior International:

400 metres 1. B. Jones 47.5 seconds 2. C. Van Rees 47.7 3. Hoffmann 47.7

1978, Edmonton I had a chat with George Donald our team manager to straighten out the early morning altercation with Frank. I'm pretty fed up. In the afternoon I went down to the South Side with Cameron Sharp and Roger; we ran a few

120s. It was roasting. When I got back I enjoyed a wee dip in the pool.

4 x 120 metres

10th August, 1974, Madrid We were up at 8.00 a.m. and down to the track to do some further baton practice. You have to hand it to them; we've been here less than 12 hours and we've practised twice for later today. A pleasant enough continental breakfast and then we went for a wee tootle around the city to get some souvenirs. I've managed to get some Spanish dolls for Josephine and others. Roger ran the best performance by anyone on the team with 46.8 seconds which may get him into the senior team for the European Championships in Rome next month. Come the late evening I felt really good and kept us nicely in contention with a 47.3 seconds relay leg for the team. Like a few of the team I felt a bit rough afterwards because of the humidity and altitude. We sat out late in to the evening in balmy Madrid at a local bar until 2.00 a.m. I've loved being part of a British team for the first time as well as the Scotland senior team last month and my first two trips abroad to Norway and Spain. It's given me the bug to push on and see just what I can achieve. Having left Thomas Graham & Sons last month and starting at college shortly, to borrow from Wullie Shakespeare's The Merry Wives of Windsor- The world's my oyster!

Evening (10.30 p.m.): Spain v Portugal v UK Junior International

1. U.K. (B. Jones (48.8); Hoffmann (47.3); C. Van Rees (47.3); R. Jenkins (47.1) 2. Spain 3. Portugal

1975 Day two of the home international against Spain and France, but this time I didn't bother with any special preparations, just taking the day as it came. Confirming yesterday's comment that I'm starting to run well, I handed the baton over after the first leg with a good lead, running the quickest split of the team too. At the evening dinner the team for Athens (European Junior Championships) was announced; fantastic, I'm in it as is Paul. Although I'm only in the relay team, Mike Farrell, the team manager told me privately that both Brian Jones and I will be entered for the individual 400 metres when we get across there; Brian's currently ranked 7th in Europe with his 47.3 seconds, whilst I'm 8th with 47.4 secs. The dinner was an absolute hoot and a great laugh with the French singing very loudly. The disco afterwards was fun and I danced most of the evening with Helen Barnett and Wendy Clarke. Unfortunately there was a bit trouble in the evening and Mike Farrell had to call the police; disappointing to see.

U.K. v France v Spain

4 x 400 metre relay 1. U.K. 3.12.6 (Hoffmann 47.7; Griffiths 48.7; Van Rees 47.9; Jones 48.3) 2. France 3.13.1

1978, Edmonton No training today as I have the relay tomorrow. In the afternoon McMaster and I played snooker across in the union. Then it was down to the stadium to watch a feast of athletics, with Wells winning the 200 metres. Boit ran a perfect tactical race to win the 800 metres; I was glad to see that; the me of June or July would have beaten him down the home-straight; the silver medal was SO WEAK. I'll have to live with that. I partly blame myself, but I haven't been right either. I changed my mind, and although I have the relay tomorrow I decided to go out for a run in the evening.

Evening: 4 miles steady run

11th August, 1974, Madrid We were all woken early to be transported out to Madrid Airport by 9.00 a.m. I managed to buy Coach Walker some brandy. Back in London, Roger and I just missed the Edinburgh flight. It's been good accompanying him; with his experience he's been able to show me the ropes and what to do; he's been very good. The poor beggar ended up losing his bag. With it being a Sunday Coach Walker was at Turnhouse to give me a lift home.

1975 The morning after the night before; it's been a worthwhile and enjoyable international. Helen Barnett and I get on very well and we're going to write to each other over the winter; along with corresponding with Bjorn and the *Mary Rand lookalike* I'm going to be busy writing. On the journey back to Edinburgh on the train, Ewen Murray was in an unusually good humour and allowed me a meal-I take it all back! Was he feeling okay? I took a taxi home, then despite racing the past two days went straight up to Meadowbank to train with Norman Gregor; he was running very well, making for a good session.

Afternoon: 8 x 150 metres (3 minutes recovery) all in 15-16 seconds; a good session; relaxed; worked hard towards the end

1978, Edmonton Rather ironic at this stage of the Games but I had my best sleep yet not awakening until 11.00 a.m. After a good brunch and an easy afternoon the 4 x 400 metres relay team ran well to break the Scottish record, although I don't think we're on for a medal. Once again I felt flat and just one-paced; off a flying start I should be running sub 46 seconds, but aint. I was daft enough to make a $100 bet with Rick Mitchell that we'd beat the Ozzies tomorrow-chutzpah on my part!

1978 Commonwealth Games

4 x 400 metres Semi-Final 4. Scotland (R. Jenkins, P. Forbes, Hoffmann, D. Jenkins) 3:06.9 Scottish record

12th August, 1974 After making the British Junior Team I'm full of enthusiasm and having given up working at Thomas Graham & Sons I'm now a free agent, so to speak! I got the first benefits being able to go up to Meadowbank in the morning to train with both Roger and Stuart Bell, who's advising him now. Although it poured with rain it was good fun and I enjoy running with class athletes who stretch me. Just after we finished Roger got the great news that after his 46.8 seconds run in Madrid on Saturday he's made the Rome team (1974 European Championships)-happy days! In the evening I went back up to Meadowbank and did a second session; I've got the bit between my teeth. I was speaking with Ann Clarkson for a while; she's a very gentle girl who lacks confidence, but she's an excellent talent. Like me she should run the 800 metres one day; she's similar, but different, as even relatively speaking, she doesn't have my zip or change of pace, but she's a very solid 200/400 metres runner.

Morning: 3 x 200 metres (3 minutes recovery) 23 seconds

Evening: Gym circuit (3 x 8 burpees; 6 pull-ups; 6 dips; 8 bent over rowing (50ilbs); 8 press-ups (chair); 6 knee-lifts (each leg); 8 hyper-extensions; 15 (3 way) sit-ups; 8 step-ups; 8 bench-jumps astride; 8 bench-jumps (feet together); 5 x 150 metres (2.30 minutes recovery) 16 secs

Before Bed: Mobility stretching

1975 An easy working day at Meadowbank with the kids; rather than going home at lunchtime I just bought something in the cafeteria. We trained early; I was sick afterwards. The motivation of Athens and the European Junior Championships I guess. Afterwards *Pixie Mia Farrow lookalike* and I spent a long time walking around the track together talking; she's absolutely fantastic! Once back home, Heather made my dinner.

<u>**Evening:**</u> **4 x 300 metres (8 minutes recovery) 34.5; 34.7; 35.1; 35.1 seconds I was sick afterwards; felt bloody terrible**

1978, Edmonton Of course I didn't sleep as well as the night before and we were all awoken up by a helicopter overhead which was commentating on the cycling road race. An easy morning. We were fortunate in that we took an early bus down to the stadium, because with it being a holiday Saturday and the last day of the Games the roads were jam-packed with traffic-it was really quite incredible. Most disappointingly we finished well down the field, but the 4 x 100 metres guys were magnificent-what a stunning victory. I thought Frank had put them in the wrong order-I would have put Jenks on the last leg and Drew on the first-so fair play to them all.
I was so depressed about my overall performance that I didn't stay for the closing ceremony and instead spent a long time discussing middle distance training with Brendan Foster. Late evening Cameron Sharp and I went down to the celebration disco for a pint. I ended up having a good chat with Frank Clement. God the racket on our floor went on well in to the early hours.

<u>**1978 Commonwealth Games**</u>

4 x 400 metres relay 6. Scotland 3:07.7

13th August, 1973 Gaga and I travelled out to Oxgangs to feed the cat for the last time. The morning at Graham's passed quite quickly, but the *office* was so hot and stuffy-it's essentially part of the warehouse-that I ended up having four *Orange Maids*! I didn't get a lift to Mayfield with Angus Maitland-a pity as I had to wait ages on a bus. I was running quite well this evening; the Edinburgh Southern Harrier girls were looking very nice.

Evening: 3 x 4 x 200 metres (30 seconds recovery) (5 minutes between sets) all in 30 seconds

1975 With the European Junior Championships only ten days away I'm continuing to put myself through the mill. I trained with Norrie Gregor at lunchtime; another hard session. An easy working afternoon with the kids. Later on I bought Norman Donnachie a meal. I went down to Mr C. (Dave Campbell, physio); I'm in really good shape.

Lunchtime: 4 x 2 x 200 metres (30 seconds recovery) (8 minutes between sets) 23.1/24.5; 23.3/24.6; 23.9/28; 23.7/26 seconds; again, I felt terrible at the end of the session

1978, Edmonton Oh, what a bore; instead of going home today, which would have been great, instead we're not leaving until tomorrow evening. Paul; Chris Black and I had a lot of fun down at the swimming pool. In the evening Paul and I had a pint or two down at The Ship.

14 August, 1975 The hard work leading up to the European Junior Championships continues apace, probably witnessed by me not awakening until 10.15 a.m. this morn. En-route to my summer job at Meadowbank I bought a birthday card for *Pixie Mia Farrow lookalike*. Heavy rain all afternoon before running another good session including a superb 350 metres;

I'm becoming more and more confident about how I might perform out in Athens. Afterwards, *Pixie* and I spent several hours together walking round the track with my arm around her, later giving her a lift home to the Braids. I'm the number one man in her life now; it's only taken about four patient years!

Evening: 350 metres 40.1 seconds (p.b.); 300m 36 secs; 200m 22 secs; 150m 16 secs

1976 I dropped Nana and Heather off at The Scotsman office before going training. It was good to get back into the old regime; I enjoyed it. I managed 27 dips-a personal best. After lunch I took a wee tootle out to Oxgangs. Iain's spent a lot of money on Gaga's car, buying a steering wheel; spark plugs and filling it up with petrol. In the evening we joined Boo-Boo Hanlon down at The Merlin for a drink. The mist and fog descended quickly; driving through Arthurs Seat back to Porty the visibility was down to ten feet. Iain and I sat reading some of my old journals; we're too tired to watch Jekyll & Hyde.

Morning: 2 x 3 x 200 metres (jog recovery) (10 minutes between sets) 24 seconds; gradually building up speed; small circuit including 27 dips (p.b.)

1977 *Diana the goddess of love and hunting* and I went up to Meadowbank; later she left to meet her father; they were going out to the Horizon Furniture warehouse. The Europa Cup wasn't too exciting. I read some Economics before running a second session on Park Avenue. It was quite enjoyable with several old ladies watching from their first floor bay windows; afterwards I gave them a bow which seemed to amuse them. Also two girls came out to ask for my autograph. I'm now sitting at the old Queen Ann table with the table lamp; books; and small radio on in the background; only *Diana* is missing.

Afternoon (12.00 p.m.): 3 x 150 metres (3 minutes recovery); 4 x 50m All FAST!

Evening (8.00 p.m.): 100m; 165m; 265m; 165m; 100m (5 mins rec)

1978, Edmonton As most of my packing had been done it was mostly a case of killing time until we were due to leave to fly back home across the Atlantic Ocean. I played some snooker with Jim Dingwall and Paul. The flight itself was delayed by an hour and had a full load-not a spare seat. I sat at the back of the plane beside the B.B.C.'s Archie McPherson. Despite his sour face he was fine to talk to. The aeroplane food was terrible. I chatted up one of the air hostess's; she was Russian, has plenty money and owns some racehorses. Meanwhile, further up the aisle I would occasionally catch sight of Paul's bare backside or his wedding tackle as he ran up and down bare naked whilst balancing a drink and entertaining the troops. What a guy! A fine reception awaited us at Prestwick Airport, mainly for Allen Wells; the awaiting crowd gave him a hell of a welcome and deservedly so. Thereafter a bus trip back to Edinburgh. Roger and I sat together discussing how Wells might cash in. I took a taxi the last leg. It was lovely to see everyone. Mum and Anne were down at Porty to greet me. As I was settling down for some lunch *Diana* phoned. I met her at 6.30 p.m.-where else but at DeMarcos, Tollcross. She took me down to the nurses' hall of residence to see her room. After our pizza, I felt very tired and went to bed at nine o'clock.

15th August, 1974 A single line entry, but an important one: I enrolled at Telford College today. I've left Tommy Graham's behind, apart from in my nightmares. I saw Gail Blades there.

Evening: 2 x 4 x 60 metres

16ᵗʰ August, 1976 After breakfast I worked with the kids up at Meadowbank on the Playschool. It was a gorgeous day. After lunch I cleaned up the cars-hard work. I ran a solid session at night. I saw *Diana the goddess of love and hunting*. It's still less than a handful of times that I've seen her. I said I'd ask her out on Friday, but I feel I should really leave it until the Friday, I mean Sunday. There's a lot of girls in my life just now, but I feel I'm irresistibly being drawn to her and am struggling to resist the magnetic pull. Nobody could replace *Pixie Mia Farrow lookalike*, but I'm sure *Diana* could help me forget her a little. I need to phone Archie Strachan to decide whether to take up a place at St Andrew's University rather than Loughborough.

Evening: 350 metres 40.2 seconds; 2 x 200m (30 secs recovery) 24/25 secs; 4 x 100m relaxed

1978 With being back in my own bed and after travelling the previous day, that's the best sleep I've had in three weeks. After all the travelling, sitting about and eating meals I went out and ran four miles; boy was the sweat pouring off me-must be all the extra weight. Thereafter I did a light circuit at Meadowbank. After a shower I looked in to Coach Walker's hoping for a quick chat, but he was pretty busy with the upcoming Edinburgh Highland Games. The world doesn't just revolve around me, especially after my dismal failure in Edmonton. In between sleeping in the afternoon several people phoned including Albert Ree.

17ᵗʰ August, 1974 Despite getting my first Scottish Senior international last month and a G.B. Junior vest a week ago, Dave Farrer refused to give me a run in the Edinburgh Highland Games; he says I'm not good enough. Whether I am or not he's a nasty piece of work. Despite his protestations I sensed an element of Schadenfreude at work partly fuelled by Edinburgh Southern Harrier antagonism. Some of the press guys were surprised. In the evening Paul and I went to the Southern dance. It was really crap; I had too much to drink and was sick when I got home.

The Passionate Shepherd to His Love

'Come live with me, and be my love,
And we will all the pleasures prove…'

Christopher Marlowe

1975 Less than a week from the start of the European Junior Championships and I'm going well, putting in another good session today. Afterwards I sat around watching a women's athletics match and spending time with *Pixie Mia Farrow lookalike*. She's absolutely fantastic-the girl for me.

<u>Morning:</u> **300 metres 33.9 seconds (8 minutes recovery); 200m 21.8 secs (12 mins rec); 2 x 150m (3 mins rec) rolling start 15.5/15.0 secs; 4 x 100m relaxed**

18th August, 1975 With Athens in mind I went up to Edinburgh to do a little shopping; a small world-I bumped in to Bob Sinclair and Ann Clarkson, the latter is on the team for the European Junior Championships too. I stopped by at Meadowbank for lunch then lay out the back sunbathing. I ran my penultimate session before flying out; in my exuberance I banged my knee badly on a hurdle; it's very stiff and sore, which has pissed me off no end given I've been working for this championship for the past year. *Pixie Mia Farrow lookalike* and I sat and watched the football and had a good time, including me giving her a lift home to the Braids. Happy days.

<u>Evening:</u> **4 x 200 metres (5 minutes recovery) 22.0; 22.2; 22.2; 22.0 seconds**

So, We'll Go No More A Roving

So, we'll go no more a roving
So late into the night,
Though the heart be still as loving,
And the moon be still as bright.

For the sword outwears its sheath,
And the soul wears out the breast,
And the heart must pause to breathe,
And love itself have rest.

Though the night was made for loving,
And the day returns too soon,
Yet we'll go no more a roving
By the light of the moon.

Lord Byron

1976 It's a funny old world, apart from the fact it isn't. Although she's been out of my life since last December (other than the lovely congratulatory card she sent after my selection for Montreal) I picked up *Pixie Mia Farrow lookalike* and we went out together for the evening to celebrate her birthday and my return from Canada. We had a few drinks at The Laughing Duck and then a baked potato, later on sitting together in the car at our old lovers spot just beyond the entrance to The Hermitage on Braid Road. I dropped her at home; as I was leaving she began to cry...

Ae Fond Kiss

'...For to see her was to love her,
Love but her, and love for ever.
Had we never loved sae kindly,
Had we never loved sae blindly,
Never met—or never parted,
We had ne'er been broken-hearted...'

Robert Burns

19ᵗʰ August, 1975 I gave Coach Walker a ring this morning and went up to Meadowbank at lunchtime do my last session before the European Junior Championships. I ran with Davie Reid. Having banged this knee I went down to the physio to have it looked at followed by an aerotone bath at Portobello Baths. In the evening Coach Walker ran Paul and me out to the airport for the flight to London, arriving at the quaint old central London hotel at 10.20 p.m. to join the rest of the small British Junior Team.

Lunchtime: 2 x 3 x 120 metres relaxed; a slight breeze against; raining; slowest run was 13.0 seconds; last run was 12.7 secs

1977 I was introduced to 1500 metres Olympic champion, John Walker's coach, Arch Jelley. A very down to earth nice bloke. It makes you think, in all sorts of ways. I was speaking to him about my proposed move up to the half mile; because I'm so fast, he recommended I shouldn't do too much mileage.

1978 A lovely sunny morn; Will and I returned the van to the SMT Garage and spun round by Oxgangs to awaken *Diana the goddess of love and hunting*. We stopped off by the nurses' home for her to get a swift change of clothing. The sunshine was streaming down and it was a pleasure to relax in the back garden with a coffee.

I had a disastrous run at the Edinburgh Highland Games. I received no monies for taking part unlike most everyone else.

Because of today's shoddy run I've been told I must put in a good run tomorrow at Coatbridge if I want to go the European Championships in Prague next Friday. To round off a mixed day I had a fall-out with Coach Walker; however on the bright side I've decided to let John Anderson help me, which should give me a lift. After the reception at the Commonwealth Pool *Diana* and I had a light Chinese at the Dragon's Castle; we stayed the night at Pollock Halls.

1978 Edinburgh Highland Games 800 metres

20th August, 1974 I signed on the dole then went out to Oxgangs for a great meal. Mum and I went down to the bank to get me some money towards going to London. I didn't actually have enough cash so I just paid for the sleeper. I failed my driving test-doom 'n gloom; everything was going swimmingly until I got caught up doing a right-hander at the lights at Milton Road Crossroads. Gaga was very supportive saying as soon as he saw the '…crabby, nippit, sour examiner…' he knew I was going to fail. I couldn't be bothered training hard tonight.

Evening: 2 x 5 x 150 metres (walk round track recovery; 15 minutes between sets) all in 16 seconds

1975, Athens, Greece We were all up early to catch the three hours Athens flight. It's a small team, but there are five Scots on it-Paul; the thrower Paul Buxton; and Ann Clarkson and Karen Williams in the 4 x 400 metres women's relay team. It's an interestingly diverse team-those with working class backgrounds such as Paul and Mickey Morris; the amiable black athletes like Aston Moore and Wilbert Greaves and the sparky Wendy Clarke; Buxton and Sebastian Coe are quite remote and keep a distance-the latter hanging out with posh Chris Van Rees; Brian Jones is a good guy and Cambridge bound next month; whilst the girls in the relay team, Ruth Kennedy; Diane Heath; and Ann and Karen are a sweet and pleasant wee group. I'm unsure where I fit in amongst that crew! As soon as I emerged from the plane in to the intense heat and smell of aeroplane fuel the nerves kicked in; I'm here on a mission. After unpacking I went down to get the feel of the Kariharris Stadium and did an easy mile jogging. My knee is still very sore which is disappointing and a wee bit worrying. We're staying at the university accommodation and the food is just awful; it's cooked in too much oil and is unbelievably greasy-the food just floats in it; I could hardly eat a thing. In the evening a relaxed time playing chess with Brian Jones, who I like very much, despite our close rivalry all year, with us trading AAA's Junior titles.

1978 We arose after a most uncomfortable night's sleep at the Pollock Halls, with *Diana the goddess of love and hunting* ending up sleeping on the floor. Outside it was a glorious, lovely Sunday morn; Edinburgh at its very best as it often is in the very early autumn as the Festival moves toward its final week. It's still slightly cool out and the sun watery in the sky, but with the promise of much sunshine and heat to come as the morning emerges from its cocoon. We strolled out to the car; down below in the sunlight and dappled shadows we could see the dew sparkling on the lower grassy slopes of Arthurs Seat. It was still fairly quiet, with Edinburgh slowly coming too; in the near distance we could hear a church bell ring out calling the local worthies to worship. I love Edinburgh.

We skipped breakfast at the halls and instead drove up the quiet cobbled Royal Mile to Burns' International Newsagents to collect the Sunday papers and then on to our favourite haunt, Demarcos at Tollcross, for some tea and hot filled rolls. What a civilised lifestyle; living the dream, as they say. We picked up Paul and Lorraine and drove through to Coatbridge. Bad luck-the silencer on the exhaust is away; the car sounded like James Hunt on the grid.

The pressure's off re Prague. I won the 800 metres in a respectable time, out-kicking everyone down the home-straight. However, I'm being slightly economical with the truth. For those watching they may have thought, that's things back to normal for Hoffmann and the status quo has been resumed, but I'm still not right. The form which deserted me after pushing Coe at the U.K. Championships last month, but which vanished in Edmonton, still isn't there. There's something awry. Anyway, John Anderson cheered me on down the home-straight shouting me on, his voice twice as loud as everyone else's! It certainly got me pumping my arms and I was able to move clear of the field, so it was reasonably encouraging, I guess, but I know it was workmanlike. Immediately after the race *Diana* and I jumped in the car and drove straight back through to Edinburgh, trusting we wouldn't come across any policemen (given the sound of the car). We arrived safely at Meadowbank where I ran a good relay leg for the club easily handling Stretford's Martin Francis on the last leg. Afterwards a steady 4 miles; all in all a good day's work. Late on *Diana* and I went to see Groucho At Large at the Fringe-quite enjoyable.

Coatbridge International

800 metres 1. Hoffmann 1:51.6; tactical

Pye Cup, Meadowbank

4 x 400 metres relay 1. E.A.C. (49.1 seconds leg, tactical)

4 miles steady run

21ˢᵗ August, 1973 I was very sleepy this morning. Gaga's car wouldn't start, but after substituting the spare battery, ye olde Singer Vogue fired up. I gave Scott a wee hand with the lines but there weren't many. Scott had a half day; old Tommy Drummond annoyed me. I took a number 5 bus home to Porty, but it took ages. I was running well over 300 metres this evening, flying around in 35 seconds; crikey! I don't think I'd even broken a minute for a quarter mile at the start of the year; over the past six weeks I've improved out of sight. Dougie gave Mary; Pat; Duncan and me a lift home.

Evening: 300 metres 35.2 seconds (personal best); Duncan Baker did 38.5 secs; 200 metres 23.5 secs (Duncan 24.6 secs); 2 x 4 x 60m back to back

Before Bed: 24 press-ups; 24 sit-ups

1975, Athens A rest day before the start of the European Junior Championships. The nightmare on the food front continues and the breakfast was…well, basically inedible. With the rest of the team we went off on an organised tour of the city, with most of the trip spent up at the Acropolis. Absolute Oxgangs heathen that I am I was unimpressed; after all it's just a pile of stones! I think that says much about me and my lack of class and imagination, although the views through the shimmering heat and smog were impressive. It seems rather sad it hasn't made more of an impact on me, especially coming from the Athens of the North and someone who when at Hunters Tryst Primary School listening to the BBC Schools' broadcast was captivated by my hero at the time, Alexander the Great. Later in the afternoon Paul; Malcolm Edwards and I took a wee tootle down to some local shops. Paul and I stocked up on these strong tasting bags of crisps, chocolate and juice-the diet of champions and super-heroes, but it's better than consuming bowls of greasy oil. I also bought a classy and rather clever T shirt, which is a rip-off of the Adidas brand. People of course read what they want to read and it actually says Adildas; very clever.

1976 I picked Roger up at Thirlestane Road and we went along to the Scotland team meeting, including having a wee chat with Coach Walker. In the afternoon we both ran well to finish first and second; with Roger being born in Liverpool my time was a Scottish Native Record. In the evening I went out with *Diana the goddess of love and hunting* on our second date; we went to see a movie then back to the Pollock Halls; afterwards I gave her a lift home. Later on *The Simone de Beauvoir Philosophy Queen* came knocking on my door and stayed the night.

1976 Scotland v Iceland v Northern Ireland

400 metres 1. R. Jenkins 46.83 seconds 2. Hoffmann 47.16 (Scottish Native Record) 3. Villi Vilhjalmsson 47.31

1977 Once again the Coatbridge International followed on from yesterday's Edinburgh Highland Games. I'd gone out very hard in the quarter inside 22 seconds, tried to ease of, which in retrospect was silly and then found I couldn't pick it up again. Today the weather was pretty foul. For fun and a wee change I ran in the half mile and did okay. I finished just behind Singh of India who ran in last year's Olympic final, but managed to beat quite a few well-known names; it's made me think seriously that come Michaelmas about moving up to 800 metres next month, and aiming for a place in next year's Commonwealth Games and European

Championships. In the evening I was up at Coach Walker's where there was a small party; I spent much of the evening having a conversation with a very interesting Indian gentleman who had studied sport in East Germany.

1977 Coatbridge International Invitation

800 metres 1. L. Johnson (USA) 1:51.6 4. S, Singh (India) 1:52.6 5. Hoffmann 1:53.2 6. R. Weatherburn 1:55.6; very windy conditions

200m 1. A. Wells 2. D. Jenkins 7. Hoffmann

22nd August, 1975, Athens I had to get up at 6.00 a.m. which is 4.00 a.m. British time! If you'll forgive the English, the heat starts at 7.00 a.m. British time because of the heat. I was already awake before Malcom Arnold, the team coach (t'other team coach is Carl Johnson) came in to Paul and my room. I was hiding behind the door and leapt out on him giving him an amused shock! We went down to the refectory but I felt very nervous and found it hard to eat any breakfast at all. We then joined athletes and officials from other countries and took the bus down to the warm-up track which is adjacent to the main stadium itself.

The warm-up track is around 300 metres and is a brilliant resource in its own right. It has a nice feel to it and I'm quite at home already. Both tracks must have been built for the 1969 European Championships-at least I assume they were. It was already pretty hot and easy to warm up; for much of the time I remained in the shade. The orange juice sellers were already out; I like the wee bottles of orange squash that they sell. I was nervous, but Malcolm Arnold is a good guy and I found him to be very helpful. I'd drawn the pre-championships favourite, Poland's Henryk Galant in my heat so I knew I'd have to run well to qualify. Despite the early

hour I felt pretty good, not to mention getting a real lift first
thing, as my stiff and sore knee had vanished overnight.
With Galant outside of me I followed him round the whole
way. With four to go through I felt good and we both eased
through to the semi-final.

1975 European Junior Championships Morning

(9.10 a.m.-7.00 a.m. British time!) 400 metre Heat

1. Henryk Galant (Poland)
2. Hoffmann 48.23 seconds

After a warm down and watching some of the athletics I
went back on the bus to the university. I had a little to eat
and lay on my bed. Of course I couldn't sleep at all, but I lay
there all afternoon. Paul was in and out as was Brian Jones
who'd also qualified this morning. We had a wee game of
chess. It's funny, although Brian has been my biggest UK
rival all year, I'm not even contemplating him-there's bigger
fish to fry, so to speak.

It was another of these challenging afternoons as you lie
back, once again half thinking about the semi-final and half
trying to put it out of your mind. I guess I'm going to have
to get used to this if I want to compete internationally. We
kept the windows open and the curtains half drawn, but it
hardly contains the light and there's a dry heat. It's in these
moments you find out a lot about yourself. Anyway, late
afternoon, I got the call to head back down to the track to
go through it all once again.

Once there I spoke to a friendly young Greek boy who I've
been buying the bottles of orange squash from. The warm-
up went fine; again I tried to keep to the shade, keeping the
same routine as this morning, including doing my stretching
in the shaded foyer area of the small building which has the

loos and water fountain. The only small change I made was to dispense with the long white socks. Malcolm was with me again; he's a very re-assuring presence. I'm building a good relationship with him; he likes me and I guess thinks I've got a little bit character-even if it's just the headband and the early morning fricht! After my strides, Malcolm said Okay, time to go and saw me to the tunnel where I walked through to the report area whilst he headed across to the main stadium. The underground is semi-dark and cooler; we hung about there for 10 minutes before emerging into the bright sunshine and dry heat. Galant was in the second semi-final which was good news. As we lined up behind our blocks I heard Paul shout out in a long, loud, drawn-out voice-'COME-ON BA-BY!'

I couldn't get over how great I felt. I completely cruised around the track. The heat brings out the best in me. Sailing down the home-straight, easing off the throttle, I just couldn't get over how easy this was feeling; so much so that as I glided on to the Finn, Kemola's shoulder, I said to him 'Relax...drop your shoulders!' It was a stupid thing to do, probably coming across as arrogance, but I just couldn't contain my excitement and exuberance. My form is back with a bang! Paul said there were some great press photos of me, but I wasn't even aware they were available for people to take; by the time I looked in to the room they were all gone, apart from one from this morning's heat which featured Galant and me. He won the other semi-final; poor Brian Jones was eliminated. However, typical Brian, he was very supportive of me. I was so excited about how well I'm running I telephoned Coach Walker and then *Pixie Mia Farrow lookalike*. They were both delighted.

1975 European Junior Championships Evening (6.30 p.m.-4.30 p.m. British time):

400 metres Semi-Final

1. Hoffmann 47.60 seconds
2. Jaakko Kemola (Fin) 47.64
3. Ludger Zander (ger) 47.88
4. Edmund Antczak (Pol) 47.92

1976 With the *Simone de Beauvoir Philosophy Queen* having stayed overnight in my Pollock Halls room I basically had no sleep at all. I breakfasted with Roger. Because of yesterday's 400 metres international against Iceland and Ireland I looked into the team physio for a rub. Most unusually, the Edinburgh Highland Games were being held today on a Sunday. I ran fairly well and set another new Scottish Native Record; two days running if you'll forgive the pun; that can't happen very often.

In the evening my fourth date with *Diana the goddess of love and hunting*. Things are happening very fast between us. We went to a local hotel for a drink, bumping in to Frank Barratt, one of the good guys; I first got to know him when I worked at Thomas Graham & Sons. He followed his father into the plumbing business, Peter Barratt & Son. Apart from being a good guy, he's a very cool looking bloke; with his moustache and fine head of hair he'd make for a particularly handsome cowboy. *Diana* and I stayed at the disco for 10 minutes before I ran her home to Silverknowes by the sea.

1976 Edinburgh Highland Games

400 metres 5. Hoffmann 47.10 seconds (Scottish native Record)

Scotland v Iceland v N. Ireland 4 x 400m relay-a good leg 1. Scotland (Hoffmann, Andy Kerr, Forbes, Jenkins) 3:14.95

23rd August, 1974 Paul and I went to see The Exorcist; boy was it scary! Emerging from the cinema we bumped in to Fay Robertson.

1975, Athens Food-wise Paul and I have been living mainly off the stuff we bought at the shops; it doesn't seem to matter what meat is served up, it's still swimming in oil. And I'm not a fussy eater, but again I just couldn't face it.

A very easy day, trying to stay as relaxed as possible so as not to use up any energy. I played cards in the morning with a few of the guys and then lay on my bed in the afternoon, managing to sleep a little. I've been given a FANTASTIC lift; one of the team officials came to my room with a telegram from *Pixie Mia Farrow lookalike* sent with love, no-less; how my spirits soared! I prepared and re-prepared my bag and kit several times-my G.B. vest which is a snug wee fit; the number 110 and my red Puma Munchen spikes.

It was good to get down to the warm-up track to go through the same routine for the third time. I felt okay when I was warming up, but not quite as good as last evening before the semi-final when I was flying; however I was very, very nervous about the final, so I knew that would help me run fast. Paul said to me that when he was returning on the bus last night to the games village, that all the Poles could do was to say Galant and Hoffmann-Hoffmann and Galant; that's given me a lift to know I'm being noticed; probably because of the ease of my run. The great nervousness and worry is a mixture of knowing I'm in with a chance of doing well after last night's performance, but the other factor is I don't want to let anyone down, including myself.

If

'…If you can fill the unforgiving minute
With sixty seconds' worth of distance run,
Yours is the Earth and everything that's in it,
And—which is more—you'll be a Man, my son!'

Rudyard Kipling

I have to say Malcolm Arnold was brilliant. I said to him that all I wanted to do was to give my absolute best. I didn't want to step off the track feeling I hadn't give it my all. He said he knew I would do that-he was great-calm, level-headed, positive and caring-just the right balance. After warming up, it was the same routine. And then once more back into the dark reporting room, only to be released like gladiators to perform in front of the waiting crowd. Once again, as everyone settled behind their blocks Paul launched in to 'COME ON BA-BY!' At least I was expecting it this time.

Galant had drawn lane 1 so I couldn't see him at all, but overall lane 4 is a good draw. The gun fired and I went out reasonably hard, but the echelon and stagger remained pretty consistent, although I suspect Galant had already moved ahead of everyone. Coming through 300 metres he was ahead and the rest of us were in a line, perhaps with Harald Schmidt of Germany slightly up on the rest of us. Initially I felt disappointed that it was so close, particularly as I didn't feel I had much else to give. I tried to stay relaxed; with 50 metres to go, Galant was several metres ahead of the field and there was now six of us in a row for the medals. From here I drove on and just felt I wanted it more than anyone else; that it was more of a fighting spirit than anything physical that saw me through to the silver medal.

If

*'...If you can force your heart and nerve and sinew
To serve your turn long after they are gone,
And so hold on when there is nothing in you
Except the Will which says to them: "Hold on!"*

Rudyard Kipling

I was very, very happy, especially as I didn't feel anywhere near as good as in last evening's semi-final where I could have registered a faster time. Throughout the race I didn't feel as if I ever quite got going; I seemed to just go through the motions; but when I realised I'd won a silver medal in a personal best I was absolutely delighted. Indeed, the whole team was pleased, especially Mike Farrell who had entered Brian Jones and me in the individual event of his own volition, so that helped justify his decision. I telephoned home including to the Walker household and spoke to Clint. I phoned *Pixie's* home and passed on the news to her Mum. If you can't share such moments, they're like dust.

1975 European Junior Championships

(6.00 p.m.) 400 metres Final

1. Galant 46.88 secs
2. Hoffmann 47.27 (p.b.)
3. Reimann (G.D.R.) 47.41
(9.00 p.m.) 4 x 400 metres relay Heat 2. GBR 3:11.1 (48.1 secs split)

Athletics Weekly Cliff Temple reports from Athens

'...The other British silver went to Peter Hoffmann, ranked only eighth before the championships at 400m, but coping with three rounds in 36 hours better than most-especially as the first round was held at the equivalent of 7.10 am British time! Hoffmann won his semi in 47.6 and came through strongly for second place in the final in a personal best 47.27, behind Polish winner Henryk Galant (46.88 in lane one). AAA Junior champion Brian Jones never looked happy, and went out in the semis...'

1976 I gave the New Zealand distance runner Rod Dixon a lift up to the Edinburgh Tattoo alongside *Diana the goddess of love and hunting*; I must be careful to avoid her for the next few weeks...

1977 I picked up Susan Rettie's tennis racket and played tennis for 3 hours. By the end, my legs were whacked. Afterwards a meal and a blether with Paul. A telegram arrived to say I'm in the relay squad for the G.B. v Russia match; I hope I get a run. I trained in the evening; afterwards Paul and I had a drink then went to see the hypnotist, Robert Halpern's Fringe show; what a fucking laugh we had; he should have been paying the two of for getting the audience laughing so much; I was almost lying on the floor in tears, my sides splitting.

11.30 a.m.-2.30 p.m.: 3 hours of tennis

Evening (7.00 p.m.): 4 x 110 metres; 300 metres 34.2 seconds

24th August, 1975, Athens The last day of the European Junior Championships. I spent most of the morning phoning Edinburgh speaking with *Pixie Mia Farrow lookalike* which was just great; she was delighted to hear about me getting a medal. I also spoke to Coach Walker who kicked off with the immortal line *What happened!* I also spoke to Nana and Davie Campbell the physio. Thereafter, I relaxed as much as possible. Come the evening back down to the stadium for the fifth and last time. Paul had a disappointing run in the final of the 800 metres, but had run well to make the final. Malcolm Edwards was barged off the track in the home-straight.

Disappointingly, we only finished fifth in the 4 x 400 metres relay, running slower than in last night's heat. We were going well half way through, lying in second place, but Chris Van Rees went a bit mad on the third leg running wide on the first bend and expending so much energy over the first 200 metres that he blew up and struggled to even get the baton to me. If only he'd just sat in all the way and given me the baton on the two leaders' shoulders we would definitely have medalled. Ce la vie. It was surprising given how posh and bright he appears to be. Anyway, there was no blame or recriminations amongst us; all I'm doing is recording the facts. I was more disappointed for the rest of the team; it would have been great to see them go home with a medal too; I've already got mine. However, the girls came up trumps and it was lovely to see them get a bronze medal, particularly the Scots, Ann Clarkson and Karen Williams, but the whole team with Ruth Kennedy and Diane Heath are lovely. Ruth did well to just hold off the Belgians on the last leg by one tenth of a second! Later the whole team relaxed.

Early evening the boys had 40 metres races along the university halls of residence corridors; I beat Coe in the final; he's surprisingly quick for a distance runner. Later on we went to a reception, which was just awful, but Paul and I were in good form and had everyone in stitches of laughter. Happy days. But I'm looking forward to getting home to let everyone see my medal and also to see *Pixie*.

Evening: 4 x 400 metres relay 1. GDR 5. UK 3:11.5

Athletics Weekly Cliff Temple reports from Athens:

'...The men's 4 x 400m was disappointing for Britain, after some excellent running in the heats, which had several foreign journalists tipping the British squad to win. Jeff Griffiths and Brian Jones kept Britain up with the leaders, and Chris Van Rees (like Ruth Kennedy, a medallist in Duisburg two years ago) went up to second place halfway through his stint. However, the effects of having run the first bend wide caught up with him and combined with a poor changeover to Peter Hoffmann, Britain were back to fifth, where they stayed...'

1978 *Diana the goddess of love and hunting* and I dropped by to see Denis Davidson. He was very good about my Commonwealth failure. Late on *Diana* and I bumped into Willie at the top of The Royal Mile. He was sitting in the car with his window wide open waiting to collect Nana and Heather from the Tollbooth Church. Surprising him from behind, I asked in a very deep *voice If Sir would mind moving the vehicle?* His reaction was priceless! *Diana* and I went along to see a couple of Fringe events: Squawk and As You Were. Enjoyable enough, but I was a little restless. Tomorrow I fly out behind the Iron Curtain to Prague for the European Championships.

25th August, 1974 A foul day; it poured with rain all day. The Scottish Relay Championships were a flop; we had a walkover in the 4 x 400 metres and were third in the 4 x 100m. At night, at the last minute I decided to fly down to London instead of taking the train. Gaga gave me a lift out to Turnhouse where I met Roger and also Drew Harley. I shared a room with the latter at the Crystal Palace Hostel in the tower block.

1975, Athens In the morning a crowd of us went shopping; I picked up some good T-shirts. The flight to London was fine; Brian Jones and I played chess for much of the journey. I'm very fond of him; he's really looking forward to starting at Cambridge. He has a nice way with him-good humoured; sensitive and bright. I'm sure he'll go far. At London we happened to bump into Frank Dick at the airport for the ongoing flight to Edinburgh; he was coming back from the Bank Holiday Monday, UK v USSR match. There was a bit of a kerfuffle where he had Ann Clarkson in tears; I jumped to her defence. He told me not to get above myself just because I was a European medallist; well, for fuck's sake, what could you say to that! Bob Sinclair met us at the airport and gave Paul; Ann and me a lift home. I went out to see Mum; it was FANTASTIC to see *Pixie Mia Farrow lookalike* again. I ran her home; we stopped off by the Hermitage…as we do.

1976 I spent the morning reading and playing a little golf. Roger telephoned; I joined him and David at Meadowbank where we ran two good 300 metres. Dad's sketched out a letter for me to apply to the army, but to borrow from an early John Buchan novel it's Half-Hearted; do I really want to do that with the option of St Andrew's or Loughborough Universities?

The road to hell is…and all that; so much for resisting the charms of *Diana the goddess of love and hunting*. We tried to get in to see a film at the Festival, but were unsuccessful. So instead we went for a drink to the Cramond Inn and then had some chips. I met her parents; we got on okay. Goodness knows what they thought of me with my dyed orange hair tied up in an Indian beaded hairband (which I'd brought back from Canada); a navy T shirt with a large Puma face on the front and Hoffmann emblazoned on the back; and my cut-away jeans; not to mention, after three weeks away, I'm still carrying an Canadian twang!

Afternoon: 2 x 300 metres 33.5; 33.3 seconds (15-20 minutes recovery)

1977 Coach Walker rang me at mid-day to say I'm running in the individual against Russia tonight. Great news, but my legs are sore and I wouldn't have trained the way I have this week if I'd known earlier on. It was a ghastly evening with torrential rain, absolutely miserable. Anyway, I ran okay. Afterwards Gavin Miller; *Diana the goddess of love and hunting* and I went out for a pleasant Chinese meal to the Mie Kwei at Morningside. *Diana* stayed overnight.

UK v USSR

400 metres 3. Hoffmann 47.78 seconds

1978 A bright, light, late summery morn. After breakfast I jogged a few laps around Porty Golf Course.

Diana telephoned and we had a long, good humoured chat. Thereafter, around eleven o'clock, Willie and Jo ran me out to the airport; we took a circuitous, roundabout route as I wanted to pick up some new screw in spikes. The flight to Gatwick was tremendous-clear views all the way. It took an unusual route out, flying over both the Forth Road and Rail Bridges. Unfortunately we were delayed in London for an hour, but the flight to Prague took only an hour and a half. After the usual million point military and officials' checkpoints we were eventually allocated our rooms. I'm sharing with Cameron Sharp, which suits me fine; I like Cameron and we get on well together. He's quite a serious bloke, but an all-round decent guy, with a nice dry humour. Although he's a P.E. jock at Jordanhill, he surprised me with his knowledge of economics. He says that each evening he likes to listen to The World Tonight on Radio 4 at ten o'clock.

26th August, 1973 I got up at 9.45 a.m. and went up to Meadowbank for the 400 metres time trial which Coach Walker had put on to decide who will get the last place in the E.A.C senior men's 4 x 400 metres relay team for the British Cup Final in London. I finished only third, with Keith Ridley winning it. I wasn't overly bothered not to make the team although as they're flying down it would have been my first time in a plane. Fair play to Keith breaking 50 seconds for the first time-he ran 49.9. I improved my personal best running 50.8 seconds; not a bad way to end the Youth season. Being a Sunday I trained in the afternoon with Duncan Baker and Steve. I was too tired to do any weights.

Morning: 400 metres time trial: 1. K. Ridley 49.9 seconds 3. Hoffmann 50.8 secs (p.b.)

Afternoon: 2 x 4 x 150m (walk 250m recovery); easy weights-work

1974, London, Bank Holiday Monday Drew Harley went out to buy a few papers. The rain was coming down in sheets and the wind was swirling; perfect conditions for a 400 metres. Not. By lunchtime it had cleared a little, but the breeze remained. Drew had a poor run in the 200 metres which Roger won. I ran a personal best to finish fourth although I felt I could have won the race if I'd distributed my effort better. Still, it's a good way to end the season and go into the winter's training. We had a little bit of trouble getting our travel expenses, but got there in the end. I actually got back to Meadowbank by 7.00 p.m. before going out to Oxgangs with Gaga; John took us for a drink.

Southern Counties AAA v AAA Juniors

1. M. Clark 48.0 2. R. Benn 48.2 3. D. Laing 48.3 4. Hoffmann 48.5 (p.b.)

1977 A relaxed day reading, playing music and sleeping before this evening's relay leg against Russia. As it was so cold, wet, windy 'n miserable Heather decided not to go up so I gave the two free tickets to Fiona Fyffe instead. I ran okay, but felt a little lethargic. In the evening *Diana the goddess of love and hunting* and I went to the reception at the Commonwealth Pool. We were at the same table as some ex-rugby mates of Dad, including Boroughmuir's Bill Noble. They were good fun. We got to bed at one.

UK v USSR

4 x 400 metres relay 1. UK 3:08.8 2. USSR 3:10.0

1978, Prague I didn't feel that great after a breakfast of frankfurters. All the complaints are flowing in already about the food and the lack of recreational facilities.

At lunchtime we went to the British Embassy for an informal buffet lunch. The diplomats do 18 month stints; Prague is seen as one of the very worst outposts. The Irish chap who is in charge of security was telling me there are significant problems with bugging.

In the afternoon Coach Harry Wilson drove a few of us out to a forest with fantastic running trails. I did a very enjoyable 5 miles Fartlek with Mary Stewart; running along smooth, soft pine-covered woodland trails is very much my thing; it's far superior to running on the road. We ran at a good pace and I felt better mentally than I have for a while. The running's still not there after Edmonton, but all I'm keen to do is run one more 800 metres and get the season over and done with. To finish off, Steve Ovett and I ran some back-to-backs. Although we ran in each other's shadow I'm not running the way I was in June and July. However, it was good for him. He's not confident about the 800 metres, telling me he's really neglected any speed work in the past two years. I bolstered his confidence by saying how quickly and smoothly he was running. Sebastian Coe didn't want to come out with us all, preferring to keep himself to himself.

Afternoon: 5 miles Fartlek with Mary Stewart; 2 x 4 x 80 metres with Steve Ovett

27ᵗʰ August, 1974 Well, then, the start of a new big adventure. Having left Thomas Graham & Sons (I feel I should be adding by Appointment to Her Majesty the Queen!) I started studying at Telford College. Just as well I was early because when I travelled out to Crewe Toll I discovered my classes are actually held at the annexe at the Dean Village, which suits me down to the ground. The Geography teacher is brilliant; he's an old guy-a retired teacher; he's opinionated and quite a character. He rammed home the message that with half a dozen key facts we can all pass any Higher exam as long as we know how to structure an essay properly. It inspired a lot of the students. I'm the youngest there; many of the students are three times my age. I think I'm going to be quite happy here; it bodes well for the future, helping confirm the wisdom of the radical change I've made to my life trajectory. With the season wynding down and as we head toward autumn and Michaelmas, I joined the middle distance guys in the evening. It was hard-going. Afterwards I warmed down with Ann Clarkson.

Evening: 6 x 400 metres (3 minutes recovery) 59; 59; 59; 59; 61; 62 seconds By the end of the fourth run my legs above the knees were like lead!

28ᵗʰ August, 1975 I went out to Telford College for the Modern Studies tutorial but discovered I'm unable to take that subject-a bit of a bugger. I felt a bit fed up today-perhaps the aftermath of the highs of Athens? After last evening's good 150s session with Roger and Gus McKenzie I did something lighter this evening.

'...Now a soft kiss-Aye, by that kiss, I vow an endless bliss...'

John Keats

I was on the end of the most beautiful kiss from *Pixie Mia Farrow lookalike* which more than transformed how I felt in the afternoon; we spent a lovely evening together.

Evening: 2 x 4 x 60 metres

1977, London An early start, with a 6.00 a.m. rise. *Diana the goddess of love and hunting's* father gave me a lift out to Turnhouse. Surprisingly, I got on a flight no problem at all; it's one of the great things about British Caledonian. The flight left at 8.00 a.m. I sat beside Madge Carruthers who's officiating at the Bank Holiday meet between the UK and Germany. She's very pleasant. When we arrived in the capital the rain was bucketing down. We travelled out to the Queens Hotel. To stretch my legs I took a 90 minutes tootle around the shops, ending up buying a knight. I spent the evening reading and watched some TV. *Diana* surprised me at 10.30 p.m. phoning me in my room; it was great to hear from her!

1978, Prague After breakfast, Harry Wilson drove us out to the forest. This time I ran five miles with many of the distance guys including Ovett; Foster; McLeod; Black; and Davies. For me I was probably running a personal best over the distance; of course part of the motivation was not getting stranded and lost in the forest for ever-only kidding, as the trails are cleverly laid out. I felt good for doing the session, although it's unlikely to do me any good for a half mile race in two days' time. Afterwards only Harry Wilson, Mick McLeod and I went back in the car.

In the early afternoon I joined the tour of Prague. After all the negativity about the athletics set-up, the city is quite stunning with its location on the River Vitava. There's a medieval feel to the capital with its olde worlde charm: Prague Castle; dozens of church spires; the old square; the Astronomical Clock; and the Charles Bridge with the statues of Catholic saints. If the producers could get in to the country it would make for a marvellous film location. The only drawback was there was more walking involved than any of us quite realised; however, it was a must see. Fortunately on my return I dived straight in to the physio for a rub. In the evening I lay and read. I'm reading John Cowper Powys's Autobiography and John Stewart Collis' The Worm Forgives The Plough; two wonderful books.

Gaga rushes to the door each morning when the post arrives and is always disappointed there's no interesting mail awaiting him, so I thought I'd write him a letter from Prague with some attractive Czechoslovakian stamps on the envelope:

Monday, 28th August, 1978, Prague, Czechoslovakia

Dobry Den Comrade Willie,

That means good morning! Well, here I am reporting from cell block 416 at Strahov University. I've settled in quite well as opposed to most other team members. They all hate the food and lack of recreation facilities to help keep themselves amused. I'm quite lucky having brought across some good books to read and pass the time.

The flight from Edinburgh to London was excellent, with the weather the clearest I've encountered on a flight; I could see the patchwork of the fields, rivers and hills down below for most of the hour. Also, with it being British Caledonian we enjoyed a meal on board-chicken curry no less.

Meg Ritchie, Brian Burgess, Chris Black were on the flight too; we were amongst the last to arrive at Gatwick which meant not too much hanging around, although the flight out to Prague was delayed by an hour. The flight most surprisingly only took one hour thirty five minutes from lift-off to touch down as we had a good following wind; the return flight will take longer.

It was good news to discover there's no time difference here. Some good news for you-I managed to pick up a litre of Johnny Walker whisky which should keep you going for a month or two in to the autumn.

You would not believe the weather; it's been dull, cold and blustery with the temperature only 13 degrees. It's like Meadowbank in March; if this keeps up the performances will be well down.

On Saturday I ran a five mile Fartlek with Mary Stewart; yesterday I ran five miles with Brendan Foster; Steve Ovett etc. we've been doing all our running in a forest located two miles away from a small village. Coach Harry Wilson has driven us out there. It's fantastic to run along the undulating heavily scented woodland trails. We can run for miles without really noticing it and it's particularly easy on the legs as the terrain is quite soft. The Czechs are clever in that the trails are clearly marked out with a continuous painted white line which you follow to complete a two and half miles circuit.

Yesterday a group of us went on a bus tour, however we ended up walking for most of the time. We were taken in to Prague Castle, the President's home. I took lots of snaps of the architecture which will be of interest to Jo who would have love to see it.

We also attended an informal buffet reception at the British Embassy. Evidently this is one of the dreaded outposts in the diplomatic service. An Irishman who is in charge of security was 'fed up to the back teeth' and the poor guy still has sixteen of his eighteen months to go! He was also complaining about the amount of bugging that goes on; private conversations have to be undertaken in the garden!

I'm rooming with Cameron Sharp of 4 x 100 metres Commonwealth Games fame. He's a nice guy and someone who I would have chosen if the choice had been given to me for a room-mate. Our room itself is very basic and is really only for one person. If I crane my neck out the window I can look down over a valley which recedes well in to the distance toward Prague itself. The university halls of residence are thus very much situated on top of a hill-like plateau.

I feel quite well; this gives you a flavour of what's happening. I'm looking forward to seeing you safe and well next week.

Best wishes and love.

Peter

Morning: 5 miles

1975 I was running so poorly this evening I've decided not to run in tomorrow's Coke Meeting. I had a really good chat with *Pixie Mia Farrow lookalike* tonight; we did our long walk together around the back of Meadowbank because K. was watching us.

'...Make me immortal with a kiss...'

Christopher Marlowe

I gave her a lift home; as usual we stopped off just past the Hermitage. God, she's beautiful.

'Close your eyes and I'll kiss you, Tomorrow I'll miss you.'

Paul McCartney

Evening: 300 metres 36.8; 200m 24; 2 x150m; 4 x 100m

1977, London I joined Nat Muir, John Robson and Mark Holtom for breakfast. It was a lovely late summer's morn out; the early coolness had evaporated and it was sunny and bright. I strolled out in just my shirt with my sleeves rolled up and picked up some of the nationals. London is so civilised. Back at the hotel I lounged around all morning, drinking coffee and reading the newspapers. One of the officials gave me a lift down to Crystal Palace. All afternoon I sat watching the athletics, just along from Olympic 110 metres hurdles champion, Guy Drut, who was doing the television coverage for Europe. In the evening, a pleasant meal, a game of pool, before retiring for the night. *Diana* rang me again.

1978, Prague I had been hoping to see John Anderson today, but didn't get the chance. I tried to have as relaxed a day as possible, laying back for much of the time reading a biography of Conan Doyle. Late afternoon I did some light jogging. I missed Cameron (Sharp) so walked back in the rain with Frank Dick traversing through the world's largest stadium, the giant Great Strahov Stadium. After writing a few letters, including one each to Anne Williamson, Gaga and *Diana,* I fell asleep reading.

29th August, 1975, London Well, that will teach me to be spontaneous. After last evening's session I'd decided not to race the Coke Meeting at Crystal Palace, but when I awoke this morning in Edinburgh, spur of the moment, I decided to take part. I met the throwers, Meg Ritchie and Chris Black at Turnhouse and flew down with them. They're both excellent company. I'd decided not to tell either Coach Walker or *Pixie Mia Farrow lookalike* and give them the surprise of watching it live on the box and seeing me suddenly appear. I ran surprisingly well-my second best ever time-47.48! I phoned both of them afterwards; Coach Walker isn't very pleased!

IAC/Coca Cola Meeting

1. D. Jenkins 5. Hoffmann 47.48 seconds

1977, London After breakfast I did a little jogging and stretching, followed by a light massage. Dave Jenkins was on the adjacent table. Afterwards a relaxed day-a cold bath; some Laurel & Hardy on the box and some lunch of steak and chips. I ran the first leg of the relay against Germany and handed us over in the lead. Because it was the last event and I knew I wouldn't catch the flight I decided to stay on and attend the reception. It was an enjoyable enough affair including a roast turkey dinner. Before bed a few games of pool and a Clint Eastwood film, Joe Kidd; Dougie McLean ended up sleeping on my floor!

Bank Holiday Monday

UK v Germany 4 x 400 metres relay 1. UK

1978, Prague Well tonight is the night as the saying goes. I had a few carbohydrates for breakfast and then wandered over to see the Karhu rep. Unfortunately the shoes were too big, although I was silly not take a pair which I could have passed on to Norrie Gregor. After a light lunch I had an easy afternoon-some writing, some reading and a little sleep. I watched Alan Pascoe and the rest of the 400 metres hurdlers get knocked out in their heats! I warmed up with Steve Ovett; he's not as confident as he really should be, however he qualified okay. I didn't, as I knew I wouldn't; all month I've been running way below par; however, ironically it was the best I've run tactically, running with group all the way. I was glad to get my last half mile of my first season out the way. The weather conditions and the poor dismal mood and morale of the British camp-there's a dissonance about this trip which I've not experienced before, somehow matched my mood as I went through the motions this evening. John

Anderson says that next year, no matter who I'm facing, I'll just take off with 100 metres to go and leave everyone in the dust. That will be great! Later on I went out for a meal with John; Dave Moorcroft; and Dick Ashton. I got back around midnight; Cameron Sharp was very tipsy after a few drinks earlier on; he was quite amusing as he regaled me about the sexual exploits of a Miss Hearnshaw-others I should say, rather than Cameron's!

1978 European Championships, Prague

800 metres heat 1. O. Beyer (DDR) 1:47.7 5. Hoffmann 1:49.3

30th August, 1975, London I was up early this morning to catch a flight from Gatwick Airport to Edinburgh. I felt a bit fed up after the reaction to my spontaneity of racing in London and the adverse reaction to it. I though *Pixie Mia Farrow lookalike* might have phoned at five o'clock, but no luck. I stayed in alone, just watching the box; *Pixie* phoned at 10.30 p.m. It was a bit fractious; however, Ann Sowersby was very good and phoned up suggesting I come up to the dance and pick them both up; *Pixie* and I stopped off at Arthurs Seat en-route to dropping her home. She's got a sore tooth.

Bank Holiday Monday, 1976, London I left Edinburgh first thing and flew down to London for the UK v France match at Crystal Palace. The team was half of our training squad as I partnered David and Roger Jenkins; warming up it felt more like a pre-season training session! We easily beat France and also a GB 'B' team. Job done, I flew back to Edinburgh getting home by 10 pm; in between I read 50 pages of Sociology. It's a strange existence; I may be a poor student, but here's me hopping on and off jets and because of the speed and reliability of transport I can go from Edinburgh to London and return again the same day, sandwiching an international race in between; a funny old world.

Great Britain v France, 1976:

4 x 400 metres relay

1. GB (R. Jenkins 47.9; Hoffmann 47.5; G. Cohen 46.5; D. Jenkins 47.1) 3.08
2. France
3. GB 'B' team

1977, London After yesterday's international against West Germany, Alan Dainton dropped me off at East Croydon Station to catch the train to Gatwick Airport. Unfortunately I had to hang around for four hours. I gave *Diana the goddess of love and hunting* a ring to let her know I'd be arriving at four o'clock. I didn't feel too good, but managed to finish my book on the flight. On arrival in Edinburgh the rain was absolutely teeming down. *Diana* was there to meet me and we took the airport bus back. As Will was out running Jo to the Edinburgh Sketching Club we had to take shelter in the old greenhouse. In the evening I felt worse; a sore stomach; I was sick. Late on the doctor was called out. I've a rumbling appendix.

End of the season: REST!

1978, Prague With the season effectively over I took a wee tootle up to the track and ran a gentle four miles and a little reflection about the future. It's been a mixed season; the indoors went well with a AAAs title and after running a 1.46 800 metres in only my fourth proper race seemed to promise incredible things with the world at my feet; then for no apparent reason come this month of August, all my running ability just seemed to disappear, running through my fingers like the sands of time. As to where it's gone, who knows.

There was a big clock in the stadium so I was able to gauge how quickly or slowly I was running. Come the evening it was back down to the main stadium to join John Anderson and a group of the girls to watch the evening's athletics. Coe won the first semi-final and Ovett the second, just in front of Beyer, who I'd raced so well against back in June; the final should be riveting. It's just a pity my form has deserted me; it would have been fun to be in the mix. It was absolutely miserable-cold and wet; autumn's arrived very early; so much so I was freezing and very glad to get back to our accommodation for a bite to eat and to dry out. Note to self and others: Don't go to Prague at the end of August that is if you're allowed in!

<u>Morning:</u> 4 miles run

31st August, 1975 I ran a pretty good session this morning, then spent a lovely afternoon sitting out the back of Meadowbank with *Pixie Mia Farrow lookalike*. Very happy days.

Tell Me Not Here, It Needs Not Saying

'...I played with you 'mid cowslips blowing,
When I was six and you were four;
When garlands weaving, flower-balls throwing,
Were pleasures soon to please no more.
Through groves and meads, o'er grass and heather,
With little playmates, to and fro,
We wander'd hand in hand together;
But that was sixty years ago.

You grew a lovely roseate maiden,
And still our love was strong;
Still with no care our days were laden,
They glided joyously along;
And I did love you very dearly,
How dearly words want power to show;
I thought your heart was touch'd as nearly;
But that was fifty years ago...'

A. E. Houseman

Once home to Porty, I enjoyed the charming *The Secret of Santa Vittoria*. Later, Gus McKenzie's dad phoned me with the arrangements for the meeting at Gateshead tomorrow.

Morning: 2 x 300 metres (15 minutes recovery) 33.9; 33.8 seconds

1977 After the doctor left, things went from bad to worse. At 2.00 a.m. I was feeling terribly sick and was to be found lying on the bathroom floor wishing that terrible feeling would go away. I forced myself to get up and took a couple of tablets managing to sleep until 7.30 a.m. I visited the doctor who gave me a line for Leith Hospital; they decided I should remain in for the night. I spent most of the time reading a fine book from their library-ironically, it was Brian Glanville's The Olympian. It's a funny old world. But it's not.

1978, Prague After breakfast, a group of went on a tour, of all things, a truck factory. Need I say more? Probably not. It was extremely boring. On the return journey on the bus I wasn't feeling too tricky. However, after some lunch I was able to join Harry Wilson who took Tony Simmons and me for a session down in the woods. It brought home to me, just how unfit I am and how much I've got to find. Come the evening I watched the best race I've seen since Montreal; the men's 800 metres was truly extraordinary and incredibly exciting.

Sebastian Coe rather heroically and characteristically took the race by the scruff of the neck in an attempt to burn off Ovett's kick and Beyer's strength. I could hardly believe the clock-49.3 seconds through the bell; 62.3 seconds at 500 metres and 76.1 seconds at 600 metres. Ovett looked comfortable, attacking off the final bend moving in to the lead, but had been run to a standstill; to everyone' surprise, apart from possibly me (I knew how strong Beyer was after his narrow win against me in the UK v GDR match back in June) nipped past Steve in the final 30 metres. Well, after that, everything was an anti-climax.

What followed however, was, in its way, illuminating and almost as extra-ordinary. Coe normally keeps himself to himself, as I know from previous trips e.g. the European Junior Championships. However, we got him talking on the main staircase of our accommodation until the small hours of the morning. There was Dave Jenkins, Brendan Foster and me; it was mainly Bren who was asking him about his training with a whole array of questions. Amongst a bing of information, one session stood out as perhaps one of the all-time greats: 4 x 800 metres in 1:51. I thought Brilliant-yes that might be manageable-what with a 10 to 15 minutes recovery? Brendan asked him about the recovery. Coe replied Oh, two minutes. Jenkins and I almost fell off our chairs! It made me question whether I want to continue middle-distance running. And to think only a month ago I quite fancied my chances of beating him at the UK Championships. I may have the physical ability, but not the mental or emotional equipment. When I retired to bed I had a terrible headache; tension at the back of my head.

Afternoon: 8 x 200 metres (45 seconds recovery) 27 seconds; with Tony Simmons

1st September, 1973 Paul and I went up to Meadowbank to watch the basketball. Come the Saturday evening I ran in the floodlight meeting between Edinburgh and Glasgow. I was pleased to win for Edinburgh. We were given T shirts to race in; Edinburgh had red ones, whilst Glasgow had white ones. It felt good to have been selected and I feel it rounds off my first serious season. I enjoyed running under the floodlights; Aunt Heather filmed the race.

Edinburgh v Glasgow Floodlit Meeting Youth 400 metres

1. Hoffmann 52.6
2. J. Wark 53.6
3. I. Callander
4. B. Dickson 54.9
5. D. Smith 55.1

1975 We (being Mark Wilson; Gus McKenzie; and Gus's lovely girlfriend, Annette Ramage; and me) left Meadowbank for Gateshead at one o'clock. I didn't run well at all; running two hard and fast 300s yesterday probably wasn't a good idea at all, as I ran over half a second slower; the minor consolation was I beat Ovett. On the return journey Gus's car broke down at a place called Belford, where we had to spend the evening at a bed 'n breakfast. I managed to telephone *Pixie Mia Farrow lookalike.*

Greenham Games, Gateshead

300 metres 1. D. Jenkins 32.9 4. Hoffmann 34.5 5. A. McKenzie 35.3 6. S. Ovett 35.3

150 metres 5. Hoffmann 16.7

1978, Prague I ran four miles this morning, going off at a fair old clip, running well, but faded badly; I need someone to run with for these types of sessions. John Anderson and I went down to the stadium to watch the championships; whilst there he sketched out a programme for me. (PC) Geoff Capes was disqualified, evidently for belting an official; as P.G. Wodehouse wrote Hallo, 'allo, 'allo! Rather tragically, Mary Stewart was tripped up with a lap to go.

Morning: 4 miles

2nd September, 1974 Now that I'm a part-time student, second-class (Telford College) I pootered around for much of the morning writing up my notebooks and journals and then spent a few hours at Porty Library. It's always peaceful there. In the afternoon Gaga kindly gave me a lift up to college; this is my new life for the next two years until I can move on to the next rung of the ladder. It's a time of great hope and aspiration. To borrow from Pressburger and Powell, I Know Where I'm Going. As we move towards Michaelmas I'm getting excited about planning ahead. For life to be meaningful it's important to have aims and objectives; goals in life to propel me forward, making the journey fun and so much more satisfying. As John Stewart Collis structured his life story-Arriving; Growing; Searching; Doing; and Finding. Come the evening I watched the

European Championships; Tony Simmons ran the race of his life to get a silver medal; Joyce Smith won a bronze whilst Roger qualified for the semi-finals; Gaga and I had a fish supper.

1978, Prague This morning I ran five miles with Tony Simmons and Dave Black in the woods, however they burned me off; I was breathing out my arse! Once again I joined John down at the track; it was tragic to see Dave Jenkins being tripped up in the relay; it actually gave me quite a start.

<u>Morning:</u> **5 miles**

3rd September, 1975 Coach Walker's taking a gamble by selecting me for the 400 metres hurdles at this weekend's Pye Cup Final. Sandy Robertson kindly took me for a hurdles session; he was very good and I enjoyed myself.

<u>Evening:</u> **400 metres hurdles technique work over the first three hurdles with Sandy Robertson**

1977 Surely a record, six letters in the post including an offer to undertake a B.A. in Business Studies at Dundee. After deciding against Loughborough or St Andrews last year I may take up the offer. The real challenge is whether I can combine it with my proposed move up to the half mile. After a very fallow year, despite several GB appearances, it's a difficult one. Dougie McLean couldn't make it, so I played a solitary game of golf at Porty. It was a crisp, cold and breezy early autumn day, but I enjoyed being out. As we move into September and I continue taking a break from athletics it's a good time for self-reflection and contemplation. I studied some Economics so I'm clearly veering toward accepting the offer. Come the evening *Diana the goddess of love and hunting* and I enjoyed a drink up town;

some chips at Henderson Row before seeing her safely on to her bus home to Silverknowes by the sea.

1978, Prague I attended a big team meeting of athletes who were complaining about the poor team management by Messrs. Goodman et al, who's been useless and never around. I had a snooze, did some packing, before going down to watch the men's 1500 metres. Ovett won it out the park, but Dave Moorcroft hung on for a gutsy third; he's the only athlete to have medalled at Edmonton and Prague. In the evening Cameron Sharp and I went along to the reception to end the championships. It summed up the whole experience-very poor and subdued, with sparse rations available; we were allowed a single beer and a small salad; back to bed by midnight. Appropriately enough, my season is petering out; who knows what the future holds. The enthusiasm I normally feel come Michaelmas, when the farmers and I sum up the year and plan ahead to the future is somewhat lacking. I'm unsure and unsettled about the future.

4th September, 1975 I'm really enjoying Maths; I have to focus and concentrate the whole time. Conversely, I've found History boring with an unimpressive lecturer, so much so I've packed it in and decided to do a Higher Biology instead. Mr C. gave me a rub and also a bottle of wine away with me. Come the evening *Pixie Mia farrow lookalike* and I had a wonderful evening out at a movie. Happy days.

1976, Cwmbran Despite feeling grim all day after the evening, before I ran okay, particularly in the long relay handing us over a 10 metres lead. Cohen ran well on the last leg to take 8 metres off Roger and pip him on the line in the same time, giving Wolverhampton & Bilston the cup; we lost out by two points. Paul had a poor run in the half finishing sixth in a winnable race. Ce la vie. Once again *Diana the goddess of love and hunting* stayed overnight. I've only known her a month and already she's become an integral part of my life; I'm having second thoughts about moving from Edinburgh to Loughborough University.

1976 Pye Gold Cup Final

4 x 100m relay

4 x 400m relay 1. W & B 3:13.4 2. EAC 3:13.4

1978, Prague Ye gads, our alarm went off at 7.00 a.m. After breakfast Cameron and I shifted our luggage to the ground floor; fortunately, the Czechoslovakian cleaner we've befriended allowed us to use the staff lift. On the flight back to London we rather ironically enjoyed our best meal for a week. At Gatwick Airport it was very amusing to see Steve Ovett avoid all the photographers as he raced past them pushing his luggage trolley. Whilst t'others headed off in the direction of Heathrow, Liz Sutherland and I spent four hours awaiting the flight to Edinburgh, however we had an enjoyable blether and some food. Will, Jo and *Diana the goddess of love and hunting* were waiting for me at Turnhouse; it was lovely to seem all.

5th September, 1973 As I was pricing plumbing invoices work passed quite quickly today. Roy had a wee dig at me as is his way from time to time. He told me I'm not a Cost Clerk; and instead I'm a Junior Cost Clerk. If it wasn't so sad in all senses you would have to laugh! Come teatime, Scott Wallace and I accompanied each other to Rankin Drive before I headed down to get the 42 bus at the Kings Buildings. Gaga gave me a lift up to Meadowbank; as Anne and Iain were down (Mum had her hospital operation yesterday) they were in the car too. It was a really tough session tonight as I joined the middle distance group. I was thinking how very lovely *Pixie Mia Farrow lookalike* is. I'd love to get off with her on Saturday at the dance after this weekend's Europa Cup. Scott Brodie gave me a lift home.

Evening: 10 x 400 metres (1 minute recovery) 66; 69; 70; 72; 72; 72; 67; 67; 66; 66 seconds

1974 I'm really enjoying this new way of life. I was at college all day; it was great stuff, beating the Dickensian world of Thomas Graham's hands down. The only drawback was because the busses were so busy I got back quite late. After training with the middle distance guys, Coach Walker gave me a lift to the Playhouse; we had a good chat in the car for half an hour. I bought a fish super and then travelled out to Oxgangs.

Evening: 4 x 600 metres (5 minutes recovery) 89; 91; 89; 86 (53 seconds last lap); the track was full of puddles

1975, London I arrived at Waverley Station fairly early this morning to join the EAC team for the Pye Cup Final in Londonshire. I sat next to *Pixie Mia Farrow lookalike* on the train, so the long journey was a joy rather than a bore. From there to Crystal Palace. However, a disastrous first day. After my successful debut back in June, Coach Walker took the risk of running me in the 400 metres hurdles; I just couldn't get my stride pattern right and finished last; to round off a terrible evening, Roger Jenkins and I mucked up our changeover in the 4 x 100 metres relay and dropped the baton, when we most likely would have won. That's the first time that's happened to me. It didn't help changing the team's order. Normally I run the first leg and have *always* handed over in the lead no matter who I've raced; this time I was placed third, with Roger on the long second leg.

Pixie was furious and in a bad mood on the bus saying I wasn't to see her this evening. However, such is the path of true love-HUH, I wish!-we bumped in to each other in the bar and she was in a FANTASTIC MOOD; being non-drinkers a bottle of wine put us on our backs; we went out for a walk and spent a lovely evening together.

Tell me not here, it needs not saying

'…Or marshalled under moons of harvest
Stand still all night the sheaves;
Possess, as I possessed a season,
The countries I resign,
Where over elmy plains the highway
Would mount the hills and shine,
And full of shade the pillared forest
Would murmur and be mine….'

A. E. Houseman

1975 Pye Gold Cup Final, Crystal Palace

400 metres hurdles 8. Hoffmann 59.3 seconds
4 x 100 metres relay; Roger and I mucked up the baton change

1976 We travelled back from the Pye Gold Cup final on the team bus. I played some cards and then *Diana the goddess of love and hunting* and I sat together for the rest of the long journey back from Wales and read The Omen. Reading the same book together was a surprisingly enjoyable shared experience; something novel, if you'll forgive the pun. I had a meal at her house. Dad came down to collect me and I ran him home.

1977 After dropping Will off at his wee part-time job I took the dog to Portobello Park for a good run about. I took care of all my correspondence including my grant form, now that I've decided to study at Dundee. Early afternoon I went out to the doctor's-sister-for an allergy jag. I've just finished studying some Economics and Maths-I'm keen! as well as writing my journals. I feel happy! Late on I took the dog back out to the park; it's been very windy all day. Late on I watched a Michael Caine film, Pulp. It was about a writer being asked to immortalise someone's life. Is that what these journals are about? Discuss!

1978 My first full day back from Prague. There was no way I was going to go in to my summer job; instead I took Will and Jo down to Gullane and ran on the sands with the dog. After a shower at Meadowbank I had lunch with Will then went out to Dalkeith. After the enjoyable experience of running in the Prague Woods I'm keen to find somewhere similar to train. I ran round the nature trail in the Duke of Buccleuch's estate; it's excellent to train in. Home for a light tea of currant bread and honey before doing some track-work in the rain. *Diana* was down to time me; thereafter we had a drink and went to the Dominion Cinema to see a lovely and rather charming film, The Goodbye Girl. A different day as I settle back in to the new world of post Commonwealth and European Games and post Coach Walker and what I'm going to do. Or not…

Morning (10.00 a.m.): Gullane 4 miles

Afternoon (3.00 p.m.): 4 miles walking/jogging exploring Dalkeith Country Park

Evening (6.00 p.m.); 150-200-150 metres clock (90 seconds-2 minutes recovery); 11 repetitions

1975, London It was one of those absolutely lovely soft early autumn days. After breakfast I wandered along to Crystal Palace for day two of the Pye Cup final. The charming Charlie Lipton was along so I spent a little time with him; what a lovely man. John Anderson was there too. We sat and blethered. He was full of praise about me getting the silver medal at the European Junior Championships two weeks ago-*I told you, you would be good*...he's always such a wonderful inspiration. I spent half an hour lying on the pole vault mat with *Pixie Mia Farrow lookalike* before the 4 x 400 metres relay. She told me if I wanted to spend the evening with her I had to hand over a 10 yards lead on the first leg-a tall order against the great Wolverhampton & Bilston team full of senior internationalists! Anyway, to cut a long story short, I ran out of my skin, with a 46.8 seconds first leg! Not a bad way to finish off my junior career and gave us a 10-15 yards lead! We went on to run a Scottish Club Record of 3:08.9; pretty good given how young that team is with Paul; Roger; and Norman Gregor and we front ran it all the way. It was a great way to finish off the final. Later John Scott; Lorna Inglis; *Pixie* and I went out for a meal, before waiting 90 minutes for the train home to Waverley Station. As ever, a turbulent, topsy-turvy journey with *Pixie-life* ranging from hellish to wonderful and all points in between. However, it ended all right; we were still pals as we emerged from the train.

A Midsummer Night's Dream

'...The course of true love never did run smooth...'

William Shakespeare

1975 Pye Cup Final:

4 x 400 metres relay 1. EAC 3:08.9 (Hoffmann first leg 46.8 seconds! Scottish Club Record) 2. W&B 3:11.9

7th September, 1973 I sat in Gaga's car at Nile Grove reading the Scottish Daily Express, before wending my way along Balcarres Street; as ever autumn's arrived early in Edinburgh town; it was overcast, breezy and somewhat cool. Given it was Friday, work was still equally unpleasant.

However, one piece of good news to cheer us up was Edinburgh's David Wilkie won the world title breaking the world record. In the early evening, Gaga ran me up to Meadowbank to watch the Europa Cup; I missed Scott Brodie and Keith Ridley so just went in with the Knowles twins, thereafter meeting a lot of friends later. It was the women's final to begin the three day event. The weather was pretty poor-people will think twice about bringing international athletics to Edinburgh at this time of the year and before we knew it, it was dark and the floodlights were on; at some deep psychological level I think that made us feel slightly warmer! Our best performance by a mile was Helen Golden who ran 23.1 seconds in the 200 metres only two metres down on the Olympic champion. She ran really well, almost holding East Germany's Renate Stecher on the bend, losing very little down the home-straight. Helen's a lovely woman who everyone likes. If she trained hard, I suspect she could be quite brilliant; after all, she won the 1970 European Junior which shows her potential. However, in some ways she seems a throwback to an earlier, gentler age.

There were a lot of attractive girls around.

8th September, 1973 I enjoyed a long lie in bed before going up to watch day 2 of the Europa Cup and the start of the men's events. Frank Clement ran brilliantly to beat a good field in the 1500 metres. Paul arrived at the house just after 7.30 pm and we went on to the dance, which was absolutely fabulous; we had a great time and got a bit tipsy. On the bus coming home the Edinburgh Southern Harriers girls were great company

1976 A game of golf on Porty Golf Course in the rain, before going out to Pentland Community Centre where I was presented with monies raised at Dr Motley's surgery towards my training expenses.

1977 Well, after some time off and although it's still a few weeks until Michaelmas, I've made the decision to move up to 800 metres. Although only Boit and Juantorena have broken 1.44 I'm aiming high!

START OF BUILD-UP
TOWARDS A SUPER-FITNESS
AIM; SUB 1:46

An atypically rainy Edinburgh September day; there was a letter in the post from Dad from the Amber Pacific at Ravenna, Italy: '...Sorry you didn't get in to Jordanhill; I guess you'll realise the error of not staying at Loughborough, however that's water under the bridge now. I've written to Bill Watt at the bank telling him to re-new your payments...'

An atypically rainy Edinburgh September day; after some studying, I dropped in to Meadowbank and played squash against Coach Walker and then Bill Cummings; in the latter match, that's the best I've ever played. I slept between 4-7 p.m. before Susan Rettie and I went to see Oxbridge down in Portobello-a fun evening, but cold walking home. Winter is coming.

Afternoon (12.00 pm); 30 minutes squash with Coach Walker

Afternoon (2.30 pm): 45 minutes squash with Bill Cummings; I'm terribly stiff and sore!

9th September, 1975 I was in for Anatomy, Physiology & Health and Biology; this DNA business is complex; so much so when I got home I had to have a sleep! In the evening I worked hard in training, then as per usual *Pixie Mia Farrow lookalike* and I warmed down together.

Evening: **2 x 3 x 300 metres (3 minutes recovery; 12 mins between sets) all in around 38 seconds; a cold, wet evening-horrible for running in; autumn is here**

1977 As Mao-Tse Tung wrote: 'A journey of a thousand miles starts with a single step.' And this morning I took my first steps on the long journey ahead if I want to move successfully from the quarter up to the half mile and make next year's Commonwealth Games team, oops, correction, WIN next year's Commonwealth Games 800 metres!
It was such a glorious crisp, fresh and clear early autumn morning I decided to drive down the lovely East Lothian coast past the little villages of Longniddry and Aberlady to Gullane to run on the sands. We all look for positive signs from the heavens so it seemed appropriate to kick off my winter training this way. It's earlier this year, well in advance of Michaelmas, but I'm keen as mustard to start making deposits in the bank, especially before Adrian and Paul start knocking fuck out of me come November.

I took the dog; en-route we stopped off for some petrol at Asda. It was the loveliest drive down, watching this slower world come alive. I consider some locations ambiseasonal and Gullane is one such, but in most respects it actually marks the clockwork-like change in the procession of the seasons; being an athlete I associate it most with autumn and winter training.

The Forth was calm and like glass, with only a gentle zephyr blowing through the marram grass and the smell of the sea air and the occasional gull on the wing. I ran five miles along the beach, in and out of little coves and up and down undulating, wyndy sand dunes and little dips, all followed by a few hard sand dune hills. The beach itself was completely empty, indeed the emptiest I've ever seen it; it was only when we reached the sand dunes there was a solitary old man and a young boy out. I wasn't charged for parking as the wee man was away on his bike.

On the way back home I picked up some Lucas ice cream and then showered at Meadowbank, before spending the rest of the day studying apart from picking up some gravel and plants for the new pond. Come nine o'clock I picked up *Diana the goddess of love and hunting* at the west end for a drink before Gavin Miller took us out to Prestonfield House for a meal. A good evening, including looking in to the Festival Club afterwards, thereafter finishing off with a coffee at the Rutland Hotel, Charlotte Square.

My life pattern over the next year needs to be broadly similar to today by focusing on three things: my studies; my training; and quality time with *Diana*. I also need to find time to fit Gaga in too. It seems easy when I put it like that! Tomorrow I'm meeting up with Coach Walker for our annual get-together to go over and agree our plans for the next year. But most importantly I'm in a happy place and full of hope about the future. I was going to quote RLS about the journey being the thing, but I'm reading David Daiches' Was, A Pastime From Time Past and this quote seems more appropriate: 'Happiness was anticipation, awareness of happiness was always retrospective.'

<u>Morning:</u> Gullane Beach 5 miles run; 4 sand dune hill runs; a lovely morning

10th September, 1973 After dropping Iain back at Oxgangs, it was down to Thomas Graham's to work; it must be close to my first anniversary here at *Dickensville*. However, the day was leavened as I had my Athletics Weekly and passed reasonably quickly, mainly because I spent all of today, day-dreaming about *Pixie Mia Farrow lookalike*. I was back home by 5.45 p.m. before going out to run a very hard session with the middle distance runners; I was 'out the box' for ten minutes afterwards. Someone must have upset *Pixie* because I noticed she was crying; I was greeting too but for other reasons, 600s by way of example! Later we played cards together; we're travelling through to Grangemouth by train on Saturday; I wonder if I'll be able to sum up the courage to suggest a game of mixed doubles at tennis next Monday on the holiday.

Evening: 4 x 600 metres (4 minutes recovery) 96; 96; 92; 94 seconds

1974 Gaga picked me up from Telford College in the Dean Village; he said the BAAB had been on the phone and I've been selected for the GB v West Germany Junior international. I phoned Coach Walker to let him know and did some speed-work; later on Dougie McLean took me for a drink.

Evening: 3 x 60 metres; 3 x 80m; 3 x 100m with a walk back recovery

1975 I was in for just Maths today. After dinner I did a wee session with *Pixie Mia Farrow lookalike*. It was very cold, so much so, I kept my tracksuit on. Ann Clarkson asked me for the £3 I owed her; OUCH! to be honest I'd forgotten all about it, but *Pixie* said she'd pay for it, which is pretty good of her. As usual I gave her a lift home to the Braids; we stopped off en-route for a baked potato and then outside the Hermitage. A lovely evening together; I feel so happy when we get on as well as we did this evening.

I Love You

'I love your lips when they're wet with wine
And red with a wild desire;
I love your eyes when the lovelight lies
Lit with a passionate fire.
I love your arms when the warm white flesh
Touches mine in a fond embrace;
I love your hair when the strands enmesh
Your kisses against my face...

...So kiss me sweet with your warm wet mouth,
Still fragrant with ruby wine,
And say with a fervor born of the South
That your body and soul are mine.
Clasp me close in your warm young arms,
While the pale stars shine above,
And we'll live our whole young lives away
In the joys of a living love'

Ella Wheeler Wilcox

Evening: 8 x 60 metres relaxed and fast; so cold I ran with my tracksuit on

11ᵗʰ September, 1973 Before making my way along Balcarres Street I sat in Gaga's car reading his Scottish Daily Express. Muhammed Ali beat Ken Norton on points. There was a nip in the air and a light frost about. I like these kind of mornings; everything is fresh with a whole new day ahead of me; it's just a shame I have to spend most of it cooped away inside Thomas Graham & Sons, however it wasn't too bad. Nana gave me a wee ring and I looked in to see Mum briefly before going out to Roy's house at Lasswade for lunch; his wife is pregnant. Later I phoned Paul. In the evening. *Pixie Mia Farrow lookalike* got on my wick calling me by my last name, Hoffmann. Scott ran Duncan, Dougie and me home; Top Thirty tonight.

Evening: **10 x 200 metres (90 seconds recovery); all in 27 seconds; some gym press-ups; sit-ups; squats**

12th September, 1977 My last week in Edinburgh before I venture forth to spend each week in Dundee. I went out for an easy run across the Braid Hills. On a fresh, early autumn day it was wonderful being out running freely across the bouncy turf. The world's at my feet, literally and metaphorically. I looked across to Edinburgh Castle, yellow aglow in the sun, with the fine buildings of Blackford and the Old Town in the foreground; from high up above the 18th green I could espy the River Forth and Fife beyond and my future in the far distance. Later, I collected Will from his wee part-time butchering job; mid-afternoon I bought ten gold-fish for the pond; watching them swim around in their new habitat; the final part of the jigsaw and to coin a phrase, the end of my little pet project. A massage from Denis and then another wee run. So went the day.

Morning (10.15 a.m.): **4 miles on Braid Hills**

Evening (9.30 p.m.): **4 miles Eastfield-Joppa and Portobello Promenade**

13th September, 1974 I was out to Turnhouse early to fly down to Birmingham for the Great Britain v West Germany Junior International. I met up with Robert Sinclair, Ann Clarkson and the *Mary Rand lookalike from the south west*. We were met at the airport and driven out to the college; we were the first to arrive so mucked about all day. *Mary* is rather gorgeous; perhaps I'll have a chance of getting off with her tomorrow evening at the dance.

1975 I left Porty quite early to take the roundabout 5 bus up to the Pollock Halls to join the senior Great Britain team meeting for this weekend's match against Sweden; I'm in the relay team but unlikely to run. Last night I told Coach Walker I'd be available to run for the club instead. Afterwards George Sinclair gave me a lift down to Meadowbank, where I immediately bumped in to *Pixie Mia Farrow lookalike*. She was smartly dressed in a white jumper and kilt for leading the teams out on parade. I spent the afternoon with her; she was in a fantastic mood. It was good to see Roger win the 400 metres in 46.7 in pretty blustery conditions. Come the evening *Pixie* and I went to the Edinburgh Tattoo and snuggled up together, before going on to a Chinese restaurant for a bite to eat. Late on I gave her a quick ring to make sure she got home safely. A very happy day spent in her company.

Perfect Day

'...Oh, it's such a perfect day
I'm glad I spent it with you...'

Lou Reed

1977 I read a bing of old Athletics Weeklies and the morning flew by; later, some work on the pool and a game of squash with Coach Walker. In the evening *Diana the goddess of love and hunting* and I went to see Confessions of a Window Cleaner. It might not have been stimulating intellectually, but what a bloody laugh; come the interval I noticed all these middle-class women walking about with a smirk on their faces. And as for the men, well, what more could they ask for, with all these young lovelies sporting themselves naked and all for £1.75! Diana and I grabbed some fish 'n chips before I drove her home via the Cramond Inn.

Afternoon (2.00 p.m.): 1 hour squash

14th September, 1975 I went up to Meadowbank to be told I'm not to be released to run for the club. *Pixie Mia Farrow lookalike* arrived just after mid-day and we mucked about all afternoon. Rather wonderfully I got a run after all-my first official British senior vest! When I was warming up with the relay team, David Jenkins told me to make sure I was completely warmed up; I don't think he was injured at all, but was just keen to see me get my first cap and to give Roger the glory last leg. The race was incredibly close the whole way with Roger snatching it on the line-great stuff and wonderful that *Pixie* was there to see it too. At nine o'clock I picked her up at the Morningside clock before we went for a couple of drinks and then on to the after-match disco. We had a wonderful evening; I'm completely in love and of course, very, very happy.

UK v Sweden, Meadowbank:

4 x 400 metres relay 1. UK (Hoffmann, Auckett, Hartley, R. Jenkins) 3:07.6; 2. Sweden (G. Moller, E. Carlgren, A. Faager, Sjoberg) 3:07.7

Athletics Weekly '...the 4 x 400m relay, the Swedes certainly made our squad of Peter Hoffmann (coming in at ten minutes notice for David Jenkins, suffering from a sore back), Jim Aukett, Bill Hartley and Roger Jenkins work for it. With no more than a stride or so in it all the way round, Jenkins took over two metres ahead and re-assured feint hearts as held off Sweden's Sjoberg in this vulnerable position-by seven-hundredths of a second. An enjoyable match...but a smoothly organised minor triumph for the Scots...well and truly an Edinburgh Festival. 'The Scotsman' sponsored the match.'

15th September, 1978 We awoke this morning to the aftermath of last night's storm. The wind was still howling and part of Josephine's greenhouse roof had been blown off. As a temporary measure I hammered down some plastic sheeting before going off to buy some wood and roofing; by lunchtime I'd manged to repair all the damage. In the afternoon Will and I went to Kwikfit for new tyres for his car; blimey, the bill came to over £46! Paul looked in to see us; he'd been appearing before a Kangaroo Court of SAAAs officials, about his wild escapades in Edmonton. At the Coke Meeting Ovett broke the world two miles record whilst Coe ran a new British record over 800 metres, both significantly different performances, but showing Ovett's amazing range. *Diana the goddess of love and hunting* is staying overnight. I'm sitting reading some Robert Louis Stevenson.

16th September, 1975 Happy days. After last year's first year at Telford College I'm studying for further Highers and I've been given a grant from Lothian Regional Council of £605 which is just wonderful news; they must have confidence in me; it says much for the City Fathers that such a grant scheme is available to people such as me giving me a second chance in life after failing at school. I zipped up to Torphicen Place to let them know that I've changed some of my courses. After tea I ran a trial with the Edinburgh relay team for this weekend's trip to meet Munich; I ran a fine last leg going past Scott Brodie. Afterwards *Pixie Mia Farrow lookalike* and I spent the evening together most happily! We had a great time and get on well!

Evening: During half-time at the Meadowbank Thistle v Berwick Rangers match we ran the 'Munich' relay team; 41.7 seconds-not bad eh!.

17th September, 1975 Only Maths today. Come the evening a session on my own. *Pixie Mia Farrow lookalike* came down later and did her session. Afterwards we were chatting away before wandering in to watch a basketball game together; she was in one of her fantastic moods!

Evening: 2 x 150 metres (5 minutes recovery) 16; 15 (10 mins rest); 2 x 120m (5 mins rec) 12.8; 12.9 secs; 2 x 100m (jog/walk round track) 10.9; 11.0 secs

18th September, 1977 Another major crossroads in life and the start of a new adventure today. After walking away from Loughborough last year I start at Dundee tomorrow. It was one of these wondrous, gorgeously soft, beautiful early autumn days. It was crisp and cold first thing as we collected the Sunday rolls and took the dog to Porty Park. However, after packing my suitcase, Will, *Diana the goddess of love and hunting* and I were able to sit out in the back garden amongst the lawns, borders and the pear and apple trees which are groaning with this year's crop. We sat happily playing cards and dominoes. It was good to spend time with Will as I know how much he'll miss me throughout the week. He dropped me off at Waverley Station for the ten to three train. It was a lovely journey up through the Fife countryside. There were lots of boats and yachts out on an azure blue Forth. I arrived at my digs and was immediately met by a couple of other students. The large house I'm staying at is fine; it's a couple with three children although one of the children stays at a residential home. We're five minutes from Broughty Harbour; after unpacking I walked out along the shore; it was just starting to get cold with the warmth of the day and the sun beginning to slowly, then quickly fade. I telephoned *Diana* (3 x 10p). I'm lying back in bed reading, with Radio Forth on in the background. I miss *Diana*.

19th September, 1975 Munich, I still couldn't find my passport so had to dash up to the Post Office to get a one year version, however when I got up to Meadowbank I

discovered that Betty Steedman had my passport all along!
The team gathered outside Waverley Station before heading
out to Turnhouse to fly out to Munich. I was taking the piss
out of McMaster; he was setting himself up for it with some
ridiculous cockiness; I just couldn't resist it.

1977 I took a number 10 bus in to Dundee but couldn't
register as I didn't have my Highers results with me. At the
railway station I bought a small map and used the day to find
my way around, including taking a bus out to Caird Stadium;
it's fine. After lunch I met Ian Brown at the university; he
was helpful and I walked down to Riverside. When I got
back to my digs I discovered that Will and Jo had driven up
from Portobello with my Higher results and handed them
into the janitor; they'd been and gone. I ran five miles
including a visit to a Dawson Park then had a bath; there's
no shower. I phoned Jo and then *Diana*. I've got my
timetable written out; jeez! I've no time at all.

**Evening (8.00 p.m.): 5 mile run from digs to Dawson
Park**

20th September, 1974 I got up to Edinburgh early on to buy
a couple of tapes; the Cat Stevens (Foreigner) was poor, but
the Neil Diamond, (Stones), was excellent. The group of us
travelling down to London were Coach Walker; Keith
Ridley; Drew McMaster and Claude Jones. After last
weekend's British Junior match I was thinking about
the *Mary Rand lookalike from the south west* who will be there
with the Edinburgh Southern Harriers women's team;
perhaps I might get off with her. The first day of the Pye
Cup went brilliantly and E.A.C. are leading. The atmosphere
is incredible; really exciting stuff; it's when athletics moves
from just being an individual thing to a shared team
experience. Norman Gregor was brilliant; he won the 400
metres hurdles in a Scottish record 51.6 seconds; then Coach

Walker fired him up to run the 800 metres and he finished second in 1:49.4; the guy's a legend! Meanwhile I ran in the 4 x 100 metres relay; we broke the Scottish Club Record but still only finished fourth. Paul just stayed in my room tonight; he's just down for the drink. And the women!

1974 Pye Cup Final

4 x 100 metres relay 4. E.A.C. 41.7 seconds (S. Brodie; A. McMaster; R. Jenkins; Hoffmann)

1975, Munich I've picked up a bad cold and felt a bit flat so didn't join the others out shopping so just stayed back at the hostel instead. I spent a fair amount of time chatting with Adrian Weatherhead. Come the afternoon I didn't run badly, especially given the way I was feeling, however McMaster annoyed me with his cockiness. Come the evening we were at a reception at the Munich Ratskeller. We had a wee drink and by this stage I was in full flow, with Drew now floundering on the end of some repartee-that'll teach the bugger! Our host was somewhat bemused about me asking about the rats of the Ratskeller; of course by now I was playing to the crowd with Paul encouraging me on, drink in one hand, whilst bent double over a chair in fits of laughter.

Munich v Edinburgh

100 metres 5. Hoffmann 11.0 seconds

200 metres 3. Hoffmann 21.8 seconds; equals my official p.b.

1977, Dundee An inauspicious start to training in Dundee at the start of the Commonwealth Games season. I had an early dinner at 4.15 p.m. then travelled out by bus to Caird Park to do a run with a chap. It's a fair walk from the changing rooms to the bus stop; I missed the 8.20 p.m. bus and had to hang around for 40 minutes. En-route back I phoned *Diana the goddess of love and hunting;* she phoned the telephone box back; some toasted cheese for supper before I lay back and read.

Afternoon: Gym circuit

Evening (7.15 p.m.): 6 miles run along the Kingsway

21st September, 1974, London We were served up a pretty rotten breakfast. I stayed in my room all morning; the lovely *Mary Rand lookalike from the south west* wandered past a few times. The weather took a very bad turn for the worse and it poured with rain. I was pretty annoyed as with the camber of the track all the water had gathered in lane one and hadn't been swept away so I found myself splashing through 400 metres whilst everyone outside seemed to have a relatively dry run. I felt my run was rubbish although it was within a few tenths of my best. However, I ran a fantastic relay leg for the club. Keith Ridley handed me the baton after the first leg pretty much last; I flew round the track in an official split of 47.3 seconds taking us up to a close second; thereafter Norman and Roger did the business taking us out to a new Scottish Club Record. A boisterous fun evening; at the dance; I got off with *Mary;* we spent the evening drinking and dancing, having a great time. George Sinclair ensured she was chaperoned safely away!

1974 Pye Cup Final

400 metres 1. G. Cohen 47.2 2. I. Saunders 47.4 3. M. Delaney 4. Hoffmann 48.8; I had the inside lane and it was full of puddles

**4 x 400 metres relay 1. EAC 3:12.6 Scottish Club Record
(K. Ridley 51.0; Hoffmann 47.3; Gregor 47.5; R. Jenkins
46.7)**

1975, Munich A touristy day. We watched the Bavarian
costume parade before enjoying some lunch at the Olympic
Stadium; we then went up the Olympic Tower. I had mixed
feelings being there because I'd enjoyed much of the
excitement of the '72 Games, but whilst up on high I
reflected on the tragic massacre only three years before.
Most people went down to the Octoberfest, but I didn't
really fancy staying so went back to the hostel and went out
instead for an afternoon run with Adrian Weatherhead and
Ray Weatherburn, through some lovely parts of the city with
beautiful houses lining the quiet streets. On such a lovely
autumn afternoon it was a joy to be out but I was hanging
on for dear life to the boys' coat-tails. I can't imagine any of
the other sprinters doing this! Anyway, knackering myself,
and ending up with sore hips and legs I managed to hang in
there. I telephoned *Pixie Mia Farrow lookalike;* it was fantastic
to hear her cheery voice.

22ⁿᵈ September, 1975 The flight from Munich left at mid-
day. Come the evening I bumped into guess who...she's had
her hair cut very short and looks like Mia Farrow. We went
for a jog come walk round Arthurs Seat, walking hand in
hand, laughing and chatting six to the dozen.

23ʳᵈ September, 1973 We ran a hard session.

**THE END of that era; on to a new training diary and
onward from 52.0 seconds towards 48.9 seconds.**

**Morning: 6 x 600 metres (5 minutes recovery) 106; 107;
103; 107; 101; 98 seconds**

1975 Back to college today followed by an afternoon reading and listening to music. *Pixie Mia Farrow lookalike* phoned at 4.30 p.m.; I picked her and Wendy up and drove them out to Dunfermline College of PE for the start of their new student life.

24th September, 1975 I was chatting with Laurie Gray at college. Despite it being such a wet, wild 'n windy Wednesday evening *Pixie Mia Farrow lookalike* and I walked around Arthurs Seat before I saw her on to her bus home.

25th September, 1975 Once again I was just in for Maths today. I wish my grant monies would arrive soon. It was a wild evening so I gave *Pixie Mia Farrow lookalike* a lift out to Cramond to Dunfermline College of PE. She took me up to her room. We had a long talk, ending up with her telling me she loved me. It was the most fantastic thing I've ever heard. As I drove home I've never felt so happy.

Evening: Walk/Jog around Arthurs Seat

26th September, 1975 When I got home from college it was good to see my grant had arrived. Come the evening I dashed out to pick *Pixie Mia Farrow lookalike* up. She looked gorgeous, the most fantastic looking girl I ever saw in my life. We went to see The Eiger Sanction. It was okay. We bumped in to another happy couple who are also in love, Helen Golden and Stevie Green. We didn't get back out to the college until 1.30 am after a really fantastic evening.

27th September, 1975 It absolutely poured with rain all day. Early afternoon I met *Pixie Mia Farrow lookalike* at Binns' Corner; she'd been standing there for almost an hour; I felt bad about that. We went to *see Enter The Dragon;* we got in to see it for free. She really enjoyed it. In the evening I met her out at the college; we had an argument, however we had a really fantastic evening at the disco.

1978 Willie and I had a half pint down in Portobello watching the Rangers match. *Diana the goddess of love and hunting* phoned me at nine o'clock for a whole hour after her first full day on the wards. She really needs me just now; I'll be there for her always. I've just heard over the radio that Paul may be banned from international athletics. Josephine has left a hot water bottle in my bed-the first of the winter.

28th September, 1975, *the day before Michaelmas*
I went up to Meadowbank and ran a session on my own before meeting *Pixie Mia Farrow lookalike* at Binns' Corner to do the club sponsored walk. She wasn't in a good mood, feeling very tired.

Morning: **2 x 500 metres (10 minutes recovery); second run through the quarter in 53 seconds finishing strongly**

Afternoon: **14 miles sponsored walk**

1978 Sandy Sutherland from The Scotsman and Brian Meek from the Scottish Daily Express had both been trying to get a hold of me to comment on Paul's one year ban from international athletics. Come the evening, *Diana the goddess of love and hunting* and I had a few drinks at the *Two Inns* and some fun winning some money on the fruit machine; thereafter to *Pixie Mia Farrow lookalike's* 21st birthday party; it wasn't up to much…

My Life Closed Twice Before Its Close

My life closed twice before its close—
It yet remains to see
If Immortality unveil
A third event to me

So huge, so hopeless to conceive   5
As these that twice befell.
Parting is all we know of heaven.
And all we need of hell.

Emily Dickinson

'Now I have told the year from dawn to dusk'

'Now I have told the year from dawn to dusk,
It's morning and its evening and its noon;
Once round the sun our slanting orbit rolled,
Four times the seasons changed, thirteen the moon...'

Vita Sackville-West

Watering the Horse

How strange to think of giving up all ambition!
Suddenly I see with such clear eyes
The white flake of snow
That has just fallen in the horse's mane!

Robert Bly

The Swineheard

When all this is over, said the swineherd,
I mean to retire, where
Nobody will have heard about my special skills
And conversation is mainly about the weather.

I intend to learn how to make coffee, as least as well
As the Portuguese lay-sister in the kitchen
And polish the brass fenders every day.
I want to lie awake at night
Listening to cream crawling to the top of the jug
And the water lying soft in the cistern.

I want to see an orchard where the trees grow in straight lines
And the yellow fox finds shelter between the navy-blue trunks,
Where it gets dark early in summer
And the apple-blossom is allowed to wither on the bough.

Eiléan Ní Chuilleanáin

Love and Age

And I did love you very dearly,
How dearly words want power to show;
I thought your heart was touch'd as nearly;
But that was fifty years ago. Then other lovers came around you,

Your beauty grew from year to year,
And many a splendid circle found you
The centre of its glimmering sphere.
I saw you then, first vows forsaking,
On rank and wealth your hand bestow;
O, then I thought my heart was breaking!--
But that was forty years ago...

But though first love's impassion'd blindness
Has pass'd away in colder light,
I still have thought of you with kindness,
And shall do, till our last good-night.
The ever-rolling silent hours
Will bring a time we shall not know,
When our young days of gathering flowers
Will be a hundred years ago.

Thomas Love Peacock

Summer Has Gone

I have tidings for you,

The stag bells;

Winter pours;

Summer has gone

Wind is high and cold;

The sun is low;

Its course is short;

The sea runs strongly...

Cold has seized

The wings of birds;

Season of ice.

These are my tidings

'Summer Has Gone' (Early Irish Lyrics, Oxford 1956)

The train puffed its way from state to state collecting more and more athletes from every station. And every nation. We met old, young faces and traded gossip. Crossing America I realised you cross several continents. Sometimes the rains teemed down and you could hardly see out the window. Then we would pass through desert lands where the temperature soared in to three figures.

I loved the journey; yet many others hated it. But then for athletes from England, Australia or New Zealand, many of them had set off weeks or even months beforehand. Some of these guys must have lost condition. At long stop stations I saw some of them get off the train and jog up and down the platform. One guy mistimed the train's departure, but we cheered him on, as he chased the train down just managing to jump back on board as it picked up speed.

On and on and on the train made its way through this magnificent land: New England; New York; Pennsylvania; Ohio; Michigan; Arizona; and finally into the beautiful state of California. One day I'd looked out on the Atlantic; now I can see the Pacific.

From my schooldays I recalled one of the great dates, the 10th May, 1869, when the Central Pacific met the Union Pacific, linking the two railways. And now my journey is nearly over. I'm going home. Home to Los Angeles, the City of the Angels.

In the hours leading up to the race I'm afraid. I'm scared. I'm scared of letting my family down; scared of my rivals; scared of the pain; scared of the oxygen debt at the end of the race and the painful lactic acids which will burn my legs and sear my lungs.

Grandfather saw only gold for me; the gold he never found when he mined for it decades ago. But grand-daddy was an innocent. Such thoughts make my pulse race. Memories are dreams. And dreams, memories. I feel hot; like I'm about to go through it all again.

Adrenalin.

Heart-rate very high.

I like Los Angeles. Back then it was a much older world than the smoggy city of today, where the glare makes your eyes smart. And the clime suited me. The warmth. The gentle zephyrs. It made for running fast. Helped me fly.

I'm about to face seven of planet Earth's finest quarter milers. Men who can run like the deer.

It's a warm still evening. Earlier, a few of us went out to a Mexican restaurant. Mary Pickford the film actress came over to our table. Just to wish the American boys well.

I feel very, very tired. Like nothing before. Voices in the distance. Echoing. And echoing. Each time I try to focus I'm drawn to the past. Reality and fantasy seem intertwined. The City of the Angels, ebbing and flowing. Ebbing and flowing. The day of the final. The final day.

I can see my family huddled around; just like families all over America, seated by the radio, tuned in to KDKA, WLW or WOR.

I've slept badly.

It's going to be a very hot day.

I've just heard some bad news.

I've got the outside lane. It's the worst draw.

I feel like a man going to meet his maker.

I can't face breakfast, yet I know I should force down some ham and eggs, pancakes and syrup and a pot of coffee. But I've no appetite.

At least high up here in the athletes' village it's relatively cool and peaceful. Contrast that with the cauldron in the valley below. And the Coliseum. I look out over Beverly Hills. A cat strolls over and rolls on its back, asking me to rub its stomach.

Roy Campbell wrote:

"For only out of solitude or strife

Are born the sons of valour and delight"

Later that morning I play a game of chequers with our great sprinter Charlie Paddock. But I can't concentrate. Kipling seems more appropriate than Campbell:

'If you can force your heart and nerve and sinew

To serve your turn long after they are gone

And so hold on when there is nothing in you

Except the Will which says to them: Hold on!'

When I enter the home straight; when I've run out of gas, I need that fortitude.

I re-check my shorts, vest, spikes and tracksuit for the umpteenth time.

A knock on the door.

It's time to go.

I walk down the corridor. Several team members wish me luck. They commence a rhythmic chant, which gets louder and louder, the sounds echoing off the walls.

The Coliseum. I begin to warm up. Despite the heat I keep my tracksuit on. Some easy jogging. I avoid eye contact with my rivals. I jog, very, very slowly; a slow, steady, hypnotic rhythm. I look down at God's earth. The cinders. The warm up settles me a little. It's an old friend. Twenty minutes to go. A few strides. God, that got my heart and lungs pumping.

Temperature is 104 degrees.

My heart-rate is way up. I'm struggling to breathe. I feel a tightness in my chest. It's strange how the rapid beat and throb of my heart seems to be more in my throat and head than in my chest.

More oxygen.

100,000 people. Yet I feel alone.

Of a sudden, I feel calm. The outside lane holds no fear. I've journeyed to the Rubicon, let the dice fly high.

Teach us oh Lord to accept the things we cannot change.

Not long now.

More tightness. It's just nerves. A fearful heat. But it will help me fly. My heart's racing. Preparing for battle.

A quick stride around the turn. This is the day. A day in time. Set aside for me. Destiny. I've known it since I was a child running on the sidewalks, feeling the joy of the gift; the gift to run fast.

Tracksuits off!

The sound of the marksman's voice breaks my thoughts. It feels like a dream. Everything unreal.

On your marks!

I feel alone.

Get set!

A long pause. And then the silence is shattered by the bang of the starter's gun. I fly out the blocks. The first 110 yards around the bend are over in a flash. I've gone out quickly, but controlled. I need to spread my effort.

Going down the back straight I hear the splash of an opponent's footsteps. It scares the life out of me. One of the Englishmen go past. I reach out and lock on to him looking for support; to ease my passage. I'm no longer running blind. Going round the turn the gap remains the same. As we hit the 275 yards mark my body begins to seize. We're all tired, I remind myself. It's beginning to hurt. A terrible pain in my chest. Approaching 330 yards I notice a raven walking in my lane. Of a sudden it takes off. And screeches. And turns into a dove.

Entering the home straight I'm in a dream, running in slow motion. I feel part of the race, yet removed. The sound of the crowd-a constant humming, droning in my ears. My legs are heavy. My arms tired, neck and shoulders tightening up. Lifeblood ebbing away.

I glance up at the flame, burning brightly on high. And for a moment, hills of green. And water, running gently. Bubbling and plashing. Everything has gone quiet. For a moment in time I am above Olympus. High up, looking down.

It is finished. John, 19:30

Printed in Great Britain
by Amazon